DIASPORIC COLD WARRIORS

STUDIES OF THE WEATHERHEAD EAST ASIAN INSTITUTE,
COLUMBIA UNIVERSITY

The Studies of the Weatherhead East Asian Institute of Columbia University
were inaugurated in 1962 to bring to a wider public the results of significant
new research on modern and contemporary East Asia.

DIASPORIC COLD WARRIORS

NATIONALIST CHINA, ANTICOMMUNISM, AND THE PHILIPPINE CHINESE, 1930s–1970s

CHIEN-WEN KUNG

CORNELL UNIVERSITY PRESS
Ithaca and London

First published 2022 by Cornell University Press

Library of Congress Cataloging-in-Publication Data

Names: Kung, Chien-Wen, 1981– author.
Title: Diasporic cold warriors : nationalist China, anticommunism, and the Philippine Chinese, 1930s–1970s / Chien-Wen Kung.
Description: Ithaca [New York] : Cornell University Press, 2022. | Series: Studies of the Weatherhead East Asian Institute, Columbia University | Includes bibliographical references and index.
Identifiers: LCCN 2021026422 (print) | LCCN 2021026423 (ebook) | ISBN 9781501762215 (hardcover) | ISBN 9781501762222 (pdf) | ISBN 9781501762239 (epub)
Subjects: LCSH: Zhongguo guo min dang. | Chinese—Political activity—Philippines—History—20th century. | Anti-communist movements—Philippines—History—20th century. | Anti-communist movements—Taiwan—History—20th century. | Anti-communist movements—China—History—20th century.
Classification: LCC DS666.C5 K86 2022 (print) | LCC DS666.C5 (ebook) | DDC 324.251/075—dc23
LC record available at https://lccn.loc.gov/2021026422
LC ebook record available at https://lccn.loc.gov/2021026423

To my parents

CONTENTS

ACKNOWLEDGMENTS

Over the past decade and more, far too many persons and institutions directly and indirectly contributed to the writing of *Diasporic Cold Warriors* to be mentioned by name in these next few paragraphs. I hope I can do some justice to their contributions, nonetheless. At Columbia, Adam McKeown welcomed me into the international and global history program, inducted me into the study of Chinese migration and diaspora, and, in a café on the northwestern corner of Central Park one spring afternoon, blessed my inchoate research topic after having left academia for greener pastures. I wish that he were still here today to read this. Thanks to Eugenia Lean, I am able to identify myself as a historian of modern China, albeit one who comes to the field from the outside in. Her colloquium in the spring of 2013 was the intellectual high point of my years in New York. Despite our vastly different approaches to the "Chinese" past, her comments have always been on the mark. "What would Eugenia think?" is still a question that I ask myself as I try to live up to her intellectual standards.

During graduate school, I was equally fortunate to be surrounded by brilliant friends and colleagues at Columbia and beyond. Collectively and individually, Clark Alejandrino, Kyoungjin Bae, Nishant Batsha, Manuel Bautista, Allison Bernard, Harun Buljina, Chris Chang, John Chen, Eunsung Cho, Kumhee Cho, Richard Chu, Jae-Won Chung, Sam Daly, Evan Dawley, Clay Eaton, Hannah Elmer, Chloe Estep, Idriss Fofana, James Gerien-Chen, Arunabh Ghosh, Yanjie Huang, Xiaoqian Ji, Colin Jones, Ulug Kuzuoglu, James Lin, Owen Miller, Sayantani Mukherjee, Jack Neubauer, Sean O'Neill, Allison Powers, Victor Petrov, Josh Schlachet, Nataly Shahaf, Ian Shin, John Thompson, Tyler Walker, Yijun Wang, Dominic Yang, Adrien Zakar, and Dongxin Zou—among many others—provided generous and thoughtful feedback; inspired me through their own scholarship and intellectual ruminations; helped me decipher sources and conceptualize narratives; kept me sane over beers, happy hours, and *Civilization V* multiplayer; and introduced me to *Game of Thrones*. I also want to thank Lien-Hang Nguyen and Michael Szonyi for offering penetrating insights at a late stage and Matt Connelly and Betsy Blackmar for their suggestions during the initial stages of the project.

Research and writing during graduate school were funded by the Weatherhead East Asian Institute, the Sasakawa Young Leaders' Fellowship Fund, the China and Inner Asia Council of the Association for Asian Studies, and the Confucius China Studies Program. In the Philippines, Taiwan, and China, respectively, the Institute of Philippine Culture at Ateneo de Manila University, the Institute of Modern History at Academia Sinica, and the Research School for Southeast Asian Studies at Xiamen University were gracious hosts during my overseas stints. I am indebted to the librarians and archivists across Asia and the United States who helped me track down materials and to the many persons, especially in in the Philippines, whom I was able to converse with about their life stories and my research. I am particularly grateful to Teresita Ang See, Teresa Chong Carino, Wesley Chua, Go Bon Juan, the late Benito Lim, Charlson Ong, Dory Poa, the late Julio Tan, Tan Tian Siong, and Solomon Yuyitung for sharing their experiences with me.

Having emigrated "overseas," I completed this book back "home" thanks to Ministry of Education Tier 2 Academic Research Fund (MOE2018-T2-1-138) that enabled me to become part of the "Reconceptualizing the Cold War" (RCW) research project at the National University of Singapore. Over the past few years, I have benefited tremendously from the social and intellectual companionship of Ang Cheng Guan, Chan Cheow-Thia, Henry Chan, Sayaka Chatani, Jack Chia, Clay Eaton, Leow Wei Yi, Jason Lim, Masuda Hajimu, Wen-Qing Ngoei, Joseph Scalice, Seng Guo Quan, Josh Stenberg, Mitchell Tan, Tan Ying Jia, Taomo Zhou, and Dongxin Zou. I am grateful to Hajimu for welcoming me into RCW; Sayaka and Taomo for our many lunches together and discussions on Asian diasporas; my old Columbia friends Clay and Dongxin for always finding the time to read one more draft and listen to one more idea; Joseph, for conversations about the Philippines, the academic job market, and communism; and Wen-Qing, for extended Facebook and WhatsApp chats.

Special thanks must go to Mike Montesano and Carol Hau. Mike has been an intellectual mentor since we met over a decade ago in Singapore and I declared my intention then to pursue a Ph.D. Over e-mail, coffee, and meals, he introduced me to the professional study of Southeast Asia, supported my research, and opened more doors for me than I can count. Very early on, Mike introduced me to Carol. Although we have met in person only once, no one has read more of my work than she has. Without Mike and Carol, I would not have known where to start and how to continue.

Emily Andrew, Allegra Martschenko, and others at Cornell University Press shepherded this book all the way through from proposal to final product.

I could not ask for a more supportive, responsive, and meticulous editorial team. I would like to thank the press's two peer reviewers and the anonymous reader for the Studies of the Weatherhead East Asian Institute series for their feedback, which helped me refine the manuscript. The excellent maps and index are the work of Mike Bechthold and Malcolm Thompson respectively, while a First Book Subvention Award from the Association for Asian Studies helped cover the costs of publication. A modified version of chapter 3 was published as "In the Name of Anticommunism: Chinese Practices of Ideological Accommodation in the Early Cold War Philippines" in *Modern Asian Studies* 53, no. 5 (September 2019): 1543–1573. That chapter and others have been enriched by comments and questions at multiple conferences, workshops, and seminars since 2013.

Lastly, I could not have done this without friends, family members, and former students. Since secondary school, Ooi Say Hien has been an inexhaustible source of intelligent conversation on pretty much everything. In the grueling, lonely, but pedagogically rewarding year that I spent at the University of the Pacific, my cousin Itamar Calmon-Huang and Aunt Isabel put me up in their home in the Bay Area and fed me during the holidays. I became interested in modern Southeast Asia during my three and a half years at Raffles Institution in Singapore, where I had the privilege of teaching several amazing cohorts of A-Level students.

I dedicate this book to my parents, who have always afforded me the freedom to pursue my interests and supported me through trying times.

Abbreviations

ACM	Philippine-Chinese United Organization in Support of Anti-Communist Movement
AFP	Agence France-Presse
APACL	Asian Peoples' Anti-Communist League
CA	Chinese Association
CCN	*Chinese Commercial News*
CCP	Chinese Communist Party
CDN	*China Daily News*
CEC	KMT Central Executive Committee
CIA	Central Intelligence Agency
CIC	Counter-Intelligence Commission
CKSC	Chiang Kai-shek College
CKSHS	Chiang Kai-shek High School
CNA	Central News Agency
COF	Congreso Obrero de Filipinas
COWHM	Chinese Overseas Wartime Hsuehkan Militia
CPP	Communist Party of the Philippines

CRP   Chinese Revolutionary Party

CUFA   Committee on Un-Filipino Activities

CVP   Chinese Volunteers in the Philippines

DA   Democratic Alliance

DND   Department of National Defense

H.B.   House Bill

IMH   Institute of Modern History

IPI   International Press Institute

Kang Chu   Philippine-Chinese Anti-Japanese Volunteer Corps

Kang Fan   Philippine-Chinese Anti-Japanese and Anti-Puppets League

KMT   Kuomintang

Lo Lian Hui Philippine-Chinese United Workers Union

MCA   Malayan Chinese Association

MCP   Malayan Communist Party

MIS   Military Intelligence Service

MOFA   Ministry of Foreign Affairs

MP   military police

NHS   Nanyang High School

NICA   National Intelligence Coordinating Agency

NPA   New People's Army

NTD   New Taiwan dollars

OCAC	Overseas Chinese Affairs Commission
OPAC	Overseas Party Affairs Committee
PACL	Philippine Anti-Communist League
PCACL	Philippine Chinese Anti-Communist League
PCCA	Philippines-China Cultural Association
PCCP	Philippine-Chinese Communist Party
PCLA	Philippine-Chinese Labor Association
PHP	Philippine pesos
PKP	Partido Komunista ng Pilipinas
PLA	People's Liberation Army
POWs	prisoners of war
PRC	People's Republic of China
R.A.	Republic Act
RMB	Renminbi
ROC	Republic of China
Shang Zong	Federation of Filipino-Chinese Chambers of Commerce and Industry
SQT	Three Principles' Youth Corps
SSC	Philippine Chinese Youth Wartime Special Services Corps
UP	University of the Philippines
UPI	United Press International
USD	US dollars

VA	COWHM Veterans' Association
WACL	World Anti-Communist League
Wen Zong	Filipino-Chinese Cultural and Economic Association
Wha Chi	Philippine-Chinese Anti-Japanese Force
Xiao Zong	General Association of Chinese Schools
Zhongxin	China News Service
Zong Lian	Grand Family Association

NOTE ON TRANSLATION AND ROMANIZATION

The translations from Chinese are a combination of my own and those of various historical actors themselves. The Philippine Chinese were accustomed to publishing dual-language texts.

Many Philippine Chinese (e.g., Pao Shih-tien / Bao Shitian) and Nationalist Chinese officials (e.g., Chen Chih-ping / Chen Zhiping) adopted Wade-Giles or nonstandard romanization systems when representing themselves in English. Thus, I have resorted to pinyin romanization only when I have not been able to find out their romanized names (e.g., Cai Yunqin). I also believe that employing non-pinyin romanization where possible better captures the historical moment that these persons lived through and shaped. For this reason, the Chinese Nationalist Party is the Kuomintang, not the Guomindang. The party itself has never used the latter. To mitigate any confusion, I have provided a glossary of selected Chinese names at the end of the book.

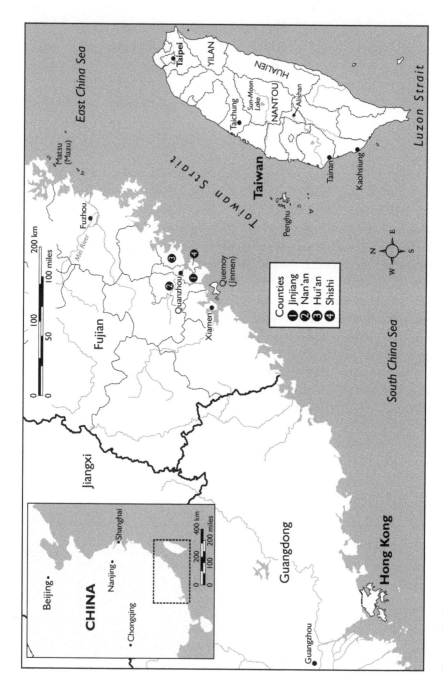

MAP 1. Southern Fujian and Taiwan

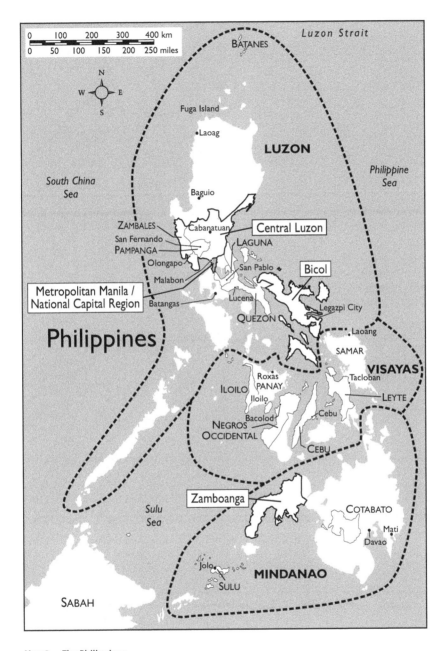

MAP 2. The Philippines

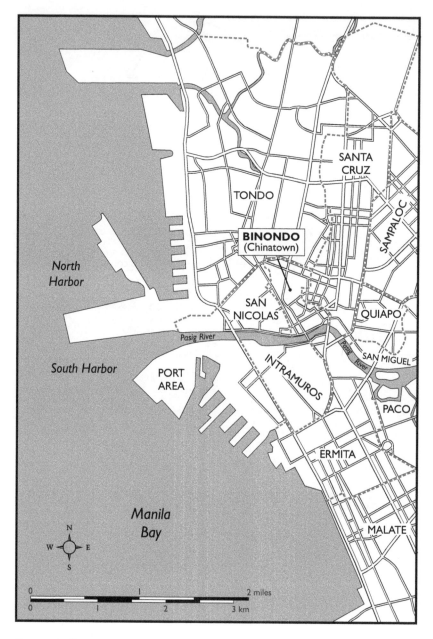

MAP 3. Manila

DIASPORIC COLD WARRIORS

Introduction

The Philippine Chinese as Cold Warriors

In the 1950s, as fears of Chinese communism swept the "free" world, a striking consensus emerged among professional observers of the Chinese diaspora. The "attitude of the Chinese in the Philippines was the best among all Southeast Asian countries," declared the chairman of the Overseas Chinese Affairs Commission (Qiaowu Weiyuanhui, or OCAC) of the Republic of China (ROC) in June 1952.[1] Six years later, OCAC's deputy chairman wrote that among the thousand or so Kuomintang (KMT) branches globally, the Philippines' was the most active and energetic in fighting communism.[2] US intelligence concurred, noting that "of all the Overseas communities, the Chinese in the Philippines have been the least attracted toward Communist China."[3] Empirical evidence substantiated these views. OCAC statistics show that in all but one year from 1951 to 1963, "patriotic voluntary contributions" (*aiguo zidong juanxian*) from the Philippine Chinese to Taiwan were the highest among all overseas Chinese (*huaqiao*) societies. In some years, such contributions from the Philippines exceeded those from all other countries combined.[4] This was despite the size of the Chinese community, one of the smallest in Southeast Asia. According to a 1959 estimate, it comprised only 270,000 persons, or 1.2 percent of the Philippine population.[5]

Relative to their diasporic counterparts then and unbeknownst to most of us today, the Philippine Chinese were the world's most exemplary Cold Warriors. For two decades from the KMT's flight to Taiwan in 1949 to the early 1970s, no overseas Chinese community was as active in identifying and rooting out suspected Reds from its midst. In no other *huaqiao* society was the KMT more dominant and communism more deinstitutionalized and less of a social and political force. Schools, newspapers, chambers of commerce, and other Chinese civic institutions in the Philippines were not openly contested between left and right until well after Manila recognized Beijing in 1975. Instead, pro-Taiwan organizations such as the KMT, the Philippine Chinese Anti-Communist League (PCACL), Chiang Kai-shek High School (CKSHS) (later, Chiang Kai-shek College [CKSC]), the *Great China Press* and *Kong Li Po* newspapers, and the community's governing body, the Federation of Filipino-Chinese Chambers of Commerce and Industry (Shang Zong), proliferated. Tolerated by the Philippine government, they overlapped in function and membership, structured associational life, suppressed heterodoxy, and propagated the party's all-encompassing political program of "Anticommunism and resist Russia" (*Fangong kang'E*). Ironically, then, the "China" with the strongest and most unchallenged ties to any *huaqiao* community was what the cultural theorist Kuan-Hsing Chen calls "a defeated, exiled regime existing under the global cold-war structure."[6]

This book examines how and why the Philippine Chinese became model Cold Warriors and traces their interlocking, often contentious partnership with the KMT and the Philippine state in opposition to Sino-communism from the 1930s to the early 1970s, especially from 1945 onward. Through this narrative, I argue for a networked and diasporic understanding of the Nationalist party-state and contend that this regime exercised a form of nonterritorial sovereignty over the Philippine Chinese with Manila's participation and consent. Before and after it seized the Chinese and Taiwanese states, what we reify as the KMT was a loosely hierarchical constellation of party branches, diplomatic organs, activists, and their affiliated civic organizations that spanned Chinese communities globally, connected them to China, and interfaced between the Nationalist state and *huaqiao* societies. Through its networks, the party aimed to mobilize a deterritorialized Chinese nation and destroy Chinese communism in pursuit of a unified China under its leadership. But it could not and did not simply assert its dominance over foreign governments such as the Philippines. Rather, Manila "shared" its sovereignty with Taipei by selectively outsourcing the management of its Chinese population to a Chinese state in a way that other anticommunist states such as Malaya and Thailand did not. Relations between the Philippine Chinese, Nationalist China, and the Philippines were thus part of what I call an intra-Asian "anticommunist ecumene"—a Cold War waged not by the United States and not only by national governments, but by Asian countries and peoples working with each other.

Contrary to depoliticized popular narratives of Chinese cultural integration, this book also argues that intra-Asian anticommunist connections decisively shaped Chinese civic identity and practices of belonging in the Philippines. Most Philippine Chinese were nationals of the ROC and suspect minorities in their country of residence; some were true believers in the KMT who had fought for it during the Second Sino-Japanese War (1937–1945) and continued doing so afterward. But more importantly, anticommunism was an expedient position for Chinese to adopt and perform given the discrimination they faced, the KMT's dominance of Chinese civic life, and the intimate ties between the ROC and Philippine states. For them, embracing the status quo was politically and personally useful; to challenge it was to risk being outed as a "communist" to the military and intelligence services in both countries, with which the KMT enjoyed close relations. Worse still, one could be deported to Taiwan. For these reasons, dissent was not absent but indirect, infrequent, and managed in ways that reinforced the KMT's near hegemony. Most nonconformists were not communists. They were, rather, non- or anti-anticommunists: persons who, by adopting less uncompromising attitudes toward the KMT–Chinese Communist Party (CCP) conflict than KMT partisans did, implicitly challenged the foundations of the KMT's influence in the country.

The Philippine Chinese: Ethnicity, Culture, and Nationality

At the heart of this book are the Philippine Chinese: residents of the Philippines of Chinese ancestry who saw themselves as culturally Chinese and were perceived as such by Filipinos.[7] This category of persons included legal citizens of both the Philippines and the ROC as well as mestizos of Chinese, Spanish, and Filipino heritage. Being "Chinese" was partly about self-identification and partly about how one was categorized and identified by other persons and states.[8] "Philippine Chinese" accommodates two popular contemporary signifiers of Chineseness. One is "Filipino Chinese," which refers to traditional or older Chinese who are largely Chinese in terms of their cultural identity but have acquired Philippine citizenship. The other is "Chinese Filipino," which has come to mean young, mostly native-born persons who identify themselves as Filipinos first but maintain their cultural Chineseness. "Philippine Chinese" can also mean those who were both culturally Chinese and ROC nationals. I prefer not to use the even broader identifier "Tsinoy" (or "Chinoy"), as this also includes individuals with some Chinese ancestry, such as the Philippine national hero Jose Rizal, who did not identify themselves as Chinese and were not identified as such.[9]

The Philippine Chinese from the 1930s to 1970s were unusual among their Southeast Asian counterparts in that an overwhelming 85 percent of them traced their ancestry to southern Fujian Province (Minnan or Hokkien) and the rest mostly to Guangdong, according to one estimate. In turn, 90 percent of Philippine Hokkien were from Jinjiang, Nan'an, and Hui'an Counties in Quanzhou Prefecture, with those from Jinjiang outnumbering those from the other two by an almost two-to-one ratio (see map 1).[10] No Chinese dialect group was as dominant in any other Southeast Asian country.[11] This considerable native-place homogeneity largely inhibited feuding between dialect groups and enabled a modified version of the Hokkien dialect to serve as the lingua franca for the entire community, Cantonese included.[12] Language aside, other markers of "Chinese" as opposed to "Filipino" identity have included participation in Chinese organizations such as dual-language schools, clan associations, and chambers of commerce; the observation of customs such as ancestor worship; occupation; and, importantly, the classificatory schemes of the states that laid sovereign claim to them.

Such schemes can be traced back to Spanish colonial rule in the Philippines (ca. 1565–1898). The Spanish labeled the Chinese *sangleys* (later, *chinos*) and in 1760 created the official legal category of "Chinese mestizo" in response to the islands' growing mixed-race population and to distinguish between mestizos and natives (*indios*).[13] From the mid-nineteenth century onward, however, increasing numbers of new Chinese emigrants gradually displaced mestizos from the professions that they had traditionally dominated, such as wholesaling and retailing. The Chinese mestizo gradually disappeared into the similarly hybrid ethnic category of "Filipino," even though a few continued to identify as "Chinese."[14] Simultaneously, ethno-cultural distinctions between Chinese and Filipinos, especially in Manila, widened in the late nineteenth century and especially during US rule (1898–1946). In extending the Chinese Exclusion Act to its new colonial possession in 1902, the United States abolished the ethno-legal category of "Chinese mestizo" and reclassified Chinese mestizos as "Filipinos." It also helped keep the Chinese occupationally separate from Filipinos and reinforced the association between ethnicity and economic occupation. Filipino and Chinese nationalisms had a similarly delineating impact on ethnic distinctions. The former principally targeted Spanish rule but also opposed "alien" domination of the colonial economy. Stereotypes of the Chinese as wealthy, corrupt merchants, opium addicts, secret society members, and petty criminals crystallized in the late nineteenth century, were reinforced under US rule, and persisted into the postcolonial period. Concurrently, efforts by the Chinese state, reformers, and revolutionaries to establish closer ties with Chinese communities overseas throughout this period reinforced how the Philippine Chinese understood themselves vis-à-vis Filipinos. In response to developments in their ancestral homeland and the Philippines, Chinese elites adopted what the historian Edgar Wickberg has called a "policy of organization and signification of their community." As others considered them a community, he writes, "so they considered themselves" one.[15]

Crucially, from the US period onward, the question of nationality also came to the forefront of the "Chinese question," as it would for all Southeast Asian states in time. By the start of the Commonwealth period in 1935, political opinion had shifted in favor of jus sanguinis citizenship. In 1939, a new naturalization law reflected this shift in the direction of populism and made obtaining citizenship for most Chinese extremely difficult. The state now controlled the "gate of citizenship," allowing it both to assign rights, privileges, and obligations to its citizens and to discriminate against the Chinese "alien."[16] After World War II, the Supreme Court cemented the Philippines' commitment to jus sanguinis. In the 1950s and 1960s, legislation that aimed at curbing purported Chinese dominance of the economy further solidified legal boundaries between Chinese and Filipinos. Only after 1972, under martial law, was naturalization simplified by presidential fiat to facilitate the mass political integration of locally born Chinese. The Philippines, in this respect, differed from other postcolonial Southeast Asian states in that its Chinese lacked a straightforward legal pathway to naturalized citizenship. Other governments—democratic and authoritarian alike—were proactive and often coercive in seeking to integrate their Chinese communities, but Manila remained indifferent to integration for the longest time. It was content to allow its small and relatively unproblematic Chinese community to remain a perpetually foreign body and largely the sovereign responsibility of another regime. This attitude goes a long way toward explaining the ideological identification of Chinese society with Taiwan and *Fangong kang'E*.

The Networked and Diasporic KMT

By the early US period, the Philippine and other overseas Chinese had become the objects of attention of the KMT. Today, the abbreviation refers to one of multiple political parties in Taiwan—the party of Sun Yat-sen and the Three Principles of the People (Sanminzhuyi). With respect to most of the twentieth century, however, we use "KMT" as a shorthand for the party-state (*dangguo*) that was founded in 1928 in mainland China and relocated to Taiwan after the KMT's military defeat in the Chinese civil war in 1949. Like its CCP–People's Republic of China (PRC) counterpart, this polity was based on the Soviet model of parallel, interlinked government and party structures. Rather confusingly—and this book is guilty as charged—we also describe this regime as "Taiwan," the "ROC," and "Nationalist China"; we freely interchange these labels even though the pre-1928 ROC was not ruled by the party that Sun founded and even though the post-1949 ROC controlled more territory than just the island of Taiwan. It is the KMT-ROC *dangguo* that historians of modern China and Taiwan focus on to produce what we might call territorialized scholarship on the KMT.[17] By contrast, the sum total of scholarship on the KMT in Southeast Asia is small and dated. Our understanding of the party overseas mostly comes by way of historians of the Chinese in the United States and, to a lesser extent, scholars of the Americas and Australasia.[18]

By focusing on the Philippines, *Diasporic Cold Warriors* underscores the need for scholars of East and Southeast Asia to think about the KMT transnationally. The party itself certainly did. In Manhattan's Chinatown, the Chinese Consolidated Benevolent Association building on Mott Street continues to fly the ROC flag today as a symbol of the association's intimate historical relationship with the KMT. In Singapore and Penang, respectively, the Sun Yat-sen Nanyang Memorial Hall and the Sun Yat-sen Museum remind visitors of the party's overseas origins—as indeed do official, KMT-sanctioned written narratives. These narratives tell a different story from most histories of modern China by depicting overseas Chinese activists and the anti-Qing predecessors of the KMT that they established as vital to the founding of the ROC.[19] For this reason, Sun supposedly called *huaqiao* the "mother of the revolution" (*huaqiao wei geming zhi mu*).[20]

The KMT's use of *huaqiao* (literally, "Chinese sojourner") throughout the twentieth century tells us how the party hoped these persons perceived their relationship to China. Coined in the late nineteenth century, this neologism emphasized one's belonging to a transnational *hua* community, temporary displacement from an imagined Chinese homeland, and sojourners' affinities for China, rather than where they happened to live.[21] It became integral to what the Asian American scholar-activist L. Ling-chi Wang calls the "loyalty paradigm" in narratives of Chinese migrant societies and to the KMT's project of "extraterritorial domination" in the United States.[22] Like its precursors, the KMT recognized, as the historian Prasenjit Duara writes, that while territorial nationalism may be the sole legitimate expression of sovereignty in the modern world, it is an inadequate basis for enabling identification with the nation-state. All nationalisms thus make use of more exclusive or broader narratives of historical community, based on common race, language, or culture, to create affective identification between the people and the nation.[23] In this way, Chinese living abroad, whom the Qing had branded traitors to the empire, were rehabilitated as members of a global, ethno-cultural nation. Such nationalist mythologizing became a feature of the KMT's diasporic mobilization, especially in the South Seas, or Nanyang, region, to which most Chinese migrated starting in the mid-nineteenth century.

During the 1920s and especially after it captured the state in 1927, the KMT consolidated its overseas networks and formulated a legal justification for "overseas Chinese affairs" (*qiaowu*). In 1929, the ROC government enacted a new nationality law that underpinned its "body-based sovereignty" over persons of Chinese descent in the decades that followed. I borrow this concept from the historian Nicole Phelps, who describes how US consuls looked to enforce their sovereignty over naturalized Americans in Habsburg territories and, in doing so, undermined the Westphalian idea that a government's citizens or subjects were only those persons who lived within the territory it controlled.[24] Underlying this legislation was the principle of jus sanguinis (*xuetong zhuyi*; "right of blood"). Like its 1909 Qing predecessor, the law treated as "Chinese nationals" (*zhongguo ren*) anyone whose father was Chinese when this person was born; anyone who was born after the death of the father and whose father was Chinese at the time of his death; and anyone whose mother was Chinese and whose father was of uncertain nationality or stateless. On paper, almost anyone born to a Chinese father, dead or alive, or to a Chinese mother and a dead or unknown father was a "Chinese national." It remained unchanged until 2000, when the new Democratic Progressive Party government of Taiwan amended it to include provisions for jus soli (birthplace) citizenship.[25]

The KMT-ROC, then, was a political network that connected China and Taiwan to Chinese communities abroad. Although it overlapped with and depended on Chinese migration networks, it was a different type of transnational formation.[26] The principal nodes of this network in foreign countries were party branches and subbranches, civic institutions such as newspapers and schools that were affiliated or ideologically aligned with the party, and diplomatic organs such as embassies and consulates. To varying degrees, these institutions were embedded in Chinese migrant societies. Party branches were formally subordinate to the KMT's highest governing organ and embassies and consulates to the Ministry of Foreign Affairs (MOFA), creating a hierarchy between the "center" (*zhongyang*) and "overseas" (*haiwai*).[27] Official party directives and ideologies such as *Fangong kang'E* flowed downward, across borders, from the former to the latter; in the opposite direction, diplomatic cables, reports on local party and Chinese affairs, and letters wishing Chiang Kai-shek a happy birthday apprised the center of its periphery. Finally, from itinerant party members to diplomats, diverse persons circulated through and built these networks, connecting *zhongyang* and *haiwai*. This was how the system was supposed to function.

Nationalist China engaged in diasporic mobilization through its overseas networks as much out of necessity as ideology. For most of its existence since 1912 and until it gave up any pretenses of "counterattacking the mainland" (*fangong dalu*), the ROC has been a territorially incomplete and partially sovereign state menaced by Western, Japanese, and Soviet imperialism from without and warlords and the CCP from within. Before 1949, the party never controlled more than a portion of the mainland; after 1949, it controlled none of it. Arguably, therefore, the ROC's need for "its" diaspora was more urgent after 1949. The party-state continued to assert that it looked out for the interests and rights of the overseas Chinese and that it protected them from discrimination and mistreatment by postcolonial states—and communism. KMT branches, schools, and other cultural and ideological organs of the party remained vital to how the center represented itself as a protector of Chinese traditions and how it mobilized this nation against a putatively despotic, materialistic CCP. The ROC persisted in employing the term *huaqiao* long after the term ceased to describe how most persons of Chinese descent living overseas understood their relationship to China. Even today, Taiwan's Overseas Community Affairs Council, the former OCAC, retains as its Chinese name the Qiaowu Weiyuanhui.

By contrast, the CCP was less interested in claiming *huaqiao* as "Chinese nationals." The PRC had no nationality law of its own until 1980.[28] From its founding to 1954, it was preoccupied with consolidating control domestically and the Korean War. It paid little attention to overseas Chinese affairs, even if there may have been party members and sympathizers everywhere. From the mid-1950s onward and especially after the 1955 Afro-Asian Conference in Bandung, the PRC explicitly encouraged *huaqiao* to become citizens of their countries of residence, adopt integrative practices such as intermarriage, and limit their pro-PRC activities to strengthen its relations with Southeast Asian states.[29] In effect, the PRC repudiated jus sanguinis citizenship and, in the words of one leading PRC scholar of Chinese migration, "decolonized" from Southeast Asia.[30] This was an important step in the transformation of Chinese sojourners into "ethnic Chinese" (*huaren*) and their descendants into "persons of Chinese descent" (*huayi*).[31]

The KMT, Shared Sovereignty, and the Intra-Asian Anticommunist Ecumene

For all the KMT's extraterritorial aspirations, its networks, organizations, and supporters were only able to entrench themselves as deeply as they did in the Philippines with the host state's acquiescence and involvement. Consequently, over time, ROC-Philippine ties with respect to the Philippine Chinese crystallized into an arrangement of what the political theorist Stephen D. Krasner calls "shared sovereignty," whereby recognized national political authorities voluntarily cooperate with external actors such as other states or regional and international organizations to jointly manage a particular issue.[32] In adopting such an approach, the Philippines stood out from the rest of the region. Other Southeast Asian states, wary though they were of the PRC and Chinese communism, were as suspicious of the KMT and its designs on their Chinese residents. At different times after 1945, Indonesia, Malaya, Thailand, and South Vietnam proscribed and suppressed the KMT. Not so the Philippines. There, the state tolerated the presence of a foreign state and a foreign political movement among foreign peoples within its sovereign territory. It inherited from the United States legislation that reinforced the foreignness of Chinese society and a predominantly laissez-faire approach toward governing the community. After independence in 1946, even though Manila intervened in Chinese commerce and education more extensively than before, it continued to allow Chinese leaders, supported by a Chinese state, to manage their own affairs. During the Cold War, Manila depended extensively on the KMT-ROC, with which it was ideologically aligned, to shore up its national security. Lacking knowledge of the Chinese language, the Philippine military relied on ROC diplomats and KMT activists to help gather and manufacture intelligence on suspected Chinese communists, who were then deported. Manila also gave Taiwan free rein to propagandize among "Chinese nationals" and mobilize them as diasporic Cold Warriors.

This sharing of sovereignty resembles but largely differs from the post-1945 Philippines' vastly more well-known relationship with the United States. The relationship was "neocolonial," in one political economist's view, because it constituted an "alliance between the leading class or classes of two independent nations which facilitate[d] their ability to maintain a dominant position over the rest of the population of the weaker of the two nations."[33] More concretely, it manifested itself in the form of US military bases on Philippine soil, control over trade policy, military and economic aid, and election interference. I hesitate, however, to treat the KMT's involvement in Philippine-Chinese society in similar conceptual terms. While Chinese and Filipino elites certainly benefited from the Sino-Philippine partnership, and while it was certainly not frictionless, it was essentially one between relative equals. However much it may have engaged in a kind of internal colonialism in Taiwan after 1945, the KMT utterly lacked the political, economic, and military might needed to act neocolonially overseas.[34] As the examples of other Southeast Asian countries that rejected its extraterritorial claims suggest, the transnational KMT depended on other national governments to survive abroad. This is further evidenced by how, in no small part due to a series of far-reaching executive decisions by President Ferdinand Marcos, the partnership unraveled within a few years in the early 1970s. That this unraveling took place immediately after the KMT-engineered deportation of two Chinese newspapermen to Taiwan in May 1970—an event that seemed to represent the zenith of the KMT's hold on Chinese society—suggests that shared sovereignty was ultimately a fragile and contingent formation.

Shared sovereignty as a conceptual framework is equally useful in helping us to think about the Cold War that Manila, Taipei, and the Philippine Chinese waged in relation to conventional narratives of the conflict. Like the United States, the two states at the core of this book shared concerns toward the PRC as what the historian Ang Cheng Guan labels a "new subsidiary communist hub in East and Southeast Asia."[35] After 1949, the fear of Sino-communism and Southeast Asia's Chinese as potential CCP agents escalated. In the Philippines, intelligence reports from this period abound with references to local Chinese as "fifth columnists," rumors of CCP operatives and propaganda being smuggled into the country, and wildly inaccurate estimates of the number of Chinese communists and their sympathizers. Likewise, the ROC was adamant that the CCP was expanding into Nanyang and viewed all its overseas work after 1949 as related to the battle against communism.[36] To this end, it churned out a stream of propaganda including one tract called *The Communist Bandits' Plot against the Overseas Chinese* (*Gongfei dui huaqiao zhi yinmou*). In it, the KMT accused the CCP not only of crimes against overseas Chinese who had returned to China but also of conspiring with "Russian imperialists" (*E di*) to corrupt *huaqiao* and, through them, destabilize Southeast Asian countries from within.[37] The responsibility of *huaqiao* was to unite and assist "the free world's struggle against communism" (*ziyou shijie de fangong douzheng*).[38] In many ways, their success in the Philippines emphasizes how Southeast Asia's Cold War was, except for Indochina, a victory for anticommunism.[39]

Diasporic Cold Warriors departs, however, from US-centric studies of the Cold War in the region by focusing on Asian state and nonstate actors. If, as the anthropologist Susan Bayly contends, Vietnamese and Indian intellectuals in the 1970s and 1980s were part of a "worldwide socialist ecumene," then our titular protagonists helped construct an intra-Asian anticommunist ec-umene: a space of interaction that united intellectuals, merchants, students, military officials, politicians, Chinese, and Filipinos under the banner of anti-communism.[40] The United States is not absent from this book, but, unlike in standard Cold War histories involving Taiwan and the Philippines, it is a mi-nor player.[41] US State Department, Central Intelligence Agency (CIA), and Asia Foundation records reveal that although the United States monitored Philip-pine *huaqiao*, it intervened minimally in the Chinese community beyond tar-geting it for propaganda. For example, as opposed to operations against Filipino communists, those specifically against suspected Sino-communists after 1945 often took place without US involvement or even knowledge. The United States, while willingly allowing Taipei and Manila to surveil and police Chi-nese society, remained mostly an onlooker.

The Cold War I am interested in was intra-Asian rather than US-driven. Yet beyond the Association of Southeast Asian Nations regional organization, we know little about anticommunist connections within the region compared to, for example, left-wing ties between Indonesia, North Vietnam, and the PRC.[42] We typically associate anticommunist movements with the nation-state, whose integrity right-wingers looked to protect against deracinated, cosmopolitan transnationals. But if the left operated across borders, it stands to reason that their enemies did so as well—mimicking and opposing them at the same time.[43] This logic animated Nationalist China and its overseas Chinese sup-porters in the Philippines and elsewhere. Their transnational networks rein-forced right-wing nationalist ideologies and were constitutive of an alternative, very much understudied, East Asian Cold War.[44]

Ideology and Chineseness

This book is also, unlike most histories of the United States and the Cold War in Southeast Asia, about society and culture as much as, if not more than, di-plomacy. If fantasies of Chinese communism's infiltration of diasporic com-munities drove right-wing mobilization throughout the region, then diplomatic history can only plumb the surface of regional anticommunism. As the histo-rians Taomo Zhou and Meredith Oyen do in their studies of China-Indonesia and US-China migration diplomacy, we must also attend to overseas Chinese communities as sites of contestation and non-contestation between states and factions.[45] Viewed from the bottom up, anticommunism and its challengers were sets of localized and transnational social, cultural, and political practices, from the arrest and deportation of Chinese communist suspects to the KMT's transformation of Chinese associational life to the staging of propagandistic rituals such as visits to Taiwan and theater performances. Collectively, these practices produced the Cold War not as external to Chinese society and as affecting it, but as a social and cultural reality that states, social organizations, and persons helped create.[46]

The KMT's diasporic networks, its collaboration with the Philippine state, and the intra-Asian anticommunist ecumene that it constituted had profound consequences for the Philippine Chinese. But we would not know this from narratives of the community that emphasize cultural integration, on the one hand, and its economic life, on the other. The first narrative is exemplified by *Tsinoy: The Story of the Chinese in Philippine Life*, a lavishly illustrated coffee-table book that spans several hundred years of history and tells the story of how the Chinese who migrated to the Philippines became Filipinized, the trials and tribulations they faced, and their many contributions to Filipino society and culture.[47] It was published in 2005 by Kaisa Para sa Kaunlaran (Unity for Progress), a grassroots civic organization that young, college-educated Chinese established in 1970 to advocate for jus soli citizenship and cultural integration.[48] Today, Kaisa promotes interethnic understanding and goodwill and the "integration of the ethnic Chinese into mainstream Philippine society."[49] Its credo reads: "Our blood may be Chinese, but our roots grow deep in Filipino soil; our bonds are with the Filipino people."[50]

Tsinoy's story is a familiar one, and not only to scholars of the Chinese diaspora who study efforts to forge what the historian Adam McKeown calls "ethnic identities appropriate to pluralist polities" in "some sort of hybrid formulation."[51] It reproduces tropes common to histories of other minorities and speaks to universal experiences of intercultural interaction, adaptation, and persecution by the dominant ethnic group. Like Kaisa's other publications, this volume tells us much about how Tsinoys wish to be seen.[52] While it offers a necessary corrective to official national histories and challenges anti-Chinese prejudices, it is also incomplete. Its postwar chapters omit any mention of Taiwan's influence, even though they refer to the establishment of PRC-Philippine relations in 1975. The KMT, one of the largest Chinese organizations in the country in the 1950s and 1960s, does not feature in the section "Network of Organizations" and is nearly completely absent from the book.[53] There is nothing in it on anticommunism or support for Taiwan.

A metanarrative of depoliticization also underpins the second narrative, which focuses on the patriarchal—overwhelmingly if not exclusively male—business community.[54] The class interests of the Philippine-Chinese businessman are depicted as synonymous with those of Chinese society in general, to the exclusion of other social groups such as intellectuals. He was "political" only to the extent that he sought leadership positions within Chinese society and attempted to forge mutually beneficial, patron-client ties with local politicians that enhanced his commercial ventures. While he may have participated in China-centric politics during the Second Sino-Japanese War, the times had changed. He could not return to China, where he faced persecution as a member of the capitalist bourgeoisie. Acknowledging that his future lay with his country of residence, he hoped to cope with the discriminatory policies toward his family, his business, and his community that his new political masters had implemented.

Diasporic Cold Warriors politicizes both narratives by arguing that the KMT's and the Philippines' intersecting anticommunist projects and sharing of sovereignty were instrumental to how the Chinese adapted themselves to the postcolonial Philippines and forged for themselves suitable ideological identities. As the historian Fredy González writes in his book on the Mexican Chinese, transnational ties between Chinese migrant societies and China did not necessarily inhibit the integration of the former into their nations of residence, but could enable it.[55] In addition to businessmen, the journalists, educators, teachers, war veterans, students, criminals, and other Chinese social groups in this book were far from indifferent to the China-Taiwan split. Instead, many exploited it in response to anti-Chinese sentiment and legislation. If, as the literary scholar Caroline S. Hau argues, the Chinese were racially territorialized as aliens loyal to China under US rule, then their racial and territorial foreignness assumed an ideological dimension after 1945, especially with the outbreak of the left-wing Hukbalahap Rebellion and the CCP's victory in the Chinese civil war in the late 1940s.[56] Filipino elites identified communism as an "un-Filipino" foreign ideology that was hostile to democracy and inclined toward authoritarianism. Discriminated against for their supposed domination of the economy and ethno-cultural distinctiveness, the Chinese were also ideologically heterodox and vulnerable to blackmail, arrest, and deportation as "communists" or communist sympathizers. As nationals of one state and residents of another, many Chinese, by aligning themselves with an ideology that these states shared, fashioned themselves as "good Philippine residents and good Chinese citizens."[57]

Ideology was thus more than a matter of belief and unbelief and Chineseness more than a matter of ethnicity and culture, narrowly defined. Numerous Philippine Chinese, KMT members especially, were true anticommunists and believers in the ROC, even after 1949; others were in it purely for political and economic self-aggrandizement; most were driven by both belief and expediency, which can be hard to pry apart. What matters is that by practicing anticommunism, they acted in ways that signaled to their fellow Chinese, Filipinos, and the ROC the "right" beliefs, irrespective of how deeply held these beliefs were. Ethno-cultural aspects of being Chinese, such as language, customs, and physical features, were difficult if not impossible to shed or conceal. Ideology, by contrast, was largely performative. In the words of the literary theorist Terry Eagleton, it is "a suasive or rhetorical rather than veridical kind of speech, concerned less with the situation 'as it is' than with the production of certain useful effects for political purposes."[58] Anticommunist practices served such suasive purposes. From forming civic institutions to fundraising in support of the ROC to informing on suspected Chinese Reds to the state, they helped Chinese mitigate racial prejudices toward them by emphasizing their ideological bona fides. They could also elevate certain individuals' or factions' reputations within the community at the expense of others'.

All Philippine Chinese had to reckon with the interweaving of anticommunism into their lives, but not all were full-throated anticommunists and supporters of the ROC—certainly not the founders of the civic organization Pagkakaisa sa Pag-unlad (Unity in Progress), for example. A secondary goal of this book is to explain how such persons' "tactics," to use Michel de Certeau's term, contested the "strategies" of anticommunism.[59] Support for communism and the CCP was the most direct tactical option available, particularly during the Chinese civil war. However, explicit commitment to communism among the Chinese declined after 1949 as anti-leftist strategies, backed by Manila, Taipei, and Philippine-Chinese elites, were institutionalized. A "desire to fight back against instituted power," as the anthropologists Judith Farquhar and Qicheng Zhang caution us, cannot be regarded as "natural, inevitable, or even the most interesting aspect of social life"—not when resistance was costly and compliance beneficial.[60] Nor should we treat the ideological positions of the Philippine Chinese as falling into the simple binary of anticommunism-communism. Instead, the obverse of anticommunism was sometimes non- or anti-anticommunism. I use this idea to designate stances and practices that, intentional or not, expressed discomfort and indirect opposition to anticommunism. For example, the *Chinese Commercial News* (*CCN*), the country's most well-read Chinese newspaper in the 1950s and 1960s, published articles that both praised and criticized the ROC and PRC, unlike mouthpieces of the KMT. The paper also supported Chinese cultural and political integration into Filipino society. In opposing the KMT's ethnocentrism and chauvinism, more liberal, multicultural Chinese such as the *CCN*'s editors questioned the association between Chineseness and the ROC and undermined the KMT's legal and cultural claims on them. Like their right-wing counterparts, these persons performed a particular civic identity to integrate into the nation.

Sources and Organization of the Book

To explain how the Philippine Chinese became such committed Cold Warriors, this book draws on sources chiefly from Taiwan, the Philippines, and the United States. Materials from the ROC MOFA Archives document, often in great detail, developments in Philippine-Chinese society. They reveal, fundamentally, the extraordinary attention that the ROC paid to the overseas Chinese and how it worked with and through the organs of the Philippine state to manage Chinese society. They are also a repository for sources that we would otherwise not have access to or that no longer exist, such as Philippine government correspondence and clippings from defunct Philippine-Chinese newspapers. By contrast, the KMT Archives are less comprehensive, especially after 1949. At the intraparty level, official written communication between *zhongyang* and *haiwai*—between the Central Committee in Taipei and the KMT headquarters in Manila—and between the party in Manila and its provincial branches, appears to have been minimal. The periphery enjoyed considerable autonomy from the center despite being formally subordinate to it.

Research and fieldwork in the Philippines have proved invaluable in helping me flesh out the social dimensions of this book. While access to government documents in the country remains uneven, collections of presidential papers at different private libraries and archives have allowed me to make sense of official Sinophobia and anticommunism from the late 1940s to the early 1950s. Most of all, I make use of the single richest collection of sources on the Philippine Chinese in the country, the Chinben See Memorial Library at the Kaisa Heritage Center, which is named after one of Kaisa's late founders and a pioneering scholar of the Philippine Chinese. The Chinese- and English-language materials from the 1950s to the 1970s deposited there represent an astonishing array of institutions, individuals, and interests. They also abound with evidence of the special relationship between Taiwan and the Philippine Chinese and the omnipresence of *Fangong kang'E* as a cultural slogan and set of practices.

The book is organized as follows. Chapters 1 and 2 set the scene for the Cold War era by tracing the emergence of the Philippine KMT before 1949. Chapter 1 explains how the KMT institutionalized itself in the country and clashed with Sino-communism there before the Japanese occupation, especially during the 1930s. It argues, principally, that despite the apparent advantages that accrued to the KMT under US rule, the party was in no position of hegemony at any point before 1942 and the playing field between it and the Chinese left was fairly level. The scales began to tip toward the KMT in the two years or so immediately after 1945. Chapter 2 covers this "period of bloody struggle" from 1945 to late 1947, explaining the party's renewed conflict with the Chinese left and collaboration with the coercive organs of the Philippine state against their common nemesis. Concurrently, legal and diplomatic developments such as the signing of a treaty of amity between the ROC and the Philippines in April 1947 legitimized the party's occupation of civic space in Chinese society and its body-based sovereign claims on "Chinese nationals" in the Philippines. In 1949, the KMT was militarily defeated in mainland China and being proscribed elsewhere in Southeast Asia. In the Philippines, however, it had carved out a sphere of influence for itself through coercive and legal means. The Chinese left, having miscalculated tactically in its bid for power after World War II, found itself deinstitutionalized; its prewar and wartime leaders had mostly departed for China.

Diasporic Cold Warriors then turns to how different groups of Chinese adapted to the anti-Chinese, anticommunist ideological climate in the Philippines in the early to mid-1950s. Chapter 3 explains the key theme of practicing anticommunism that runs through the entire book. It describes the activities of three clusters of Chinese "anticommunists"—including two men closely affiliated with the local KMT—in pursuit of social status, political patronage, and economic profit. It argues that Chinese anticommunism in this particular Cold War and postcolonial context was just as much about—and often only about—ideological self-fashioning, self-aggrandizement, and class warfare as it was about commitment to the KMT's cause. Chapter 4 details two interconnected episodes involving the detention and trials of Chinese charged with being communists. The first saw around three hundred, virtually all innocent, individuals—including multiple KMT members—arrested by the Philippine military in late December 1952 largely based on testimonies by the sole communist among them, Koa Chian; the second involved a group of high school students from Cebu who self-radicalized and became communists. The examples of Koa and the Cebu students reveal that Chinese communism in the Philippines persisted as a limited alternative to the solidifying, KMT-approved ideological status quo. Crucially, though, ROC officials and local Chinese leaders reacted to both episodes by negotiating with the Philippine state to rectify the pursuit of Chinese communists in the country and turn crisis to their advantage.

The next three chapters of the book describe the KMT's dominance of Chinese society and culture in the Philippines and the transnational ties between this society and Taiwan that were part of the intra-Asian anticommunist ecumene. Chapter 5 examines how conservative, pro-ROC elites restructured the community in the mid-1950s in response to anti-Chinese measures and in doing so transformed it into a more effective vehicle for propagating *Fangong kang'E.* Institutions such as CKSHS and the PCACL helped create a more ideo-logically uniform diasporic society that was linked to Filipinos, the ROC, and indeed global anticommunism. In the same thematic vein, chapter 6 analyzes a handful of the many visits that Chinese civic groups in the Philippines such as the PCACL organized to "Free China." I use these visits to explore how the ROC represented itself to the world as a "homeland" for the overseas Chinese and shaped the diaspora's perceptions of the ROC through experiential nation-alism. Yet those who organized and went on the visits, I show, did not necessar-ily subscribe to *Fangong kang'E* and instead demonstrated diverse understandings of patriotism and what the ROC stood for.

Chapter 7 focuses on the most infamous incident in relations between Na-tionalist China and the Philippines: the Yuyitung affair. Quintin and Rizal Yuy-itung, respectively the editor and publisher of the *CCN*, were arrested by the military on May 4, 1970, and deported to Taiwan as pro-communist "Chinese nationals" by order of President Ferdinand Marcos. The affair vividly illustrates how the KMT regime laid sovereign claim to the Philippine Chinese through its diasporic networks and conspired with Manila against their common Cold War enemy. It also provides valuable insights into how more liberal Chinese articulated their dissent from the ideological status quo through what I call non- or anti-anticommunism. The paper's nonconformist approach to report-ing news on China and vocal support for Chinese cultural integration indi-rectly challenged the hegemony of anticommunism and the KMT's grip on Chinese society. At the same time, the affair makes clear how the diasporic Cold Warriors who represented and sought to protect the status quo reacted to perceived heterodoxy.

Finally, picking up from where chapter 7 leaves off, the Conclusion explains how, during the first three years of martial law in the Philippines from 1972 to 1975, Marcos nationalized Chinese schools, simplified the naturalization pro-cess for foreign nationals, and paved the way for the Philippines to recognize the PRC in 1975. Together with longer-term social and cultural changes, these executive decisions accelerated the large-scale localization of the Philippine Chinese and the un-sharing of its sovereignty with the ROC. The KMT did not simply disintegrate without a trace though. Institutionally attenuated, it lived on in the political imagination of its loyalists. I then recapitulate the book's core narrative on the Philippine Chinese as Cold Warriors and its principal ar-guments: namely, on the diasporic and networked KMT; how the KMT's net-works enabled the sharing of sovereignty between the ROC and the Philippines and gave form to an intra-Asian anticommunist ecumene; and how these net-works politicized Chinese identity formation and civic integration. In the fi-nal few pages, I reflect on how the book can serve as a starting point for thinking about China and the Chinese in Southeast Asia more generally, both during the Cold War and in our time. More broadly, I sketch the outlines for a global Chinese history that focuses on the experiences of Chinese peoples and polities and how Chineseness was made and unmade, in diverse settings in and beyond China.

CHAPTER 1

The KMT, Chinese Society, and Chinese Communism in the Philippines before 1942

On March 2, 1947, the Kuomintang's (KMT) general branch in the Philippines officially reopened, having been destroyed during World War II. Of those who addressed the twelve hundred in attendance for the reopening ceremony at the party's headquarters on Benavidez Street in Manila's Chinatown, three are especially significant. The first was the Chinese consul Chen Chih-ping, who presided over the ceremony. Chen, who later became the Republic of China's (ROC) first ambassador to the Southeast Asian nation, stressed that the KMT and the Chinese diaspora were inseparable, describing the latter as "vanguard troops" (*xianfeng budui*) of the former and exhorting those present to preserve the party's glorious history and "carry forward [Sun Yat-sen's Three Principles of the People] into the world" (*hongyang yu shijie*). The second speaker of note was sixty-one-year-old Ong Chuan Seng (see figure 1.1). The founder and principal of Chiang Kai-shek High School (Zhongzheng Zhongxue, or CKSHS) in Manila, Ong was also a member of the Central Executive Committee (Zhongyang Zhixing Weiyuanhui, or CEC), the KMT's highest decision-making organ, in Nanjing. Ong recalled being present at the founding of the general branch on October 11, 1921, exactly a decade and a day after the start of the Xinhai Revolution, which overthrew China's last imperial dynasty, the Qing. Looking backward, Ong traced the history of the Philippine KMT to early twentieth-century anti-Qing groups in the archipelago and to precursors of the party such as the Revive China Society (Xingzhonghui) and the Revolutionary

FIGURE 1.1. A bust of Ong Chuan Seng at Chiang Kai-shek College. Author's photograph.

Alliance (Tongmenghui). Reflecting on his present, he described the party's nation-building project, following the ratification of a new constitution in late 1946, as entering its third and final stage, that of creating a constitutional government. The third person of importance, although not physically present, was Chiang Kai-shek, who spoke to the audience through "instructions" (*xunci*) that he had written to commemorate the occasion. In it, he reminded the attendees of their responsibilities to the Chinese nation and urged them to "collectively encourage loyalty" (*tong li zhongcheng*).[1]

This ceremony challenges Sinologists' mainland-centered understandings of the pre-1949 KMT by emphasizing how the party represented itself diasporically and was linked to overseas Chinese societies through the institutions and individuals that formed its transnational networks. CKSHS, the CEC, the ROC Consulate, and the party's general branch constituted just a few of the many organizational ties between the party-state and the Philippine Chinese. Each of the three individuals in question linked the KMT-ROC party-state in China to the party and its constituents overseas by crossing borders—in Chiang's case, figuratively—to be in the Philippines. As the leader who had overseen China's victory against Japan in the war, Chiang personified an imagined Chinese nation that extended beyond China's borders and that Chinese everywhere were supposed to owe their loyalties to. Chen Chih-ping, in his capacity as an official diplomatic representative of the ROC, articulated China's solicitude for the overseas Chinese—a key pillar of its foreign policy.[2] As both a local school principal and one of only several overseas Chinese members of the CEC, Ong Chuan Seng symbolically straddled China and the Philippines— the center and its periphery. A founder of the Philippine KMT, Ong, like Chiang, embodied the ties between the party's prewar history and the postwar scene. His speech joined these temporal segments to each other in a stagist, teleological narrative, driven by the KMT, that he believed was culminating in the realization of Sun Yat-sen's vision of a democratic China.

In the same historical spirit of this ceremony and to set the stage for the rest of the book, this chapter examines how the KMT established itself in the Philippines from the late 1920s to the eve of the Japanese occupation, the Philippines as a setting for overseas Chinese history, and the clash between the KMT and the Chinese left in the country. Throughout the prewar period, despite the KMT-ROC party-state's increasingly institutionalized efforts at diasporic mobilization after 1927, the party's position in Philippine-Chinese society was less secure than it became after World War II. US colonialism, it is true, facilitated the emergence of a Chinese capitalist class that was largely unsympathetic to communism; excluded from the islands Chinese laborers who might have formed a critical proletarian mass for left-wing mobilization; permitted the KMT to operate openly; and suppressed communism until the late 1930s. Some of these factors propelled the KMT's ascent after 1945. But unlike in the 1950s, Chinese communism in the Philippines grew during the 1930s in partnership with the Filipino left and in spite of seemingly unfavorable structural conditions. The KMT faced financial difficulties and was generally unpopular among members of the Chinese community's de facto governing body, the Philippine

Chinese General Chamber of Commerce in Manila (Feilübin Minlila Zhong-hua Shanghui). Internal factionalism bedeviled the party from the 1930s on-ward, even during the Second Sino-Japanese War (or the War of Resistance, as it was known in China), supposedly the high-water mark of overseas Chinese nationalism. In December 1941, with Japan poised to invade and occupy the archipelago, it is difficult to say which of these two Chinese factions held the upper hand.

KMT Networks beyond China, 1894–1930s

The political organization that we describe as the KMT emerged in the first half of the twentieth century by embedding itself in a landscape of Chinese mobility that extended across and beyond a globalizing, modernizing China. It began as a decentralized, heterogeneous aggregate of anti-Qing societies held together by a small group of committed revolutionaries and was transformed after 1927 into a bureaucratized, hierarchical network that radiated outward from the National-ist capital in Nanjing. Similar to chambers of commerce in the early twentieth-century lower Yangtze delta region, the overseas KMT developed into what the historian Zhongping Chen calls an "associational network," within which inter-personal and institutional relations were intertwined with each other and with broader socioeconomic and political forces.[3] Yet, while the KMT in some ways resembled existing kinship and commercial networks, it is irreducible to and dif-fered from them in other ways. As the examples of Ong Chuan Seng and other Hokkiens whom we will encounter suggest, native-place migration routes un-derlay the itineraries of many nationalists who moved between China and the Philippines. However, the KMT's ecumene was not a closed space and could ac-commodate those not from the typical Philippine-Chinese home villages in Jinji-ang and other counties in Quanzhou. Both the party's networks and migration networks joined the overseas Chinese to China. But if the former linked emi-grants' villages and places of sojourn through real and imagined ancestral rela-tions, party branches abroad connected these emigrants to each other and to their imagined counterparts in China by perpetuating an ideology that suppos-edly transcended native place. The party did not contribute to migration as what Adam McKeown calls "a viable economic strategy and stable system for the cir-culation of goods, people, information, and profit," but rather leveraged existing migration patterns to network the Chinese national revolution.[4]

In official and semiofficial narratives of the KMT's history such as Ong's, the party traces its origins to Sun Yat-sen's founding of the Xingzhonghui in Honolulu on November 24, 1894. Eleven years later, after twice trying and failing to overthrow the Qing, Sun merged the Xingzhonghui and other anti-Qing organizations into the Tongmenghui. In accordance with its constitution, five Tongmenghui branches were established in China and four overseas: in Nanyang (Singapore), Europe (Belgium), the Americas (San Francisco), and Hawai'i (Honolulu).[5] Each of these branches was responsible for revolutionary activities in a particular world region. In Southeast Asia, with guidance from Singapore, Tongmenghui branches were created in Siam, Burma, and the Dutch East Indies in the years leading up to the fall of the Qing dynasty in 1911. In that year, just a few months before the revolution, the Philippine branch was founded at the initiative of a Hong Kong Tongmenghui member.[6] The first KMT was constituted from these branches, in and beyond China, and from several smaller revolutionary parties, to contest the republic's first national elections in 1912. A year later, however, Sun was again forced to seek refuge overseas when the ROC's first president, Yuan Shikai, banned the KMT. Sun's newest political party, the Chinese Revolutionary Party (Zhongguo Geming Dang, or CRP), was born in Tokyo and of his disillusionment with democracy and KMT members' ill discipline and disunity. Henceforth, Sun required that all CRP members swear oaths of secrecy, fully devote themselves to the revolutionary cause, and obey him unquestioningly.[7] The CRP was reorganized into the second KMT after the May Fourth Movement in 1919, but it remained unable to operate openly in China.

In these early years of the KMT, there was no bureaucratic mechanism to ensure coherence between party branches in China and those overseas. In lieu of a fixed, institutionalized center and overseas branches, there was the itinerant leadership of Sun Yat-sen, his ever-changing coterie of loyalists, and their interpersonal, transnational webs of political friendship. Wang Jingwei, for example, was instrumental in organizing the Tongmenghui in Siam in 1908.[8] In the Philippines, the establishment of the CRP there owed much to Ong Chuan Seng, a Tongmenghui member whom Sun sent to the islands after the KMT's failure to overthrow Yuan in 1913.[9]

Refounded in 1919, the KMT was reorganized again in 1923, this time with support from the Comintern, into a Leninist vanguard party, becoming the senior partner in an anti-imperialist united front with the Chinese Communist Party (CCP). This was a vital juncture in the history of the KMT's efforts at overseas mobilization and at ensuring that, to quote one of its main slogans, "the party was present wherever there were large numbers of overseas Chinese."[10] Now based in Canton (Guangzhou), Sun laid down detailed regulations for the establishment and functioning of party branches abroad. These included requiring general branches (zongzhibu) in large or capital cities to "accept an executive appointed by the Canton party headquarters to carry out party duties or resolutions." On paper, *zongzhibu* also had jurisdiction over lower-level party branches (*zhibu*), subbranches (*fenbu*), and sub-subbranches (*qufenbu*) in smaller towns with a Chinese presence.[11] In January 1924, forty overseas representatives attended the KMT's First National Party Congress in Canton, right after which the party created the Overseas Department (Haiwaibu), which Sun chaired, to provide centralized direction to *zongzhibu* abroad.[12] Overseas party branches proliferated as the KMT mobilized the diaspora against warlordism. By June 1925, the party's overseas membership was estimated at 43,612 and its reach had expanded beyond East Asia, the United States, Canada, and continental Europe to include Cuba, Mexico, Australia, India, South Africa, and England.[13] By the Second National Party Congress in 1926, *zongzhibu* and around three hundred *zhibu* and *fenbu* had been established in every Southeast Asian country.[14]

The KMT and CCP's successful Northern Expedition and subsequent split in 1927 ushered in a new organizational and ideological phase in the KMT's diasporic project; it is from this point on that distinctions between the KMT as a political movement and the ROC as the government become blurred because of the former's incorporation into the latter. As part of its anticommunist purge and drive toward administrative centralization, the CEC instructed all overseas branches to reorganize themselves and reregister their members in 1928.[15] After *qufenbu* were abolished, the three tiers of the party and its collective leadership overseas were restructured, as table 1.1 illustrates.[16]

In 1932, Sun's Overseas Department was renamed the Overseas Party Affairs Committee (Haiwai Dangwu Weiyuanhui, or OPAC). Subordinate to the CEC, it was responsible for organizing and expanding the party abroad, disseminating information through party newspapers, disciplining and indoctrinating members, working with the CEC's Organization and Propaganda Committees on propaganda plans, coordinating between party branches and consulates, and protecting overseas Chinese from discrimination.[17] State agencies such as the Ministry of Foreign Affairs (MOFA), the Education Ministry, and the Overseas Chinese Affairs Commission (OCAC) complemented and overlapped with OPAC in engaging the diaspora; within the regime's parallel party-state structure, these institutions were subordinate to the Executive Yuan, rather than to the CEC. OCAC, for instance, which was founded in 1926, worked with ROC diplomatic missions, compiled textbooks, and established schools throughout Southeast Asia.[18] Figure 1.2 diagrams how these agencies mediated between the party-state in China and Chinese societies abroad in the 1930s.

One further KMT diasporic organization was specifically vital to the rise of the Philippine KMT. During the Nanjing Decade (1927–1937), the KMT was convulsed by internal disputes and the emergence of factions that lay outside

Table 1.1 Organizational structure of KMT *zongzhibu, zhibu,* and *fenbu* overseas as stipulated by the Central Executive Committee in 1928

	EXECUTIVE COMMITTEE (ZHIXING WEIYUANHUI)	STANDING COMMITTEE (CHANGWU WEIYUANHUI)	DEPARTMENTS (*KE*) / SECTIONS (*GU*)
General branch (*zongzhibu*)	9 or 11 persons, elected by *zongzhibu* members	3 persons, chosen by the Executive Committee	9 *ke* (Organization, Propaganda, Training, Overseas Nationals, Investigation, Public Relations, Secretariat, Accounting, General Affairs); heads of each chosen by the Executive Committee
Branch (*zhibu*)	5 or 7 persons, elected by *zhibu* members	1 person, chosen by the Executive Committee	7 *ke* (the above, but less Investigation and Secretariat)
Subbranch (*fenbu*)	3 or 5 persons, elected by *fenbu* members	1 person, chosen by the Executive Committee	7 *gu* (same as above)

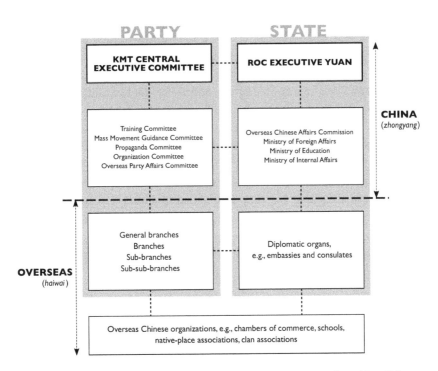

FIGURE 1.2.   The KMT-ROC's overseas Chinese bureaucracy in the 1930s. Adapted from Yoji Akashi, *The Nanyang Chinese National Salvation Movement, 1937–1941* (Lawrence: Center for East Asian Studies, University of Kansas, 1970), 4–5; and Yang Jiancheng, *Zhongguo Guomindang haiwai gongzuo de lilun yu shijian, 1924–1991* ([Taipei], 2001), 14.

the party-state structure but vied for power within the regime. The most extreme of these factions was the Blue Shirts (Lanyi She), a paramilitary group formed in response to the Japanese invasion of Manchuria in September 1931. Its core members were graduates of the Whampoa Military Academy and fanatically loyal to its first commandant, Chiang Kai-shek. Historians describe the structure of the Blue Shirts as pyramidal or consisting of concentric circles. At the top of the pyramid, or within the innermost circle, was the Forceful Action Society (Lixingshe), which Chiang led. Beneath this were two groups, one of which, the Chinese Young Comrades Association, became the main front for the Lixingshe. The Lixingshe also organized a third tier or ring, the Renaissance Society (Fuxingshe), which included as many as five hundred thousand members by the time Chiang disbanded the Blue Shirts in 1938.[19] As we will see, the Blue Shirts, specifically the Fuxingshe, were very much active in the Philippines, where they left a lasting imprint on the KMT for decades.

By the early Nanjing Decade, therefore, the Nationalist regime in China had established a network of central and peripheral institutions with which to mobilize the overseas Chinese. It was also during this period, in 1929, that the state passed its Nationality Law and affirmed jus sanguinis as the ideological basis for diasporic mobilization. Do these institutions and laws corroborate the diplomat and historian Stephen Fitzgerald's claim that the "nearest approach to a simple colonial position on China's relations with Chinese in Southeast Asia was represented by the policies of the Kuomintang"?[20] They do—but we should not confuse the KMT's colonialist aspirations with reality. The KMT's efforts to modernize China during the Nanjing era were beset by factionalism, corruption, fiscal problems, and bureaucratic inertia.[21] Unable to reorder social relations in rural China, for example, the state had even less control over its overseas branches. These branches were supposed to obey directives from *zhongyang*, but they were financed entirely by their members and subject to conditions beyond Nanjing's control, such as the migration policies and laws of other states.[22] The regime, to a large extent, depended on diasporic loyalists to ensure that its overseas networks functioned effectively in territories beyond its sovereign control.

Philippine-Chinese Society and the KMT in the 1930s

In the Philippines, one node among hundreds in the KMT's overseas Chinese networks, US colonial rule shaped a social structure and legal framework that was advantageous to the party-state. In the late 1920s, the islands had been an insular territory of the United States for three decades and were a few years from becoming a self-governing commonwealth in 1935. On the eve of the Great Depression, the Philippine economy was booming, underpinned by free trade with the United States and a vibrant domestic sector. Chinese merchants were among those who benefited from this sustained growth. Like Spain before it, the United States desired a stable, law-abiding, and economically viable Chinese society. To realize this objective, it cultivated Chinese elites through the General Chamber of Commerce to develop profitable industries, such as lumber, tobacco, and sugar.[23] Although their role in the Philippine export sector diminished over time, Chinese businessmen were able to exploit the rising purchasing power of a growing population to expand their share of the domestic economy. Besides serving as intermediaries between producers and consumers in the exchange of goods, they also moved into new manufacturing activities and began providing financial services to a mostly Chinese clientele.[24] Unsurprisingly, Wong Kwok-chu, the foremost economic historian of the Chinese in the Philippines, describes 1909–1929 as a "golden era" for Chinese capitalists.[25] Over the course of more than three decades, the proportion of Chinese who self-identified as engaged in trade or commerce increased, according to official census data. In 1902, 55 percent of Chinese surveyed (23,364 out of 42,097) were categorized into the occupational group of "trade and transportation." By 1918, this figure had increased to 58 percent (28,501 out of 48,337), and in 1939, 62 percent (41,864 out of 67,035) were involved in what the authorities deemed "trade."[26]

US immigration laws also played an important role in entrenching merchant capitalists as the dominant class in Philippine-Chinese society. In 1902, the United States extended its 1882 Chinese Exclusion Act almost wholesale to the Philippines to stem the inflow of Chinese "coolies." Consequently, the Chinese community there was smaller than elsewhere in Southeast Asia, both in absolute terms and relative to the native population. Those who managed to gain entry were largely merchants, teachers, professionals, and students and were able to exploit loopholes in the system or evade immigration controls entirely. Many arrived as or pretending to be the children or relatives of local merchants, who drew from among their male kin in China to work for them as clerks and shopkeepers' assistants. Others took advantage of the Philippines' island geography and corrupt local officials to enter via illicit channels such as the "Sulu route" connecting Jolo and Zamboanga to Borneo and the rest of the Philippines.[27] Colonial law thus virtually eliminated coolie labor while reinforcing chain migration between the islands and a few sending counties in southern Fujian, especially Jinjiang.[28] For such reasons, one historian has attributed the seeming weakness of Chinese communism in the Philippines to the absence of a "significant" proletarian base in Chinese society and to kinship ties between employers and employees that precluded and mitigated "antagonistic relations" between them.[29]

That being said, we should not overstate the extent to which the preponderance of merchant capitalism and a relatively small working class explain the KMT's and the Chinese left's influence among the Philippine Chinese. Shared native-place ties were no obstacle to one's participation in organized labor as, for instance, an assistant to a shopkeeper, a student, or indeed a communist revolutionary from Jinjiang. It is likewise problematic to assume that the Chinese capitalist ethos enjoyed, to use Max Weber's term, an "elective affinity" with the KMT's nationalism.[30] Despite attempts by Sun Yat-sen's supporters to cultivate them, the historian Andrew R. Wilson argues that "there is little to suggest that the majority of the community was fired by national issues," even after the Xinhai Revolution in 1911.[31] The General Chamber of Commerce was a traditionalist and pragmatic organization that had been founded in 1906 with official support from the Qing state, and it would never be on entirely friendly terms with the KMT. For the leaders of the General Chamber and other institutions such as native-place associations, guilds, and kinship organizations, linkages to sources of authority external to the Chinese community such as the Qing, Yuan Shikai, Republican, and Spanish or US colonial governments were primarily for the purposes of enhancing one's reputation within the community itself. Unlike those of revolutionaries such as Ong Chuan Seng and the even more militant KMT operatives who arrived in the Philippines in the mid-1930s, Chinese merchants' affiliations with political movements were multiple, fluid, and stemmed less from ideological commitments than from a desire for legitimacy and communal cohesion within a local context. In particular, these "liminal virtuosos," as Wilson labels them, through appealing to whichever government happened to be in power in China, safeguarded their class and ethnic interests in the face of Filipino anti-Chinese sentiment.[32]

Thus, when Chiang Kai-shek and the KMT came to power in 1927, it became expedient for Chinese elites to cultivate the Nationalist government in the hopes of reciprocal support for the community. On April 6 of that year, the *Manila Times* published a message from them expressing "great sympathy" with the nationalist movement and wishing the generalissimo the "quickest success in the unification of China." Three weeks later, in a similar message, they congratulated Chiang for his "energetic effort to rid China of Bolshevism" and for the "organization of the Kuomintang government," which they understood would have "no other policy than that of Dr. Sun Yat-sen and no other object but the protection of [their] rights." That summer, the General Chamber conducted an extensive campaign to apprise local Chinese across the

Philippines of developments in China and to rally them behind Chiang.[33] To be sure, these patriotic performances may have been born of antipathy toward "Bolshevism" and fears that it would spread to the Philippines (which it did). But more telling was Chinese leaders' call for the "protection of [their] rights," which they believed that a succession of anti-Chinese measures in the 1920s threatened. In 1921, for example, the Philippine legislature approved the Bookkeeping Act, which required foreign businessmen to keep their accounts in English, Spanish, or a Filipino language. Chinese merchants waged a concerted and ultimately successful five-year lobbying and legal campaign against the act with the backing of the Chinese government; Chinese diplomats in Manila and Washington, DC; the press; and private sector interests.[34] In 1924, an immigration bill, eventually vetoed by the US governor-general, proposed that, within one year of its passing, Chinese residents had to present certificates authorizing them to reside in the Philippines. That year, race riots in Manila marked the first real, albeit still relatively small-scale, outbreak of anti-Chinese violence during the US era.[35] With tensions between Chinese and Filipinos growing and the new Chinese regime in a position to intercede with Manila on their behalf, Chinese elites' support for Chiang can hardly be regarded simply as part of what one historian in 1972 called a "national awakening."[36]

More important than the capitalist orientation of Chinese society in shaping the KMT's fortunes was the United States' generally laissez-faire approach to Chinese affairs and tolerance of the party's diasporic activism. In the Philippines, the KMT was able to openly pursue its goals among persons that the racist colonial state categorized as perpetual foreigners who could not be assimilated into the national polity.[37] US paternalistic colonialism was premised on tutoring Filipinos in the ways of liberal democracy and guiding them toward self-rule and independence. To preserve "the Philippines for the Filipinos," the United States implemented new laws that made it difficult for Chinese not born in the islands to obtain naturalized citizenship if they did not meet a long list of qualifications, which included owning real estate worth at least 5,000 Philippine pesos (PHP) and being able to speak and write English or Spanish and a Filipino language.[38] Eager to reap the rewards of overseas Chinese capitalism, the United States was more willing than any colonial power in Southeast Asia to delegate responsibility for Chinese society to the diplomatic representatives of the Chinese state and to local Chinese elites. This was similar to how it collaborated with Filipino elites to govern the country as a whole.[39]

After 1927, therefore, the Philippine KMT was legitimized as a semiofficial organ of Nanjing and could mobilize an ethnically and legally "foreign" minority with little interference by the authorities. Elsewhere in prewar Southeast Asia, states tended to be suspicious of the KMT as a foreign political organization that had designs on their "internal" affairs. This was certainly the case in the two countries with the largest Chinese populations in the region and where the KMT was the most active. In Malaya, the British banned the KMT twice, first in 1925 and—despite recognizing the ROC in 1928—for a second time in 1930, fearing that the party aimed to construct an *imperium in imperio* in British territory.[40] Thailand repeatedly refused to even recognize Chiang Kai-shek's government because it believed that an official ROC diplomatic mission in Bangkok would enable the KMT to directly control the Chinese population. Like the British, the Thais also restricted the KMT's propagandizing in Chinese newspapers and schools.[41] These interventionist approaches persisted after 1945 and underpinned nationalizing projects in both countries. In the Philippines, the colonial state's accommodation of the KMT likewise carried over into the postwar and postcolonial era, with far-reaching consequences for the Philippine Chinese and the party during the Cold War.

The KMT was free to expand its diasporic infrastructure and membership throughout the prewar Philippines. In 1931, according to a report by five members of the Philippine KMT to the Fourth National Party Congress, the party's membership in the country stood at around 4,000.[42] Data compiled by the Taiwanese scholar and KMT official Yang Jiancheng in 2001 indicates that 1,706 of them had joined in 1927 alone; however, the rate at which its membership grew after that year slowed down.[43] By 1931, the party had expanded across the archipelago despite the challenges that geography posed to communications and travel between Manila and other islands. Manila was the location of the *zongzhibu* and Luzon *zhibu*; five other *zhibu* were based in Cebu, Sulu, Davao, Iloilo, and Zamboanga, and subordinate to these six branches were fifty-one *fenbu*. Through its networks, the party made inroads into multiple sectors of Chinese society, particularly education. Among the ways in which US rule benefited the Chinese was the freedom that it afforded them and other residents to found and run private schools. By 1931, forty-five of them had been established, mostly by local chambers of commerce, to accommodate the growing number of teenage migrants who had entered as merchants' kin. These institutions taught in English, to prepare students for careers in the Philippines, and in Chinese—Mandarin after 1926—to prepare them for higher education in China and to cultivate traditional Chinese values.[44] Several were founded, largely after 1924, by KMT branches in cities large and small, such as Baguio, Cebu, Manila, Iloilo, Roxas City, and Mati, and named Zhongshan schools after Sun Yat-sen.[45]

Despite these signs of expansion, the Philippine KMT was scarcely in a position of strength in the 1930s, as evidenced by the relatively slow growth in party membership after a sudden spurt in 1927. For all their rhetorical enthusiasm for Chiang in 1927 and despite their propensity to affiliate with diverse civic organizations, Chinese elites were slow to join the KMT. Until the mid-1930s, relatively few General Chamber leaders were also KMT members.[46] The same 1931 report to the Fourth National Party Congress that described the KMT's progress in Chinese education also noted with alarm that Chinese communists were increasingly active in the country and had formed their own labor organizations to compete with KMT-sponsored unions. Of greater concern at the time was the party's parlous financial situation caused by the Great Depression. Nanjing provided very little direct economic aid to its overseas branches, which depended almost entirely on their members' contributions and monthly dues to survive. The *zongzhibu* had only just begun receiving a small, 1,000-yuan monthly subsidy from the CEC, which kept it afloat. With its chief supporters hit hard by the economic downturn, its main newspaper, the *Kong Li Po* (*Gongli bao*)—the oldest Chinese newspaper in the country—faced bankruptcy.[47] Four years later, in 1935, the *Kong Li Po* remained in print, but the *zongzhibu* feared that the paper's ongoing financial woes deprived the party of an effective propaganda apparatus with which to contest the opinions of what it cryptically referred to as a "reactionary faction" (*fandong pai*). Its report to Nanjing made clear that the party's operating environment in the islands was "extremely dire" (*elie zhi ji*).[48]

Chinese Communism in the Philippines, 1925–1942

Relative latecomers to the Philippines, Chinese communists focused on mobilizing their working-class co-ethnics and by the early 1930s had carved out a space for themselves in Chinese society, much to the consternation of the KMT. The earliest Chinese labor organization in the country was likely an early twentieth-century reformist organization, which Ong Chuan Seng was a member of. The first "progressive" (*jinbu*) labor union, according to one communist account, was the 1925 Workers' Association (Gongren Xiehui), which counted teachers, clerks, and shop assistants among its members and helped set up other Chinese unions.[49] A pivotal figure in its formation and the history of Chinese communism in the Philippines was Co Keng Sing. Born in 1905 in Jinjiang, Co studied Marxism and English in Hong Kong. In 1925, at his father's urging, he traveled to the Philippines. A year later, after meeting a CCP agent there, Co joined the Chinese Communist Youth League (Zhongguo Gongchan Zhuyi Qingnian Tuan) and soon became one of its leaders. In 1927, Co helped organize the Workers' Association and smaller Chinese unions into the Philippine-Chinese Labor Association (Feilübin Huaqiao Zong Gong-hui, or PCLA).[50]

Co's activities in the 1920s brought him and other Chinese communists into the fold of the emerging Filipino communist movement. This coming together was by no means straightforward. Following its establishment in 1927, the PCLA attempted to forge ties with its Filipino counterpart, the Congreso Obrero de Filipinas (COF), but it was kept at a "segregated distance" because of the COF's racial politics.[51] In 1929, the COF split into radical and conservative factions as Comintern influence on the movement grew. The latter faction proved more amenable to Chinese participation and integrated the PCLA into its ranks, after which the PCLA was renamed the Philippine-Chinese Labor Federation (Feilübin Huaqiao Ge Laogong Tuanti).[52] By March 1930, it had a membership of around fifteen hundred workers in twelve unions and two hundred more in a Chinese young workers' club, which included singing, calisthenics, drama, and other cultural groups.[53] Later that year, the radical COF faction founded the Partido Komunista ng Pilipinas (PKP), a broad-based, multiethnic coalition of "the proletariat, the peasantry, the urban poor, and the revolutionary students—the Moros, mountain tribes, and Chinese toilers, as well as the Christian Filipinos," according to the Comintern. The Politburo consisted of sixty-two Filipinos and twenty-five Chinese, including Co.[54] Its composition, in this respect, differed from the majority Chinese Malayan Communist Party (MCP), which was founded in the same year.

The decade from 1927 to 1937, which overlapped with the Great Depression, the KMT's rise to power in China, and the start of the Commonwealth era in the Philippines, was an eventful period for Chinese communism. Peasant and labor unrest had been steadily growing in the 1920s and escalated dramatically during the Depression as the price of export crops plummeted, businesses failed, and unemployment surged.[55] In reaction, the state suppressed organized labor and suspected communists, most dramatically by banning the PKP in early 1931 and jailing several of its leaders on charges of sedition. As ideologically problematic foreigners, Chinese communists and their sympathizers were subject to arrest, harassment, and deportation by the authorities. In 1930, for example, five hundred Chinese who had participated in Labor Day demonstrations were charged with disturbing the peace and issued with an ultimatum to cancel their membership in communist organizations or face deportation.[56] In January 1935, what one Chinese communist labor organizer referred to as the "largest strike by workers in a furniture factory in the history of the Chinese labor movement" erupted, resulting in clashes between the workers and police. The crackdown that ensued caused the strike to fail and significantly weakened the Chinese left, which now found itself at a "low ebb" (*dichao*).[57]

Chinese communism's history in the country thus differs from the KMT's, even though these histories were intertwined. By the early to mid-1930s, the KMT in the Philippines had been organized into a networked hierarchy of branches and their affiliated institutions, especially schools. Partially autonomous by virtue of their geographical remove from China and their financial dependence on local Chinese merchants, these branches were nevertheless formally connected, bureaucratically and ideologically, to OPAC and the CEC in Nanjing. But no such multitiered, transnational infrastructure existed in the case of the Chinese communists. Although Co Keng Sing may have been a CCP member, the multiple Chinese communist organizations that he was a part of had no institutional ties to any CCP organ in China, as far as we can tell. None of them cohered into something that we might call the "CCP in the Philippines" in the same way that the *zongzhibu, zhibu, fenbu,* and schools constituted the Philippine KMT. Chinese communism was not quite driven by the "uncoordinated actions of individuals" seeking refuge abroad, but there is no direct evidence that the CCP in China had a systematic program for promoting its organizational work in the Philippines.[58]

While the KMT was an anti-imperialist organization until the Second Sino-Japanese War, its focus after 1927 was on transforming China.[59] Chinese communists such as Co Keng Sing were distinct from KMT operatives in that they actively forged ties with like-minded Filipinos in pursuit of transformative political change in the Philippines. They were, to use Caroline S. Hau's term, "revolutionary cosmopolitans." Animated by the "spirit of internationalism," overseas Chinese such as Co committed themselves to revolution in and beyond China and viewed these projects as complementary. Leveraging their facility with languages and exploiting the long-distance transportation networks made possible by imperial globalization, they ranged across the colonial world to assist national liberation movements and to promote solidarities between leftist forces. In the long term, however, partially because of ethnic and cultural divisions between them and native actors, they privileged the cause of radical revolution in China and would commit themselves fully to transforming their homeland in the late 1940s.[60]

Much as it did in China, the Second Sino-Japanese War energized the Chinese left and the KMT in the Philippines even as it exacerbated tensions between them and divided the latter. With fascism and militarism ascendant globally, the Commonwealth authorities decided to legalize the PKP in 1937. In the years that followed, it merged with other smaller left-wing parties to contest the 1940 municipal elections. Chinese leftists were similarly allowed to operate openly. On Labor Day in 1938, Co Keng Sing, who had spent much of the first half of the decade in Shanghai, Moscow, Hong Kong, the Dutch East Indies, and Xiamen, again helped bring together different Chinese labor unions under a single umbrella organization. Consisting of over forty smaller groups, this Philippine-Chinese United Workers Union (Feilübin Huaqiao Ge Laogong Tuanti Lianhehui, or Lo Lian Hui) focused on anti-Japanese propagandizing, raising funds for the resistance effort, and encouraging its members to return to China to serve and fight.[61] Like its predecessors, the Lo Lian Hui was closely linked to the Filipino left. It did not shy away from opposing the KMT.

Three days before the Japanese captured Manila, Co and four hundred other Chinese leftists fled the city with the aid of Filipino peasant leaders for the mountains of Central Luzon, where they created their underground movement.[62] By late 1942, three guerrilla organizations had emerged. The first and most famous was the Philippine-Chinese Anti-Japanese Force (Feilübin Huaqiao Kangri Zhidui, or Wha Chi), which was affiliated with the PKP's armed wing, the Hukbong Bayan Laban sa Hapon (People's Anti-Japanese Army, or Hukbalahap) in Central Luzon, and commanded by Wong Kiat.[63] The second, closely tied to the first, was the Philippine-Chinese Anti-Japanese Volunteer Corps (Feilübin Huaqiao Kangri Chujian Yiyongjun, or Kang Chu), headed by Co Chi Meng and affiliated with the Chinese Freemasons. The third, mostly working underground in Manila but with a presence in Iloilo, was the Philippine-Chinese Anti-Japanese and Anti-Puppets League (Feilübin Huaqiao Kangri Fanjian Da Tongmeng, or Kang Fan), led by Co Keng Sing.[64]

The Factionalized KMT and Its Enemies Without, 1937–1942

Like the Chinese labor movement with Co Keng Sing, the KMT was shaped decisively by "traveling nation-makers" such as Ong Chuan Seng. Their border-crossing political itineraries corresponded closely to entrenched migration patterns between the Philippines and China.[65] Yet Chinese political movements in the islands owed just as much to persons who were unattached to the kinship networks of Chinese society, non-conversant in its Hokkien lingua franca, and thus neither "insiders" nor "outsiders." One such right-wing traveling nation-maker was a man from Jiangsu named Mah Soo-Lay. Born in 1908, Mah led a peripatetic political life comparable to that of Co, Ong, and other overseas Chinese nationalists in the early twentieth century. While in high school, he planned to study physics but became politicized after reading a copy of the

Three Principles that a cousin, who had been studying at the Whampoa Military Academy, gave him. In 1925, Mah left China to study at Meiji University in Japan, where he became interested in Southeast Asia and in 1927 joined the KMT. In his unpublished memoirs, Mah recalled squabbling with young left-wing party members while in Japan. After graduating, he embarked on a career as a high school principal, teacher, and journalist in Malaya for three years. To improve his English, which he believed was necessary for promoting the KMT's cause in Nanyang, he traveled to Manila. At the University of the Philippines (UP), he took classes in Philippine and Southeast Asian history and then transferred to the University of Santo Tomas to study accounting, all while continuing to teach and write. In 1936, when vacationing in China, Mah joined the Fuxingshe. This marked the beginning of his involvement in internal party affairs. Once back in the Philippines, he and another Fuxingshe member, Fang Chih-chou, gathered nine KMT members to found the Philippine-Chinese Mutual Aid Society (Feilübin Huaqiao Huji She), which they named after an existing Fuxingshe group in China. In 1953, seven of these nine persons had become ranking members of the *zongzhibu*.[66]

Fang, like Mah, was from the world of education and journalism, not business. In 1935, he was already a member of the Mutual Aid Society in China when OCAC sent him to the Philippines to be the principal of Sun Yat-sen High School in Iloilo. Working with Mah, he and others established the society's main branch in the Philippines in Manila in the winter of 1937. Fang served as its secretary and the head of its General Affairs Department while working as a newspaper editor. In his history of the Mutual Aid Society, he is instrumental in its expansion beyond Manila as a parallel structure to the "official" KMT. Its first provincial subbranch was formed in Cebu in 1938; in Leyte in 1939, it essentially merged with the local KMT. When Japan invaded, preparations were under way to establish subbranches in Lucena City, Iloilo, and Negros Occidental.[67]

The Mutual Aid Society's quasi-fascist origins and ideological program are hard to discern from the sole extant piece of documentary evidence that it has bequeathed to posterity. In this special commemorative volume published in Manila in January 1948, the secretary-general of the CEC and former head of OPAC, Wu Tiecheng, called the society a "mass organization" (*minzhong zuzhi*) that most people did not know of, but which also did not seek to be known. Wu hailed it for attacking "careerists" (*yexinjia*) and the "Red communist bandits" (*chise gongfei*) who sought to destroy the Nationalist revolution. Employing a striking agricultural metaphor, he compared the society to a "sharp knife that mows down weeds" (*shanyi youcao de lidao*) in a time of revolution but a mere farming implement to "transplant rice seedlings" (*chayang*) in a time of rebuilding.[68] But this volume dates from 1948, not 1937, and in it, Wu's language is the exception, not the norm. Elsewhere, we find much talk of opposing communism and descriptions of the society's numerous contributions to the War of Resistance against Japan, but no real attempt to define "mutual aid" ideologically. The introductory essay, for example, speaks only of the need for patriotism to be blended with a "spirit" (*jingshen*) of mutual aid, understanding (*liangjie*), and cooperation (*hezuo*) or else risk indirectly helping the communists.[69] Fang Chih-chou recounted the group's past but offered little in the way of explaining its core ideology.

Mah's autobiography and what we know about the founders of the Mutual Aid Society in the Philippines suggest that some but not all of them were committed ideologues. What all of them had in common was ambition. Mah explained that these men were drawn from commercial, professional, and intellectual circles in the country and had become "dissatisfied and dejected" (*buman yu kumen*) with the existing leadership of the *zongzhibu* and the likes of Ong Chuan Seng.[70] By December 1941, several Mutual Aid Society members had successfully insinuated themselves into the *zongzhibu* and were jostling with party elders such as Ong for influence. Two of the most fanatical society members were Shih I-Sheng, a former insurance agent, and Koa Chun-te, a journalist and teacher. Shih was on the Standing Committee, and Koa became the *zongzhibu*'s secretary-general around 1940;[71] both reprised these roles after the war while recruiting like-minded persons to the cause. But not all Mutual Aid Society members were as uncompromising as these two men were in opposing the Japanese, and membership of the society and the KMT did not necessarily supersede one's primary identification with other organizations such as the General Chamber of Commerce.

Mah and these two comrades of his were the products of institutions that aimed specifically at indoctrinating and training party cadres for the struggle against China's enemies. Shih graduated from the Central (formerly Whampoa) Military Academy in 1938, and in 1940, he, Koa, and Fang enrolled in a monthlong course at the Central Training Corps (Zhongyang Xunlian Tuan) in Chongqing.[72] Mah had earlier attended a similar course there in 1939. The corps was established in late 1938, with Chiang as its commander, as part of the KMT's wartime attempt to expand the scope of training for members and would-be members. Believing that the nation's problems lay in individual weakness, the corps' leaders sought nothing less than the complete militarization of everyday life to militarize society as a whole. The four men underwent an intensive, four-week program of leader worship, lectures on wartime government policies in the morning, drill sessions in the afternoon, political study and small-group discussions in the evening, and journal-writing as a way to gauge one's assimilation of the regime's values and norms.[73] Suitably transformed, they then returned to the Philippines to carry out the KMT's agenda beyond China.

The War of Resistance galvanized Chinese nationalism in the Philippines but, with persons like Shih and Koa coming to the fore of the KMT, also caused friction within the party and between the party and the General Chamber of Commerce. In the 1930s, Chinese merchants contributed significantly to anti-Japanese movements that raised funds for the defenses of Manchuria and Shanghai.[74] By September 1937, the chamber, the KMT, its new united front communist partners, and the ROC Consulate had jointly launched a large-scale donation drive, which assigned each Chinese family a contribution quota and required that wage earners provide 10 percent of their monthly income to the war effort.[75] From 1937 to 1941, despite the relatively small size of the Chinese community, its average monthly per capita contributions to the Nanyang Chinese National Salvation Movement were the highest in Southeast Asia.[76]

Chamber and party diverged, however, when it came to boycotting Japanese goods in the Philippines. Led by the *zongzhibu*'s head of propaganda, Justo Cabo Chan, and with the support of left-wing Chinese groups, a militant KMT faction pushed hard for this boycott and severing business ties with Japan. More conservative General Chamber members feared that this would adversely affect local Chinese businesses that handled Japanese goods and perhaps remembered that similar boycotts in the early 1930s had only facilitated the growth of Japanese department stores.[77] Cabo Chan eventually arm-twisted enough moderates to get what he and other radical nationalists wanted in February 1938, but having alienated many of his fellow merchants, he was removed from the board of the Philippine-Chinese Resist-the-Enemy Committee (Feilübin Huaqiao Kangdi Houyuan Hui), which coordinated anti-Japanese diasporic mobilization.[78] Later, according to Japanese government sources, the Japanese military was even able to coerce several merchants into not attending boycott meetings by threatening to confiscate their property in Xiamen, which Japan occupied from May 1938 onward.[79] Fault lines also emerged within the KMT, even within the ranks of the Mutual Aid Society. The textile merchant and *zongzhibu* Standing Committee member Say Kok Chuan, for example, was less supportive of the boycott than Shih I-Sheng, Koa Chun-te, and Justo Cabo Chan were. Tensions between them worsened to the point of requiring mediation by Wu Tiecheng, the head of OPAC, in 1940.[80] Mere membership in the Mutual Aid Society was not necessarily a reliable indicator of one's ideological convictions and absolute willingness to put nation above profit.

Intraparty factionalism was exacerbated by the creation of KMT-linked paramilitary youth groups in the islands. Three principal organizations were formed, each under different party leaders and each reflecting the multifarious connections between the party in China and the Philippines.[81] In May 1941, Chiang Kai-shek personally dispatched the Zhangzhou-born Lin Tso-mei to Manila to form the first organization, the Philippine Chinese Youth Wartime Special Services Corps (Feilübin Huaqiao Qingnian Zhanshi Tebie Gongzuo Zongdui, or SSC). Consisting largely of students from KMT-controlled high schools in Manila such as CKSHS, the SSC functioned as a branch of the Three Principles' Youth Corps (Sanminzhuyi Qingnian Tuan, or SQT), whose members swore an oath of loyalty to Chiang himself.[82] The second group, the Chinese Overseas Wartime Hsuehkan Militia (Huaqiao Zhanshi Xuegan Tuan, or COWHM), was founded in March 1942 as the Loyal Soul Fraternity (Huaqiao Zhonghun She) by several Philippine-Chinese who had undergone basic military training at the Thirteenth Reserve Officers Training Camp in Nanping, Fujian; it came under the nominal leadership of Lin's second in command in the SSC, Lee Hai-jo, in July 1944.[83] Both these organizations focused on anti-Japanese propaganda during the occupation; the COWHM also fought alongside US forces during the Battle of Manila in early 1945.[84] The third group, the Chinese Volunteers in the Philippines (Feilübin Huaqiao Yiyongjun, or CVP), was established as the military wing of the *zongzhibu* with guidance from the director of OPAC, who was then visiting the Philippines.[85] Commanded by Shih I-Sheng, the CVP was supported by the ROC Consulate and, somewhat surprisingly, the General Chamber of Commerce.[86]

Despite their ideological similarities, these organizations differed in ways that illuminate the structural complexity and factionalism of what historians refer to as the KMT. The COWHM was essentially a grassroots militia group. Despite Lee's becoming its commander in July 1944, the Loyal Soul Fraternity's founders retained effective control of the organization. The other two groups were affiliated with rivalrous party factions. Lin Tso-mei's SSC and its parent organization, the SQT, had comparatively little grounding in local Chinese society compared to the CVP and the Philippine KMT. Lin was Hokkien and had joined the Fuxingshe in 1932. He did not consider himself an overseas Chinese and appears never to have left China before 1941, but he was nonetheless familiar with Chinese affairs in the Philippines. For this reason, he was ideally placed to ensure that the SSC did not become overly embedded in Chinese society and answered only to the center. As Lin explained to researchers from Academia Sinica in 1993, when the CEC sent him to the Philippines it covered all his expenses for three years to guarantee that the SQT was financially independent and did not need to rely on local Chinese merchants. Unsurprisingly, Lin was not universally welcomed, even though he was a direct emissary of Chiang himself. Shih I-Sheng opposed him, but Lin eventually secured the backing of Ong Chuan Seng and the chair of the Resist-the-Enemy Committee, Yu Khe Thai.[87]

Conflict between the KMT and the Chinese left further complicated efforts to forge a unified opposition to Japan, with each side blaming the other for disrupting the fragile peace between them. The KMT accused the "other party" (*moudang*) of continuing to incite labor unrest and damaging the interests of Chinese merchants. In 1940, it claimed that communists were openly attacking the party by slandering Justo Cabo Chan as a "traitorous businessman" (*jianshang*) and conspiring to overthrow the Resist-the-Enemy Committee.[88] In response, the KMT would have us believe that it took the high ground. In April, Koa Chun-te was speaking at an anti–Wang Jingwei event organized by a KMT youth organization when he noticed members of the "other party" whispering among themselves and trying to tear down a banner with the slogan "Long live the Republic of China." Koa felt that he had to respond immediately. In his speech, he called for an end to attacks on the KMT and the government and urged all in attendance to "obey the sole leader, support the sole government, and believe in the sole ideology" (*fucong weiyi lingxiu, yonghu weiyi zhengfu, xinyang weiyi zhuyi*) for the sake of national unity. Taking aim at liberals and communists, Koa said that "individualism" (*geren zhuyi*) and "classism" (*jieji zhuyi*) were harming the nation at a time when its fate hung in the balance.[89]

However, Koa's attempt at ideological suasion had little effect on one communist member of the audience, Wu Ziqing. Straight after Koa had finished, Wu, without asking for permission to speak, stood on a chair and began cursing the government for its corruption and unfair treatment of the Eighth Route Army, one of two communist battalions fighting alongside KMT forces during the war. Wu's broadside was followed by loud cheering and applause from a portion of the crowd. The atmosphere grew tense. Koa warned Wu that this was traitorous behavior and demanded that he personally substantiate his charges before the *zongzhibu* leadership the following day or else be branded a reactionary. According to Koa, the communists only became angrier and threatened violence. Koa and several other KMT leaders gathered at the *zongzhibu* the next day to hear from Wu, but Wu did not show up. He instead mailed them a copy of a telegram from the Eighth Route Army to central command to prove his accusations.[90]

The twenty-six-year-old Wu appears not to have been acting at the instigation of the Lo Lian Hui, for after his outburst came to the attention of communist leaders, they worked with the *zongzhibu* and ROC Consulate to tamp down the incident.[91] Several months afterward, Wu was summoned to the consulate, where Ong Chuan Seng and others "harshly admonished" (*yanjia xunjie*) him.

However, the ROC consul was concerned that Wu's fundamental beliefs might not have changed and that he would continue to act improperly. He recommended that Wu be made to apologize for his actions publicly, in writing, or be deported.[92] The consulate added Wu's name to a twenty-seven-person list of the most important Chinese communists in the Philippines whom it was actively looking to have expelled.[93] Wu, however, was not deported and later became a Wha Chi platoon leader.[94]

Naturally, left-wing narratives such as that of the Lo Lian Hui's postwar secretary-general Shen Fushui finger only the KMT for undermining the anti-Japanese coalition in pursuit of narrow partisan ends. In his account, the KMT and US authorities were "collaborating" (goujie) to destroy the united front. Differences between them even extended to the realm of semantics. The Lo Lian Hui insisted on using "saving [the nation] from extinction" (jiuwang) to describe the anti-Japanese movement rather than "saving the nation" (jiuguo), which was the KMT's preferred expression. It believed that wang (extinction) emphasized the critical juncture at which the nation found itself and the certainty of this happening if the Chinese people did not fight back. Somewhat pedantically, Shen said that the KMT was "talking nonsense" (hushuo) by claiming that a nation that had not yet been vanquished ought not to employ language such as jiuwang. The communists apparently viewed the more sensational term jiuwang as appealing to a wider audience.[95]

Far more serious for the Lo Lian Hui was the political and military situation in China and how it exacerbated tensions between the Chinese left and the KMT. In Shen's account, the Lo Lian Hui paid particular attention to exposing the corruption and misadministration of the KMT governor of Fujian, Chen Yi, and bringing to light KMT forces' attack on the CCP's New Fourth Army in southern Anhui in January 1941, ostensibly because it had disobeyed Chiang's orders. In leveling these criticisms, Chinese leftists in the Philippines clashed with the KMT zongzhibu, which tried to "whitewash" (tuzhi mofen) Chen's crimes and blamed the New Fourth Army for wrecking the united front. Shen was adamant that Chinese supported the Lo Lian Hui's position and saw through the KMT's lies. Divisions between left and right across national boundaries were amplified within Chinese society by the KMT's formation of a shop assistants' union to rival a similar organization on the left, one that Shen was a member of. Not content with simply defending Chen Yi, the KMT supposedly also concocted false criminal charges against communist-aligned shop assistants and the Lo Lian Hui.

Shen's history of the Lo Lian Hui, when juxtaposed with the KMT's narratives, suggests that the two most actively anticommunist members of the Mutual Aid Society before the Japanese occupation were Koa Chun-te and Shih

I-Sheng. It reveals, too, an informal division of labor between the two men: Koa, the journalist and teacher, supplied the rhetoric with which to assail the left, while Shih, drawing on his military training, acted as troublemaker. On Labor Day in 1941, Shen described how Shih and a gang of thugs infiltrated and tried to disrupt demonstrations organized by the Lo Lian Hui. After leftists printed leaflets denouncing Shih, Shih filed a legal case against the Lo Lian Hui and accused Co Keng Sing of libeling him. A violent, vain, and litigious man, Shih leveled similar charges against the Shop Assistants' National Salvation General Union. Both cases were still being heard by the courts when Japan invaded in December, and they were never resolved. Having been thwarted on May 1, Shih took revenge when he and a group of police officers forced their way into the union's headquarters and arrested or beat up those present.[96]

Chinese schools, like the labor movement, were sites of intense political mobilization and contestation between the left and the KMT. Nanyang High School (NHS) in Manila, in particular, was a hotbed of communist-driven student activism. One student there, Santos Ong, ended up joining the Kang Fan and studying Marxism at the home of a former teacher after the Japanese shut down all Chinese schools.[97] Many NHS students traveled to Yan'an during the war, and twenty of them joined the CCP's Eighth Route and New Fourth Armies. In one ex-student's words, they did so in the belief that these were the most resolutely anti-Japanese of all Chinese forces and also because the future China should embrace Soviet socialism.[98]

Prior to the Japanese occupation, NHS—which, unlike CKSHS, does not survive today—was also at the center of a fierce struggle between left-wing students and the KMT-friendly school administration. According to the recollections of one such student, Shi Chunliang, the conflict erupted when the principal announced one day that two students, Xu Jingbo and Shen Yongcai, were being expelled for disrupting the school's anti-Japanese activities. Xu and Shen worked part-time in a dressmaking shop and were members of the Chinese Dressmakers' Union. All that they had done, apparently, was distribute communist publications to their fellow students. Incensed, Shi and other left-wing students questioned how anyone could be "guilty" of patriotism and launched a series of protests against their elders. At one point, they urged students to boycott their exams or to refuse to answer the questions and instead fill their exam papers with slogans supporting Xu and Shen. When the administration banned them from meeting in school, the Assembly of the Seven Gentlemen (Qi Junzi Jihui), as they called themselves, met at each other's houses or at Luneta Park under the pretense of "going for a stroll in the park" (guang gongyuan).

NHS, unlike schools established by chambers of commerce or the KMT, had been founded in 1934 as an engineering school by a group of left-wing activists and was supposed to be governed collectively by both an administrative committee and the student assembly. But by July 1937, even before the expulsions of Xu and Shen, it had been penetrated by what Shi referred to darkly as a "reactionary force" (*fandong shili*) and had gravitated toward the KMT. Shi did not elaborate on this, but we know that Mah Soo-Lay taught there around then as head of moral education (*xunyu*).[99] Mah may have been responsible for devising military-style drills that kept students within school premises and prevented them from taking part in external National Salvation activities. In response to the protests, school authorities further charged Xu and Shen with inciting other students to not study hard, warned parents that the CCP was manipulating their children, and tried to alter the composition of the student assembly's executive committee. Unfortunately for Shi and his compatriots, the school administration was victorious. Shi blamed this on the youthful naïveté of the Seven Gentlemen, who were unfamiliar with "strategy" (*celüe*) and driven only by emotions and a sense of justice. Consequently, they were never able to coordinate a mass movement. The administration proceeded to fail Shi and those who took part in the exam protests, before expelling them. In April 1938, Shi left the country for Hong Kong and then Yan'an.[100] Many Chinese leftists did so as well. Their departures, during and after the war, helped thin the numbers of the KMT's enemies in the Philippines.

By the eve of the Pacific War, the KMT and the Chinese left had established footholds in the Philippines and clashed with each other in their contest for allies and influence. The KMT, as this chapter has explained, bureaucratized and rationalized its approach to overseas Chinese affairs after coming to power in China in 1927. Yet for all its extraterritorial legal claims and the formal institutions that it developed, the party continued to rely on individual nationalists such as Ong Chuan Seng, Mah Soo-Lay, Shih I-Sheng, and Lin Tso-mei, operating between China and the Philippines, to implement Nanjing's diasporic agenda on the ground. In effect, these right-wing traveling nation-makers localized the KMT and its affiliated organizations such as the Mutual Aid Society even as they maintained the local party's connections to the center.

In late 1941, neither the KMT nor its former and future nemesis on the left could claim primacy over the other in the Philippines. By fortifying the social dominance of a Chinese business class that was unsympathetic to political radicalism, by limiting the entry of Chinese coolies into the islands, and by adopting a laissez-faire attitude toward the party's interventions in the Chinese community, US colonial rule seemed structurally and legally advantageous to the KMT. This may have been so in the longer term. But despite these advantages, the Philippine KMT's social and political reach before 1941 was never as extensive as it was at the height of the Cold War in the mid-1950s. The party faced competition for hearts and minds from the communists, who were able to organize a labor movement despite the Chinese Exclusion Act. The party was challenged, too, from within its ranks by peripatetic ideologues such as Mah, Shih, Koa, and Lin and from without by traditionalist Chinese business leaders who were less enthusiastic about opposing Japan than these true believers were. The General Chamber of Commerce remained largely unfriendly toward and separate from the party, in stark contrast to how, decades later, the Federation of Filipino-Chinese Chambers of Commerce and Industry (Shang Zong) vociferously championed Taiwan's anticommunist program.

Japan's invasion and occupation of the Philippines temporarily suspended conflict between the KMT and the Chinese left. But, as in China, the former emerged from the war weaker and the latter stronger. KMT branches and schools were destroyed or closed, and the disunity that plagued the party before the war persisted into wartime. The CVP, SSC, and COWHM did not cooperate or communicate with each other or Filipino resistance forces and remained for the most part separate organizations. Some KMT members and many pro-KMT businessmen even collaborated with the Japanese, compromising their reputations and inviting retribution from the communists. On the left, by contrast, the Wha Chi, Kang Fan, and Kang Chu, having come out of the prewar Chinese labor movement, worked more closely with each other. They were relatively more experienced at underground work than the KMT, as many of their leaders such as Co Keng Sing had traveled to the CCP's Yan'an base of operations in China or served in the New Fourth Army. The Wha Chi also coordinated its activities with the Hukbalahap and early during the occupation was designated as the Huks' Squadron 48 in a gesture of interethnic ideological solidarity toward the New Fourth and Eighth Route Armies.[101] In early 1945, this left appeared poised to entrench itself into Philippine politics and exploit the weaknesses of its ideological competitor.

CHAPTER 2

A "Period of Bloody Struggle"

The Rise of the Philippine KMT, 1945–1948

In the spring of 1947, around the time that the Kuomintang (KMT) *zongzhibu* in the Philippines officially reopened, the general manager of the *Chinese Guide* (*Huaqiao daobao*), Gong Taoyi, traveled to Hong Kong. There he met Co Keng Sing, who had relocated to Hong Kong in September 1946, and other Chinese leftist leaders.[1] The *Guide*, the wartime newspaper of the Philippine-Chinese Anti-Japanese and Anti-Puppets League (Kang Fan), had begun publishing openly following the end of the Japanese occupation, but it was now struggling financially because the KMT had been intimidating subscribers and advertisers into withdrawing their support. Co, his fellow anti-Japanese guerrilla Du Ai, and their contacts among Hong Kong's left-wing press advised Gong on how best to save the *Guide*. On returning to Manila, Gong implemented some of their suggestions to cut operating costs and boost subscriptions and advertising revenue, ensuring that the *Guide* survived until its five-year anniversary in April. Later that year, however, the Philippine authorities, supported by the KMT, stepped up their harassment of Gong's wife, Huang Wei, who had become the paper's editor in chief after her predecessor had left for China. Accused of being a communist and Soviet surrogate and faced with deportation to Xiamen, Gong and Huang decided to shut down the *Guide* and leave the Philippines. On October 30, 1947, shortly after the *Guide*'s final issue had gone to print, Philippine military police (MPs) went to its offices searching for them but were told that they had just left the building. Barely avoiding arrest, both left the country for Hong Kong shortly afterward.[2] They never again returned to the Philippines.

The flight of Gong, Huang, Du, Co, and other like-minded revolutionaries in the late 1940s brought to a close a brief, vicious, and poorly understood period of conflict between the Chinese communists and the KMT in the early postwar Philippines. From the end of World War II there in March 1945 to late 1947, the Chinese left was openly active, emboldened by its resistance to Japan and the difficulties faced by the Philippine state in reconstituting itself. As in China, it came to blows with the KMT, which had likewise faced down Japan and was seeking to rebuild its diasporic networks in the country. But in 1948, amid the Hukbalahap Rebellion and the Chinese civil war, Chinese communism in the former US colony was spent as an organized political force. A few communists went underground, throwing in their lot with the Huks, but most departed for the more propitious ideological climes of Hong Kong or China. Conversely, the KMT was driven from mainland China in 1949, but by then it had reestablished itself in the state closest to its new center of operations in Taiwan.

How and why was the KMT able to consolidate itself in the Philippines, at the expense of the Sino-communist movement there, in the five years after World War II? And how and why did the Chinese left disengage from the country? This chapter answers these questions by focusing on developments after Japanese rule, beginning with the Chinese left's simultaneous conflicts with the KMT and the Philippine political establishment over the issue of wartime collaboration. The left's extrajudicial pursuit of Chinese collaborators, including many KMT members and supporters, precipitated a violent struggle between the two sides. Concurrently, Chinese leftists' relationship with the Partido Komunista ng Pilipinas (PKP) and perceived meddling in domestic politics, partly over collaboration by Filipinos, antagonized the newly elected president of the country, Manuel Roxas. The KMT exploited these tensions between the communists and the new government. Positioning itself as a stabilizing force, it collaborated with the Roxas regime to construct and oppose the "Chinese communist problem." Starting in the fall of 1946, the KMT's and Philippine authorities' prosecution and persecution of the Chinese left intensified, putting pressure on its institutions to shut down and its leaders to leave the country. Several years later, with Chinese communism as an organized political and social movement in the country having collapsed, the arrest and deportation of a Chinese businessman and triad leader with close financial ties to the left symbolically sealed the KMT's victory.

Besides explaining how such informal anticommunist partnerships were forged, this chapter also examines legal and diplomatic developments during the same period that propelled the KMT's rise. Chief among these were the signing of a treaty of amity between Manila and Nanjing in April 1947 and a September 1947 Supreme Court case on the issue of citizenship. Collectively, these affirmed the KMT's control over Chinese education, its legitimacy in the Philippines as a civic organization, and the Republic of China's (ROC) body-based sovereignty over persons both states considered "Chinese nationals." As the final section of the chapter shows, such arrangements did not obtain in other Southeast Asian states, whose governments tackled the Chinese question and Chinese communism by marginalizing the KMT rather than sharing sovereignty with it.

The Japanese Occupation and the Question of Collaboration

As in Malaya, Japan's occupation of the Philippines from 1942 to 1945 proved uniquely divisive and violent for the Chinese and would profoundly shape the political direction of the community in the three years that followed. Mindful of how the Chinese had supported the ROC government's war efforts, the Japanese military arrested, tortured, and confiscated the property of dozens of Chinese businessmen who were at the forefront of the anti-Japanese movement before 1942. Shortly after the fall of Manila in January, the Japanese compelled Chinese business leaders into forming the Chinese Association (Huaqiao Xiehui, or CA). Go Co-Lay, who had extensive business dealings with the Japanese before the war, became its president, and the KMT's Tee Han Kee its vice president. Provincial CA branches, answerable to their respective Japanese military garrisons, were also founded. Collectively, the CA mobilized Chinese to raise funds and galvanize support for the Greater East Asia Co-Prosperity Sphere, tried to persuade the Nationalist government to surrender, and helped provide "voluntary" Chinese labor for Japanese military projects. To further win them over, the Japanese released numerous Chinese from imprisonment on three ceremonial occasions in 1943, including five hundred guerrillas on October 14, the day that the Japanese-sponsored Second Philippine Republic (1943–1945) was founded.[3]

Such gestures did little to placate Chinese guerrilla organizations, among whose wartime activities targeted CA officials for assassination. Tee Han Kee, who had been a founding member of the Tongmenghui in the Philippines and later an executive committee member of the *zongzhibu* in the 1930s, was murdered by a member of the Chinese Overseas Wartime Hsuehkan Militia (COWHM) at the end of July 1943; Go was killed in September 1944.[4] Following Go's death, the CA was reconstituted under the direction of the Kempeitai (Japanese MP) and tasked with eliminating the Chinese resistance. Japan's first choice to lead the CA was former Philippine Chinese General Chamber of Commerce president Alfonso Sycip, but he fled to Fuga, a remote island off Northern Luzon, immediately after being released from custody in February 1943 and remained there until the end of the war.[5] The Japanese then turned to Justo Cabo Chan, the former propaganda chief of the KMT and a vociferous supporter of the anti-Japanese boycott movement before 1941. During the occupation, he led a small anti-Japanese force in the mountains of Luzon, until the Japanese threatened his family and forced him out of hiding in November 1943. As CA president, he was responsible, according to the *zongzhibu* after the war, for forming a special forces team (*biedong dui*) to assassinate his party comrades Shih I-Sheng, Koa Chun-te, and other leading KMT figures.[6] Unlike his predecessor Go, however, Cabo Chan survived an attempt on his life by the Kang Fan in December 1944.[7]

Born from self-preservation, Cabo Chan's dramatic conversion from KMT propagandist and resistance fighter to collaborator suggests, on the one hand, that we might avoid treating responses to Japanese rule in terms of a heroic, moral-ideological binary of collaboration and resistance, as historians have argued.[8] Go Co-Lay's and Tee Han Kee's stories are similarly more complex than they initially seem. Go, for example, may have had self-interested reasons for "collaborating" because of commercial relations with Japan, but as president of the CA he also interceded with the Japanese to call for the release of Chinese and Filipino guerrillas. By urging persons whose family members had been detained to give themselves up to the authorities in return for amnesty, he may also have helped save lives. Tee, a drugstore owner, supposedly secretly donated medicine to prisoners in Japanese detention camps.[9] On the other hand, in our pursuit of nuance and efforts to question the resistance-collaboration binary by "look[ing] through the moral landscape to the political one underneath," in the historian Timothy Brook's words, we must remember that many did not do such looking.[10] For particular factions within the Chinese resistance, especially on the left, the involvement of Go, Tee, Cabo Chan, and others in the CA, irrespective of their motivations and the pressures they faced from Japan, outweighed any private actions to ameliorate the violence of occupation or their earlier anti-Japanese stance.

The Postwar Conflict over Collaboration

In the aftermath of Manila's liberation from Japanese control in March 1945, Chinese resistance movements officially demobilized and pursued divergent political agendas that would quickly lead to conflict between them. With respect to overseas Chinese policy, the postwar KMT government was keen on recapturing the enthusiasm that many *huaqiao* had demonstrated toward the party during the War of Resistance. To this end, and recognizing that party-affiliated Chinese merchants were too preoccupied with recovering their own businesses to devote their full attention to party affairs, the KMT dispatched high-level cadres to oversee the restoration of its diasporic networks in Southeast Asia. In this way, it hoped to accelerate the process by avoiding the delays that back-and-forth written communication between the center and the periphery might have caused.[11] One such operative, Tong Xingbai, the director of the Overseas Party Affairs Committee (OPAC), traveled to the Philippines in early 1945, with Manila still in ruins, to help rebuild the party around a small group of members who had fought the Japanese; prior to the occupation, Tong had visited the country and encouraged the creation of the Chinese Volunteers in the Philippines (CVP).[12] In May, the rivalry between Shih I-Sheng and the Philippine Chinese Youth Wartime Special Services Corps' (SSC) leader, Lin Tso-mei, which had been put on hold during the occupation, was resolved in favor of the former when Lin was recalled to Chongqing.[13] By mid- to late June 1945, KMT *zhibu* in Manila and Luzon, along with the *fenbu* under them, had been reestablished. In a move that signaled the party's ideological direction, a ten-person reorganization committee was formed that included Shih, Koa Chun-te, Say Kok Chuan, Chua Lamco, and Sy En, the future president of the General Chamber of Commerce. The five men were members of the Mutual Aid Society that Mah Soo-Lay and Fang Chih-chou had helped found, and all except for Sy En were CVP members. Shih, Say, and Chua were appointed to the Standing Committee of the *zongzhibu*, while Koa reprised his position as secretary-general.[14] Fang, Sy, and the others refounded the Mutual Aid Society in November 1945, and, by January 1948, four subbranches and three regional branches of the society had been established beyond Manila, together with an office in Xiamen to assist returning *huaqiao*.[15]

While this was a challenging period for the Philippine Chinese in general, a reorganized and militarized KMT was able to exploit the weaknesses of Chinese leadership organizations in early to mid-1945 to position itself as a major power broker in the community. The ROC Consulate, which was supposed to defend the community's interests on behalf of the Chinese government, was understaffed and its acting consul unpopular with many Chinese because he had kept a low profile during the occupation. The General Chamber of Commerce, many of whose members had collaborated with the Japanese, and whose relations with the KMT were anything but friendly, was in no position at the time to support shop owners who had suffered major property losses due to fires and looting during and after the Battle of Manila.

The KMT's main rival for leadership of the Chinese community at this time was a resurgent and emboldened Chinese left, with which it swiftly renewed hostilities. A mass rally on Labor Day in 1945, organized by the Kang Fan, reignited this conflict. Co Keng Sing's official biography, published in China in 1995 by the Quanzhou-based Xu (Co) clan association of the Philippines on the ninetieth anniversary of his birth, depicts this rally in vague, hyperbolic language. Co described the parade that followed the rally as celebrating the Philippines' retrocession and manifesting the "formidable strength of anti-Japanese progressive forces" (*kangri jinbu liliang de qiangda*). It was the "grandest of its kind since the founding of the Philippine nation" (*Feilübin jianguo yihou zui shengda de yici*) and an unforgettable occasion for those involved.[16] The KMT's representation of events, by contrast, was written a few years after 1949 and retroactively incorporated into an expansive, righteous narrative of anticommunism going back to before the civil war. In its lengthy report to the Seventh National Party Congress in Taipei in October 1952, the *zongzhibu* traced the beginning of a two-year "period of bloody struggle" (*xuedou shiqi*) with the Chinese communists to that day in 1945. Kang Fan and Philippine-Chinese Anti-Japanese Force (Wha Chi) protesters, it said, openly called for the murder of ROC Consulate officials, prompting the CVP and COWHM to stage a counterprotest in their defense.[17] CVP member and future KMT secretary-general Cua Siok Po wrote in his memoirs that the communists affixed a cartoon of two caged turtles with their heads in their shells to the doors of the consulate to mock the consul for lying low during the occupation, after which they loudly called for all "turtles to be overthrown" (*dadao wugui*).[18] If Cua is to be believed, the protesters had forgotten that the previous consul and his entire staff had been executed by Japan in April 1942 for refusing to collaborate.[19] Cua's anecdote is telling, for it depicts Sino-communists as conflating the moral binary of resistance versus collaboration with the ideological binary of left versus right. It also emphasizes how the left understood "collaboration" as inclusive of multiple forms of wartime behavior, including inaction.

In China, popular justice and clandestine operations against "traitors to the Han race" (*hanjian*) during the Second Sino-Japanese War gave way to semiregular judicial procedures after 1945.[20] No such transition took place among Chinese guerrillas in the Philippines, however. Official responsibility for identifying and arresting Chinese and Filipino collaborators lay with the US military's Counter-Intelligence Commission (CIC) and their sentencing, after their deportation to China, with the ROC. By July 1946, 146 Chinese residents had been detained and scheduled for deportation as "undesirable aliens." But Chinese communists, more so than the KMT, were able and willing to bypass these procedures in pursuit of retributive justice on their own terms. At least two Chinese, including a former member of the Kempeitai, were killed in such a way immediately after the liberation of Manila as a wave of violence and kidnappings began to sweep Chinese society.[21] Contrary to the KMT, such disorder can hardly be attributed solely to the communists acting in concert against innocent Chinese. The postwar Philippines was awash in nearly a million infantry weapons from the occupation and from the bloody US military campaign to retake the country. Unable to recover most of these firearms, the state ceded its coercive capacities to provincial warlords, peasant guerrillas, and street thugs and struggled to prevent the country from becoming enmeshed in wider arms-trafficking networks that supplied buyers as far away as Israel and Argentina.[22] Seizing on these loose weapons and the absence of a functioning police force, Chinese resistance fighters and criminal elements carried out individual acts of retribution and took advantage of vulnerable members of Chinese society.

To purge collaborators, the Chinese left also established on May 30 the Anti-Collaboration Commission, which they described to the US military as a body to "help the government authorities to distinguish the Chinese traitors under the Japanese regime from that of loyal ones."[23] Justo Cabo Chan was summoned to appear before it. The commission also sought out Yu Khe Thai, the owner of Yutivo and Sons, one of the largest Chinese hardware companies in the Philippines.[24] Although not a KMT member, Yu had chaired the Resist-the-Enemy Committee before 1941 and was Ong Chuan Seng's ally, having helped finance Chiang Kai-shek High School (CKSHS) in 1939. Yu was among the first Chinese to be arrested and jailed at the start of the occupation in 1942. On the emperor's birthday in April 1943, Japan granted amnesty to him and several other Chinese leaders in return for a public display of gratitude toward Japan and a promise to cooperate with the occupying regime.[25] Yu was forced to become the secretary of the CA and was also threatened by the Kang Fan. Neither he nor Cabo Chan, who was in CIC custody in mid-1945, attended his trial before the commission.[26]

Fearing communist attacks on their members and supporters, the various KMT factions set aside their differences and created what one ex-guerrilla called an "invisible organization" (wuxing jigou) against the left.[27] On the matter of collaboration, the party adopted a flexible and pragmatic approach, in effect anticipating the arguments of historians such as Yumi Moon who have called for an understanding of the phenomenon based on the "choices and consequences of local actors in the changing political, normative, and material contexts of a conquered society."[28] For radicals, for whom even nonresistance deserved opprobrium, the likes of Yu and Cabo Chan who had surrendered to the Japanese automatically forfeited their right to return as community leaders, even if they had acted under duress. This moral binary, if enforced, would have sapped the KMT's foundations in the Philippines by delegitimizing many of its key financial supporters.

KMT-affiliated groups had also fought against collaborators during the occupation, but the party shifted its stance afterward and won over the Chinese business community in the process. Through its Committee for the Investigation of Collaborators and the Maintenance of Peace and Order, the KMT argued that only those who caused or sought to cause harm or death to their fellow Chinese ought to be branded collaborators.[29] Based on this definition, Yu Khe Thai was innocent for having used his position of leadership within the CA to protect Chinese society. On April 15, 1945, Ong Chuan Seng wrote to his colleague Wu Tiecheng, now the secretary-general of the Central Executive Committee (CEC), describing Yu as a patriot who should be rewarded for his contributions to the War of Resistance and omitting any mention of Yu's involvement in the CA.[30] (Ong himself left the Philippines for Chongqing at the start of the Pacific War, became a Legislative Yuan member in 1943, and helped organize the relief effort in Fujian.[31]) Vouched for by Ong and the KMT, Yu became one of the most respected Chinese leaders in the country—and, having been threatened by the Kang Fan, a staunch anticommunist.[32] Cabo Chan's was a more complicated and unresolved case. Justifiably or not, most KMT members considered him guilty but allowed the CIC to try him. When the CIC released Cabo Chan because it lacked the evidence to convict and deport him, he simply retreated from public life. Stripped of any influence within the party he was once fiercely committed to, he paid only a social penalty for his wartime conduct.

To secure friendly relationships with merchants such as Yu Khe Thai, the KMT focused on its worsening struggle with their common nemesis, the Chinese left. To counter the Anti-Collaboration Commission, which it blamed for acts of violence and blackmail, such as the politically motivated murder of the manager of the KMT's *Great China Press* (*Da hua ribao*), CVP guerrillas formed *biedong dui* in Manila and elsewhere.[33] Clashes between the Chinese left and right began erupting beyond the capital. Following the establishment of an Anti-Collaboration Commission branch in Iloilo, for example, the KMT assisted local authorities in October 1945 in arresting the entire leadership of the Iloilo Kang Fan on charges of disturbing the peace. Only after the testimony of a fellow Kang Fan member were the leaders released.[34]

On its part, the CIC grew frustrated with the communists' and the KMT's usurpation of its authority and the violent clashes between them. On July 18, 1945, seeking an end to killings carried out by secret assassination squads in Chinatown, the CIC's Chinese Section convened a meeting of representatives from both parties' anti-collaboration commissions and from the General Chamber of Commerce, the Homicide Squad, and the Provost Marshal's Office. It stated that while it did not "sponsor, encourage or recognize" any Chinese organization over the other, it was the "only one duly authorized and constituted authority for the investigation, apprehension and incarceration of Japanese collaborators" in Manila. Local Chinese should turn over information on collaborators to the CIC and not publish accusations of collaboration or conduct any investigations themselves. Those present, including Co Chi Meng on the left, Chua Lamco and Lee Hai-jo on the right, and the General Chamber of Commerce's representative Sy En, signed these provisions.[35]

However, the meeting did little to stop violence from continuing or the communists from pursuing collaborators. In August, the CIC reported that despite being warned not to conduct its own investigations, the Anti-Collaboration Commission had put Yu Khe Thai (again) and Say Kok Chuan on trial. Like Yu, Say had been imprisoned by the Japanese and then released in 1943 on the condition that he thank the emperor and cooperate with the occupying regime. The trial of the men did not go ahead, after the CIC and MPs dispersed the proceedings. In response, the *Chinese Guide* and the *Chinese Commercial Bulletin* (*Qiaoshang gongbao*, the Philippine-Chinese Anti-Japanese Volunteer Corps' [Kang Chu] newspaper) denounced the CIC as "fascistic" and "Japanese Kempeitai-like," even accusing it of taking bribes.[36] In December 1945, KMT and Mutual Aid Society member Vicente Dy Sun, who had been tortured by the Japanese, received a letter from the commission that threatened his life if he did not cough up 200,000 Philippine pesos (PHP).[37] He hired a bodyguard, reported the threat to the police, survived, and rose through the ranks of the General Chamber of Commerce to become its president many years later. Also in December, a bomb exploded in Manila at the New England Hotel and Restaurant, whose owner had been threatened by KMT guerrillas for employing communists. The *zongzhibu* officially denied any responsibility for the bombing and declared that its members had been told to act in a law-abiding manner in accordance with the ROC government's instructions.[38]

The Chinese Left and Philippine Politics

As the attacks on the CIC suggest, collaboration was just as much a source of friction between Chinese communists and the Philippine and US authorities as it was between them and the KMT. Despite the CIC's arrest of prominent collaborators such as Jorge Vargas and Jose Laurel along with the cabinet members of Laurel's Second Philippine Republic, many of these politicians had eluded justice in the eyes of the left and resumed their political careers after the war. The most prominent offender was Senate president Manuel Roxas, who had briefly served as Laurel's "food czar" in 1944 after resisting earlier entreaties by the Japanese to join the puppet administration.[39] Roxas was President Sergio Osmeña's chief political rival within the divided Nacionalista Party and defeated the incumbent in the first postwar elections in April 1946 to become the first president of the independent Philippines. But he won only because he never went on trial for collaboration. After arresting Roxas and other members of Laurel's wartime cabinet in the spring of 1945, the CIC handed them over to the Philippine government. In accordance with Washington's policy on collaboration, the People's Court was established to try them. However, Roxas was personally pardoned by General Douglas MacArthur, the supreme Allied commander in the Southwest Pacific area, in breach of his own government's legal protocol. With MacArthur having undermined Osmeña's authority, Roxas and his congressional supporters were able to sap the functioning of the People's Court by denying it funding and manpower. Roxas was also under attack for being soft on collaborators because two of his sons were implicated in pro-Japanese activities during the war.[40]

The Chinese left's anger at the government's failure to deal effectively with collaborators was compounded by the persecution of their Filipino allies and by Sinophobia. Unlike the KMT, Chinese communists had consistently sought out their Filipino ideological counterparts in pursuit of an internationalist, multiethnic coalition against fascism and imperialism. During the war, Chinese communists served as interpreters and advisers to the Huks and, at their Filipino comrades' suggestion, formed the Wha Chi as a Huk squadron in May 1942; Huk leader Luis Taruc later hailed the Wha Chi for shattering Filipino stereotypes of the Chinese as greedy capitalists by going out of their way to aid Filipinos who had been ravaged by the war.[41] While tensions between the Wha Chi and the Huks persisted because of disputes over tactics and what Taruc called the Wha Chi's "chauvinism and self-interest," their partnership endured for the first three years after Japan's defeat as the US and Philippine authorities attempted to marginalize the left.[42] In late February 1945, sixteen Huk leaders were arrested, including Taruc and his second in command, Casto

Alejandrino, for allegedly failing to cooperate with the US military in San Fernando, Pampanga.[43] Separately, at the first postwar special session of the Philippine legislature from June to July 1945, the House of Representatives introduced two bills aimed at restricting alien dominance of the economy by nationalizing the retail trade. Its Committee on Commerce and Industry consolidated them into House Bill (H.B.) No. 355 and sent it to President Osmeña for his approval in mid-September.[44]

Demonstrations in support of the arrested Huk leaders and in opposition to anti-Chinese legislation proliferated. The largest took place in Manila on September 23, 1945, and was sponsored by the newly formed Democratic Alliance (DA), a PKP-led coalition party that included the Philippine-Chinese Democratic League (Feilübin Huaqiao Minzhu Da Tongmeng), the political wing of the Kang Fan.[45] Scarcely a week after H.B. No. 355 had reached Osmeña's office, over twenty thousand demonstrators brandished communist flags and Maoist and Stalinist slogans, marched to Malacañang Palace, and demanded that Osmeña both release Taruc, Alejandrino, and other Huks and act against "traitors." Among them were around one thousand Chinese, who demanded "the removal of collaborators from Congress," which "caused a strain in Philippine-Chinese relations by passing anti-Chinese laws," according to the pro-Roxas *Daily News* tabloid. During the rally in front of the palace, Co Keng Sing exhorted Chinese workers and peasants to unite against the remnants of fascism in the country. He conflated the Chinese left's antifascism and opposition to anti-Chinese legislation, attacking Congress for "doing what Hitler did to the Jews."[46]

A week later, Co expounded on his remarks in an article titled "We Demand Justice" in the *New China Review*, the *Chinese Guide*'s English supplement. Co claimed that there were only twenty-five non-collaborators out of ninety-five members of Congress. Roxas, despite being a cabinet member under Laurel and the head of the economic planning board, had not only regained his position as a congressman but also had the "nerve" to run for president. To distract the people from their wartime activities, Congress and the Senate, aided by the *Daily News*, had launched an anti-Chinese campaign to "please those who [had] racial prejudice so that they [could] maintain their political positions," a "method [viewed as] similar to what Fuehrer Hitler tried on the Jews." Although the Chinese, as foreigners, had no right to interfere in Philippine politics, they had the right to demand justice against collaborators because they had suffered during the war and fought with Filipinos against the Japanese. Co also criticized the United States for rehabilitating collaborators. The article ended by calling for unity in Chinese society, which, it declared ominously, could be achieved only by "wiping out Chinese collaborators."[47]

Roxas and his allies in Congress and in the media wasted no time in striking back. On September 25, the front page of the *Daily News* featured the headline "1,000 Chinese in Huk Parade."[48] Its editorial excoriated these Chinese for interfering in the domestic political affairs of the Philippines, labeled them "undesirable aliens," and demanded that the president arrest and deport them immediately. Osmeña, who had apparently "received them on the grounds of Malacañan [*sic*] and kowtowed to them," was denounced by the same paper the following day as the "Chinese puppet leader."[49] Roxas himself demanded the expulsion of Chinese "who [were] not needed in the country," and the House formed a committee to investigate Chinese involvement in the protests. Co was nowhere to be found when the sergeant at arms of the House went searching for him on September 29, and he did not show up at the committee's hearings the next day. On October 10, Co reappeared and was subpoenaed to attend the hearings—but did not. To the dismay of Roxas's supporters and the KMT, nothing came of the investigation. Frustrated by Manila's inadequate efforts to prosecute collaborators, the United States refused to support the committee.[50] Filipino nationalists, meanwhile, were dealt a setback when the president vetoed H.B. No. 355 on October 16, citing the incompatibility of protectionist measures with the Philippines' membership of the United Nations and commitment to internationalism.[51]

The "Chinese Communist Problem"

By late 1945, Co's repeated evasions of the state and the Kang Fan's involvement in the September 23 protests crystallized in Roxas's mind the emerging "Chinese communist problem" and how it figured into his own political ambitions. The DA endorsed Sergio Osmeña for president. Despite reservations about Osmeña, DA leaders viewed Roxas as a fascist and collaborator.[52] For Roxas, any future anticommunist measures doubled up as retribution against Osmeña's supporters, including Chinese leftists. As president of the Senate, he was not lacking for information on the Chinese left and its ties to Filipino communists. Sometime after September 23, Roxas received a document titled "Big Head of the Chinese Communist Party." In it were the names of eight Sino-communists, including Dy Eng Hao, the "secretary of the Chinese Communist Party (Cantonese)," who spoke "Chinese, English, Tagalog & Spanish"; Wong Kiat of the Wha Chi; the *Chinese Guide*'s Smin Chang; and Co Keng Sing, "alias Gam Kim Seng," who "delivered speech of Sunday against the Congress of the Philippines at Malacañang" and had "a case before the war not yet finished up" and "charges brought to him by the Chinese Nationalist

Party."[53] The *Guide* and *Commercial Bulletin* were also listed. The ungrammatical English of this typewritten and anonymously authored text indicates that it was either composed or translated by a nonnative speaker.

In the same box as this document in the Roxas Papers at the University of the Philippines (UP) is a letter titled "Deport Undesirable Chinese." Its author, Chua Peng Leong, claimed to be representing "Chinese neutrals and residents of Manila," and his missive was intended for the US authorities. The letter is typewritten in excellent English on plain paper and has no return address or date. The year "1945" and the acronym for the Philippine Military Intelligence Service, "MIS," are handwritten in its margins, which suggests that MIS forwarded it to Roxas (or vice versa). It begins with a powerful thesis: the "real disturbers of the peace" are the Chinese communists, who not only were actively involved in Philippine politics but also were committing kidnapping, robbery, and murder, "sometimes in connivance with Filipino gangsters and hoodlums." Chua accuses them of collaborating with Japan and deceiving the CIC into thinking that they were fighting the Japanese. Unsurprisingly, leading Chinese Reds were also in league with the Huks and had connections with the Soviet Union and the Chinese Communist Party (CCP). Having already collected PHP 1 million through means such as kidnapping and extortion, Chinese Reds had "extended their power and influence" over the Huks and had created the DA to transform the Philippines into an "instrument of communism." This organization was "sowing the seeds of discontent, terrorism, and banditry, with murders here and there." The letter ends with a plea to the United States on behalf of "all law-abiding and peaceful Chinese and Filipino citizens" to act swiftly against this menace.[54]

The letter contains just enough factual details, such as the names of Chinese communist leaders and their organizations (the "Hua Chee," "Khong Huan," and "Khong Thu"), as well as a list of the secret societies they were in league with, to persuade the reader of its author's familiarity with Chinese affairs. The factuality of this piece, however, is beside the point. Its principal effect was to play to Filipino and US prejudices toward the Chinese population while attributing Chinese criminality to a specific ideological faction and thus distinguishing between "good" and "bad" Chinese. For example, while there is nothing to suggest that Sino-communists controlled the Huks, this assertion resonated with perceptions of the Chinese as self-serving and stoked fears of communism as a "foreign" ideology. Similarly, by claiming—not without reason—that the communists engaged in kidnapping, robbery, and murder and were linked to Filipino and Chinese gangsters, the letter reinforced stereotypes of the Chinese as inclined toward criminal behavior. Whether Chua, whose signature is at the end of the letter, was an actual person is unclear, but by declaring themselves to be law-abiding "neutrals," he and those he represented distanced themselves from communal politics and framed their letter as born of mere civic-mindedness.

As its conflict with the Chinese left worsened, the KMT sought increasingly to prove itself useful to the coercive organs of the Philippine state and pin the blame for criminal behavior on the communists. While the provenance of Chua's letter is unknown, its blurring of the distinction between communism and gangsterism and its provision of intelligence to the authorities are consistent with this broader trend. By early 1946, incidences of kidnapping and blackmail in Manila's Chinatown had reached epidemic proportions, much to the frustration of the metropolitan police. On March 2, the *Philippines Free Press*, the country's oldest news weekly, reported that wealthy Chinese were being blackmailed into handing over large sums of money to Chinese gangsters. Pretending to be guerrillas, they targeted individuals who had profited from buying and selling war materiel to the Japanese and informed their intended victims that only by contributing to the resistance could they "redeem" themselves. If their targets failed to do so within a day, they would be shot or kidnapped and then killed.[55] One kidnap victim was the deputy manager of the *Great China Press* and a CVP veteran, Cai Yunqin, whose kidnappers accused him of being "reactionary by nature" (*fandong chengxing*) and said that he deserved death. He was set to be drowned but remarkably, although we know not how, escaped to tell his tale.[56]

For the KMT, an organization committed to protecting the interests of Chinese abroad and seeking to expand in the Philippines, it was politically expedient to help the police tackle Chinese-related crimes and to attribute these crimes to communism. Chinese society was something of a black box to law enforcement officials. Linguistic and cultural barriers between Filipinos and Chinese made crimes involving these challenges uniquely difficult to solve. As Manila's exasperated chief of police explained to the *Philippines Free Press* in May 1946, in response to the kidnapping spree: "Tracking down Chinese criminals, particularly the murderers, in Manila is like chasing the legendary will-o'-the-wisp. It is next to impossible to get them for the simple reason that both the victims and their relatives—even if they personally know the culprits—refuse to talk. Mortal fear of violent reprisal from the killer or killers grips them and keeps their lips closed." Unable to understand Chinese, the police usually confronted a "blank wall" when investigating Chinese suspects and witnesses, who insisted on speaking Chinese even if they knew Tagalog well.[57] The KMT helped the police overcome this linguistic divide by reorganizing one of its special forces teams and establishing a communications network with the authorities in opposition to Chinese criminals and communists.[58] In this manner, the KMT rendered Chinese society legible to its host government and insinuated itself into the coercive apparatus of the state.

KMT intelligence reports and propaganda from mid- to late 1946 give us a sense of how party members assessed the threat of communism during a critical period that spanned Roxas's election, the outbreak of the civil war in China, and armed conflict between the Philippine state and the Huks. Chinese communists in the country were supposedly providing the Soviet Union with confidential military and political information, encouraging the Huks to adopt Sinophobic attitudes, and establishing base areas in Central Luzon to retreat to in difficult circumstances.[59] In October, three months after Chiang Kai-shek launched a large-scale attack on the CCP in north China, the *zongzhibu* relaunched its wartime publication, *Soul of the Great Han* (*Dahan hun*), as a monthly magazine. In its inaugural issue, Secretary-General Koa Chunte (see figure 2.1) reprised his role as chief polemicist for the KMT in the islands. He warned that while *hanjian* previously operated covertly, the new *hanjian* were behaving boldly and using democracy as a cover to propagate their "treasonous theories" (*maiguo lilun*). Because the ROC had failed to disband the "bandit special agents" (*feite*), a "Red disaster" (*chihuo*) and "new imperialism" (*xin diguo zhuyi*) were menacing the globe and threatening World War III. The party had revived *Dahan hun* to confront this new enemy of the Chinese nation.[60]

Koa's richly suggestive language here anticipated Chiang Kai-shek's branding of the CCP as *hanjian* by five years and shows that the KMT was grappling with how to define its communist enemy.[61] His prose dovetailed with contemporaneous fears of communism as a global threat and anticipated the Cold War. It also evoked the KMT's revolutionary heritage and struggles against Western and especially Japanese colonialism: Koa employed the same label—*hanjian*—used to describe Chinese collaborators during the War of Resistance to represent the communists. Finally, he described the communists as *fei*, a term that the KMT attached to the CCP during the Nanjing Decade and resurrected during the civil war as the main signifier of Sino-communism in its propaganda.[62] (After 1949, the CCP likewise described the KMT as *fei*.) By using it, Koa was comparing the CCP to anti-dynastic "bandits" from imperial times, such as the Taiping rebels, to delegitimize the communists and legitimize the ROC. Like Chua Peng Leong's letter to Roxas, Koa's article forged a link between crime and communism that informed the KMT's collaborative policing of Chinese society. It was no coincidence that the same issue of the magazine featured articles on how the COWHM had helped capture thirteen kidnappers (*bangfei*) and on Cai Yunqin's kidnapping by a separate gang of "bandits." Both strongly implied that the *fei* in question were

FIGURE 2.1. Former Philippine KMT secretary-general Koa Chun-te (second row, third from left) in Taiwan in 1950. Reprinted with permission from Academia Historica.

communists. The former declared *fei* (not *bangfei*) the biggest enemy of wealthy and poor Chinese alike, while the latter, as we have seen, described how the kidnappers accused Cai of being a reactionary.[63]

Persecuting and Prosecuting the Chinese Left

As fears of communism grew, the ideological climate in the Philippines shifted decisively rightward and in favor of the KMT. Relations between the Filipino left and the state deteriorated swiftly following the presidential and congressional elections in April 1946. At the new president's orders, Huk leader Luis Taruc and five other DA candidates were prevented from taking their seats in the House on charges of electoral fraud and terrorism. Subsequently, clashes in Central Luzon between the Huks and the police, which had served as Roxas's pretext for banning Taruc and other Huks from Congress, worsened. Anti-Chinese sentiment was also growing. The failure of earlier efforts to national-ize the retail trade only galvanized populist politicians such as Senator Vicente Sotto of Cebu, who alleged that Chinese economic practices such as remitting money to China and black marketeering were making the Philippines a "weak nation." Sotto also protested the growing number of Chinese entering the is-lands illegally following the start of the civil war, believing it to be "one of the gravest national problems" of the day.[64]

In the autumn of 1946, recalled the daughter of Kang Chu leader Young Ching-tong, "reactionary forces started to intensify" (fandong shili kaishi xiaozhang).[65] For left and right, the turning point was what the KMT later called the "September 5 incident."[66] It had been a long time in coming. In May, while visiting Washington, Manuel Roxas told the ROC's ambassador to the United States that there were many Chinese communists in the Philippines who were functioning as intermediaries between Moscow and the Huks and were using terrorist methods to attack other Chinese. The president and the ROC consul pursued cooperation between their countries against these Reds, in the inter-ests of protecting the ROC's overseas nationals. Roxas believed that it would not be difficult to find legal reasons to deport the Reds.[67]

The arrests that took place on September 5 followed swiftly on the heels of the "pacification" campaign that Roxas had launched against the Huks in Central Luzon in August.[68] That evening, MPs raided the Chinese Guide, the Chinese Commercial Bulletin, Union High School, the Chinese Labor Federation, the Hong Kwong Institute, and several other sites. The entire circulation staff of the Chinese Guide was detained, as was Young Ching-tong, who was teach-ing at the institute. Over the next two days, around sixty-one persons were arrested and their residences and shops searched. However, this operation proved unsuccessful. To deport the arrested, the state required evidence of their active interference in the internal politics of the Philippines, such as in-volvement in the Huk movement, or of other violations of the law and forms of criminal activity. For this reason, those arrested were questioned about ties to the Huks, the organizations they belonged to, whether they had legal resi-dence papers, and what they had done during the occupation. Unable to find such evidence, Roxas was forced into halting the arrests and releasing those detained. His office explained that the raids were conducted in response to complaints that "lawless elements," some involved in a kidnapping ring, reg-ularly visited the places raided. The palace stressed that it had no desire to become involved in political disputes within Chinese society so long as they did not touch on Filipino affairs.[69]

All signs pointed to Shih I-Sheng and the CVP. Shih had connections to law enforcement and the military (see chapter 1). Witnesses identified the Chinese agents involved in the raids as active KMT members, while according to the *Chinese Commercial News* (*CCN*), Shih was present at MP headquarters after the arrests.[70] Detainees released a few days later told the *Manila Times* that they had been subjected to third-degree torture by those agents, among whom was a member of the "Overseas Chinese Volunteer Corps."[71] In response to accusations in the left-wing Chinese media, Shih denied any role in the raids.[72] But six years later, the *zongzhibu* smugly described the incident as a KMT "plot" (*yinmou*) against the communists in recounting its achievements to the Seventh National Party Congress.[73]

September 5, although an embarrassing climbdown for the Roxas administration, was in hindsight the start of what Chinese communists described as the White Terror campaign against them.[74] Two days later, in a seemingly unrelated episode, a Philippine-Chinese Democratic League member and teacher in the provinces named Wang Jiawai was seized and killed in a raid on the local league headquarters, triggering protests by the league, the Philippine-Chinese United Workers Union (Lo Lian Hui), and the *Chinese Guide*. Wang's corpse was shipped to Manila, where an autopsy proved that he had been shot. A week afterward, he received a martyr's funeral in Manila, at which the Lo Lian Hui's secretary-general, Shen Fushui, angrily denounced the KMT and the Philippine government for collaborating to oppress local Chinese. The legal case that Wang's supporters brought before the courts was never settled, according to Shen. But it drove home to the Chinese left that they had to be on their guard going forward.[75] Although Shen did not provide concrete evidence of the KMT's involvement in Wang's murder, party records make it clear that armed force was used to purge communists from schools.[76]

Violence against leftists aside, the KMT also consolidated its hold over the school system by providing funding, through businessmen affiliated with the party, for the building of facilities, and by assisting schools in vetting applicants for teaching jobs at the start of each academic year.[77] Where appropriate, it also assisted the state in its legal prosecution of alleged Chinese supporters of the Huks. One noteworthy episode involved five men associated with Kipsi Primary School in Batangas City in southern Luzon. In 1946, they were taken into custody by MPs on suspicions of involvement in communist activities but were released due to a lack of evidence. On August 13, 1947, following directives from the Office of the President, MPs raided the school and confiscated many books and papers. Two weeks later, they rearrested the principal, Lu Bon King; the trustees Gan Ping (president of the board of trustees), Yap Lim Son, and Lao Tang Bun; and a regular contributor to the school, Ng Bun Ho. On September 1, the men, all Chinese nationals, went before the Bureau of Immigration's Deportation Board, which, after several hearings, ordered them deported. In its report to the Seventh National Party Congress, the KMT incorporated the *wu huagong an* (case of the five Chinese communists) into a list of milestone events during its "bloody struggle" against the left after 1945. The *zongzhibu* noted with approval the role played by Uy Ting Bing, a businessman and the secretary of the Batangas KMT, in testifying before the Deportation Board and the support that he received from the Philippine authorities. It described the deportation order as a "major victory" (*da shengli*) and as dealing a "fundamental blow" (*genben dongyao*) to the "bandits' spirit and faction" (*feitu jingshen zhenying*).[78]

Some of the Deportation Board's findings were as follows. On March 30, 1946, the five men demanded PHP 10,000 from Uy to finance Luis Taruc's electoral campaign. When Uy refused to pay this sum, Gan Ping threatened him with death. Another merchant, Lim Yu Ching, who was not a KMT member, said that he was similarly threatened; he also testified that the petitioners had preached that Roxas was "bad" and criticized the ROC, US, and Philippine governments while in Lim's restaurant. Sometime that year, Lu Bon King drew the Soviet flag on the blackboard in a classroom and said that this flag should be "up" while the flags of other countries should be "down." On July 7, Gan likely delivered a "fiery speech" advocating revolution against the Philippine government. Gan, Yap, and Lao were said to have transported war materiel in a jeep from Batangas to the Huks in Pampanga in 1947. Finally, many documents confiscated from the library had "communistic leanings," according to brief translations or synopses that the ROC Consulate provided to MPs.

Lu, Gan, Yap, Lao, and Ng were not the first Chinese nationals whom the Philippines sought to deport, but they were the first to challenge the deportation order in the Supreme Court, to which they petitioned unsuccessfully for a writ of habeas corpus. Two statutory provisions governed the deportation process in the country, the first of which this case was tried under. According to Section 37 (a) of the Immigration Act of 1940 (Commonwealth Act No. 613), the immigration commissioner, a political appointee, was authorized to issue warrants for the arrest of aliens for, inter alia, illegal entry; possessing, consuming, or trafficking in prohibited drugs; crimes of "moral turpitude"; prostitution or managing a brothel; becoming a public charge; credit fraud; profiteering, hoarding, and blackmail; and, finally, unacceptable political beliefs. Any foreigner who "believes in, advises, advocates or teaches the overthrow by force and violence" of the Philippine or indeed any other government could be ejected from the country.[79]

On October 22, 1948, in a 6–3 decision on *Lao Tang Bun et al. v. Engracio Fabre et al.*, the Supreme Court denied the petitioners habeas corpus and, in doing so, reaffirmed the judiciary's nonintervention in deportation proceedings and thus the sovereign authority of the government in these matters.[80] Justice Jose Bengzon, summarizing the majority opinion, reminded them that the court had "time and again . . . announced the view that the decisions of the customs or immigration authorities are final, unless there has been an abuse of discretion or power, or where they have acted in open violation of the law." The burden of proof to show that the Immigration Bureau had abused its power rested with the accused. Furthermore, deportation was not a criminal procedure, and a deportation order did not have to be justified by "preponderance of the evidence" or by "evidence beyond reasonable doubt"; "some evidence to support the order" was enough. Observers sensed the implications of this verdict for the campaign against the Hukbalahap. A US Embassy official wrote his secretary of state that it was "certain to be a great aid to the Philippine authorities in tightening up deportation procedures and bringing about the actual deportation of undesirable aliens, particularly those known or suspected to be engaged in Communist activities"—regardless of the legal arguments in play.[81] In no other deportation cases involving Chinese after 1948 did the accused seek redress for unlawful detention from the Supreme Court, only from which habeas corpus could be obtained.

What, then, of the evidence and the persons whose testimonies the Deportation Board had used to identify the five Chinese as communists? In a lengthy and scathing dissent, Justice Gregorio Perfecto questioned the reliability of the immigration commissioner's witnesses, highlighted the contradictory testimonies of the five petitioners, and slammed the conclusions that the board had drawn from the scanty evidence that was presented to it. For example, there was no proof that the materiel that Gan and others had transported in a jeep from Batangas was meant for the Huks. Even if the publications confiscated from the school library were "communistic," that did not mean that the petitioners were communists, since persons of all ideological persuasions could reasonably be expected to read works such as the *Communist Manifesto*. In response to the charge that the petitioners had criticized Roxas and the governments of China and the United States while showing partiality toward Russia, Perfecto defended their right to free speech, even as foreigners.

Turning to the petitioners' testimonies before the Deportation Board, Perfecto pointed out that Gan Ping denied ever extorting Uy Ting Bing to help Luis Taruc and did not even know who Taruc was. Gan had also spoken at

Uy's house on Chiang Kai-shek's birthday in 1946. Ng Bun Ho testified that he knew nothing about communism and had only ever gone to Uy's house to ask for contributions in support of the relatives of those killed by the Japanese. The school had been established in memory of Chua Kipsi, a KMT member and the president of the Chinese Anti-Japanese Association in Batangas, who had been martyred during the war. Its nine-member board of trustees included three KMT members and the "communists" Gan, Yap Lim Son, and Lao Tang Bun, all of whom were elected by the school's financiers, including Uy.

Perfecto reserved his harshest remarks for Uy Ting Bing and the other main witnesses for the prosecution, whom he deemed untrustworthy. Uy had collaborated with the Japanese by selling them scrap iron, coal, and bread and had earlier been convicted of illegal possession of morphine. (In 1949, Philippine military intelligence reported that Uy was part of a weapons smuggling ring operating out of Batangas.)[82] Furthermore, Uy bore a grudge against Lu Bon King because Uy had asked Lu to support his candidacy for president of the board of trustees, but Lu refused. Lim Yu Ching had been imprisoned for knifing someone. During the investigation into the five men, Lim perjured himself by first denying that he had been convicted in the knifing and then admitting that he had been convicted in his second testimony. Lim had sought to secure payments in advance for meals that his restaurant served to two petitioners and became angry when they refused. Armando Valdez, the MP officer who had arrested the five men, was operating purely on hearsay—and orders from above. In 1946, he went to the school twice and saw the building packed with Chinese. Someone was speaking in Chinese, which Valdez did not understand. Another Chinese told him that the speeches were "communistic." Valdez admitted to having no real evidence that the accused were Huk members but said that "Malacañang pounded on us and we had to act." Two army intelligence operatives, Agents 176 and 591, had demonstrated inadequate knowledge of communism by alleging that two former Philippine solicitors general were members of the "communist" Civil Liberties Union. Agent 176 had "received information regarding communist movements from a Chinese ex–guerrilla captain," while Agent 591 confessed that he had "not come across a definite individual whom [he could] positively point [to] as a member of the Chinese Communist Party in the Philippines." Perfecto concluded that the "evidence for the prosecution was an utter failure."

The Supreme Court's decision can also help us reconstruct how and why the arrests came about and how information circulated and was generated to incriminate the five men. Uy Ting Bing and Lim Yu Ching were most likely responsible for their being summoned for questioning by MPs in 1946 (the decision does not say when exactly). As was often the case in ideologically inflected arrests, native informants such as Uy and Lim—some part of the local KMT, others not—were the first points of contact between Chinese society and the Philippine authorities because of the latter's linguistic inadequacies and lack of familiarity with the former. In 1947, President Roxas pressured Armando Valdez to arrest the men. Presumably, Roxas had acted based on intelligence from government agencies, which in turn relied on Chinese sources: it is not a stretch here to argue that Uy and the KMT helped generate the pressure that Manila applied to Batangas. The arrests were part of a larger anti-Chinese anticommunist crackdown that had begun with the September 5, 1946, raids in the capital. Uy had ample reasons to report the men. He may have acted out of spite because of their failure to support his bid for board president, or as a KMT partisan who despised communism, or to deflect attention from his smuggling activities and collaboration with the Japanese. As a ranking KMT member in Batangas, Uy was integrated into the KMT's nationwide organizational structure and had access to the *zongzhibu*'s leaders such as Shih I-Sheng, who then conveyed his intelligence to the Philippine military.

Uy and other Chinese played an active role during the other stages of the Philippine state's investigation into the five men. According to Lu Bon King, the four hundred books that were seized from the school library were brought to Uy's house, whereupon Uy selected fifty-two for use as evidence during the deportation hearings. ROC Consulate officials helped summarize their contents for the prosecution. An anonymous Chinese informed Armando Valdez when the latter visited Kipsi Primary School in 1946 that the speeches Valdez did not understand were "communistic." Agent 176 had also received similarly second-hand intelligence from "a Chinese ex–guerrilla captain."

Perfecto's dissent and the inadequacies of the evidence against them notwithstanding, the five men could very well have been communists. Shen Fushui, in his insider's history of the Lo Lian Hui, described them as "patriots" and revealed that two were members of the Shopkeepers' Mutual Aid Association of Batangas, a group affiliated with the Lo Lian Hui, while another two were part of the Kang Fan. However, Shen was adamant that they had been "falsely accused" of engaging in communist activities in the school.[83] The question, in any case, presumes that in the late 1940s, there was widespread agreement among official circles in the Philippines on what it meant to be a "Chinese communist" and on what evidence could be used to demonstrate this—when there was not. As Justice Perfecto argued, the existence of some "communistic" library books, which Uy Ting Bing handpicked and ROC officials summarized, in no way proved that the principal and the president of the board of trustees were communists. But for the Deportation Board, such partial and cherry-picked evidence, which would have been inadmissible in a court of law, was adequate. Secondhand intelligence, such as what Valdez and Agent 176 had collected from unknown sources, was permissible. So too were the leaps of logic required to bridge the gap between material evidence (books) and ideological belief. This and similar cases did not establish the guilt of the accused but rather established the criteria with which individuals were identified as legible, legal-ideological subjects that could be acted on by the Philippine and ROC states. The *wu huagong an* reflected and helped define the Sinophobic anticommunist climate in the country and region.

The story of the five men ends with an unexpected twist in the tale. Following the Supreme Court's decision, the immigration commissioner Engracio Fabre, announced that he would arrange for their immediate deportation, but their counsel, a former secretary of labor, was able to secure a temporary suspension of the deportation order with the Immigration Bureau.[84] When, in July 1949, they were deported to KMT-controlled Xiamen, the Lo Lian Hui worked out a deal with a KMT official and former Philippine resident who realized that his party's demise on the mainland was looming and was looking to switch sides. To prove his new loyalties, this official agreed to identify the five men not as Chinese communists (*huagong*) but as KMT members who had fallen victim to an intraparty feud. Four swiftly left the city, but the fifth remained and was soon reapprehended by a KMT special agent and sent to Taiwan before the CCP captured Xiamen in October.[85]

The End of the Chinese Left

As anticommunism in the Philippines intensified and the civil war tilted in favor of the CCP after 1947, Chinese leftist leaders began to quit the islands for their homeland, usually returning via Hong Kong. From there, Gong Taoyi, Huang Wei, and Co Keng Sing returned to China in early 1949, on the eve of the CCP's victory; they went on to work for the CCP's United Work Front Department (Tongyi Zhanxian Gongzuo Bu) while living in the same residential compound in Beijing. Like many other "returned overseas Chinese" (*guiqiao*), they were accused of counterrevolutionary behavior and persecuted for their cosmopolitanism during the Cultural Revolution. A Gang of Four agent in Fujian compared the Wha Chi to a "lychee tree which bore fruits with red skin, white meat, and black hearts."[86] Huang and Gong were taken into custody for investigation, with Gong allowed to return home during the evenings and on Sundays to care for their young child. Co Keng Sing suffered the most. Denounced as a reactionary for having cooperated with Filipinos and the US military during the war, Co fell ill and was admitted to a hospital, where Gong would secretly go to see him. In 1968, after being discharged and despite not having fully recovered, Co was sentenced to hard labor in Heilongjiang and Henan. In 1973, Gong was in Beijing when he found out that Co had died two years earlier, on August 8.[87]

By the end of 1947, the KMT's "bloody struggle" was largely over. Looking back on the two-and-a-half-year period that began in mid-1945, the *zong-zhibu* assessed that while it had paid a large price, it had protected itself and "calmed" (*anding*) *huaqiao* society and was gaining support among the Chinese.[88] Despite the violence and deception that it had employed and the questionable extent to which there was genuine enthusiasm for the party, there was some truth to what party leaders reported. The majority of Chinese communist leaders had left the country. Their movement had been deinstitutionalized and driven underground.

On November 22, 1950, MIS's arrest of Chinese businessman Co Pak capped the KMT's triumph over not only Sino-communism in the Philippines but also one of the few organizations whose scope and structure rivaled the party's. The evidence that MIS had gathered against one of the "wealthiest members of the local Chinese community when the war broke out," to quote the *Philippines Free Press*, appeared substantial.[89] The fifty-three-year-old Jinjiang native was president of the local chapter of the Chinese Freemasons (Hongmen), a secretive fraternal association that had branches globally and throughout the Philippines.[90] According to the ROC Embassy, Co was the preeminent financial supporter of Chinese communism in the country. In 1935, Co began molding the Hongmen into an instrument of communism by admitting into its fold Sino-communists who had recently arrived in the islands. These included his kinsman Co Chi Meng, whom the embassy believed had exploited common native-place ties to further this alliance. During the war, Co Pak funneled money and supplies to the Kang Fan, Wha Chi, and Kang Chu, as indeed the Chinese left acknowledged.[91] After the war, he provided these organizations with names of Chinese collaborators; continued funding them and their publications, such as the *Chinese Guide* and the *Chinese Commercial Bulletin*; bailed out Chinese Reds who had gotten into trouble with the authorities; and even paid Huk leader Luis Taruc protection money.[92] After the CCP captured Jinjiang in 1949, Co remitted PHP 20,000, via Young Ching-tong, to the new authorities in his hometown.[93] That he was "completely a member of the traitorous party was without question" (*chuncui zhi jiandang fenzi juewu yiwen*), wrote Shih I-Sheng to the ROC Executive Yuan in March 1951, right after Co's deportation to Taiwan.[94] ROC ambassador Chen Chih-ping summarized this deportation as "benefiting our party-state's prestige in the Philippines" (*liyu wo dangguo zai Fei weixin*).[95]

This account, however, tells only half the story. Despite his support for Sino-communism, Co Pak was not a communist in the way that Co Chi Meng, Co Keng Sing (another kinsman), and Young Ching-tong were. Chen explained that Co Pak began collaborating with Chinese Reds in 1935 so that he could exploit their "terrorist strength" (*kongbu liliang*) to further his ambitions within the Hongmen. Without communists serving as his enforcers, Co would not have become an "elder brother" (*dage*) of the organization.[96] Beyond the Hongmen, Co was not involved in the Chinese labor movement. To the contrary, before the occupation, Co made his fortune from opium and morphine trafficking, gambling and prostitution dens, smuggling, and counterfeiting. During the war, the Japanese availed themselves of his narcotics business and brothels; Co also purchased scrap iron and war materiel for the administration and helped it track down KMT guerrillas—all while covertly supporting left-wing Chinese resistance groups.[97] After the war, Co was charged with collaboration and set to be deported, but this first of two deportation cases against him was dropped in March 1947.[98] By this point, the Sino-communist movement that Co Pak had financed was in decline. In the three and a half years that followed, although we cannot say for sure based on extant archival materials, the KMT and the ROC Embassy worked with MIS to have Co rearrested.

The Co Pak affair, like the *wu huagong an*, typified the KMT-ROC's partnership with Manila against Sino-communism. Ironically, it reveals that when circumstances demanded it, the KMT was as capable as the Chinese left was of imposing an ideological-moral binary onto the ambiguities of individual agency and motives. Chinese communists branded Yu Khe Thai, Justo Cabo Chan, and many KMT members as "collaborators" to advance their own cause in opposition to the KMT, while at the same time turning a blind eye to their financier's support for the Japanese. Conversely, the KMT largely disregarded its own members and supporters' "collaboration" but gave no quarter when the opportunity arose to boil Co Pak's ruthless, manipulative pursuit of self-interest down to "communism."

Diplomacy, Citizenship, and Shared Sovereignty

From 1945 to 1948, the KMT's conflict with the Chinese left and collaborative relationship with the Philippine security state were part of a larger political process through which the party's authority over the Philippine Chinese

was legitimized. Following the Pacific War, KMT branches and operatives constituted an advance vanguard for the rebuilding of Nationalist Chinese influence in Southeast Asia. Synchronously, the ROC sought to leverage its position
as one of the four major Allied powers to establish diplomatic ties that facilitated diasporic mobilization and safeguarded the interests of "Chinese nationals" overseas. In the Philippines, such interstate diplomacy was not directly
connected to anticommunist cooperation between KMT guerrillas and the
Philippine military on the ground, but it created a legal basis for shared sovereignty and would have similar lasting consequences.

Formal diplomatic relations between the ROC and the Philippines were established almost immediately after Philippine independence on July 4, 1946.
The two governments then began negotiating a treaty of amity to "re-assert
the friendly relations of the two nations" and "define the rights and privileges
of one in the territory of the other," as one ROC diplomat put it. While these
negotiations proved far from straightforward, they eventually yielded a short
statement of principles that was meant to guide relations going forward and,
indeed, became a touchstone for future disputes over issues such as immigration, economic nationalization, and education. On April 18, 1947, President
Roxas and Chen Chih-ping signed this treaty, which was soon ratified by the
Philippine Senate and the ROC's Legislative Yuan.[99] Of concern to us is the
sixth of the treaty's ten articles, which read:

> The nationals of each of the high contracting parties shall be accorded,
> in the territories of the other, the liberty to establish schools for the
> education of their children, and shall enjoy freedom of peaceful assem-
> bly and association, of publication, of worship and religion, of burial
> and building cemeteries, upon the same terms as the nationals of any
> third country in accordance with the laws and regulations of the other.
>
> The nationals of each of the high contracting parties shall have the
> right to acquire, inherit, possess, lease, occupy and dispose of, by sale,
> testament, donation or otherwise, any kind of movable or immovable
> property and to engage in trade and other peaceful and lawful pursuits
> throughout the whole extent of the territories of the other upon the
> same terms as the nationals of any third country in accordance with
> the constitution, laws and regulations of the other.[100]

The two paragraphs of this article reproduced and formalized the liberal ethos
of US colonial policy toward Chinese society in the Philippines and in doing so
paved the way for the expansion of Nationalist China's diasporic sovereignty in
the country. Nanjing was authorized to found and operate its own schools, and
since many of these private institutions were KMT-run, the treaty effectively

sanctioned the party's control over much of Chinese education. As Chinese nationals were guaranteed freedom of peaceful assembly, association, and publication, as well as the right to engage in "other peaceful and lawful activities," the treaty also legitimized the KMT itself and other civic organizations that Nationalist China supported.

Just as important is what the treaty did not say about citizenship. Deliberations between the two states and among members of the Senate's Committee on Foreign Relations prior to the treaty's ratification did not define what it meant to be a "Chinese national." By providing no such definition, the Philippines signaled its acceptance of the ROC's Nationality Law of 1929 and the principle of jus sanguinis enshrined within it. There was little need for the treaty to explicitly define Chinese citizenship in terms of jus sanguinis, as this implicit understanding of legal Chineseness was already in practice in early 1947. It was not always this way. Starting in 1911, the Supreme Court selectively applied the principle of jus soli (right of the soil) to grant citizenship to mestizos born in the Philippines to Chinese fathers and Filipino mothers. The transition toward blood-right citizenship was informed by growing anti-Chinese populism under US rule and can be traced back to the 1935 constitutional convention, whose delegates mostly argued that citizenship resided in a set of immutable personal and political characteristics in one's "blood." After 1945, judicial, as distinct from political, opinion shifted away from jus soli and toward jus sanguinis.

This shift is evident in the Supreme Court's landmark September 1947 verdict on the case of *Jose Tan Chong v. The Secretary of Labor*. Born in San Pablo, Laguna, in 1915 to a Chinese father and Filipino mother, Tan Chong was denied entry into the Philippines in 1940 after spending the previous fifteen years in China. Ordered to be deported by the secretary of labor, he sued for habeas corpus in Manila's Court of First Instance and secured his release from custody, only for the solicitor general, representing the executive branch, to appeal this decision. On October 15, 1941, the Supreme Court affirmed the lower court's judgment that Tan Chong was a citizen, but the solicitor general filed a motion for reconsideration a week later. The case was unresolved when the war came. After independence, the Supreme Court reversed its earlier verdict. It argued that birth alone did not make someone a citizen and that Tan Chong was a Chinese national because he had not spent his youth in his country of birth and lacked intangible attributes of citizenship such as "knowledge and pride of the country's past." Citizenship was a "political status." "The citizen must be proud of his citizenship," the court ruled.[101]

By embracing jus sanguinis, the Philippine Supreme Court legitimized the same principle that informed the ROC's Nationality Law. This was satisfactory to both states, as it meant that the ROC had legal jurisdiction over and the freedom to mobilize Chinese who had been born in either China or the Philippines and who resided in the latter. For such persons, it was possible to become a citizen in accordance with the Revised Naturalization Law (Commonwealth Act No. 473) of 1939. But this law itself was a product of the post-1935 political environment that favored jus sanguinis and made obtaining citizenship "prohibitively complex, costly, unsure, and slow," one critic of the process wrote in 1974.[102] Wealthy Chinese seeking citizenship to mitigate the effects of anti-Chinese legislation typically bribed their way through this process, while those of limited financial means tended to have little incentive to naturalize. Furthermore, even naturalized citizens such as Yu Khe Thai continued to support the KMT, participate in ROC-sponsored activities, and visit Taiwan regularly. Ethnic Chinese Philippine nationals remained exceedingly mobilizable *huaqiao* subjects for the KMT and "foreigners," because of their "blood," to Filipinos.

The KMT in Southeast Asian Perspective

Beyond the Philippines, comparable legal arrangements did not obtain between states and the KMT in other parts of Southeast Asia. In pursuit of their own nation-building or decolonizing projects, many of which explicitly addressed the Chinese question, independent and colonial governments proved just as or more wary of the KMT's extraterritorial designs on their Chinese populations as the Chinese left's. For this reason, despite comparable attempts by the ROC at diasporic mobilization and diplomacy, no similar configurations of shared sovereignty emerged elsewhere in the region.

Thailand, for example, was the first of two regional states to sign a treaty of amity with the ROC, doing so on January 23, 1946, during a brief period of civilian rule from 1944 to 1948. Unlike the Philippines, however, Thailand did not enjoy cordial relations with the ROC in part because it had sided with Japan during the war. The ROC's distrust increased following the Thai military's suppression of Chinese rioters during the Yaowarat Incident of September–October 1945. For Nanjing, the treaty was a means of resolving tensions diplomatically, while Bangkok needed regular relations with the ROC to forestall a possible Chinese veto against Thailand's application for membership of the United Nations.[103] Still, relations did not improve; to the contrary, with the return to power of the military and wartime prime minister, Field Marshal Plaek Phibunsongkhram (Phibun), in 1948, they worsened. Concerned that the conflict in China would spill over into Thailand, Phibun regarded all

Chinese political activity as problematic: his was a country of 3 million Chinese persons in 1950, by the anthropologist G. William Skinner's estimate, compared to 230,000 in the Philippines.[104] In June 1948, in violation of the Treaty of Amity, Phibun began shutting down Chinese schools, and, in July, the Interior Ministry declared the KMT an "illegal, unregistered alien political party."[105] His repression of the KMT was so severe that Nanjing even asked the United States to help it overthrow him.[106] During this period, Phibun was less tolerant of the KMT than the communists, so much so that the latter came to dominate the Chinese Chamber of Commerce by the end of 1949.[107]

The KMT in Vietnam and Malaya faced comparable opposition from the state in 1948 and 1949. Like Thailand, these were countries with significantly larger Chinese populations than the Philippines.[108] In Vietnam, the KMT sought to mobilize the ethnic Chinese (Hoa) in part by taking over the Association of the Overseas Chinese and neutering its dialect-based subcommittees. As in the Philippines, the KMT also had its own paramilitary organizations in Vietnam. These groups were disguised as Boy Scouts and supported by the ROC Consulate and the Chinese Chamber of Commerce in the twin cities of Saigon and Cholon. In 1948, however, amid the First Indochina War, the French dissolved the association's subcommittees and, in 1949, the KMT's militias.[109] In doing so, the French curbed the KMT's mobilizational capacities. They also disrupted the party's illicit provision of goods to the communist-led Vietminh— whose anticolonialism the KMT identified with and with whom direct relations could help protect Hoa in the Vietminh-controlled north.[110] As for the Chinese communists, they were weaker in southern Vietnam than in Thailand and Malaya in the late 1940s. In Saigon-Cholon, the CCP had few supporters because it had made few inroads into the working class and labor unions. The French did not consider Hoa communism in the south a threat to Indochina's security.[111]

There was no love lost between the Malayan Communist Party (MCP) and the Malayan KMT after the occupation; in some respects, as historians such as Cheah Boon Kheng, C. F. Yong, and R. B. McKenna have shown, a comparable, frequently violent contest to that in the Philippines also erupted there. The Malayan case differed in several ways, however. First, in the two years immediately after the end of Japanese rule, MCP- and KMT-aligned guerrilla organizations occupied towns throughout the peninsula and in doing so partially territorialized their rivalry. Second, their rivalry was overshadowed by racial violence between them and the Malay population in the areas they occupied.[112] Third, and most of all, the KMT was not able to forge a collaborative security relationship with the colonial state during the Malayan Emergency, despite their common antipathy toward the MCP. Although the KMT encouraged its members to enlist in the British Special Constabulary and the Civil District Watch Corps, the British ended up banning the KMT for a third and final time in May 1949. Britain disapproved of the KMT's connections to Chinese triad organizations such as the Hongmen and feared that its fundraising abilities would result in the potential loss of foreign exchange through the remittance of KMT-controlled money to China.[113] More than that, the KMT's Sinocentric, nationalizing project was incompatible with Britain's political strategy of combating the MCP by "Malayanizing" the Chinese population and supporting the conservative, pro-British Malayan Chinese Association (MCA).[114] Many KMT members, it is true, joined the MCA, including H. S. Lee, Malaya's first finance minister. But without official sanction and as party hardliners mellowed or died, the Malayan KMT declined—slowly. By independence in 1957, celebrations to mark the ROC's National Day on October 10 had largely disappeared.[115]

Other states, too, were more proactive than the Philippines in seeking to naturalize their Chinese population to advance nationalizing projects and formally limit Chinese state interference. In 1946, during its anticolonial struggle against the Dutch, the Republic of Indonesia automatically recognized as citizens any Chinese who had been born in the country and resided there continuously for five years. This citizenship law aimed to minimize the number of Chinese over whom the ROC could exercise jurisdiction and, unsurprisingly, upset Nanjing.[116] In South Vietnam, the Ngô Đình Diệm government stipulated in 1955 that all children of Chinese-Vietnamese parents were Vietnamese citizens. A year later, all locally born Hoa were nationalized, and, in 1957, in response to protests by Chinese merchants and Taiwan against a succession of anti-Chinese policies, Saigon allowed foreign-born Chinese to acquire Vietnamese citizenship through a simple process of registration.[117] Malaya's 1957 constitution, in keeping with aims of Malayanization, allowed all persons in the country to qualify as citizens either by birth or by fulfilling residency and language requirements and then swearing an oath of loyalty.[118] No such measures were forthcoming in the Philippines until 1972, despite calls by Philippine-oriented, anti-KMT Chinese liberals for jus soli citizenship and a less onerous naturalization process.

These comparisons underscore how the postwar trajectory of the Philippine KMT diverged from that of the party in China and elsewhere in Southeast Asia. The first three years after the Pacific War, this chapter has shown, are crucial to understanding this divergence. In this period, supported by many members of the Chinese business community, the KMT entered into an alliance of convenience with the Philippine police and military against a resurgent Chinese left. The violent conflict between these ideological factions at first revolved around the question of wartime collaboration by their ethnic compatriots, which the left adopted a hard-line stance toward but the KMT was willing to overlook in search of supporters from among the business class. However, as relations rapidly deteriorated between Manila and the Huks, and between the KMT and the CCP in China, the conflict between the Philippine KMT and the Chinese left became entangled in domestic and regional Cold War politics. Exploiting the Chinese communist movement's tactical missteps and the Roxas government's anticommunist drive, the KMT and its Philippine partners succeeded in driving from the country left-wing "revolutionary cosmopolitans" such as Co, Huang, and Gong and in deinstitutionalizing the movement by 1948.

What the KMT called a "bloody struggle" and the Chinese left described as the White Terror unfolded contemporaneously with the establishment of a legal-diplomatic framework for ROC-Philippine relations that also benefited the party in the long term. State sanction, as examples from the rest of Southeast Asia suggest, was vital to the KMT's ability to project extraterritorial influence and to carve out civic institutional space for itself within a given national territory. Other states looked askance at external Chinese involvement—communist or otherwise—in their (larger) Chinese populations, but Manila did not. Instead, the Philippines outsourced the management of a relatively small community of "Chinese nationals" living within its borders to China. The Treaty of Amity legitimized the ROC's legal claims on these persons and enabled the local KMT to operate more openly there than anywhere else, especially in the sphere of Chinese education. The extent to which the party capitalized on this particular manifestation of Philippine liberalism would become evident in the decades to follow.

CHAPTER 3

Practicing Anticommunism

Chinese Self-Fashioning in the Cold War Philippines

On January 28, 1954, *The Bullseye* newspaper in Manila printed a letter to President Ramon Magsaysay from a "group of nonpolitical but patriotic local Chinese merchants" who had resided in the islands for over twenty years and come to regard the Philippines as their "second mother country." Its author, Lim Tian Seng, said that the purpose of the letter was to point out "bad elements among the local Chinese who have utilized convenient facilities accommodated to them by some corrupt government officials to enrich themselves." He singled out two individuals for special blame. The first he did not name and gave only this description: "[a] naturalized alien whose citizenship is even now under question and whose notoriety is so well-known to the Filipinos as well as the Chinese that no further introduction is necessary." Lim identified the second man as the former Kuomintang (KMT) secretary-general in the Philippines, Shih I-Sheng ("Sy Yek Sheng" in the letter). Lim proceeded to describe how Shih blackmailed wealthy Chinese. According to Lim, Shih simply picked up the telephone and called someone well-off. Flaunting his KMT credentials, Shih claimed to have connections with the Philippine military and told his victim that he had been reported to the authorities as a communist or communist sympathizer. Shih then offered to clear his name if he paid Shih 10,000, 30,000, or 50,000 Philippine pesos (PHP), depending on how wealthy he was. Shih had made, by a "very conservative estimation," no less than PHP .5 million from this scheme and, although no longer secretary-general, remained in the country as "head of the Chinese Volunteers of the Philippines Fraternity."

Lim also claimed that the previous week "thousands of local Chinese commercial establishments received by mail supposed communist propaganda literature in Chinese, sealed in envelopes allegedly issued by the 'Propaganda Department of the Chinese Communist Party in the Philippines.'" Reasoning that such a large quantity of propaganda could not have been mailed by actual Chinese communists because of the government's "relentless" anticommunist policies and Chinese Reds' lack of organization in the country, he concluded that the materials must have been forged. The real culprits, he conjectured, were "well-organized racketeers" who hoped to deceive the state into believing that Chinese communists were active and profited from any arrests that it made. He had reasons to believe, he said, that in the Department of National Defense (DND) there were many "Chinese operatives" who were in league with these racketeers and had been feeding their Filipino superiors "biased and inaccurate or even false and malicious" reports on the political activities and leanings of local Chinese. Finally, the letter mentioned the military's arrests of over 300 Chinese on December 27, 1952, on charges of communism. That at least 170 detainees had been released revealed that the DND was relying on flawed intelligence. Lim modestly hoped that no further arrests would be made unless they were well supported by substantial evidence.[1]

Lim's letter recalls Chua Peng Leong's 1945 missive to Manuel Roxas. Both Lim and Chua fashioned themselves as civic-minded, law-abiding, and nonpolitical Chinese who felt ethically compelled to report crimes by their co-ethnics to the leader of their country of residence. However, each blamed a different group. Chua accused Chinese communists of being the "real disturbers of the peace" and was complicit in strengthening the association between communism and crime that propelled the KMT's postwar ascendancy.[2] Eight years later, its former secretary-general was denounced for the same crimes of blackmail and extortion that his nemeses on the left supposedly engaged in. This new category of *huaqiao* criminal included Shih as well as "Chinese operatives" who were working for the Philippine military and providing the government with deliberately false information on other Chinese.

Lim had more in common with Shih and the "Chinese operatives" who had infiltrated the DND than his letter to the newly elected president condemning them suggests. Blackmail, forgery, rumormongering, and similarly criminal or ethically questionable behavior were aimed at tearing down the reputation of people like Lim by having them identified as communists. In a perverted way, Shih and these operatives were practicing anticommunism in the name of Filipino national values. Until exposed, they were perceived as anticommunists or as aiding anticommunism. Similarly, Lim's carefully worded letter was a performance of his ideological affinities. By informing on his fellow Chinese to the public, Lim was playing to Filipino prejudices toward the Chinese and proved that he was a "patriotic" Chinese merchant who regarded the Philippines as his "second mother country." Lim understood "patriotism" as a civic disposition that was unrelated to his place of birth or nationality, neither of which we know. He might not have spoken Tagalog or been able to pass as racially Filipino. But in exposing Shih and the operatives, he was enacting his opposition to corruption and strengthening the Magsaysay administration's capacity to distinguish between genuine and fake Reds.

Much of this book is about what it meant to be a Chinese "anticommunist" in the Cold War Philippines and how anticommunism enabled Chinese civic integration into the Philippine nation-state. This chapter explicitly addresses these questions. As Shih's behavior here and elsewhere implies, anticommunism was not simply a question of ideological authenticity—an elusive and problematic quality for scholars to measure. Rather, anticommunism as a social phenomenon was just as much, and often exclusively, a diverse repertoire of tactics that Chinese from different social classes employed to consolidate their reputations, forge useful ties with Filipino elites, and attack or defend themselves against each other. Anticommunism entailed inventing a Chinese communist threat in the absence of one. It became crucial to factional struggles between and within established and emerging centers of power in the Chinese community such as the KMT, the Republic of China (ROC) Embassy, and the Philippine Chinese General Chamber of Commerce in Manila. For law-abiding Chinese or Chinese who wished to be seen as such, anticommunism was an ideological bulwark against blackmailers and extortionists. Conversely, it enabled Shih and other criminal entrepreneurs such as the Chinese operatives to wage class warfare against the established social order from below rather than from above. Ironically, anticommunism and not communism became a means of redistributing wealth, status, and power within a small, fractious, and legally precarious ethnic minority community. Its practitioners' "tactics," to adopt Michel de Certeau's language, did not so much subvert the state's "strategies" as partially complement them.[3]

Three case studies, representing an assortment of classes, tactics, and institutions, are featured in the pages that follow: ex–General Chamber president Alfonso Sycip and the organization that he served as the figurehead of, the Philippine-Chinese United Organization in Support of Anti-Communist Movement (Feilübin Huaqiao Fangong Kang'E Houyuanhui, or ACM);[4] Shih I-Sheng and a Korean-Chinese doctor, Edward Lim, who manipulated their association with the KMT for self-aggrandizement; and a gang of operatives, led by

Antonio Chua Cruz, whom the DND employed to gather intelligence on Chinese society. Collectively, these Chinese on all sides of the law pursued ideological and self-interested ends by practicing anticommunism.

Anticommunism and Sinophobia in the Early 1950s

Chinese communism in the Philippines declined rapidly after September 1946. By 1948, faced with an increasingly unfavorable political environment, its leaders had mostly returned to China, and where left-wing organizations such as the Philippine-Chinese United Workers Union (Lo Lian Hui) had once operated openly, only small, secretive fragments of the movement remained. Yet, fears of Sino-communism persisted precisely because it had vanished from the public eye. Throughout Asia, communism in general seemed to be cresting in the late 1940s. In the Philippines, the Huk Rebellion intensified after negotiations between the government and the Huks broke down in August 1948. That year, communist uprisings, some more short-lived than others, erupted in Malaya—whose communists were predominantly Chinese—Burma, and Indonesia, seemingly at the instigation of the Soviet Union at the Calcutta Youth Conference in February.[5] In Indochina, the French colonial state had been at war with the Vietminh since 1946. The Chinese Communist Party (CCP) was on the verge of driving the KMT from mainland China. Even before the People's Republic of China (PRC) entered the Korean War in October 1950, therefore, Chinese communism had become a distinct, territorialized, and racialized subset of the global Red threat.

In the Philippines, Filipino fears of Chinese communism in the late 1940s and early 1950s were inseparable from anxieties over porous borders and immigration policy. State officials and politicians feared that communists lurked among the twenty-seven hundred or so Chinese "overstaying temporary visitors" who had entered the islands during the civil war and then refused to leave for China after their three-month visitor visas had expired.[6] Reports by the National Intelligence Coordinating Agency (NICA) lay bare the state's fears that pro-communist Chinese smugglers and corrupt local officials were facilitating the inflow of CCP propaganda, gold, drugs, and similar contraband into the country and the outflow of foreign exchange and illicit arms to China. CCP agents were believed to have entered the country to work with local Chinese communists and the Huks and infiltrate Chinese society. The immigration commissioner testified to the House Committee on Un-Filipino Activities (CUFA) in October 1948 that of the 561 known communist agents in the islands, at least 50 were Chinese, some of them "prominent socially and in business."[7] In language that typified Filipino fears of the Chinese as fifth columnists, an intelligence report declared: "If nothing is effectively done in advance" to stop the "Chinese Menace," the Philippines "may later become a 'Little China.'"[8] A similar report asserted, without evidence: "Of the officially estimated 200,000 Chinese residents in the Philippines, 36,000 have been identified as communists and communist sympathizers. This figure exceeds even the native communist forces."[9] In 1951, Magsaysay, as secretary of national defense, reduced this figure to a still alarmingly high 30,000.[10]

Officials perceived Chinese communism as part of the larger Chinese question in the country. Sinophobia and anticommunism were distinct yet overlapping phenomena that the Cold War and Filipino nationalism melded, compounding fears of alien economic dominance, moral degeneracy, and insularity that went back to colonial times.[11] To many, the Chinese were "passive and individualistic in temperament" but capable of being "energized by propaganda" and hence susceptible to indoctrination.[12] Local Chinese "nurtured their ties with the motherland, operate[d] cohesively as a race, and in many instances claim[ed] dual citizenship." "[Their] unassimilability and their financial or commercial influence make them effective instruments of probable aggressive Chinese foreign policy," NICA argued in 1948.[13] Contrary to the historian Philip A. Kuhn, the "Chinese problem" was not only inseparable from the "China problem" but in many respects integral to it.[14] As reflected in the Philippines' jus sanguinis citizenship law, race and nationality were in Filipino eyes intertwined aspects of Chineseness.

Populist expressions of these frequently inconsistent anti-Chinese prejudices took multiple forms. Politicians and journalists frequently inveighed against Chinese in the newspapers to drum up support for their election campaigns and to boost their readership, respectively. On the legislative front, Congress members and lobbying groups persisted with their campaign to curb perceived Chinese economic dominance. In 1954, despite countervailing efforts by Chinese merchants, Magsaysay enacted the Retail Trade Nationalization Act, forbidding non-Filipinos or corporations not wholly owned by Filipinos from engaging in retailing.[15]

Relative to other countries in Southeast Asia, in particular Indonesia, violence against the Chinese population in the postwar Philippines tended to be small-scale. Individual Chinese were often the targets of corrupt, unscrupulous, or simply clueless representatives of the state. The police were known to raid Chinese commercial establishments, carrying with them search warrants and small quantities of opium, ammunition, and Chinese communist propaganda. If merchants refused to pay them off, the police pretended to have found such contraband on their premises and arrested them.[16] Intelligence agencies and the police were also ignorant of Chinese and thus subcontracted the gathering of intelligence on Chinese society to other Chinese, rendering themselves vulnerable to inaccurate or fabricated reports on alleged communists. Because of their legal status, Chinese who were arrested by the state and found guilty by the Deportation Board were deported as foreign nationals to China or Taiwan. Police criminality was such a serious matter that the ROC foreign minister raised it with a Philippine official in Taipei in April 1951. The police "act in such a way that the Chinese people live in a constant fear," he said. "They have instilled a feeling of insecurity among the Chinese nationals and a reign of terror [has] spread among them."[17]

Fears of extortion, arrest, and deportation by the Philippine authorities were compounded during the 1950s by demands for money by the CCP. In December 1949, in response to a foreign exchange crisis, the Philippine Central Bank imposed currency controls that prohibited Chinese from remitting money to family members in China; this was circumvented by having remittances channeled through third-party brokers in Hong Kong.[18] After the disruption of these remittance networks, it became increasingly common for Chinese to receive letters from their relatives, written at the instigation of CCP officials, asking for further sums of money, in either small amounts on a regular basis or an immediate lump sum.[19] A KMT member informed the US Embassy in Manila that at least half of those who received such demands acceded to them, fearing for their relatives if they did not.[20] Reporting them to the Philippine authorities was not an option because remitting money overseas was now illegal. Those who admitted to doing so could also easily be charged with aiding the CCP.

From the late 1940s onward, it thus became expedient for Chinese to adopt anticommunist positions in their everyday lives. As the actions of anti-Chinese politicians, corrupt police, and Chinese communists suggests, opportunities abounded for individuals or groups—even from beyond the country—to profit from the social instability caused by Filipino anti-Chinese prejudices and fears of communism. In the absence of authentic Chinese communist threats to national security, anticommunism became a new and valorized ideological resource that Chinese competed to accumulate and transform into social and political gains. For them, practicing anticommunism signaled their conformity, despite being foreigners, to a national identity that the state defined in ideological and racial terms. As anti-Chinese legislation and institutions such as CUFA made abundantly clear, to be Filipino was to not be Chinese or communist. ROC citizenship and ethno-cultural markers of Chineseness such as language, customs, and physical features were difficult if not impossible to conceal. Ideology, by contrast, was a positive quality of being "Filipino" and easy to show off.

Chamber, Embassy, and Party

By the early 1950s, commercial elites had regained their leadership of Philippine-Chinese society. Mindful of the Co Pak affair and having been assailed by the left for "collaboration," many merchants eagerly jumped on the anticommunist bandwagon. Seemingly little had changed about the composition and leadership of their class. As before the war, wealth generated in sectors such as banking, insurance, manufacturing, and especially retailing remained the leading criterion of social status. Except for those who had perished during the occupation, nearly all who had held prewar leadership positions in the General Chamber of Commerce had been reinstated, including its president, Alfonso Sycip.[21]

The General Chamber had long been dominated by what the political scientist James Roland Blaker calls "traditionalists" and was never on especially good terms with the KMT (see chapter 1). These traditionalists were men such as Sycip and his brother Albino, for whom leadership centered on maintaining a single organization for arbitrating internal community disputes, mediating between the community and the Philippine state, and preserving what they considered to be Chinese values. Insofar as they identified themselves as "Chinese" and retained ties to China, they did so primarily in a cultural sense and to enhance their own influence and prestige within the Philippines. While they may not have been, as Blaker claims, apolitical—for what could be more political than the maintenance of power within a given community?—he draws an important, if overly schematic, distinction between them and their "nationalist" competitors. The latter group, comprising KMT members, was more oriented toward China and sought to leverage the financial and political resources of Chinese society to influence the mainland, such as during the War of Resistance.[22]

Over the course of the Second Sino-Japanese War and the Chinese civil war, traditionalism and the avoidance of Chinese nationalist politics became increasingly untenable for the likes of Alfonso Sycip. The rise of anti-Chinese nationalism threatened the livelihood of Chinese businessmen and called into question the ability of their representatives to protect their interests and negotiate effectively with the government. Threats against them from the left remained fresh in their collective memory. Thus, fears of communism, the desire to be perceived as "good" Chinese, and a ubiquitous Cold War discourse incentivized them into taking the right side in the KMT-CCP conflict. Doing so was consistent with their support for Nationalist China during the Pacific War and the long-standing practice of cultivating ties with external state authorities to legitimize their leadership of Chinese society.[23]

The problem for the General Chamber in this Cold War environment was that organizations that manifested external state authority were competing to influence the Chinese community. One was the ROC Embassy, whose influence was growing. Diplomatic developments after the Treaty of Amity in 1947 enhanced Nationalist China's profile in the Philippines, in particular Chiang Kai-shek's July 1949 visit to the Philippines, during which he met with prominent Chinese leaders such as Alfonso Sycip, Yao Shiong Shio, Chua Lamco, and Ong Chuan Seng (see figure 3.1). Having recently resigned as ROC president in January, Chiang arrived in the country as chairman of the KMT, at the invitation of President Elpidio Quirino, to discuss plans for a North Atlantic Treaty Organization-esque "Pacific Pact."[24] Although nothing came of these plans, the optics of Chiang's visit and his continued association with the ROC as its de facto head of state stimulated Chinese anticommunist initiatives. Buoyed by expanding diplomatic ties, the embassy became increasingly outspoken on local Chinese issues, for example, by opposing anti-Chinese legislation and supporting Manila's initiatives against communist and other "undesirable" aliens."[25]

The local KMT espoused a similarly hard-line ideological position and, by the early 1950s, was entering what it called a "period of flourishing" (pengbo shiqi) despite a number of setbacks. Financially, for example, the situation remained precarious, with two out of five party newspapers forced to shut down and two to merge. Although party membership increased to 16,590 in 1950, it declined by well over 50 percent to 7,369 by the Seventh National Party Congress in October 1952, likely because of the loss of mainland China.[26] Factionalism, which had subsided during the party's "bloody struggle" with the Chinese left, flared up again both within and outside the party. Conversely, the zongzhibu reported to Taipei that it had tightened its hold on Chinese education. Among the 136 Chinese primary and secondary schools in the Philippines, the KMT enjoyed close relations with eighty-four boards of trustees and had vetted and recommended fifty-nine principals. An estimated 95 percent of these schools, it believed, upheld national policies.[27] But perhaps most importantly, staunch KMT members and nonmembers who supported the KMT were finally making inroads into the General Chamber of Commerce, whose capture had been a target for the party since the 1930s. Mutual Aid Society members such as Sy En and Yao Shiong Shio were part of this generation of chamber leaders, as was dedicated anticommunist Yu Khe Thai;[28] Sy in fact succeeded Alfonso Sycip as president in 1950. Four years later, the Manila-based chamber was supplanted as the community's governing body by the Federation of Filipino-Chinese

FIGURE 3.1.   Chiang Kai-shek poses for a photo with Chinese leaders on his visit to the Philippines in 1949. Alfonso Sycip, a friend of the generalissimo, is on his immediate right. Reprinted with permission from Academia Historica.

Chambers of Commerce and Industry (Shang Zong), a pro-KMT organization that aggressively infused anticommunist ideology into all aspects of Chinese life. Its formation and the concurrent withdrawal of leaders such as Sycip from public life signaled the definitive collapse of traditionalism as a political position and a major victory for the party and Taiwan.

A "Very Smooth Operator"

The Philippine-Chinese United Organization in Support of Anti-Communist Movement, or ACM, was founded in January 1951, two months after Co Pak's arrest and a month after San Francisco's Chinese leaders had formed a similar organization, the Six Companies Anti-Communist League.[29] Established at the height of an anti-Red conjuncture of events in early 1950s East Asia and beyond, the ACM represented one of the decade's most visible efforts by Philippine-Chinese elites to bolster their credentials as good anticommunists and loyal residents of the country. Like grassroots associations such as the Philippine Anti-Communist League (PACL), the creation of retired US Army major Frank Tenny, the ACM complemented official anticommunist initiatives such as CUFA and made it clear where the Philippine Chinese stood in the Cold War. By 1952,

Chinese communities in Burma, Malaya, Indonesia, and the Americas had launched similar anticommunist groups.[30]

Globally, pro-KMT overseas Chinese leaders reacted to the Nationalists' flight to Taiwan in 1949 by mobilizing their communities and launching fundraising drives in support of the ROC. In a sign of things to come, the most significant contributions during this initial stage of *Fangong kang'E* from any *huaqiao* community were from the Philippines. As both a ranking member of the *zongzhibu* and the president of the General Chamber of Commerce, Sy En played a vital role in drumming up enthusiasm for this cause. Taipei commented approvingly on how efficiently its diasporic networks functioned in the Philippines because of the party's and the chamber's overlapping membership. In August 1950, after months of planning, the Philippine Chinese became the first overseas Chinese to send an official delegation to Taiwan. The forty-six persons who joined this "observation and study" (*kaocha*) trip, including Cua Siok Po and Koa Chun-te (but excluding Sy En, who had prior commitments), were granted access to the likes of Chiang Ching-kuo and Soong Mei-ling and visited ROC forces stationed on the offshore island chain of Quemoy (Jinmen). In total, they donated PHP 200,000, 1,600 radios, and 240,000 towels to the war effort.[31] Their visit also coincided with Chiang Kai-shek's launching of a comprehensive reform program to transform the corrupt and factionalized KMT into a streamlined, democratic centralist instrument for recovering mainland China.[32]

Following this visit, ROC ambassador Chen Chih-ping urged its participants to form an anticommunist organization that "displayed the facts of their anticommunism" (*biaoxian huaqiao fangong zhi shishi*) to the Philippine government.[33] The ACM's objective, Chen explained, was to "redouble and coordinate the efforts of the Chinese nationals in the Philippines in aiding their legitimate government, now temporarily seated in Taiwan, to which they [had] all along manifested their loyalty, in its determined struggle against [the] evil force of Communist aggression." As the first such organization among overseas Chinese, it also hoped to inspire others to "[unite] together in the same manner so as to achieve greater strength to bring about the early defeat of Communism." To avoid being perceived as an exclusively "Chinese" organization, the ACM welcomed Filipinos into its ranks and was endorsed by President Quirino. To further legitimize itself, the ACM had Chiang Kai-shek directly approve its twenty-five Standing Committee members, who then nominated the Executive Committee and chaired its four subcommittees.[34]

Backed by the ROC state, the ACM united under the banner of *Fangong kang'E* members of the two largest Chinese organizations in the country. Alfonso Sycip, who had just stepped down as president of the General Chamber in 1950 after a record ten terms in office over a decade and a half (1934–1935, 1937–1941, 1946–1949), was elected its chairman.[35] Sycip was ideally placed to lead an institution that sought to gain favor with both Manila and Taipei. Born in the Philippines in 1883 and fluent in English and Chinese, Sycip was a naturalized citizen and one of the richest people in the country, having made his fortune from the import and export business. He was detained by the Japanese during the war and then released, on account of his old age. Unlike his counterparts who were forced to join the Chinese Association (CA), Sycip went into hiding until the end of the war.[36] After the war, he was summoned to appear before the Philippine-Chinese Anti-Japanese and Anti-Puppets League's (Kang Fan) Anti-Collaboration Commission. Sycip was on personal terms with Filipino and ROC politicians, including Chiang Kai-shek, whom he would meet with in Taipei to lobby for the release of innocent Chinese charged with being communists.[37] He also maintained a regular correspondence with US officials. In 1956, a US Embassy official offered his unvarnished opinion on Sycip in commenting on a letter from Sycip to the director of Southwest Pacific Affairs about the need for greater US support for Taiwan. He described Sycip as a "very smooth operator" and a "slippery person" who "ingratiate[d] himself into high American circles" and to "build his prestige" displayed to his Chinese friends the letters that leading US officials had sent him.[38]

Sycip had never been especially nationalistic, certainly not compared to KMT ideologues, who were as distrustful of him as the US Embassy was. At the height of the Second Sino-Japanese War, he only reluctantly supported the anti-Japanese boycott that radical KMT members pressured the General Chamber to launch. In 1939, with the boycott taking its toll on Chinese commerce, Sycip told a gathering of Chinese businessmen that they should "regain their primary mission" and "must not be excessively indulged in military and political affairs."[39] In 1941, the *zongzhibu* accused him of urging provincial Chinese chambers of commerce to exclude KMT members from their ranks and supporting the election of communists to leadership positions within them.[40] The ROC consul was forced to clarify to the Ministry of Foreign Affairs (MOFA) that Sycip was neither a KMT member nor a communist and that his political affiliations were unknown.[41] After the war, Sycip resumed his leadership of the General Chamber and remained disengaged from China's politics until 1951, his friendship with Chiang notwithstanding. Only after becoming the ACM chairman did he start taking firm ideological positions in public. Ever the "very smooth operator" looking to "build his prestige," Sycip sensed the direction in which the ideological winds were blowing and, in the ACM, an opportunity to prove his commitment to the Chinese nation after his nonresistance during the war.

Among the ACM's four vice-chairmen were the incumbent president of the General Chamber, Sy En, and Gonzalo Gawhok (another Mutual Aid Society member), who in Sy's absence had led the August 1950 delegation to Taiwan. Sycip, Sy, Vice-Chairmen Yu Khe Thai and Yao Shiong Shio, and Standing Committee member Peter Lim were all official advisers to the US Embassy on matters concerning the Chinese community, such as communist infiltration, criminal activity, and the guilt or innocence of Chinese charged by the state with being communists or criminals. Other Standing Committee members were mostly merchants and General Chamber members, except for those who represented the media and education. These included Go Puan Seng, publisher of the center-right *Fookien Times* (*Xinmin ribao*), which Sycip had helped found in 1925, and Ong Chuan Seng. Shih I-Sheng, the *zongzhibu*'s secretary-general at the time, was also on the committee.[42] In total, twelve committee members were also KMT members, many far more ideological than Sycip would ever be.

Following its founding, the ACM focused on fundraising in support of the ROC, building its membership beyond Manila, and propagandizing in support of anticommunism in both the ROC and the Philippines. According to its charter, branches would be asked to make monthly and special "national salvation" contributions to its general headquarters in Manila. Chen Chih-ping, the ROC ambassador, estimated that PHP 5 million could be raised this way. Some of this money would be channeled secretly to Taiwan, bypassing the foreign exchange controls that the Philippines had put in place.[43] Chinese leaders had also earmarked a significant portion of these contributions for President Quirino's National Peace Fund, which had been established in September 1950 to solicit private donations in support of operations against the Huks.[44] Contributions to such projects were a simple means by which wealthy Chinese proved their value to their host country, performed good citizenship, and assuaged Filipinos' doubts about their political inclinations.

The highlight of the ACM's early years was its tour of the southern Philippines from March 27 to April 5, 1951, led by Sycip, Sy, Yao, and Ambassador Chen. The tour aimed to establish branches of the organization in provinces like Iloilo, Cebu, Davao, and Cotabato (in the same way that the KMT had done with its own branches); induct new members; and raise funds through the selling of bonds. On one occasion, Chen reported that when presiding over the founding of an ACM branch in Mindanao, he and the others discovered, much to their disgust, that the portrait of Chiang Kai-shek that usually hung in the ceremonial hall had been "maliciously" (*e'yi*) removed. They blamed this on the weakness of the KMT branch in the city and on communist intimidation of local businessmen.[45] Despite this, Chen summed up the tour as a success. The results of the tour could not be quantified, but he believed that it had made an enduring impact on anticommunist cooperation between the two governments.[46] Statistics compiled by the Overseas Chinese Affairs Commission (OCAC) show that in 1951, the Philippine Chinese made 251,096.14 US dollars (USD) in "patriotic voluntary contributions" (aiguo zidong juanxian) to the ROC. This was by far the largest amount among Chinese communities overseas that year. Second place belonged to Chinese Americans, who raised over eight times less.[47]

The ACM also propagandized in local newspapers to raise its profile among Chinese and Filipinos. Go Puan Seng's Fookien Times Yearbook was a favorite platform because it was a dual-language publication and ideal for reaching out to a wide audience. As the designated spokesperson for the ACM, Sycip took frequently to the pages of the yearbook to inveigh against communism, drawing on a common pool of talking points that the ROC used to reach out to overseas Chinese communities. In 1952, for example, he wrote an article titled "The Role of the Overseas Chinese in the Worldwide Struggle against Communism." Besides exhorting huaqiao in the Philippines and elsewhere to strengthen their anticommunist beliefs, help the authorities root out communism, and assist Taiwan in every possible way, he also criticized other Southeast Asian governments for not recognizing and reacting to the Red threat "in as clear and as energetic a manner as the Philippines." Official ROC organs were thus far from being the only ones who promoted the idea of Philippine-Chinese ideological exceptionalism. The same article also allowed Sycip to update readers on the ACM's achievements. Since its establishment, it had formed fifty provincial chapters and begun an "extensive educational campaign" that involved sponsoring journalism, distributing literature, and hosting speakers in Chinese schools.[48] A year later, Sycip wrote another hortatory piece called "An Appeal to the People of Free Nations," which contained suggestions on how ordinary people could help their governments fight communism. One was helping those who had been "forced to become Communists return to the fold of democracy." Another was reporting communists to the authorities. But, he cautioned, it was important to avoid false accusations.[49]

For Philippine Chinese like Sycip and other members of the ACM's Standing Committee, anticommunism as an ideology and a sociopolitical movement (respectively, the elimination of communists from the Philippines and reclaiming China from the CCP) was inseparable from and did not necessarily take precedence over the fashioning of one's civic identity as a "respectable," ideologically correct alien. The complicated relationship between these commitments was evident at a committee meeting in December 1951 that Ambassador Chen attended and reported on. Because materials that shed light on the internal workings of such organizations are hard to come by, Chen's report deserves close attention for what it says about Chinese anticommunists' beliefs, sensitivity to the political climate, and desire to be perceived in the right way to the right authorities.

The occasion for this meeting seems to have been Britain's continued recognition of the PRC despite Winston Churchill's becoming prime minister for the second time in October 1951. The main topic for discussion was not, however, Churchill's "betrayal" (*chumai*) of the ROC, but Sy En's proposal that the ACM change its English name to that of a charitable organization in case the PRC entered the United Nations and Manila recognized Beijing. Were this scenario to unfold, the ACM, under a different registered name, would still be able to collect donations from Chinese to support anticommunism in the Philippines and Taiwan. Sy's pragmatic suggestion met with an impassioned reaction from other Standing Committee members. Dy Huan Chay, the only other person to support it, believed that it would help protect Chinese society and was consistent with popular views. (Dy, who was not a KMT member, had served as head of the wartime Young Men's Christian Association, which Japan had used to indoctrinate Chinese youth. Consequently, he was put on trial by the Anti-Collaboration Commission after the war.)[50] Most of those present, however, resolutely opposed this seemingly superficial change. Chen Chih-ping denounced Sy as "myopic" (*yanguang duanshi*) and his proposal as a "cowardly compromise" (*pasi tuoxie*). Yao Shiong Shio said that since the ACM's goal was to oppose communism, changing its name would render it meaningless; in any case, Chiang had appointed the committee and thus had the final say on the proposal. Say Kok Chuan asserted that acting in response to what he called "Anglo-French imperialist schemes to sell out Taiwan" would signal to others that the Philippine Chinese had flip-flopped. Chen echoed this concern when he said that since Quirino had approved the organization, changing its name would suggest to both the ROC and the Philippines that the ACM's core ideology had changed. In the end, the ACM did not change its name at that time. The last word belonged to Sycip, who acknowledged Sy's and Say's concerns but sided with the status quo. "Whatever happens to Taiwan in the future," Sycip said, "we Chinese in the Philippines should adhere to the Philippine environment. As it is an anticommunist country, the name of the organization does not need to be changed."[51]

This dispute appears to pit Sy and Dy as pragmatists against ideologues such as Chen, Yao, and Say, but this distinction may be too categorical. Sy and Dy, despite being more flexible than their opponents when it came to the ACM's name, did not seek to change its fundamental mission, which was to propagandize on behalf of the ROC. To the contrary, they believed that the ACM, under a different name, might be able to achieve its aims more easily if geopolitics shifted in an untoward direction. Their opponents' reaction, while couched in highly charged rhetoric, was also informed by a sensitivity toward the political environment. Chen, for example, was concerned about how a change in the name of the organization would affect how Manila and Taipei perceived it, while Say was likewise worried that dropping "anticommunist" from its official title would cause others to treat the Philippine Chinese as unreliable. Reputations and perceptions mattered, in other words, to all who participated in this organizational exercise in ideological self-fashioning. Sycip nicely summed up the entanglement of self-interest and ideology at the end when he said that "anticommunist" was pragmatic because of the ideological position of the Philippine state and the perception of ideological commitment that the organization wished to create.

Thorough-Going Opportunists

In the late 1940s and early 1950s, challenges to the reputation and social status of Chinese business elites came from within and beyond their own class, manifesting themselves in the form of accusations of wartime collaboration, blackmail and extortion attempts, and gossip. The efforts of elites to burnish their law-abiding reputations and to inoculate themselves against charges of crime or communism were a constant uphill struggle. Some who practiced anticommunism did so to exploit the establishment. Two such figures emerged from within the KMT, an organization that drew on this establishment but also empowered those who sought to destabilize it.

Shih I-Sheng parlayed his wartime achievements as a guerrilla leader into becoming the elected representative of the Philippine Chinese to the ROC's National Assembly in Nanjing in 1946.[52] From 1948 to October 1951, he served as the *zongzhibu*'s secretary-general and after resigning from his position went on a tour of the United States, Central and Latin America, Europe, and Southeast Asia. Shih returned to the Philippines in April 1952 and remained on the party's Executive Committee well into the 1950s.[53] We know less about his contemporary Edward Lim. He claimed to have been born in Shanghai, but ROC and US sources indicate that he was born in Pyongyang, Korea, and grew up in China. After studying pharmacy in the United States, Lim served in the US military in World War I and then returned to China to practice medicine. Before arriving in the Philippines in the late 1930s, Lim worked as a doctor with the rank of lieutenant general for a pro-Chiang warlord, through whom he acquired a Chinese passport and became involved in intelligence work. Lim spent World War II in the company of anti-Japanese guerrillas on Panay Island, where he was involved in anti-Japanese broadcasting. Because of Lim's fluency in Chinese and English, the KMT employed him after the war as an intermediary between the party and the Philippine government. Until June 27, 1950, he was, in his own words, the party's "general secretary of foreign relations" (*waiwu zongganshi*), but he was then demoted to a "liaison officer" after claiming to speak on behalf of the entire party to the state. Our paper trail on him runs cold around the time Shih left for his world tour. At this point, Lim, once described as "thoroughly pro-American" by US intelligence, was under investigation by Philippine intelligence on suspicions of being a communist. The outcome of this investigation is unknown, but Lim does not appear to have been arrested and deported to Taiwan. He may have remained in the Philippines and faded into obscurity, beyond the grasp of its legal system, as so many were.[54]

Shih and Lim were not like Sy En or Yao Shiong Shio, whose status owed chiefly to their wealth, nor could either claim to be a party elder like Ong Chuan Seng.[55] Although Shih may have worked as an insurance agent at one point and was described by the *Manila Times* as the owner of the Capitol Commercial Company, he was not part of the General Chamber; nor was Lim. Neither possessed the wealth needed to forge durable social relations, for regardless of their commercial dealings, both were basically political operatives. If Chinese communists such as Co Keng Sing and Shen Fushui hated Shih, his own party and embassy disliked him only slightly less. According to US intelligence sources, Shih was a "thorough-going opportunist whose proprietary attitude toward the party [had] been a matter of concern to the Chinese Embassy," he had an "arrogant personality," and he was disliked by the chamber.[56] The embassy described Shih as a "swindler and bluffer" (*zhaoyao zhuangpian*) fond of "speculation" (*maikong maikong*). It claimed that he only became a Standing Committee member of the KMT and then its secretary-general because others were too busy running their own businesses and organizations to dedicate themselves entirely to party affairs. Moreover, they hoped that Shih's "foolhardy and extravagant" (*yuyong haochu fengtou*) behavior might be useful to them. Consequently, left to run the party, he frequently got away with issuing orders contrary to party regulations without the prior knowledge or consent of his fellow Standing Committee members.[57]

What Shih and Lim did have going for them were an affiliation with the KMT and skills that were valuable to the state in a time of heightened ideological tensions. By virtue of his guerrilla activities during the occupation, Shih had built up connections with US and Filipino military and intelligence officials, and he continued to leverage them afterward. His party's reputation was high, at least among the military and intelligence agencies, because of its role in helping them combat the Chinese left after the war.

Shih's background as both an anticommunist and an intelligence operative helped him carve out a special, albeit temporary, role for himself in Philippine society. Although he did not hold a leadership position in the ACM, he represented the Chinese community in Frank Tenny's PACL, of which he was a vice-chairman. Through the PACL, Shih cultivated ties with leading Filipino anticommunists such as Colonel Agustin Gabriel of NICA and CUFA chairman Tito V. Tizon, becoming a go-to expert within the intelligence community on Chinese communism.[58] To burnish his reputation even further, Shih also published the *Free China Magazine* (see figure 3.2), which was staffed by KMT members and written in English so as to keep his contacts in the government abreast of the party's propaganda activities and cooperation with the authorities. Its "Double Tenth" issue in 1951 featured photographs of Shih donating radio sets to the Philippine Army and gifts of food, wine, and cigarettes to Philippine soldiers returning from Korea. Shih was also described as participating, alongside Tenny, in a PACL rally in Tacloban, Leyte.[59] Like Sycip's articles in the *Fookien Times Yearbook*, print publications such as *Free China Magazine* were less about their content than maintaining the visibility of particular individuals and institutions. But whereas Sycip and the ACM targeted the general public, Shih's audience was more specific. Lacking Sycip's wealth and connections to Chinese and Filipino elites, Shih sought to impress a different social circle from Sycip's.

FIGURE 3.2. Shih I-Sheng greets US major general Leland Hobbs at the United Nations Club in Manila for the inauguration of the Philippine-Chinese United Organization in Support of Anti-Communist Movement on March 1, 1951. On the far right is ROC ambassador Chen Chih-ping. Image courtesy of the Hoover Institution Library and Archives.

From the late 1940s, by which time most Chinese communists in the Philippines had left the country or gone underground, the intelligence that Shih provided to his Filipino contacts was poor at best and often maliciously false. Invited by Tizon to testify before CUFA on June 18, 1950, he skirted any analysis of Chinese communism and instead engaged in fearmongering. He declared that corruption within the government was similar to that in China three years earlier. The security situation was so dire, he said, that "the Philippines [would] be overcome by the communists" in three years. But while Manila could "not deal with the Huks," Shih bragged: "If we Chinese were allowed to do so, we would be able to get rid of them in a very short time." This self-aggrandizing boast was aimed at stoking the anticommunist climate that his career depended on. He did not necessarily substantiate these claims. On one occasion, Shih claimed that the CCP had secreted a staggering USD 200 million into the Philippines.[60] On another, he warned the US Embassy that over a hundred Chinese communists, mostly ex–Philippine-Chinese Anti-Japanese Force (Wha Chi) guerrillas, were posing as security guards at Clark Air Base to steal and sell weapons to the Huks. Shih provided no proof of this and did not respond to a request for details. Four days later, the embassy received a verbatim copy of the same letter, on the same KMT letterhead, signed by Edward Lim, who was similarly unresponsive to further inquiries.[61]

When Shih did furnish the authorities with lists of Chinese communists, the names on them were of individuals whom he was unable to extort money from or against whom he had a grudge.[62] Shih's criminal activities were inseparable from more respectable anticommunist tactics, such as civic associationism and self-fashioning through the media, because the social and political capital that accrued to him from these practices put him in a position of power vis-à-vis other Chinese. As he was the *zongzhibu*'s secretary-general, his words carried weight among many with the coercive, legal, and illegal means to affect the Chinese community. Lim Tian Seng's letter to Magsaysay shows that Chinese at the time knew that Shih was well connected to Philippine intelligence and military officials. Lacking these connections, his targets often found it simpler to pay him off rather than risk being harassed, arrested, and deported. In the early 1950s, losing one's personal wealth to a blackmailer was often preferable to risking one's reputation as a law-abiding, noncommunist Chinese resident of the country.

The importance of reputation is also underscored by Shih's downfall, which was brought about by a combination of his own missteps, an all-too-familiar factionalism within the KMT, and cooperation between the Philippine and ROC authorities. In mid-1951, Pua Chin Tao, head of the Philippine chapter of the Anti-Communist and Resist Russia League of Chinese Youth (Zhong-

guo Qingnian Fangong Kang'E Lianhehui; the successor to the Three Principles' Youth Corps [SQT]), accused Shih of breaking the law. Shih, who was
already under investigation by the Philippine government, retorted in signature fashion by forging a memorandum featuring the signatures of well-known
Chinese Reds who had left the country for China and placing it in Pua's possession. This document "revealed" that Chinese communists had infiltrated
Philippine military intelligence and established an assassination squad whose
targets included four Philippine politicians and Shih himself. It also spoke of
a submarine base on Hainan Island that the PRC planned to use for covert operations in Vietnam, the Philippines, Singapore, and other countries in Southeast Asia. When the Philippine authorities obtained the text, they suspected
that Shih was behind it and sought the ROC Embassy's cooperation in dealing with him. Unlike suspected communists and other "undesirables," Shih
was secretary-general of the KMT in the Philippines. By sanctioning his deportation to Taiwan, as the DND hoped to do, the embassy would compromise the reputation of the KMT in the country at a challenging time for the
party, the ROC, and Chinese society. Citing a classical proverb on the need for
"brothers quarreling at home" to "join forces against external attacks" (xiongdi xi qiang, wai yu qi wu), the embassy decided against supporting Shih's deportation even though it had little affinity for his antics. Instead, it advised the
rest of the Standing Committee to urge Shih to resign from his position and
requested that the Philippine government allow him to leave the country.[63]
Separately, a committee of elder statesmen from Taiwan, including Chiang
Ching-kuo, intervened in the quarrel between Pua and Shih and persuaded
each to withdraw his accusations against the other.[64] With Taipei knee-deep
in reforms aimed at eliminating factionalism and corruption from the party's
ranks, it could ill afford to allow this matter to get out of hand.

The case of Edward Lim offers useful parallels with Shih's and sheds further light on the media's role in the self-fashioning of one's political identity
as a Chinese "leader" (qiaoling) in the Philippines. Many Chinese, observed a
KMT educator on his first visit to the country in 1948, called themselves or
were referred to as qiaoling because of the many Chinese civic organizations
there.[65] Lim was one such self-described qiaoling. In January 1947, at the urging of Koa Chun-te, the KMT's secretary-general, Lim founded the Philippines-
China Cultural Association (Zhong Fei Wenhua Xiehui, or PCCA) to
"promote trust and understanding" between Chinese and Filipinos through
the study of Tagalog, Chinese, and the history, customs, and culture of both
countries and by helping Filipino students pursue their higher education in
China. On paper, the PCCA boasted impressive credentials. Secretary of the
Interior Jose Zulueta, a staunch anticommunist, served as its president and Lim

its secretary. On its board of directors were the likes of Yu Khe Thai, the mayor of Manila, Supreme Court justice Jose Bengzon, Albino Sycip, a senator, and Manila's chief of police. Other members included KMT bigwigs such as Shih, military police (MP) commanders, governors, educators, and journalists. The PCCA had branches beyond the capital and was backed by the KMT and the embassy but not the General Chamber of Commerce.[66]

The PCCA also published the *Philippines-China Cultural Journal*, which featured poetry, fiction (including a serialized version of Lim's novel *Two Beauties of the South*), inspirational quotations, and articles on topics such as Philippine-China relations, opera in the Philippines, and "Manchuria, China's Mindanao." Lim's contributions to the monthly periodical included "Oriental Democracy," which argued that democratic freedoms had taken root in ancient China, and "Why Americans Are Reluctant to Help China." The second, written in late 1947, reflected the darkening, conspiratorial mood among KMT partisans at the time. It warned that if China fell to the CCP, the rest of Asia would soon follow and spoke of the US government and society as being "honey-combed with Moscow-paid agents" seeking their destruction. The journal was not explicitly about politics in the way that *Free China Magazine* was. Anticommunism was, rather, both the subject of occasional articles and encoded into other pieces, from "Oriental Democracy" to Chinese proverbs emphasizing filial piety, an essay on the role of women in the ROC's war effort, and an article by Soong Mei-ling on the New Life Movement.[67]

Beyond publishing this periodical and establishing provincial branches, the PCCA did little. In the provinces, PCCA activities seem to have been occasions for Lim to eat, drink, and socialize with Filipino and Chinese officials. In practice, promoting "trust and understanding" between the two ethnic groups was limited to the forging of personal relations between the PCCA's founder and a handful of supporters like Zulueta whose patronage sustained the association and who might also pen an occasional article for its journal. Most of its members appear to have contributed nothing to it except their names. By the time Lim was demoted from his position within the KMT in June 1950, it was apparent that the PCCA was one among several fronts for Lim's shady dealings. The party's former "general secretary of foreign relations" was also the head of the Southeast Asia Association and the Edward Lim Hospital in Davao. The latter, in reality, was a drugstore. Through them, Lim extorted around PHP 50,000 from Chinese in the southern Philippines and employed a modus operandi that was virtually identical to Shih's. The embassy obtained a letter that he wrote to one of his victims, which stated simply: "Recently, someone has reported to the Defense Department that you have close connections to underground communist agents. I heard that the Department has ordered your arrest. I am shocked at this news and hope to reach a compromise with the authorities before this happens. What are your views on this? Please reply to my letter as soon as possible."[68]

More so than Shih, Lim participated actively in the culture of intelligence trafficking and rumormongering within Chinese society at the time. One of his many targets, it appears, was Shih himself; sadly, no further details are available. Lim also tried to smear Ambassador Chen Chih-ping when the Philippine and ROC authorities were investigating Lim. In October 1950, Lim reported to NICA that a communist agent was working in the embassy to facilitate the escape of Chinese communists from the Philippines and had secured employment on the recommendation of Chen's university classmate Young Ching-tong, the former Philippine-Chinese Anti-Japanese Volunteer Corps (Kang Chu) leader. Two months later, Lim retracted this claim and instead accused the embassy, the KMT, and the General Chamber of shielding a Chinese man whom the Philippine authorities had found guilty of smuggling arms to China and would soon deport to Taiwan.[69] By April 1951, Lim's accusatory counteroffensive had fizzled out. A last-ditch appeal by his son to, of all people, Soong Mei-ling, was met with a firm response from Chen to Soong describing Lim's crimes. In a doubly ironic twist, Lim, by all accounts a committed Nationalist, was now tarred with the same ideological brush that he had used against others despite a conspicuous lack of evidence proving that he was a communist.[70]

Shih I-Sheng's and Edward Lim's escapades suggest that the KMT's expanding influence in the Philippines did not stem from the party's internal cohesion or popularity. To the contrary, the party was deeply factionalized and, because of its ties to the Philippine military and blackmailers, unpopular among many Chinese such as Lim Tian Seng. Yet the party's power over associational life and education remained directly unchallenged, to a large extent because of the climate of fear that Shih, Edward Lim, and others had helped create. Fear incentivized both silence and participation in the party's anticommunist cause.

"Lacking a Patriotic National Mentality"

Shih and Lim's personal rivalry, as exemplified by the identical letters that each sent to the US embassy in quick succession, sheds light on the competitive, mimetic nature of anticommunist accumulation in the early Cold War. Anticommunism was not a scarce resource, the scramble for which yielded only overt social conflict with clear winners and losers. Organizations such as the ACM and the PCCA could coexist and overlap in membership and social function, without mutual antagonism. Yet certain tactics resulted in gains for some at the expense of others and could backfire on their exponents, as Shih's and Lim's downfalls show. Providing intelligence to the authorities was inherently risky because no one person or group had a monopoly on access to these authorities and faulty intelligence could result in a swift reversal of one's reputation as an informant. The state's limited capacity to surveil the Chinese community created opportunities for diverse Chinese actors to prove their usefulness to their country of residence and further their own ambitions.

One such group of actors was, until November 1951, employed by the Military Intelligence Service (MIS) and led by Antonio Chua Cruz. Born in Jinjiang as Cai Wobai, Cruz was banished from his home village at the age of sixteen for an unspecified crime and subsequently joined a gang in Shishi that menaced villages in Fujian and engaged in smuggling along the southern coast of China. After the leader of this gang was arrested in 1932, Cruz escaped to the Philippines, where his father lived, and registered himself as Cai Jie. Multiple such aliases and the absence of standardized romanized forms of their Chinese names made it difficult for the state to monitor persons like him. Cruz later faked his Philippine citizenship and obtained a counterfeit passport. During the war, he headed the overseas department of the CA and helped Japanese naval intelligence against the Chinese resistance. Right after the war, he was shot by several Chinese snipers for collaboration but survived to further his criminal career.[71]

Cruz's postwar criminal network started from the very top of the military establishment with Major General Calixto Duque, chief of staff of the Philippine Armed Forces. Besides Duque, Cruz also counted among his friends the secretary of justice, two senators, and the Speaker of the House of Representatives. How Cruz forged these friendships is unclear. The intelligence gathered on him by the ROC Embassy describes his "beautiful" Filipina second wife as close to the justice secretary and implies that she played a vital role in her husband's social prominence. Through ties to his patron Duque, Cruz secured the appointment of George Co, Celestino Cua, and Ching Boc as MIS operatives at a time when the agency desperately needed Chinese speakers. Claiming that they had in their possession a list of three thousand communists that their new employer had furnished them with, these three men worked with a Filipino MIS agent to blackmail and extort local Chinese. Proceeds from their exploits also lined the pockets of Duque and his crony, intelligence chief Ismael Lapus. By late 1951, Cruz's gang had made PHP 1.5 million in this manner. It also reported to MIS on the ROC's and the KMT's doings in the Philippines, in effect enabling the military to play off one group of informants against another and avoid overdependence on any one source.[72]

Cruz's other "anticommunist" practices after 1945 also resembled those of Lim and Shih, except that he had no ounce of belief in the Nationalist cause. A self-founded, appropriately titled civic organization, the Free Asia Publishing House, served as the pretext for Cruz to strong-arm individuals into paying him—in this case advertising fees for its journal, the *Free Asia Magazine*—or be denounced as a communist to the military. At a time when visits to Taiwan were becoming increasingly popular in the Philippines for Chinese and Filipinos, Cruz planned one for Filipino journalists in the name of promoting "Sino-Philippine relations" and promised to reimburse part of their traveling costs. When the ROC Embassy refused to grant Cruz clearance for the trip, he not only pocketed the money that the unsuspecting journalists had given him but also retaliated against Chen Chih-ping, who was an easy target for criminals like him and Edward Lim.[73] In June 1951, he leaked rumors to *The Bullseye* that the ACM was sheltering communists and that Chen had pocketed the PHP 5 million that the ACM received from the Chinese community during the early years of the Korean War. Chen, it turned out, had friends on the paper's board of directors, which withdrew the article immediately.[74]

Several months after his failed attack on Chen, Cruz met his political demise. In late 1951, Cruz's associates were arrested and Cruz himself, not for the first time, was targeted for assassination—this time by a bomb. After surviving this latest attempt on his life, he reported to the authorities that cigarette tycoon and ACM member Peter Lim was responsible for it. Lim had apparently paid a communist called Tang Huancheng to kill Cruz, but Tang was one of Cruz's lackeys at the Free Asia Publishing House. Cruz betrayed Tang to save his own skin. When the authorities arrested Tang, they also discovered eighteen telegrams about secret arbitrage agreements with communist banks in Hong Kong. Tang, defending himself, accused Cruz of forging these documents to extort money from Chinese merchants. Cruz had failed to bribe Tang into confessing that the telegrams were authentic and that Peter Lim had ordered the botched assassination of Cruz. In desperation, Cruz accused a Chinese Volunteers in the Philippines (CVP) member—whom he said was a communist, despite being in a KMT organization—and special agents of the ROC Embassy of trying to murder him. Who actually did so and who ordered the bomb attack remain a mystery. By this point, the Philippine government had figured Cruz out and charged him with forging his identification papers and with multiple counts of bribery and blackmail. In January 1952, Cruz was arrested and sent before the Deportation Board, which ordered him to be deported to Taiwan.[75]

It was symptomatic of the political environment in the Philippines at the time that criminals who made a living from accusing others of being communists frequently ended up labeled as Reds themselves. Cruz himself was merely "lacking a patriotic national mentality" (*haowu guojia minzu guannian*), according to the ROC authorities, but his associates were accused of being communists and former Wha Chi members. In its recommendation to President Quirino, the Deportation Board said that they had propagandized and solicited financial contributions on behalf of the remaining Chinese communists in the country, attended their meetings, and maintained ties to Chinese Reds previously based there. Ching Boc and Celestino Cua were charged with employing blackmail and forgery to extort money from one Chinese man, who, after refusing to pay them, was arrested by the police for having in his possession a (forged) communist pamphlet. Ching and Cua were also reported to have delivered to another person the equivalent of 1 million renminbi (RMB) for remittance to China and then demanded PHP 10,000 to "fix" his violation of exchange control regulations; the amount was meant to bribe MIS chiefs and Defense Secretary Magsaysay. George Co and six other men had also posed as MIS agents and threatened to arrest the wife of a Chinese businessman unless she paid them—which she did. Police raids on their residences had yielded large quantities of guns and ammunition, which they did not have licenses for.[76]

Coming from different social backgrounds, Alfonso Sycip, Shih I-Sheng, Edward Lim, and Antonio Chua Cruz helped create an anticommunist Chinese social order in the early Cold War Philippines. Of them, perhaps Shih and Lim were true anticommunists given their involvement in KMT intelligence before and during the occupation. We also glimpse manifestations of ideological authenticity in the semiprivate language of others such as Chen Chih-ping, Yao Shiong Shio, and Say Kok Chuan. Yet while these traces of belief are undeniable, it is also true that one's outward behavior as an "anticommunist," including one's utterances, need not have sprung exclusively or at all from faith in the Nationalist cause or a hatred of communism. Instead, as this chapter and the book argue, we can also focus on the ways in which anticommunism was useful for its practitioners in a given social and political setting. Through civic associations such as the ACM and Edward Lim's PCCA, local Chinese secured the patronage of Filipino and ROC politicians and officials and raised their profiles as *qiaoling*. English-language propaganda had a similar purpose. Through the *Fookien Times Yearbook*, *Free China Magazine*, and the *Philippines-China Cultural Journal*, Sycip, Shih, and Lim ensured their visibility within the public sphere and fashioned their ideological credentials to a wide audience.

In a country whose politicians, officials, and thus power structures became increasingly anticommunist, and in which the Chinese were suspect and vulnerable, it was pragmatic to be ideological.

Anticommunism was also a source of conflict and factionalism. Shell organizations such as the PCCA and Cruz's Free Asia Publishing House masked various criminal or ethically dubious activities. Acting as providers of intelligence on Chinese communism to MIS, Shih, Lim, and Cruz incorporated themselves into positions of power over other Chinese that their nonelite social backgrounds would not ordinarily have allowed them to hold. By leveraging the organizations that they were affiliated with—such as the KMT—and their connections to the Philippine state, they were able to threaten their targets with accusations of communism and by planting forged evidence if they did not pay up. Even the ROC's ambassador and the ACM Standing Committee member Peter Lim were vulnerable to being smeared as communists or communist sympathizers. Elites like them and Sycip were well aware of the damage that false accusations could inflict on their reputations and acted accordingly to ensure that their ideological credentials were unimpeachable. In this sense, the distinctions between the respectable and criminal dimensions of anticommunism were blurred.

CHAPTER 4

Anticommunism in Question

"Communists" and ROC-Philippine Relations in the 1950s

In the early 1950s, following the entry of the People's Republic of China (PRC) into the Korean War, Southeast Asian regimes escalated their operations against communists and Chinese communists in their midst. From early August to late October 1951, the Indonesian government under the Islamic Masyumi Party arrested fifteen thousand alleged Reds or Red sympathizers, including many pro-PRC ethnic Chinese.[1] In Thailand, at the instigation of police chief Phao Siyanon, the military forced through the National Assembly the Prevention of Communist Activities Act on November 13, 1952, which gave it broad discretionary powers to imprison almost anyone accused of being in a communist organization. Synchronously, and for three months afterward, Phao went on the offensive against persons associated with the Communist Party of Thailand. By the end of January 1953, some six hundred Chinese had been detained and questioned and numerous Chinese businesses, schools, and civic associations raided.[2] In both countries, the Republic of China (ROC) government and Kuomintang (KMT) informants had aided and abetted these crackdowns.

A comparable security operation unfolded in the Philippines on December 27, 1952, with one difference being that it specifically targeted the Chinese. Over that day, Philippine military forces fanned out across the archipelago and arrested around three hundred persons. Well over half of them—185, according to ROC ambassador Chen Chih-ping—were apprehended in Manila and the rest in Bicol, Cebu, Iloilo, and Central Luzon.[3] Among those arrested, according to the Military Intelligence Service (MIS), were the leaders of a secretive organization known as the Chinese Bureau.[4] While raids on Chinese homes and workplaces were commonplace at the time, this roundup was on a much larger scale. Never before had the authorities seized so many alleged Reds—Chinese or otherwise—all at once; in one journalist's assessment, it was "without doubt, the greatest single operation yet attempted" by MIS.[5] Yet because of how the *jinqiao an* (case of the detained *huaqiao*), as local Chinese called it, unfolded, never again would such a campaign take place.

The key difference between the Philippine mass arrests and those in Indonesia and Thailand was that the ROC was not involved in them. Many *jinqiao* were, in fact, members of the KMT and the Philippine-Chinese United Organization in Support of Anti-Communist Movement (ACM), and none were guilty of the charges against them. Approximately half were released in mid-1953, before the Deportation Board hearings against the remaining detainees began. More would be found innocent over time, but only in late December 1961 did the final few *jinqiao* secure their freedom, thanks to the persistent lobbying efforts of the ROC Embassy and local Chinese leaders over a tortuous nine-year period. The only Chinese communist implicated in this affair was a man whom MIS had arrested in April 1952 and whose false testimony, provided under duress, helped authenticate the evidence needed to conduct the arrests in the first place. Koa Chian, a courier for the Chinese Bureau, was eventually deported to Taiwan on July 26, 1957. On the Taiwanese air force plane with Koa to Taipei that day were three young men, Lao Han Keng, Sy Bun Chiong, and Go Chi Kok, and a woman of twenty, Sy Yan Wan.[6] As high school students in Cebu in the early 1950s, they were members of a left-wing reading club, which, in response to the *jinqiao an*, they renamed the Philippine-Chinese Communist Party (Feilübin Huaqiao Gongchandang, or PCCP). In July 1954, they were arrested, and their fates became intertwined with those of the *jinqiao*. Nine other members of this organization, which was not connected to the Chinese Bureau, were arrested in early 1962.

When paired with the examples of Alfonso Sycip, Shih I-Sheng, Edward Lim, and Antonio Chua Cruz from chapter 3, the *jinqiao an* and the Cebu reading club affair illustrate the diverse ways in which Philippine Chinese adapted to the anticommunist political and social climate in the 1950s. The former practiced anticommunism, profited from it, and, in the cases of Shih, Lim, and Cruz, indirectly paved the way for the December 27, 1952, arrests by arrogating to similar Chinese intermediaries the power to produce "Chinese communism" as a national security problem. In contrast, Koa Chian, the Cebu students, and the embassy and Chinese leaders who supported the *jinqiao* navigated the same environment differently. The cases of Koa and the students reveal that Chinese communism persisted in old and new forms despite and because of Manila's and Taipei's ideological orientation; support for Nationalist China among the Philippine Chinese, while considerable, was not absolute. They show that Chinese who were arrested in the Philippines and deported to Taiwan possessed a limited agency in being able to confound both states' efforts to render Chinese communism legible. This chapter also explains how the Chinese establishment, comprising ROC diplomats and local Chinese leaders, tried to turn this crisis to their advantage. Working together, the embassy and Chinese elites mounted a legal defense of the *jinqiao* and skillfully negotiated a political settlement with the Philippines and Taiwan to enhance the ROC's reputation in the Chinese community. Far from categorically rejecting Manila's operations against local Chinese, the embassy instead sought to rectify anticommunism by positioning itself between the military and Chinese society as a provider of information, ensuring that future arrests targeted only the "right" persons and that their sharing of sovereignty over the Chinese would be equitable.

Koa Chian and the Chinese Bureau

Koa Chian, the man known to us only through his interrogations at the hands of MIS, was a relative newcomer to the Philippines. He arrived in the Philippines in 1937 from Fujian, though where exactly and when he was born are unclear. During one of his first interrogation sessions, he claimed to be twenty-nine and have been born in Xiamen, which would have made his year of birth 1922 or 1923.[7] But in 1957, when in custody in Taiwan, he said that he was originally from Quanzhou and was twenty-six when he left mainland China.[8] Entering the country legally, he studied at various night schools and worked at the general store of his older cousin during the day. In 1941, he was a typesetter for the *Chinese Commercial News* (*CCN*). As a student at Nanyang High School (NHS) before the occupation, he joined the Chinese Youth Association, otherwise known as the Philippine-Chinese Students' Anti-Japanese and Anti-Traitors Association (Feilübin Huaqiao Xuesheng Kangri Fanjian Da Tongmeng), becoming one of its leaders, but he claimed not to know that it was communist at the time. After the war, Koa represented his school in reorganizing the Chinese Youth Association and realized in the second half of 1945 that it was, in fact, the Education Department of the Chinese Communist Party's (CCP) Overseas Chinese Bureau in the Philippines (Zhongguo Gongchandang Feilübin Huaqiao Ju).[9]

At this point, Koa was not a fully fledged Chinese Bureau member. Full membership, in true Leninist fashion, required that one be observed and then approved by existing party cadres. In 1947, with his general goods business faring poorly, Koa became a primary school teacher for a year. He eventually entered the ranks of the bureau, most likely in 1948, having apparently been coerced into doing so by another member, who had discussed with him the favorable situation for the CCP in China and threatened to harm him if he did not join the group. From 1948 to 1950, Koa worked again for the *CCN* and studied English at the Araneta Institute of Agriculture in Malabon. In June 1951, Koa was promoted to head of propaganda.[10]

The Philippine authorities and, through them, US intelligence had known about the Chinese Bureau since documents seized by the military in raids on Huk centers in Manila in October 1950 revealed the existence of the Chinese Branch or Chinese Board of the Partido Komunista ng Pilipinas (PKP).[11] Consisting of high-level communications among PKP leaders, these materials helped MIS initiate its subsequent two-year operation against the Chinese Bureau, culminating in the December 27, 1952, arrests, but do not seem to have been shared with ROC officials. The bureau represented what became of the Chinese left in the Philippines after the exodus of prominent Red leaders such as Co Keng Sing, Young Ching-tong, Gong Taoyi, and Huang Wei to China in the late 1940s. It did not, as the military declared shortly after the mass arrests, date back to the Philippine-Chinese Anti-Japanese Force (Wha Chi), but was rather nominally separate from it and other more well-known and more active Chinese communist organizations in the country such as the Philippine-Chinese Democratic League, the Philippine-Chinese Anti-Japanese and Anti-Puppets League (Kang Fan), and the Philippine-Chinese United Workers Union (Lo Lian Hui).[12] In 1948, the bureau assumed leadership of the Chinese communist movement in the country, supported members of these other organizations financially, and absorbed some of them into its ranks.[13] In March 1950, PKP leaders estimated that membership of the bureau was around two hundred, but in August 1952, Koa put this number at four hundred.[14]

Based on the October 1950 documents, US intelligence conjectured that while the bureau was affiliated with the PKP, it probably enjoyed a closer relationship with the CCP in China. Tensions between the PKP and the bureau were many and communication between them lacking. Strategically, the bureau and the Huks were at odds. "Many CBs want to go back home," the PKP's secretariat reported in March 1950, and many did so without permission from the secretariat; others, despite not leaving for China, remained unhappy and became "discontented and talkative." As the bureau focused on "mobilizing comrades and followers back to China to join the officer training class," it lacked a "complete, over-all plan and concrete organizational measures" and "did not mobilize [the] whole Party to discuss this problem fully." Luis Taruc himself commented that the PKP's Chinese "comrade-advisors" had an "over-zealous desire for continuous attacks on the enemy," motivated by "national opportunism."[15] In late 1951, following the seizure of an additional collection of PKP materials in September, US agents asserted that a split had emerged between the PKP and the Chinese Bureau going back to the early postliberation period. Chauvinistic and believing themselves more well versed in Marxist theory than their Filipino comrades, bureau members consistently refused to provide financial and organizational reports to the PKP's leadership.[16] Koa confirmed this split, if not its specific details, when he stated that while bureau members had to agree to be placed under the PKP and paid monthly dues to the party in "theory," they "did not like to follow the theory concerned."[17] He explained that the bureau aimed primarily to unite Philippine Chinese in support of the CCP and only secondarily to help the PKP liberate the Philippines from US neocolonialism and establish a new government of national capitalists, intellectuals, laborers, and peasants. The role of the bureau in the PKP's armed insurgency was thus "purely spiritual, moral, and financial," and were the PKP to achieve its aim, the bureau would call on Chinese to follow the country's new laws.[18] Koa and PKP leaders' remarks about the bureau are consistent with how Taruc characterized the relationship between Chinese and Filipino communists in his memoirs, as we saw in chapter 2.

As with earlier Chinese communist groups in the Philippines such as the Lo Lian Hui, the bureau had no institutional ties to the CCP. Its connections with the mainland were limited, first, to the smuggling of money by local Chinese banks and other legal businesses to China, typically via Hong Kong. Second, through the mail, the bureau obtained communist propaganda for distribution. Third, it received news on China from the CCP's radio broadcasts. Fourth, it helped Chinese leave the Philippines for China. These links were fragile and easily disrupted, as Philippine intelligence reports on efforts to curb Chinese smuggling suggest. Koa said that following the outbreak of the Korean War, the bureau stopped receiving propaganda from China via the mail.[19]

Within the Philippines, the bureau scraped by on what little money it could raise from its members and supporters, aided by the extreme secrecy with which it operated. Party members paid dues but, according to Koa, they could pay any amount they wished. Bureau sympathizers were also to be found throughout the country and belonged to a group called the Merchants' Association, which the bureau's Organization Department controlled. The bureau also conducted fundraising campaigns to support the CCP in China and help members in need of financial assistance because of unemployment or ill-ness. Koa named three such campaigns: first, to help the People's Liberation Army (PLA) buy food and, second, to fund the bureau's own expenses; he did not elaborate on the third. The bureau was also supposed to send money to the PKP, but, apparently, raids on the Central Post Office prevented that.[20]

Koa was aware of others in the bureau—or at least he was in August 1952. In April, during one of his first interrogations, he claimed to know little about its inner workings. The bureau had five main departments—secretariat, education, organization, finance, and communications—but Koa said then that he did not know their heads.[21] By August, however, Koa had changed his tune in reaction to being tortured. Koa confessed to being head of education, and other names began to come forth: the bureau's secretary was Chi Sen, and its communications head was Bong Ah. Two other men, Eng Sek and Kia Sen, were youth committee members, while Lee, one of Koa's first contacts in the bureau, was Ng Le Chiao, head of the Organization Department. While the bureau as a whole never held group meetings, Koa occasionally met Chi Sen, Eng Sek, Bong Ah, and Kia Sen at rendezvous points throughout Manila, which he drew on a map for his interrogator. In photos that were shown to him, he also identified several other bureau members, including Eng Sek and Bong Ah.[22] These were the names of individuals whom MIS later believed that it had apprehended, but in fact had not.

In 1948, Koa became a regular member of the Chinese Bureau and was taught the tenets of its underground work by one Tan It. He began using the aliases Yu and Yang Renlun in his daily life and Benito in his underground work.[23] In 1950, before leaving Manila for the Visayan Islands, Tan It introduced Koa to his new contact, whom Koa knew only as Lee and suspected of being one of the bureau's leaders.[24] Lee (or Ng Le Chiao, as Koa later revealed to MIS) gave him the task of liaising with the Huks through Koa's former English teacher, Purificacion Bolatao y Feleo, whom he had known since 1946. Feleo may have been a relative or the wife of the late Huk leader Juan Feleo, and, through her, Koa met Tessie, a courier for Taruc, in July 1951. Together, Koa and Tessie traveled to meet with the Huk leader in the Sierra Madre of Central Luzon.[25] Koa stayed there for an unknown length of time and remained in contact with Taruc as the bureau and the PKP sought to mend their relations. In September, Koa informed Taruc, "We are now operating our work smoothly," and included in his letter 800 Philippine pesos (PHP) for the Huks.[26]

In March 1952, Feleo informed Koa that Taruc again wished to meet with him and would send a courier to guide him to Taruc's hideout. On March 29, Koa met with this courier, a teenager nicknamed Baby Zenaida, at Feleo's house. Tessie, it transpired, was wanted by MIS and would not be coming to

Manila anymore. After discussing "Uncle" Taruc's whereabouts and the situation in the mountains, Zenaida agreed that she would take him to Taruc. Two weeks later, on April 13, Zenaida and Koa met at the junction of Paseo de Azcárraga (renamed Recto Avenue in 1961) and Ylaya Street on the outskirts of Chinatown. Koa was then having his shoes shined near a magazine stand and, on seeing Zenaida, motioned her inside a nearby bus station. Koa told her to wait for him while he went to fetch his belongings, but on his way home he was arrested by three MIS agents.[27] Eight months later, the military exploited what it had gleaned from torturing and questioning Koa and arrested several hundred innocent Chinese.

Identifying "Communists": The Military, Koa Chian, and Operation Chopsuy

Compared to the Huks and to the situation in other countries such as Malaya, Chinese communism in the Philippines from the late 1940s onward never amounted to a serious national security threat as defined by conservative Filipino elites. Before the capture of Koa and the *jinqiao an*, MIS's record of identifying and eliminating "foreign" communist threats to the Philippines was minimal. Its operating costs were high and its political enemies many. During the Senate, gubernatorial, and mayoral elections of 1951, the military under Defense Secretary Ramon Magsaysay refused to take political sides and, in so doing, angered the incumbent Liberal Party, of which he was still a member. In 1952, citing costs, a faction of Liberal Congress members took revenge against him by looking to veto MIS's budget for the fiscal year and cripple an agency that the ROC ambassador called Magsaysay's "political capital" (*zhengzhi ziben*). Magsaysay was riding high because of his successful counterinsurgency campaign against the Huks and appears to have given MIS's future little regard. Instead, armed forces chief of staff Calixto Duque and MIS head Colonel Ismael Lapus responded to this threat. A thoroughly corrupt man, Duque was Antonio Chua Cruz's patron and had filled MIS with loyalists such as Lapus. Unbeknownst to Magsaysay, Duque, Lapus, and a third man had begun planning Operation Chopsuy, a large-scale counterintelligence operation against "undesirable" Chinese. This operation transformed MIS's long-standing fears of Chinese communism, which the likes of Cruz and Shih I-Sheng had stoked, into a useful actuality. They presented their plan to President Elpidio Quirino, but he was too busy with affairs of state to bother with it.[28]

Even before arresting Koa Chian, MIS already had in its possession a list of Chinese aliens suspected of nonideological crimes such as arson, insurance fraud, smuggling, prostitution, illegal entry, and visa overstays, but it could not demonstrate them to any reasonable degree. Since the ROC accepted only deportees who were suspected communists and not all "undesirables," MIS sought to tar these persons with the same ideological brush.[29] To reinvent them as communists and pad its list with "real" communists, MIS went after the Chinese Bureau. Huk documents seized in October 1950 had revealed the existence of the bureau, and among the persons they mentioned was Benito, which was one of Koa's aliases. A captured Huk guerrilla informed MIS that Benito was Chinese, giving MIS a lead to pursue.[30]

To infiltrate the organization and capture Benito, MIS could no longer rely on Cruz or Shih: the former had been deported and the latter forced to resign as the *zongzhibu*'s secretary-general. The person it turned to was a teenage Chinese mestizo, Profiteza Que, who went by the Chinese names of Guo Zhubao and Guo Xiuzhi and was nicknamed Baby Zenaida. Born in Laoang City in Samar to a Chinese father from Zhangzhou and a Filipina mother, she attended Laoang Chinese School for three years and had spent time in Zhangzhou as a child. In 1948, she relocated to Manila with her father, a businessman.[31] Thereafter, she started working for MIS and joined Operation Chopsuy. Like Cruz, Que was a mestizo who spoke Chinese. Both straddled Chinese and Filipino societies and were ideally placed to engage in what Caroline S. Hau calls the "politics of strategic hybridity" by offering their services as "native" informants to the coercive state.[32] In return, both gained allies within the military establishment.

Unlike Cruz or Duque, however, Que does not appear to have been driven by a desire for corrupt self-aggrandizement. She was incompetent at best and, at worst, dishonest. In March 1952, as we have seen, she posed as a courier for Taruc and met with Koa, after which Koa was arrested. However, Que had no further success in identifying actual members of the Chinese Bureau, whose leaders operated in extreme secrecy, never met as a group, and knew each other by various aliases. Testifying before the Deportation Board during the trials of the *jinqiao*, she claimed, astoundingly, that she had gained the trust of the bureau's leaders *after* Koa's arrest and on meeting them for the very first time. She said that she worked her way down its organizational structure and quickly familiarized herself with its rank and file, which is how she identified many of the *jinqiao*. When pressed further, however, she admitted to meeting ninety of them only once and for about five minutes each, twenty-one of them twice, and only thirteen four or more times. She was similarly unable to prove that she had infiltrated the bureau, as all that MIS could offer as evidence of her supposed infiltration were Horlicks bottles, comic books, altered dresses, typed letters, and a few peso bills.[33]

The capture of Koa Chian allowed MIS to augment its ever-growing list of "communists." Through Koa, MIS learned about the bureau's leaders, including Chi Sen, Ng Le Chiao, Bong Ah, Eng Sek, Kia Sen, and others who may or may not have been affiliated with the bureau. We do not know how many names in total Koa provided, but he signed at least three written confessions during the eight months leading up to the December 1952 arrests. MIS also had other means and sources. For example, to prove her trustworthiness to Koa Chian, Profiteza Que used a forged letter to Koa from Luis Taruc. Copies of this letter were then delivered to addresses that Koa provided, and agents were dispatched to secretly take photos of the people living there. Names were also extracted from other persons, including a CCP agent from Hong Kong named Chen Jiading, who had entered the Philippines from North Borneo. After traversing the entire length of the country, he was caught trying to leave Batanes for Taiwan, where he had planned to link up with underground communists. Chen named names before retracting his confession entirely, but MIS used what he had originally confessed.[34] According to the ROC Embassy, MIS was also reliant on an ethnic Chinese interpreter and interrogator named Felix Bonaobra, who had provided many names to MIS and later tortured the arrested Chinese into confessing crimes that they had not committed.[35]

Consolidating a list of suspects' names was one thing; apprehending the individuals named was another entirely. The suspects did not resist arrest, but many were not who MIS thought they were. Koa, it transpired, did not unmask the bureau and its leadership. In this sense, he and Que were both unreliable sources of intelligence—the former far more deliberately so. Under pressure, Koa supplied his captors with the names of communists who had left the country, died, or already been outed. Many names that he provided were incomplete; sometimes he gave family names but not first names and at other times first but not last names.[36] Koa's English was poor, but as far as we know he was interrogated only in English and not in Hokkien. He lied to protect himself and the bureau, but he could not have known then that the intelligence he provided to MIS would result in the mass detention of innocent Chinese. When he did find out, he felt remorseful, or at least that is what he told ROC officials several years later.[37]

Koa deceived MIS by exploiting the agency's ignorance of Hokkien, the Chinese written script, and in particular how Chinese deliberately (mis)identified themselves to the Philippine state. Chinese persons, especially those who had entered the country illegally, often kept multiple aliases in English and Chinese and relied on registration certificates that either were forged or belonged to dead people to "legally" remain in the country under its restrictive immigration laws, during and after US rule.[38] Consider the names of the bureau's leaders. In Koa's statements to MIS, he identified the secretary of the bureau as "Chi Sen," which was how his Filipino interrogator phonetically transcribed Koa's verbal response. After the mass arrests, however, this person became known, in both legal records and the *Philippines Free Press*, as Chin Sang.[39] The man arrested was a carpenter who went by the Chinese characters "Huang Jichi" and whose name in his alien registration certificate was indeed Chin Sang. But the actual communist Koa was referring to was Huang Zixin, also a carpenter. This man's registered name was not Chi Sen, despite its phonetic correspondence with his Chinese name, but Lee At, and he had left the country in June 1951. MIS detained Chin Sang because of what it perceived were phonetic similarities between "Chin Sang" ("Huang Jichi") and "Chi Sen" ("Huang Zixin" / "Lee At").[40]

As ROC intelligence showed, MIS similarly misidentified the heads of the Organization, Communications, and Finance Departments. The Chinese names of the arrested persons were Lin Jing'an, Li Wenyun, and Wang Shitong, who were registered, respectively, as Ng Le Chiao, Dy Bon Un, and Yu Dy. Ng Le Chiao, whom Koa had originally known as Lee, had four Chinese aliases and was registered as Toh Chu. He had left the Philippines in January 1951. It may have been that MIS brought up Ng Le Chiao when interrogating Koa about Lee and that Koa had affirmed that the two were the same person. The person Koa named as communications head was Bong Ah, who resided at 543 Elcano Street. This was the former address of communist guerrilla Zhang Luogang, whose name sounded like "Bong Ah" in Hokkien; so too did the name of Dy Bon Un (Li Wenyun), whom MIS insisted was Bong Ah. Finally, Koa named the head of finance as Yu Lan and said that he was a fluent English speaker. ROC intelligence conjectured that Koa was referring to a

Table 4.1 Partial list of Chinese Bureau leaders named by Koa Chian from April to August 1952 and the persons mistaken for them and arrested by MIS on December 27, 1952

	PERSONS MISTAKENLY ARRESTED		ACTUAL BUREAU LEADERS	
RANK IN BUREAU	CHINESE NAME(S)	REGISTERED NAME	CHINESE NAME(S)	REGISTERED NAME
Secretary	Huang Jichi 黃積池	Chin Sang	Huang Zixin 黃自新	Lee At
Organization head	Lin Jing'an 林景安	Ng Le Chiao	Li Huanlai 李煥來; Cai Huanlai 蔡煥來; Li Wenfa 李文法; Li Qingyu 李清玉	Toh Chu
Communications head	Li Wenyun 李文允	Dy Bon Un	Zhang Luogang 張羅綱	[Unknown]
Finance head	Wang Shitong 王詩桐	Yu Dy	Chen Youren 陳有任	Yu Lan

"Chen Youren"; MIS ended up arresting Yu Dy (Wang Shitong), who spoke no English and was a common laborer with only a third-grade education. Table 4.1 summarizes the bureau leaders named by Koa and the persons mistaken for them and arrested by MIS.[41]

"I Want Adventure, Sir": The Cebu Reading Club Affair

December 27, 1952, shook Chinese society and ROC-Philippine relations to their core and produced unexpected reverberations. In Manila, Chinese leaders and the ROC Embassy scrambled to mount a legal and political defense of the detainees and to save anticommunism from itself. But in Cebu, the country's second city, a few young Chinese felt sufficiently angered by what had transpired that they moved in the opposite direction, identified themselves as communists, and sought to radicalize their peers. This is what we learn from their testimonies to MIS and the ROC authorities. In the absence of evidence unmediated by the state and not shaped by the needs and prejudices of anticommunism, we have little choice but to engage with this documentary record. Doing so allows us to reconstruct, imperfectly, the agency, experiences, and motivations of Lao Han Keng, Sy Bun Chiong, Go Chi Kok, and Sy Yan Wan. Their narratives hint at the emotional foundations of ideological belief and show that the four students were far from powerless even after being arrested. Like Koa Chian, they sought to complicate the state's attempts to gather intelligence on Chinese communism.

Lao, Sy, Go, and Sy met in Cebu City in the late 1940s. By September 1952, three months before the *jinqiao an*, all four of them had joined a reading club, whose members went on weekly outings to discuss leftist literature and engage in self-criticism and mutual criticism.[42] The de facto leader of this club at the time proposed changing its name to the Philippine-Chinese Communist Party (PCCP) in response to the December mass arrests. In June 1953, the PCCP was founded as a sui generis organization of self-radicalized youth that had no connections to the CCP and, unlike the Chinese Bureau, to the PKP.[43] Lao recalled that they rented a house in which they hung up pictures of Marx, Engels, Lenin, Stalin, and Mao; conducted a founding ceremony; and mimeographed their own membership cards.[44] They met regularly at "party headquarters" to attend and deliver lectures and discuss communist pamphlets and magazines that were mailed to them from Hong Kong.[45] In the middle of 1954, their "training" complete, Lao and three female party members, Lim Yan Yan, Ang Giok Lun, and Uy Bee Siong, embarked on their first mission as "communists." Posing as students, they looked to infiltrate the KMT-controlled Sun Yat-sen High School in Iloilo City.

Partly because of their inexperience and suspicious behavior, they were quickly found out by the Iloilo KMT. Through their relatives in Iloilo City, the party contacted their parents, who immediately flew in to pick up their wayward children and escort them back to Cebu. A search by the KMT of their residence in Iloilo yielded training manuals, the PCCP's constitution, propaganda, and letters from Lao to the others. But with Deportation Board hearings against the *jinqiao* still ongoing, the KMT elected not to report them to the Philippine authorities for fear of upsetting Chinese society even further. Handing them over would also deprive the party of an opportunity to interrogate them and learn more about their activities and organizational structure. Instead, the KMT had them write confessions in English and Chinese and promise not to repeat their actions, or else be reported to the state along with this evidence. Lao was shown letters that he had written exhorting Lim, Ang, and Uy to remain steadfast in the face of difficulty, after which he confessed to being a communist. The KMT then counseled him "not to live this kind of life" and released him with a guarantee of good behavior from his father, who was a ranking member of the KMT in Cebu. The three female students were also taken in by their parents and watched over by the embassy.[46]

While PCCP members may have called themselves communists, their backgrounds suggest reasons for participating in the reading club and PCCP beyond ideology. Lao was not like Co Keng Sing, who had been a Chinese Communist Youth League member and labor organizer. He claimed to have had no prior involvement in communist activities before entering the Philippines in January 1949 as a legal quota immigrant.[47] Lao subsequently acquainted himself with leftist books. He had a strained relationship with his KMT-supporting father, but we do not know if it was politics that divided them. In April 1953, he found himself unemployed and left home in shame. Through the PCCP, Lao and Sy Yan Wan fell in love, and after she was beaten by her father in July that year, she left home temporarily to live with Lao, who was nine years older than she.[48] Sy's father, David Sy Gaisano, also occupied a prominent social position as a scion of one of Cebu's wealthiest families.[49] After her arrest, MIS asked her why she had joined the PCCP. She responded simply, "I want adventure, sir."[50]

Lao and Sy's romance helps explain why the two of them and Sy Bun Chiong were arrested later that July. At that time, Sy Yan Wan was living with her relatives in Manila and had not been given any assignments by the PCCP. Once free of the KMT's clutches because of his father, Lao went to Manila to find her, knowing that Lim Yan Yan had revealed her existence and that of other PCCP members to the KMT.[51] Lao had thus broken his promise to the KMT and his father "not to live this kind of life," prompting the KMT to inform the Philippine authorities about him. While in Manila, Lao reunited also with Sy Bun Chiong, who had been tasked with infiltrating Philippine-Chinese High School and mailing letters to other Chinese denouncing Magsaysay's anti-Chinese economic policies. He ended up moving in with Lao and Sy Yan Wan. Fearing a crackdown on the PCCP, the three decided to destroy Sy Bun Chiong's letters and flee Manila for Mount Banahaw, a Huk stronghold in Quezon Province that was under siege by the Philippine military. But in their hurry to leave, they did not dispose of all the letters, and those that remained were later seized by MIS. They made it as far as a city at the foot of Mount Banahaw, which was crawling with troops. There, on the night of July 27, the military found them roaming around suspiciously and arrested them.[52] Go Chi Kok was arrested two days later in Manila. Other, although not all, PCCP members were arrested over the next year and a half; fourteen, including Lim Yan Yan, Ang Giok Lun, and Uy Bee Siong, were detained in various cities across the country on November 26, 1955.[53]

Like Koa Chian's confessions, the narratives that PCCP members produced were born out of some combination of an instinctual desire for self-preservation and an intent to both confuse and persuade the states that were prying into their lives. Lao Han Keng, for example, claimed after his arrest that he had given up his "communistic activities" under advice from the KMT and was hoping for a chance to redeem himself.[54] Adopting a similar emotional logic, Sy Yan Wan made a heartfelt plea for leniency when she spoke of her love for Lao and desire for adventure and said, "I no longer want to be a communist."[55] Go Chi Kok furnished both Manila and Taipei with an account that exonerated himself and scapegoated Lao. He claimed to MIS, testified before the Deportation Board, and later told the ROC authorities that he had left the reading club in January 1953, before its transformation into the PCCP, because he had come to realize the true nature of the organization. He said that he had been reading US Information Service propaganda, resulting in this realization. Go also singled out Lao as the founder and leader of the reading club and called him a communist agent from China. But Go's reliability is significantly compromised by his admission that he was Lao's rival for the affections of Sy Yan Wan. Thus, according to Go, Lao exploited his leadership of the reading club to excoriate Go's failure to rid himself of his "petty bourgeois tail" (*xiao zichan jieji weiba*). Lao also supposedly forbade any talk of love between Go and Sy because love was selfish and would hurt the organization's morale. That was Lao's ploy to separate him from Sy, Go said. When Go wished to quit the club, Lao threatened to kill him.[56] Unsurprisingly, no such details can be found in Lao's narrative, which in fact describes Go as a PCCP leader.[57] Sy Bun

Chiong's testimony corroborates that. Sy was uninvolved in the love triangle and had no vendetta against either Lao or Go. But, like Lao, Sy identified Go as a leader of the reading club and PCCP and his and Lao's instructor.[58]

For the Deportation Board, such distinctions were inconsequential because deportation was not a criminal procedure and required only that deportees be found "undesirable." But in martial law Taiwan, where they were deported to in July 1957, Lao, Sy, Sy, and Go were "Chinese nationals" who had to be subjected to an official judicial process in accordance with the July 1949 Act for the Control and Punishment of Rebellion (Chengzhi Panluan Tiaoli). This act sentenced persons found guilty of treason by either a military or common court to death, life imprisonment, or at least ten years in jail, and it therefore required that the "treasonous" activities of the four deportees be transmuted into a hierarchy of guilt and responsibility.[59] Thus, the ROC determined that Lao was the leader of the organization in part on the basis of the letter that he had written to Lim Yan Yan in Iloilo in early July 1954 instructing her on the principles of their struggle; this letter had been confiscated by the Iloilo KMT.[60] In sentencing Lao, Taiwan leaned heavily on Go Chi Kok's accusations against Lao. Taiwan's Garrison–General Headquarters (Jingbei Zong Silingbu) believed Go's claims that he had left the reading club before it became the PCCP and that Lao had told him about his communist activities in China before 1949. This was because none of Lao, Sy, or Sy had mentioned Go as a PCCP member in their statements to the ROC authorities.[61] But in the paperwork that the Philippine government had generated on them, which the ROC explicitly stated that it possessed, Lao and Sy Bun Chiong referred to Go on multiple occasions as a leader or instructor of the party. If the ROC was aware of these documents, it ignored them. For reasons that we will explore in the next section, Lao (and Koa Chian) was given a death sentence in September 1959, but it was later commuted to life imprisonment in March 1960. Similarly, Sy Bun Chiong's life sentence was reduced to a decade, while Sy Yan Wan's term of seven years in jail was reduced to six. Go Chi Kok was sentenced only to an unspecified period of "reformatory education" (ganhua) for apparently having left the reading club early on.[62]

Rectifying Anticommunism

If the December 27, 1952, mass arrests proved ultimately to be a massive intelligence failure for the Philippine military, then it was a crisis of intelligence, diplomacy, and reputation for Taiwan and Chinese leaders. Two major issues dominated the foreign policy thinking of the ROC (and the PRC) in the 1950s, according to Meredith Oyen: national security and international image.[63] Both of these were implicated in the overseas Chinese question. The KMT regime had long staked its reputation in the world on its ability to protect the interests and institutions of Chinese communities globally against economic and cultural nationalism and racial discrimination. After 1945, overseas Chinese affairs became an even greater concern for the state in the contexts of the Cold War, the loss of the mainland, and a rising Sinophobic nationalism globally, especially in Southeast Asia. Taipei may have been willingly complicit in state-directed anti-Chinese anticommunist operations in Indonesia and Thailand, but it also confronted diplomatic crises triggered by, for example, Ngô Đình Diệm's anti-Chinese nationalization drive in South Vietnam from 1955 to 1957 and a similar campaign by the Sukarno government from 1959 to 1960 that saw the KMT banned in Indonesia.[64] Further afield, in 1956, KMT-affiliated Chinese leaders in San Francisco and New York appealed to the ROC in response to an investigation by the US Justice Department into immigration fraud that saw blanket subpoenas issued for all the records from multiple Chinese American businesses and organizations. The investigation had been sparked by a report from the US consul general in Hong Kong alleging that CCP spies could easily enter the United States by exploiting the loopholes in its immigration system.[65]

The *jinqiao an* differed from the South Vietnamese and Indonesian crises and bore more than a passing resemblance to the US one in that it exposed a contradiction in the ROC's Cold War mission. The ROC was committed to, but not necessarily capable of, protecting overseas Chinese interests, and this included defending and mobilizing them against communism in the name of *Fangong kang'E*. But with the *jinqiao an*, safeguarding "Chinese nationals" meant safeguarding them against an illegitimate version of anticommunism and a corrupt exercise of state sovereignty. Failing to do so would have been a further sign of Nationalist China's weakness in international and diasporic affairs. Similar concerns obtained among Chinese elites, whose own reputations and interests were on the line during this and other episodes of intensified state intervention in their community in the 1950s. Anti-Chinese economic and cultural nationalism escalated during and after the Magsaysay administration. Subsequently, Manila also tried to nationalize Chinese schools in response to the *jinqiao an* and the Cebu students' affair, in seeming contravention of the Treaty of Amity. Chinese leaders believed that they had done enough to signal their political commitments by forming the ACM in 1951, but the arrests of ACM and KMT members in December 1952 drove home the need to inject ideological substance into the institutional forms of anticommunism.

The mass arrests caught almost everyone by surprise and were particularly troubling to the ROC Embassy. Like the Philippines and the United States, the embassy knew that most of the Chinese communist movement's leaders had fled the country by mid-1948, existing organizations had disbanded, and the remaining members had gone underground. But it was in the dark when it came to the Chinese Bureau, which only US and Philippine intelligence knew about. In the wake of Antonio Chua Cruz's and Shih I-Sheng's criminal exploits, relations between the embassy and MIS, and intelligence sharing between them, had declined.[66] Ambassador Chen Chih-ping not only was unaware of the bureau but also only learned about the military's plans on the afternoon of December 27 in a phone call with Defense Secretary Magsaysay. Even Magsaysay had not been informed about the arrests, which were spearheaded by an agency within his own department, until the last minute.[67] Equally shocked was the United States, which had nothing to do with the arrests, as a Central Intelligence Agency (CIA) agent privately told Chen after December 27.[68]

The ROC Embassy, in an immediate response to the arrests, issued a statement to Chinese residents calling for calm, contacted the relatives of the arrested, and sent officials to Camp Murphy to reassure the detainees of the ROC's support for them and ask that they abide by camp protocol.[69] It also initiated its own investigation of the suspects and, by early February 1953, had recommended that 118 be released. Among them were persons with unimpeachable anticommunist credentials. Qua Chi Peng, for example, was the president of the Legaspi Chinese Chamber of Commerce and the Legaspi chapter of the Chinese ACM and a Standing Committee member of the KMT in Bicol; in October 1952, he had traveled to Taipei to attend the inaugural Overseas Chinese Conference there. Another detainee, Lao Kiat, was the president of the Tabaco Chinese Chamber of Commerce and also a ranking member of the Bicol KMT and his local ACM chapter. In a letter to the Philippine secretary of foreign affairs, Chen wrote that it was "beyond any doubt that they [had] ever been Communist sympathizers" and hoped for their swift release. The long delay in releasing them had "occasioned great privations" for them and their families, which were mostly of limited means.[70]

Right after the arrests, the embassy also joined with Chinese leaders from organizations such as the KMT, the General Chamber of Commerce, the ACM, and the Chinese Welfare Association to form a "united working group in support of the innocent *jinqiao*" (*ge huaqiao tuanti yuanzhu wugu jinqiao lianhe xiaozu*). Led by Welfare Association president Yu Khe Thai, the working group hired the law firm of Quisumbing, Sycip, Quisumbing, and Salazar to represent the respondents.[71] The Sycip clan member in the firm was Alexander,

Albino's son and Alfonso's nephew. He served as a legal adviser to the embassy, and his firm was often contracted by the Chinese community in cases involving Chinese and the state; his uncle was also part of the working group.

When Deportation Board trials began in May 1953 after months of interrogations, charges were filed against only around half of the three hundred or so persons, including Qua Chi Peng and Lao Kiat, thanks in part to the embassy's own investigations.[72] What followed was the longest and most complex case in the Deportation Board's history. The hearings alone lasted for one and a half years, from July 1953 to January 1955.[73] During this period, 34 jinqiao were freed on January 23, 1954, and 105, including Qua, released on bail shortly afterward. The united working group raised funds and its members even contributed their own money to help the respondents post bail.[74] Of these 105, 5 had charges dropped against them in the coming years, while 1 died. The respondents' attorneys, as explained earlier, based their defense on the questionable veracity of Baby Zenaida and MIS's Operation Chopsuy before December 27, 1952. Following the conclusion of these hearings in January 1955, the board focused on the thirteen remaining individuals in detention at Camp Murphy who had not been allowed to post bail. These were the supposed leaders of the Chinese Bureau, including Koa Chian, Chin Sang, Ng Le Chiao, Dy Bon Un, and Yu Dy.[75]

A decision, whether on these thirteen persons or the ninety-nine out on bail, was not forthcoming for the next one and a half years, much to the dismay of the jinqiao themselves, ROC officials and Chinese leaders, and the military officials such as Ismael Lapus who had hatched Operation Chopsuy in an effort to prove their utility to their political masters—a group that now included Ramon Magsaysay, who had become president on December 30, 1953. A major reason for the delay was the changing composition of the three-person Deportation Board and the sheer volume of paperwork that had been generated during the hearings. In July 1956, the new ROC ambassador, Chen Chih-mai, estimated that records from the hearings amounted to 11,626 pages, a quantity of information that the board's members could not possibly be familiar with in great detail.[76]

As time passed, ROC officials in the Philippines and Taiwan became increasingly anxious about the harmful effects of the jinqiao an on their struggle against communism and the reputation that the ROC was trying to uphold as a protector of overseas Chinese communities and its nationals. From early on, Chen Chih-ping believed that the arrests had dealt a blow to the ROC's ideological struggle and exposed the weaknesses of the KMT and ACM.[77] In Taiwan, the tribulations of the jinqiao did not escape notice either, and not only among agencies such as the Ministry of Foreign Affairs (MOFA) and the KMT

Central Committee's Section Three, which focused on overseas Chinese affairs. At the second session of the ROC's First National Assembly in February 1954, representative Huang He-de, who had spent an extended period of
time in the Philippines, gave a detailed report on the Chinese in the islands,
part of which focused on the *jinqiao an*. Huang's report crystallized a general
sense of impatience among ROC legislators over the seeming lack of progress
of the trials. Claiming that Sino-communists must have infiltrated MIS for the
arrests to have taken place, Huang denounced the ROC Embassy for not taking the case seriously and supporting the detainees sufficiently and thus for
damaging the morale of the ROC's two hundred thousand or so Chinese compatriots in the Philippines.[78] Even before then, antipathy toward the Manila
Embassy was so widespread that in December 1953, Alexander Sycip's law firm
took the unusual step of writing to the ROC foreign minister to defend how
the embassy had conducted itself.[79]

Efforts by the united working group over the course of 1955 and 1956 to
have the ninety-nine *jinqiao* out on bail released entirely and twelve out of the
thirteen persons still in detention—excluding Koa Chian—released on bail
proved unsuccessful. Magsaysay, Vice President and Foreign Secretary Carlos
Garcia, and the secretary of justice were amenable, but bureaucratic inertia
and the military's insistence that Chinese communism continued to pose a
grave threat to the country prevented any progress from being made. The arrests of PCCP members in July 1954 and November 1955 only seemed to
confirm this. Yet precisely because of these fears, the embassy and the Philippine military during this period took steps to institutionalize intelligence cooperation between them, a move that both sides welcomed. According to an
agreement that they signed, embassy personnel with special training in intelligence affairs would serve as "consultants" to MIS by helping the military acquire and evaluate information on Chinese communists in the Philippines,
after which MIS reserved the right to act as it saw fit.[80] For the ROC, this was
a political gesture that might help with bargaining over the *jinqiao*. More than
that, it was an important step toward improving the anticommunist relationship between Manila and Taipei and legitimizing a mode of cooperation that
had existed earlier—such as during the *wu huagong an* in the late 1940s.

In the autumn of 1956, the Deportation Board finally delivered its verdict on
the thirteen *jinqiao*, recommending to Magsaysay that eleven of them be deported and two released entirely. Following the president's deportation order
on December 26, attorneys for the remaining detainees appealed to Magsaysay
and presented fresh evidence to the board, requesting that it retry the case.[81]
When the board rejected this request, the ROC attempted a political bargain. In
May 1957, President Garcia—Magsaysay had died in a plane crash on March 17

that year—ordered the deportation of Lao Han Keng, Sy Yan Wan, Sy Bun Chiong, and Go Chi Kok.[82] After consulting with the united working group, the embassy proposed that these four Cebu students along with Koa Chian be deported to Taiwan. In return, Garcia would release the ten innocent *jinqiao* into the custody of the embassy under the personal guarantee of the ambassador and on the condition that any or all of them would be produced within forty-eight hours if so required by the Philippine government.[83] Garcia was agreeable to this, and on July 26, Koa, Lao, Sy, Sy, and Go were deported to Taiwan. But this was not before the five of them threatened to commit suicide, using poison, knives, and metal rods that they had somehow acquired. The police had to subdue them with tear gas and force them onto the ROC military aircraft that had been sent to return them to their "motherland."[84]

The ten still in detention would have to wait longer before being released. Domestic politics and bureaucratic obstacles again proved complicating factors. Presidential elections were set for the end of 1957. The release order that Garcia issued on September 6, a Friday, reached the Immigration Bureau after its working hours, allowing military officials to meet with him over the weekend and persuade him to delay the order. The opposition Liberal Party, it said, would try to use their release against him; other members of Garcia's Nacionalista Party, including its chairman, shared the same concerns. Garcia promised that he would free them after the election, regardless of its outcome, and as a sign of his good faith instructed that Dy Bon Un be allowed to seek hospital treatment for having fallen seriously ill during his confinement.[85] Following Garcia's reelection, the number of imprisoned *jinqiao* decreased even further; Chin Sang was one of two detainees who successfully petitioned to self-deport to Hong Kong. Garcia eventually fulfilled his end of the bargain by ordering the last seven *jinqiao* released on bail on September 3, 1958.[86] Despite legally not being fully free, they do not appear to have ever again gone before the Deportation Board.

Three years later, in December 1961, a few days before he stepped down, President Garcia ordered the ninety-nine respondents in Deportation Cases Nos. 488 and 489 freed, citing the unsatisfactory evidence against them that Baby Zenaida and Felix Bonaobra had provided to the board.[87] The fourteen remaining Cebu reading club and PCCP members who had been arrested in late November 1955 also met their fates then. While their objective involvement in a communist organization could not be denied, their youth, naïveté, and vulnerability to propaganda rendered them sympathetic figures in the eyes of both the military and Chinese community leaders. Both parties tried to persuade the students to confess and apologize for their crimes and forswear communism. A former communist from England even addressed them on the evils of the ideology.[88] In 1960, the two states reached an agreement over how best to manage their situation: the Philippines would deport them but, in principle, allow them back into the country if Taiwan subjected them to *ganhua*.[89] In December 1961, Garcia first ordered twelve of the fourteen deported, but then modified his order to free an additional three persons. In exonerating one of them, Garcia said that she—much like Sy Yan Wan—appeared to have joined the club to be close to its leader, Lao Han Keng, whom she deeply loved, and not because of its ideology. She was therefore the "victim of an uncontrollable affection for a man."[90]

Koa Chian, Lao Han Keng, Sy Yan Wan, Sy Bun Chiong, and Go Chi Kok were sentenced differently in Taiwan, and all except Go (who received *ganhua*) had their initial sentences reduced. A great deal of credit for this must go to their families, attorneys, and the ROC Embassy, all of which persisted in seeking compassionate treatment of them. Sy Bun Chiong's father, for example, made an appeal to Chiang Kai-shek through the embassy.[91] Status, personal connections, and ideological credentials could amplify these appeals. Sy Yan Wan's father, David Sy Gaisano, arranged for a friend, who was a lawyer and senator, together with kinsman and former General Chamber of Commerce president Sy En, to meet with Ambassador Chen Chih-mai four days after his daughter's deportation.[92] Lao Han Keng's father hoped that his involvement in the KMT and ACM would help mitigate Lao's sentence. As for Koa Chian, who had no well-connected relatives to lobby on his behalf, Alexander Sycip argued that he not only had been tortured into providing names to MIS but had also later openly confessed to falsifying his testimony. In fact, Chinese leaders believed that it was only with Koa's help that the innocent detainees were freed.[93] In its appeal to the ROC Ministry of Defense, on whose judgment the case rested, the embassy expressed its view that the death penalty for Lao and Koa would damage the ROC's reputation among Chinese in the Philippines. Conversely, a more lenient sentence would enable the relatives of the accused and Chinese society to feel "gratitude and respect" (*gandai*) and strengthen their "affection toward their ancestral land" (*xiangwang zuguo zhi qing*).[94]

Chinese communism in the Philippines had not totally withered away by the early 1950s, and neither was diasporic support for Nationalist China as absolute as the KMT would have liked. Through the *jinqiao an* and the Cebu reading club affair, this chapter has used the experiences of Koa Chian, Lao Han Keng, Sy Yan Wan, Sy Bun Chiong, and Go Chi Kok to show that communism persisted among some Philippine Chinese as an ideological alternative to the Cold War status quo; not all trod the same self-serving ideological path as the practicing anticommunists in chapter 3. The Chinese Bureau that Koa joined and later "exposed" was a remnant of the older Chinese leftist movement in the country. The reading club and PCCP, by contrast, were a sui generis organization whose young members were driven by ideology and opposition to a Sinophobic, corrupt Filipino establishment as much as by love, anger, and jealousy. While these "communists" were ultimately victims of the state, there was nonetheless space for them to confuse and, in Koa's case, subvert Manila's and Taipei's attempts to produce intelligence on Chinese communism. In seeking to protect the bureau and himself, Koa exploited Manila's linguistic incapacities and ignorance of Chinese naming practices but ironically ended up contributing to the December 1952 mass arrests.

These arrests, and those of the PCCP a few years later, precipitated a crisis for Nationalist China and Chinese leaders in the Philippines, both of whom claimed and sought to protect Chinese society. In response to events, state and diaspora came together to contest a particular manifestation of anticommunism that threatened to destroy their reputations and *Fangong kang'E*. They raised money, hired lawyers to expose the inadequate evidence against the *jinqiao*, and bargained directly with the president to free these detainees. In the cases of Koa and Lao, they even appealed to their own government. Finally, the ROC aimed to mend its anticommunist relationship with the Philippine military and rebalance their relationship of shared sovereignty. By seconding its consultants to MIS, the embassy hoped to influence any future attempts at identifying and arresting Chinese communists and prevent any reoccurrence of what happened on December 27. In the long term, this rectification of intelligence collaboration was arguably the most significant consequence of the drawn-out, overlapping sagas of the *jinqiao* and the Cebu students.

In June 1965, the embassy summarized the state of Chinese communism in the Philippines to Taipei. No reliable statistics existed, it concluded, implicitly questioning a recent Senate report that estimated that there were five thousand Chinese Reds in the country. A year earlier, the Philippine authorities captured PKP leader Jesus Lava, who corroborated the existence of the Chinese Bureau. According to the ROC Embassy, the bureau had contributed PHP 20,000 to the Huks every three months for over a decade, from 1946 to 1956. However, after 1958, the bureau was "dissolved" (*chexiao*), and there was nothing to suggest that the Huks and Chinese communists continued to collaborate with each other after then.[95]

In July 2016, on a visit to the Philippines, I met a member of the Sy Gaisano family through a mutual acquaintance and learned what happened to Sy Yan Wan. It appears that she was treated well in prison and that her father eventually succeeded in having her freed before her sentence ended. Sy then lived in Australia. Sometime around the Cultural Revolution, however, she left Australia for mainland China with the help of a CCP-supporting aunt who had attended Peking University and without informing other family members. She then vanished. Possibly in the early 1970s, an uncle of hers visiting China tracked her down. Today, she lives in the western United States. I was asked not to inquire further about her or the traumatic events of her young adulthood. Was she searching for adventure when she abandoned her life in Australia and fled to China, and had she been lying to her captors all those years ago when she claimed to "no longer want to be a communist"? We may never know.[96]

CHAPTER 5

Networking Ideology

Chinese Society and Transnational Anticommunism, 1954–1960

On January 21, 1972, a month before US president Richard M. Nixon visited the People's Republic of China (PRC), the sixth volume of *Youth World* (*Shijie qingnian*) was published by the Federation of Filipino-Chinese Chambers of Commerce and Industry (Feihua Shanglian Zonghui, or Shang Zong). It featured an assortment of essays, poems, short fiction, photographs, and illustrations, many explicitly ideological in nature, others implicitly so. Articles on international affairs updated readers on geopolitical issues, and among these pieces was the translation of a speech that Anthony Kubek, a right-wing US political scientist connected to the pro-Chiang "China Lobby" and former visiting professor in Taiwan, had delivered during his recent visit to the Philippines. In it, the author of such McCarthyite polemics as *Communism at Pearl Harbor: How the Communists Helped to Bring on Pearl Harbor and Open Up Asia to Communization* and *How the Far East Was Lost: American Policy and the Creation of Communist China, 1941–1949* warned that Red subversion posed a greater danger to the United States than ever before because of, not despite, the PRC's entry into the United Nations half a year earlier.

Complementing these analyses were pieces that transposed what the Republic of China (ROC) and its advocates considered a global struggle against communism into personalized, localized, and sentimentalized registers. For example, an unnamed sixty-year-old Jinjiang native who had managed to visit his ailing mother in China described the poverty, backwardness, and despair that had greeted him on his bittersweet return to his hometown. It is unclear how far his narrative was genuine or embellished from generic tropes about mainland China in Kuomintang (KMT) propaganda. Still more concrete than that was an essay titled "I Love the Republic of China" ("Wo ai Zhonghua min-guo"). Its author, Cai Liyi, studied at one of the Philippines' premier Chinese schools, Chiang Kai-shek College (Zhongzheng xueyuan, or CKSC; Chiang Kai-shek High School [CKSHS] until 1965). The essay waxed lyrical about Cai's love for Chinese history and bemoaned the communists' role in dividing the Chinese nation into two. Despite being born in the Philippines, she declared that her "person, blood, bones, skin, and heart in particular" (wo de ren, wo de xue, wo de gutou, pifu, tebie shi wo de xin) forever belonged to the ROC, her ancestral land (zuguo). In concluding, she confidently repeated a standard KMT talking point by claiming that the communists would soon be vanquished and that the ROC would imminently unite all Chinese people to reconquer the mainland.[1]

It is easy, in hindsight, to read these three items as embodying the ROC and its supporters' futile, reactionary defiance of the international situation in the early 1970s. However, in the context of Philippine-Chinese society, the views expressed reflected the ideological mainstream as shaped by the makers of Chinese civic opinion and would not be out of place in a school classroom, speech, or newspaper at virtually any moment from the 1950s to the mid-1970s. These pieces highlight the connections between international and local manifestations of anticommunism; they suggest that readers of Shijie qingnian were supposed to imagine themselves as members of a transnational ideological community participating in a struggle that was simultaneously personal, China-centric, and global. This and other editions of the magazine and similar publications reveal that while not every aspect of Chinese society in the Philippines may have revolved around the reproduction and transmission of anti-communism, the threads of ideology were woven into the fabric of society and cannot be disentangled from it.

Comparable communities to the Philippine Chinese in this period were politically more diverse. Despite the conservatism of its elites, Filipino society was a space for considerable political contention and its public sphere was marked by an openness toward the PRC, especially during the Ferdinand Marcos administration. Although Marcos opposed diplomatic relations with Beijing until the early 1970s, he allowed Filipinos to visit the PRC from the start of his presidency in 1965. Commenting on the significance of such visits, the Philippines Free Press even said in June 1966: "It is the success of Communist China that the beneficiaries of the present social order—the rich, the comfortable, the government officials that serve them, the Establishment—must fear."[2] No Chinese-language publication in the Philippines would have dared publish something like that. In Indonesia, a "communal battle between the Red and the Blue," as Taomo Zhou puts it, unfolded during the 1950s among Sino-Indonesians. By the end of the decade, pro-communist groups in Indonesia had gained greater control over the Chinese media, schools, and organizations than their pro-Nationalist rivals had.[3] The KMT was banned there in the late 1950s and its highest-ranking member, Mah Soo-Lay, expelled in 1960.[4] Chinese society in Indonesia had moved in the opposite ideological direction from that in the Philippines. Elsewhere in the Chinese diasporic world, anticommunism became decoupled from supporting the KMT regime. In the United States, most Chinese publicly claimed to support "Free China" and hate communism. But, as the historian Charlotte Brooks argues, the US KMT's anticommunist collaboration with the federal government compromised its reputation among ordinary Chinese Americans. After the 1956 immigration fraud investigation, they recognized that the ROC could not defend them.[5]

In the Philippines, anticommunism and pro-KMT sentiment among Chinese went hand in hand. The outward ideological uniformity of Chinese society there from the mid-1950s onward, I argue, stemmed significantly from the reorganization of its leadership institutions and networks. Beginning with the Shang Zong, commercial and cultural leaders consolidated the social foundations of Chinese anticommunism in the Philippines in response to developments such as the *jinqiao an*, the Cebu students' affair, and Manila's efforts to regulate Chinese commerce and education. By the end of the 1950s, community governance was concentrated in five federated organizations and in the hands of a small group of pro-KMT figures. These individuals defined society's priorities, high among which was the propagation of anticommunism as a centripetal force and worldview that could unite Filipinos, Chinese, and their respective governments. The Shang Zong, KMT, Philippine Chinese Anti-Communist League (Feilübin Huaqiao Fangong Kang'E Zonghui, or PCACL), General Association of Chinese Schools (Feilübin Huaqiao Xuexiao Lianhe Zonghui, or Xiao Zong), and Grand Family Association (Feilübin Ge Zongqin Hui Lianhehui, or Zong Lian)—the "Big Five"—overlapped in leadership, facilitated useful relations with Filipinos, and enabled the seemingly frictionless diffusion of anticommunist ideology and practices. Cultural life and schools in particular became the principal sites for propagandization, mobilization, and activism in support of the ROC and *Fangong kang'E*.

These institutions and networks and the persons who participated in them were part of not only an intra-Asian anticommunist ecumene but also a global anticommunist movement. Like Chinese revolutionaries and reformers in the early twentieth century, pro-KMT ideologues within and beyond the Philippines

after 1949 hoped to mobilize the diaspora in support of "China" by situating local and national struggles against communism within a wider ideological landscape. As the work of Anna Belogurova on Chinese communist networks in
Southeast Asia and Tim Harper on the prewar Asian revolutionary underground
shows, left-wing notions of anti-imperialism have long shaped how we think
about internationalism and cosmopolitanism in the decolonizing world.[6] This
chapter, by contrast, maps some of the connections between Taiwan, the Philippine Chinese, Filipinos, and world anticommunism, emphasizing how
events such as the Hungarian Revolution against Soviet rule in 1956 and organizations such as the Asian Peoples' Anti-Communist League (APACL) intersected with the diasporic Cold War being waged in a particular Southeast Asian
country.

Restructuring Chinese Society in the 1950s

The events of December 27, 1952, and their long, drawn-out aftermath were
part of a series of uncoordinated efforts by the postwar Philippine state to exercise greater sovereignty over its Chinese population and align it more closely
with Filipino national interests. In the 1950s, interventions into trade and commerce, education, and individual security helped effect a top-down restructuring
of Chinese society, starting in 1954 with the displacement of the General Chamber of Commerce from its position of leadership. Anticommunism was integral
to social reorganization. Whereas linguistic and physiognomic differences, separate school systems, de jure differences in nationality, and internalized prejudices
on both sides could make ethno-cultural divisions difficult to bridge, ideology
was a common ground for Chinese and Filipinos alike. To an extent, it helped
mitigate the factionalism within Chinese society that social restructuring exacerbated. For such reasons, anticommunism was amplified and institutionalized from the mid-1950s onward to a much greater degree than before.

The impact of Filipinization, like that of other anti-Chinese nationalization
movements in Southeast Asia, was felt in both trade and commerce, on the one
hand, and education, on the other. Filipino nationalists had long sought to curb
what they perceived to be Chinese domination of the national economy, but it
was only after Ramon Magsaysay's election and the Nacionalista Party's overwhelming victory in the presidential and legislative elections of 1953 that the
political climate shifted decisively in a populist direction. In the first half of
1954, legislators capitalized on the new president's receptiveness toward nationalization and introduced a total of forty-seven bills targeting alien control
of economic and social sectors and covering everything from the retail trade to

universities to duck rearing. With Magsaysay's support, and despite concerted opposition from Chinese leaders and the ROC, one such bill was eventually signed into law on June 19, 1954, as Republic Act (R.A.) No. 1180.[7] The Retail Trade Nationalization Act, as it was known, required corporations involved in retailing that were not 100 percent owned by Filipinos to shut down within a decade. The legal campaign by Chinese leaders to have it overturned in the Supreme Court failed in 1957, and further limits on foreign economic activity followed under the "Filipino First" policy of the Carlos Garcia administration.[8]

Unlike the protracted and ultimately successful campaign to limit Chinese involvement in the retail trade, government intervention in the Chinese cultural sphere took place quickly but with minimal effect. Prompted by the *jinqiao an* and especially the Cebu arrests, the Committee on Un-Filipino Activities (CUFA) alleged communist infiltration of Chinese schools in early 1955, resulting in a systematic investigation by the Board of National Education. The August 1955 report that resulted from it affirmed the need for greater state control of the country's 160 or so Chinese private schools, only a handful of which had registered with the Department of Education. It described the Chinese curriculum of these dual-language schools as a "separate and complete system of education aimed at the training of the students for good Chinese citizenship" and whose every aspect, from programs of instruction to course materials to teacher qualifications—was supervised by the ROC. With intelligence reports "tending to show the danger of subversive influences infiltrating these courses," Philippine supervision of them was necessary, the report concluded. The investigatory committee was adamant, furthermore, that even the Chinese-language curriculum come under Manila's jurisdiction, for while the Treaty of Amity had guaranteed Chinese nationals the right to establish schools for their children, it also subjected this right to Philippine law.[9] Beyond the Department of Education, some officials, including the immigration commissioner, even called for all Chinese schools in the country to be shut down.[10]

Following the report, discussions commenced between the two states and local Chinese educators on how to address the concerns that it raised. In December 1955, a memorandum of understanding signed by Vice President Garcia and the ROC ambassador outlined the terms of cooperation going forward. All Chinese schools not registered and any that were to be established had to be registered with the Bureau of Private Schools. Furthermore, while they had the freedom to teach any subjects that were required by the ROC, in accordance with the Treaty of Amity, they also had to meet minimum curricular standards required of all Philippine public and private schools. To ensure that, a joint technical committee was formed to draw up a new curriculum for all Chinese schools. This went into effect in the 1956–1957 school year and eliminated separate Chinese and English departments, integrating Chinese and English subjects into a single program of study.[11]

As state interventions in Chinese education in Southeast Asia went, this was far from being disruptive and radical. Filipinization left Chinese-language instruction and thus the KMT's control of the education system essentially untouched. One reason, admitted the director of private schools, was that the Education Department lacked the funds to hire Chinese-speaking employees, so it had no actual means of supervising the Chinese curriculum, let alone designing a new one.[12] Another reason, as the political scientist Robert O. Tilman has argued, was that Philippine politicians did not truly believe that assimilating local Chinese was possible and emphasized anticommunism over assimilation. They argued, "The one way to make certain that the Chinese schools are anti-communist is to permit the Nationalist government to oversee them," even if that entailed perpetuating cultural differences between Chinese and Filipinos.[13] Still, Chinese educators feared further encroachment on their bailiwick by an increasingly activist state.

The Shang Zong, founded on March 29, 1954, was born of and into an atmosphere of crisis that the *jinqiao an* and the stream of nationalization bills after Magsaysay's election had created. Its origins, however, lie in both factional disputes within Chinese society and dissatisfaction with the General Chamber of Commerce. The organization's official history and the memoirs of its first secretary, Tang Tack, rationalize the movement toward federation from the late 1940s onward as an attempt to establish an integrated leadership structure for the Chinese community. This structure would protect the interests of Chinese trade and commercial associations throughout the Philippines more effectively than the Manila-centered General Chamber did.[14] But when the General Chamber resisted calls for organizational reform, pro-federation members from within the chamber's ranks rallied around the youthful and charismatic president of the Rice and Sugar Association, Antonio Roxas Chua, while also canvassing for support from three senior leaders of the community: Yu Khe Thai, Peter Lim, and Yao Shiong Shio.[15] Discussions followed between Roxas Chua and others, on one side, and the General Chamber faction, led by chamber president Sy En and supported by ROC ambassador Chen Chih-ping, on the other. While Sy verbally backed the idea of a federation, he hoped that the General Chamber would govern it, rather than be reduced to one among hundreds of similar institutions. The contest between these factions was resolved by popular referendum at a three-day meeting of Chinese business organizations in Manila on March 26–29. Elections for the new federation's board of directors reflected the power shift that had taken place. Yu, Lim, Yao, and Roxas Chua garnered the most votes, with Sy coming in a distant fifth— enough to secure a place on the Shang Zong's board alongside several other General Chamber loyalists.[16] Despite this conciliatory gesture, the chamber refused to join the Shang Zong until 1968, by which point Sy had died. In 1991, the chamber seceded from the Shang Zong.[17] It remains separate from and in the shadow of the Shang Zong today.

Official and semiofficial narratives of the Shang Zong depict its formation as a principled, forward-looking, and popular response to the elitism, insularity, and shortcomings of the General Chamber. Other accounts, including those of contemporary scholars of the Shang Zong, are more attentive to power dynamics. In Chen Chih-ping's analysis, for instance, Yu Khe Thai, Peter Lim, Yao Shiong Shio, and Antonio Roxas Chua belonged to what he called the party— that is to say, KMT—faction in opposition to Sy En, Alfonso Sycip, Dy Huan Chay, and chamber loyalists. For Chen, the formation of the Shang Zong represented the climax of a long-running feud between the chamber and the KMT for control over the Chinese community. In other words, as Sy En exclaimed angrily after coming in only fifth in the board elections, the Shang Zong was a KMT organ.[18] Two historians of the Shang Zong make this very argument, although neither appears to have read Chen's report.[19] The problem with this distinction between factions is that Sy was a KMT member, while Yu Khe Thai was not. Other scholars have tried to resolve this discrepancy by arguing that Sy did not belong to the "party" faction because he was indifferent to party affairs and did want the KMT to become involved in the chamber, whose leadership he sought to dominate. Conversely, Yu was not a KMT member but was supported by the party because he was a strong and respected leader.[20]

As the ROC Ministry of Foreign Affairs (MOFA) Archives and the KMT Archives feature virtually nothing of the *zongzhibu*'s internal deliberations on this squabble, the degree to which the party influenced proceedings may never be known. In 1994, Lim Soo Chan, the *zongzhibu*'s secretary-general from the mid-1960s to 1987, said that the KMT "never interfered" (*congbu ganyu*) in the Shang Zong's elections and had no way of doing so.[21] It is clear, however, that the party had incorporative designs on Chinese organizations outside its ambit, especially those that had been its enemies. One of these was the Chinese Freemasons. Following the deportation of the Chinese communist movement's financier and Hongmen leader Co Pak in February 1951, the KMT moved swiftly to install two ranking party members as chairman of the Hongmen Association and principal of its main school.[22] The Hongmen, from that point onward, was a thoroughly pro-KMT association.

It is also evident that the *zongzhibu* had long detested the General Chamber for refusing to submit to party control and being insufficiently committed to the KMT's anticommunist agenda. Conversely, the party was openly supportive of the Shang Zong from the outset. On March 28 and 29, 1954, the *Great China Press*, run by Koa Chun-te, praised Magsaysay's speech at the opening ceremony of the new organization. Addressing an audience of merchants, Magsaysay said little about economic affairs and focused on exhorting them to do more to oppose communism:

> You cannot combat this menace by wishing that it will disappear, by merely standing with folded arms and hoping it will never disturb you. You can defeat it only by constant vigilance and action. To exercise such vigilance and to take active part in the effort against Communism is the duty you owe to the community, the safeguard you owe to yourself and your children. . . .
>
> . . . [Y]our duty is to unite in the struggle against Communism regardless of the differences that may divide you in other matters. . . .
>
> In a community as large as yours, there are bound to be a few who spoil the reputation of the many. Clean your own house of these undesirable elements and you will achieve stronger unity with your Filipino neighbors.[23]

In fewer than eight hundred words, Magsaysay spelled out to Chinese leaders and ROC officials what his administration expected of them. In describing anticommunism as a unifying force within Chinese society and between Chinese and Filipinos, he provided *huaqiao* elites a ready-made justification for intensifying their ideological activism. His speech came as no surprise to those in attendance, as the ROC Embassy had worked with the Shang Zong's leaders beforehand to prepare these very talking points.[24]

The *Great China Press* concurred with Magsaysay's thinly veiled criticism of the Chinese community. So-called Philippine-Chinese leaders, it said on March 28, enjoyed boasting that they were the foremost anticommunists in Southeast Asia, but this claim deceived both themselves and others. Its editorial on March 29 went further. His speech was a warning, it said; failure to heed it would result in dire consequences for the community. Responsibility for the lack of an active and united Chinese anticommunist movement in the Philippines lay primarily with the ROC Embassy, which had provided ineffectual leadership by not heeding calls to reform the Philippine-Chinese United Organization in Support of Anti-Communist Movement (ACM).[25] That the PCACL was formed in September 1956 to replace the ACM suggests not only that the

KMT influenced the Shang Zong but also that the two organizations shared ideological goals.

The community's response to Manila's intervention in Chinese education was led by Pao Shih-tien, the principal of CKSHS. Born in Hubei, Pao did not speak Hokkien, nor did he own any businesses, and because of that he was twice removed from mainstream Chinese society. His ideological credentials, by contrast, were immaculate. Having taught at the KMT's political reeducation school in Nanchang in 1935, Pao helped establish CKSHS in 1939 with Ong Chuan Seng. During the Japanese occupation, he drafted the constitution of the Chinese Overseas Wartime Hsuehkan Militia (COWHM). After the war, when the KMT recalled Ong to China to serve on the Legislative Yuan, Pao became the school's acting principal and then principal after Yu Khe Thai stepped down in 1959.[26]

Time and again, in English and Chinese, Pao sought to counter the arguments put forth by the Department of Education in favor of greater state control of Chinese schools. Far from being an obstacle to assimilation, Pao believed that Chinese schools hastened it and facilitated interracial understanding by admitting Filipinos, encouraging interactions between Chinese and Filipino students and staff, and teaching Filipino and Chinese history and culture.[27] As for the accusation that they fostered divided loyalties among their Chinese students, Pao noted that these students were citizens of the ROC and permanent residents of the Philippines by law and that naturalization was a difficult and expensive procedure. Therefore, schools should not be blamed for "simply doing what they should do" and preparing students to be "good citizens of China"—on top of teaching subjects that had been prescribed by the Philippine state such as Philippine history and government and Philippine social life. Referring to the Treaty of Amity, Pao argued that there was no constitutional basis for abolishing Chinese schools and that doing so would be tantamount to confiscating private property without just compensation.[28] A final argument that he and others made to justify the existence of Chinese schools was that they were bastions of anticommunism and that their (Chinese) students were utterly loyal to Nationalist China. There was "absolutely no possibility of red infiltration into these schools," which were "the vanguards of the anti-Communist movement," he proclaimed on multiple occasions, dismissing the Cebu reading club arrests and other evidence to the contrary as isolated incidents.[29]

Similar to what Chinese businessmen had done in 1954, Chinese educators worked swiftly to federate themselves in response to Filipinization and present a common front to the Philippine authorities. In April 1957, 131 Chinese principals or school representatives from across the country gathered at the

ROC Embassy for a four-day conference that established the General Association of Chinese Schools.[30] Led by Pao and featuring a constitution that was drafted by the embassy, the Xiao Zong joined the KMT, Shang Zong, and PCACL as the fourth of the Big Five.[31] The joint declaration that it issued signaled the organization's priorities. The Chinese nation (*minzu*) was under attack by "Red imperialism" (*chise diguo zhuyi*). It fell on educators to unite and train the next generation of youths to fight for the recovery and restoration of their homeland. Only after this ritualized gesture toward the ideological status quo did the declaration turn toward the history of Chinese education in the Philippines. In a revealingly chauvinistic expression, it stated that had Chinese schools not existed, *huaqiao* youth in the country would have long since become "barbarians" (*yi*).[32]

Transnational Anticommunism and the Founding of the PCACL

The origins of the PCACL, more so than the Shang Zong's and Xiao Zong's, lie both within and beyond the Philippines. By the mid-1950s, it was apparent that the ACM had done little except pad the resumes of its members. After the *jinqiao an*, the ACM came under criticism from the ROC ambassador for existing "in name only" (*youming wushi*).[33] Calls to revitalize the Chinese anti-communist movement were made at the first meeting of the June 1954 Shang Zong conference, partly in response to Magsaysay's speech. Two years later, discussions began in earnest between Chinese leaders and Taiwan to form the PCACL.

The occasion that sparked these discussions was the second meeting of the Asian Peoples' Anti-Communist League (APACL) in Manila in March 1956. Formed in June 1954 by Taiwan and South Korea (but without US input), the APACL was a transnational organization of activists from across Asia that met annually to denounce the evils of communism and neutralism and exhort its members and the world to redouble their efforts against the Soviet Union and its puppets in China, North Korea, and North Vietnam. Individual chapters of the APACL, based at the time in Taiwan, South Korea, the Philippines, South Vietnam, Hong Kong, Macao, and the Ryukyu Islands, coordinated propaganda activities among like-minded government and civic groups in their countries or cities. The APACL chapter in the Philippines, for instance, was connected to the state security apparatus through Undersecretary of Defense Jose M. Crisol, among other military and defense officials, and headed by Catholic intellectual Jose Ma. Hernandez, an admirer of Taiwan and a staunch defender of Chinese education in the Philippines. Through civic organizations such as the Philippine Anti-Communist League (PACL) and links with the ROC state, Chinese anticommunists in the country became part of this network of ideologues that transcended ethnic and national divisions, the local and the transnational, and the boundaries between state and society. Three "local" Chinese were members of the Philippine delegation at the Manila meeting of the APACL, including Sy En, who was then a vice-chairman of the ACM, and four were part of the ROC delegation, including Cua Siok Po. Among the "experts" on communism who attended the meeting was "Colonel" Shih I-Sheng.[34] His antics in the late 1940s and early 1950s seemingly forgotten or forgiven, Shih had reentered public life and was even elected to the Shang Zong's first board of directors.[35]

The rising tide of Asian anticommunism in the mid-1950s and the special relationship between Taiwan and the Philippine Chinese hastened the ACM's transformation into the PCACL. Following a speech by APACL chairman and ex-ROC Interior minister Ku Cheng-kang calling on the ACM to intensify its activities, Ku and ROC ambassador Chen Chih-mai met with Chinese leaders to organize the PCACL.[36] Transnational in orientation, the PCACL was also supposed to mitigate some of the factional divisions that the formation of the Shang Zong two years earlier had exacerbated. Thus, Sy En and Dy Huan Chay were both involved in organizing the PCACL, with Sy maintaining his reputation as one of the leaders of Chinese anticommunism in the Philippines by participating in the preparatory committee for the new organization. Sy even secured his place on its five-person Standing Committee (which also included Yu Khe Thai, Chua Lamco, Yao Shiong Shio, and Peter Lim), despite finishing in nineteenth place out of sixty in the PCACL's ranked elections in September 1956.[37] That same year, the Shang Zong even invited the chamber to become part of it, but Sy rejected this offer.[38] A less obvious social division that the PCACL transcended was between merchants, represented by the Shang Zong, and the intelligentsia, comprising journalists and educators such as Pao Shih-tien, Cua Siok Po, the *Fookien Times*' Go Puan Seng, and the historian and principal Liu Chi-tien. By incorporating Pao, Cua, Go, and Liu into its ranks, the PCACL drew on their expertise in cultural propaganda to ensure that vital spheres of Chinese public life were filled with the right kind of information.

Yet it was also clear that the PCACL reflected the power shifts that had taken place within Chinese society. Alfonso Sycip, for example, for many years the president of the General Chamber, resigned as chairman of the ACM in April 1956, citing work and old age (he was seventy-three).[39] Shang Zong president Yu Khe Thai became chairman of the PCACL while continuing to head the Chinese Welfare Association. He and other Shang Zong leaders, along with intellectuals like Pao and Cua—who was at the time secretary-general of the KMT *zongzhibu* and later served as the PCACL's secretary—dominated the highest echelons of political, economic, and cultural power in Chinese society across a network of interlocking civic institutions that was the densest across Southeast Asia. According to the Overseas Chinese Affairs Commission (OCAC), the ratio of Chinese civic organizations to the size of the Chinese population in the Philippines in 1958 was 1 to 20 (5 percent), compared to only 1 to 143 (0.7 percent) in second-placed Burma and 1 to 250 (0.4 percent) in Malaya.[40]

Like the APACL meeting in March, the three-day inaugural convention of the PCACL in September 1956 was a transnational moment that straddled the boundaries between the state and society. As a social occasion hosted by the ROC Embassy, it was an opportunity for Chinese elites to cultivate officials in the Magsaysay administration and represent their ideological bona fides to their host country. In this way, the ceremonial dimensions of anticommunism were not incidental to or separate from its substance. As the anthropologist Jacques Amyot's fieldwork in 1950s Manila suggests, Chinese gatherings to which Filipinos were invited were fundamentally transactional in nature and dictated by the advantages to be gained from associating with the right people.[41] Jose M. Crisol, Jose Ma. Hernandez, and Ku Cheng-kang were present, as was a US diplomatic representative, all of whom spoke to the 310 delegates from 182 organizations across the country that had gathered in Manila. In what typified the global dimensions of high-profile ideological occasions such as this, messages of congratulation and well-wishes poured in from Chiang, Magsaysay, Garcia, and other politicians, military officials, and right-wing groups in the Philippines, Taiwan, the United States, and elsewhere in the anticommunist ecumene.[42] Coming just a few months after the ROC Embassy had agreed to second intelligence agents to serve as consultants to the Military Intelligence Service (MIS), the convention symbolically affirmed the closer anticommunist ties between Manila, Taipei, and Chinese society that Magsaysay had called for in June 1954. An important step toward finding a political solution to the *jinqiao an* was winning over persons like Crisol and the armed forces chief of staff, who spoke at the convention.

Preparatory meetings during the six months before the convention and meetings during the convention itself make it clear how Chinese leaders understood anticommunism and the PCACL's role in society. The preparatory committee agreed from the outset that the KMT, Shang Zong, and General Chamber, together with schools, clan associations, and the Women's Association, were to be represented within the PCACL.[43] In September, the convention stressed the importance of cultural propaganda and the media to the

PCACL's work. For instance, the assembled delegates agreed to increase the volume of anticommunist periodicals then in circulation and to create a radio station specifically for anticommunist broadcasting. Other proposals that passed muster involved the use of praise and censure as tactics to shape civic and political attitudes. The delegates agreed, for instance, to commend Singapore's chief minister Lim Yew Hock for his crackdown on leftist trade unions, teachers, and students, in the hope of encouraging a similarly vigilant attitude toward the dormant but ever-present threat of communist subversion in the Philippines.[44]

By the end of the 1950s, therefore, the Big Five had come to define Chinese civic identity in the Philippines. They were led by a small group of persons and overlapped in both structure and function, allowing for the rapid propagation of ideology across social fields. Redundancy, rather than specialization, was central to this ideological uniformity. With Chinese society heavily institutionalized and hierarchically structured, its elites were able to mobilize its members more effectively. Shang Zong membership fees, for example, were easily channeled into propaganda events, publicity for which could be rapidly disseminated through the Shang Zong, the KMT, schools, and newspapers such as the *Great China Press* and *Kong Li Po*. Schools and the KMT *zongzhibu* provided convenient, symbolically meaningful venues and captive audiences of party members and students for large-scale PCACL events. In fact, the PCACL, KMT, Xiao Zong, and Zong Lian were all headquartered in the same building, later named Liberty Hall (Ziyou Dasha) at Benavidez Street.[45] One Filipino journalist called it a "resplendent, enormous, six-story building sprawled over a block on a commercial street."[46] The Shang Zong was within walking distance; Binondo, Manila's Chinatown, is not a large area. Beyond Manila, this compression of institutional, ideological, and physical space was even more acute. Schools, local chambers of commerce, and KMT branches often occupied the same building and were indistinguishable from each other. These compound organizations served as the structural basis for PCACL branches. A local chamber of commerce or school event might double up as a PCACL rally, for example.

The closest parallels here are not between the Philippine and other overseas Chinese, but between the Philippine Chinese and Taiwan. In 1950, a defeated and demoralized KMT set about reforming itself to transform Taiwan Province, counterattack mainland China, and defeat the Chinese Communist Party (CCP). For the economist Ramon Myers and the historian Hsiao-ting Lin, the reforms that Chiang Kai-shek presided over from 1950 to 1952 were "probably [his] greatest achievement as leader of the KMT."[47] By the end of this period, aided by martial law, hierarchical party organs had been installed at all levels of the state and representative bodies and reached into all organized social sectors, from labor unions to schools. The KMT had laid the foundations for what the political scientists Yun-han Chu and Jih-wen Lin call the "structural symbiosis between the party and the state" and what historians of the Nanjing-era KMT describe as "partification" (*danghua*). The party was the only coordinating mechanism among disparate state organs and the only organizational link across different social sectors. It regulated the access of social actors to the state, suppressed any efforts to form alternative power blocs, and, through a system of recruitment, training, and promotion for senior government officials and military officers, ensured widespread ideological coherence.[48]

Chinese leaders and KMT members in the Philippines were all too aware of Taiwan's progress under the new-look Nationalist party-state. The modus operandi of the KMT overseas was broadly similar to that of the party in "China." In Taiwan, the KMT's incursions into society were backed by a partified state apparatus within its sovereign territory and empowered by extra-constitutional legal arrangements and emergency decrees under a state of national emergency. This precise configuration of enabling institutions and laws did not obtain in mainland China from 1927 to 1949 and certainly not in the postcolonial Philippines. There, as the *jinqiao an* shows, the state could be an obstacle to the KMT. Still, as the examples of collaboration between the Philippine military and the ROC against suspected Chinese communists suggest, there were frequent moments of convergence between the interests of Nationalist China and those of the "foreign" state that it sought to influence. In other respects, particularly with regard to Chinese cultural affairs, Manila did not stand in the way of the KMT's expansion of sovereignty and efforts to create ideological coherence.

Chinese Culture, Education, and the Taiwan Connection

For Chinese anticommunists in the Philippines, culture was a particularly important sphere of social life for reproducing ideology and inculcating nationalism, much as it had always been to the KMT as a mainland Chinese, Taiwanese, and overseas political movement. In February 1934, eight months before the end of the KMT's campaign against the Jiangxi Soviet, Chiang Kai-shek launched the New Life Movement, which aimed to regenerate the Chinese nation by transforming the everyday lives and moral values of its citizens. From personal hygiene and sartorial choices to walking on the correct side of the road and avoiding spitting and urinating in public, the movement prescribed ideal forms of personal conduct that were meant to subsume the individual to the nation. In this sense, as the historian Arif Dirlik has observed, it shared with communist mass movements the objective of "fashioning a citizenry responsive to national needs, willing to endure hardship for the good of society, and ready to exert the maximum effort for the achievement of national progress." However, whereas communist movements were premised on the indispensability of class struggle to political transformation, the KMT sought to "substitute the reform of individuals for all structural change" and to avoid social conflict.[49] Its goal, as the historian Brian Tsui writes, was to create an "everyday culture that engaged the masses in renovation of the spirit, rather than realignment of property relations" and to "offset the alienating effects of capitalist modernity," to which the party was not entirely hostile.[50]

After 1949, the KMT's culture war against the CCP assumed a further dimension with its invention and weaponization of "Chinese tradition" and its self-fashioning as the guardian of this tradition. In Taiwan, this notion of guardianship was reflected in the KMT's proprietary attitude toward historical artifacts, classic texts, and especially language. These were core elements of a national culture, on which identification with the party-state was to be built and which the materialistic CCP was supposedly bent on destroying. After half a century of Japanese rule, the Taiwanese had to be re-Sinicized by being forced to speak standard Chinese (Mandarin), the "national language" (*guoyu*), and forbidden to use colloquial Taiwanese or Japanese. Simplified Chinese characters were likewise prohibited, and using them could be interpreted as a sign of communist sympathies. In late 1966, in reaction to the Cultural Revolution, Chiang proclaimed the Cultural Renaissance Movement (Zhonghua Wenhua Fuxing Yundong). With state support, an "all-encompassing culture industry" emerged to promote the Confucian classics; encourage a new literary and art movement based on ethics, democracy, and science; preserve historical artifacts; finance tourism; construct cultural infrastructure such as art galleries and museums; and, like the New Life Movement, inculcate in persons conservative ethical values and "correct" social and individual behavior.[51] If communism targeted Confucius and other symbols of "feudal" China for elimination, the KMT sought to cultivate a respect for traditional values in the name of legitimizing the existing social order and the "rightful" Chinese government.

Culture was similarly the foundation for the KMT's promotion of overseas Chinese affairs. Nationalist China's diasporic networks and mobilizational efforts were grounded in the imagined reality of a Chinese cultural nation that transcended territorial borders but that could be made to support the territorial nation-state. With the KMT having lost the mainland to the CCP in 1949, it was all the more important for the state to nurture the ties of Chineseness that supposedly bound *huaqiao* to "China." Like the "Taiwanese" whom the KMT had to reconvert into "Chinese" national subjects, *huaqiao*, and mestizos in particular, had to be continually Sinicized to mitigate indigenization. No aspect of *qiaowu* thus mattered more than education. To control schools was to control bodies; schools that the KMT controlled were crucial mechanisms for Sinicization and ideological indoctrination and critical nodes in the party-state's transnational networks.

Contrary to Pao Shih-tien's apologetics, therefore, the Philippine Department of Education was not inaccurate in assessing Chinese schools as a force for ethno-cultural malintegration. The US political scientist Gerald A. McBeath, in his 1973 study of the Chinese community, concluded that the education system represented "the last stand of Chinese communalism." His view was shared by supporters of integration such as the social activist Teresita Ang See and the Jesuit priest Charles J. McCarthy, both of whom were active in the movement for jus soli citizenship in the early 1970s. Ang See, whose siblings attended either CKSC or the Anglo-Chinese School (Zhongxi Xuexiao), describes these institutions as "bastions of ultraconservatism and ethnocentrism."[52] It is easy to find in Chinese-language texts that were not meant for Filipino consumption abundant evidence of the attitudes and values that liberals alluded to. In a 1958 book on Chinese education in the Philippines, for example, the principal of Cebu Eastern High School (Suwu Dongfang Zhongxue) and KMT stalwart Chen Lieh-fu described overseas Chinese and native Southeast Asians as utterly different from each other because of climate. Efforts by Southeast Asian states to assimilate their Chinese populations would not succeed, he said, because China possessed a "more advanced and mature" (*jiao gao jiao chengshu*) civilization that had Sinicized the Manchus despite their greater military strength.[53] Chen's views here betrayed long-standing fears among KMT ideologues of marriages between overseas Chinese men and local women that would result in the "nativization" (*tuhua*) and "foreign-ization" (*yanghua*) of their offspring and descendants.[54] *Huaqiao* thus ought to marry each other to preserve "relations within the national bloodline" (*minzu xuetong guanxi*).[55] For the KMT, ensuring that overseas Chinese identified themselves as culturally "Chinese" rather than Filipino, Thai, Vietnamese, Malayan, or Indonesian was integral to rallying them behind the "Chinese" state.

Dual-language Chinese schools were at least partially malintegrative in a cultural sense for the same reason that they were largely a bulwark against leftist ideology: ROC control over them. "Literally the Chinese Departments are Taiwan schools set down in a Philippine environment," wrote one US sociologist who conducted research on the Philippine Chinese in the 1950s.[56] Similar to many of their counterparts elsewhere in the region at the time, they relied on textbooks compiled by OCAC and sold through government-run publishing houses such as the Cheng Chung Book Company (Zhengzhong Shuju) and the World Book Company (Shijie Shuju).[57] Through OCAC, Taiwan also supplied teachers with instructional materials that were a part of series such as Textbooks for Nanyang Chinese Schools (Nanyang huaqiao xuexiao jiaokeshu) and the Overseas Series (Haiwai wenku), the latter of which included Chen Lieh-fu's 1957 *The Philippines and China* (*Feilübin yu Zhongguo*).[58] In a survey of these textbooks for senior high school students, Robert O. Tilman found that they were not unequivocally anticommunist and, intermittent references to the Chinese nationalist revolution aside, featured little overt political content. Instead, many tended to present factual material in a straightforward and didactic manner in keeping with how lessons ought to be conducted, while excluding anything that might be construed as anti-KMT. The most directly ideological of the texts were civics (*gongmin*) textbooks, which drew from the New Life and Cultural Renaissance Movements' precepts in reminding students to stand erect, greet their parents in the morning and evening, bow to show respect to their elders, be punctual, and cover their mouths when yawning. Letter-writing exercises, which consumed a significant portion of curricular time, reinforced these moral injunctions by exposing students to model letters between children and adults that featured exhortations to embrace traditional Chinese virtues such as thrift, filial piety, and industriousness.[59] By reproducing the form and language of these missives in their assignments or even their own letters, students supposedly internalized values that inoculated them against the germs of radical leftism.

Nationalist China similarly exercised significant influence over Chinese-language teachers at these schools. While only a minority of schools such as CKSHS and Cebu Eastern were helmed by principals such as Pao Shih-tien and Chen Lieh-fu who were strongly supported by or members of the KMT, the *zongzhibu* (and, after 1956, the PCACL and Xiao Zong) played an indispensable role in vetting most Chinese teachers for approval by the embassy. The party was even responsible for hiring at sectarian schools run by Catholic, Protestant, and Buddhist missions. In the absence of a sufficient number of qualified Chinese teachers in the Philippines, some schools also employed teachers from Taiwan: fifty such teachers were sent to the Philippines from 1952 to 1968. These kinds of hiring practices minimized the likelihood of political dissent and ensured that teachers were politically innocuous at worst or KMT hard-liners at best.[60]

During their summer holidays, teachers often visited Taiwan for training and indoctrination or were exposed to intensive propagandizing by Taiwanese visitors to the Philippines. In April and June 1955, for example, four KMT instructors spent six weeks in the Philippines as part of a series of training visits to countries across East Asia. One of them was Wang Sheng, commandant of the Political Warfare Cadres Academy (Zhenggong Ganbu Xuexiao) in Taipei, which trained Soviet-style political commissars for assignment to military units.[61] Another was OCAC's director of overseas Chinese education, and the remaining two were from Taiwan's Teachers' College. Collectively, they conducted a series of lectures, workshops, and small-group training sessions for teachers and KMT members in Manila to improve the quality of teaching and promote *Fangong kang'E*. In addition to academic topics such as Chinese history and literature and practical topics such as school administration and pedagogy, the attendees also learned about other subjects in sessions titled

"The Current State of the Revolution" (Dangqian geming xingshi)
"A Basic Treatise on 'Anticommunism and Resisting Russia'" (Fangong kang'E jibenlun)
"The Life of the Leader" (Lingxiu shenghuo)
"Why We Need the Party" (Women wei shenme xuyao dang)
"How to Be a KMT Member" (Zenyang zuo yige Zhongguo Guomindang dangyuan)
"The Party and the Work of the Youth Movement" (Dang yu qingyun gongzuo)
"How to Conduct Ideological Warfare" (Zenyang zuo sixiang zhan)
"How to Conduct Psychological Warfare" (Zenyang zuo xinli zhan)
"How to Conduct Intelligence Warfare" (Zenyang zuo qingbao zhan)
"How to Conduct Organizational Warfare" (Zenyang zuo zuzhi zhan)
"How to Conduct Propaganda Warfare" (Zenyang zuo xuanchuan zhan)

Wang also gave public lectures in Manila, Cebu, Iloilo, and Bacolod on the international situation and the situation in China; they were attended by over five thousand people in total.[62]

Chinese schools in the Philippines were thus at the very least noncommunist institutions by virtue of the teachers and textbooks that they employed, the close ties to the KMT and the ROC that these personnel and teaching materials embodied, and the political environment in which they operated. KMT-run schools went even further than that by mobilizing students and teachers against communism and strengthening their ties with Nationalist China.

No school was more enthusiastic about propagating anticommunism and more closely linked to Taiwan than CKSHS (see figure 5.1), as the following snapshot of the institution in October 1957, just after the establishment of the Xiao Zong, shows us. Chiang Kai-shek's latest book, *Soviet Russia in China*, had been published earlier in the year.[63] It argued that a Nationalist counterattack against the Chinese mainland was the key to stopping the Soviet drive for world domination. All that was required from the West was moral and some material support, but not any military support. Instead, Nationalist troops and anticommunist Asian peoples would spearhead the offensive, joining forces with the Chinese masses once a beachhead had been established on the mainland. In the Philippines, the Xiao Zong purchased copies for all Chinese schools, and at CKSHS, one of only two schools outside Taiwan to be named after Chiang (the other being Chung Cheng High School in Singapore), the book became a canonical text for students and teachers.[64] Multiple volumes were put on display in the school library for borrowing; every teacher received a copy and was asked to read it and encourage students to do the same. History and civics teachers were told to incorporate it as supplementary material into their lessons, while Chinese literature teachers were to assign it as an extracurricular reading for the semester and have students write book reports on it. Lastly, students would be divided into groups and participate in a competition to test their knowledge of the text. Should they wish, they could also take part in a community-wide essay contest on the book, jointly organized by the PCACL, KMT, and Xiao Zong.[65]

FIGURE 5.1.   Chiang Kai-shek College in January 2020. Author's photograph.

The October 1957 edition of the CKSHS *Student Journal* (*Zhongzheng xuesheng*), which reported on these efforts to promote Chiang's book, gives us a further sense of the school's special relationship with Taiwan. One news item noted that OCAC had approved changes to the board of directors' constitution. Another reported that students and teachers were responding eagerly to fundraising campaigns and donation drives, such as Chiang's call for a "cultural counterattack" (*wenhua fangong*) against mainland China and to the KMT *zongzhibu*'s call for donations of books, which would be airdropped onto the mainland. The journal also listed thirty-six recent graduates who were going on to pursue university degrees in Taiwan. One such graduate, Zheng Tingting, would even be attending National Taiwan Normal University to study history and literature with financial aid from her alma mater. Zheng had topped an examination to select the recipient of this scholarship, which stipulated that she would return to teach at CKSHS after graduating from the university. The school planned to continue this scheme to improve the quality of its teachers and incorporate alumni into its staff.[66] Zheng would have gone on to become one of approximately a hundred overseas Chinese from the Philippines studying in Taiwanese universities at the time.[67]

The journal also published student essays to reward well-written and ideologically correct prose. A good example in this issue was "My Recollections of Studying at a School in the Mainland Bandit Province" ("Wo zai dalu feiqu xuexiao dushu de huiyi"), by a first-year junior middle school student. As becomes quickly apparent from reading it, this was a complete work of fiction, as we are not told where the school was, its name, or when, how long, and at what level he studied there. Nor do we learn how he managed at such a young age to leave the PRC for the Philippines. Such details mattered little. Although we do not know the exact circumstances in which this essay was written, it was likely an in-class assignment, the objective of which was to have students reproduce propagandistic stereotypes about the horrors of student life under CCP rule. CKSHS students and those at other Chinese schools in the Philippines were bombarded with such stereotypes in the classroom and beyond on a constant basis. They were likely to have absorbed them reading tracts such as *A True Account of How the Communist Bandits Have Brought Disaster upon the Overseas Chinese* (*Gongfei huoqiao shilu*) and *How the Chinese Communists Treat Overseas Chinese Students* (*Zhonggong zenyang duidai qiaosheng*), which had been published in 1955 and 1956, respectively, and were likely available in the school library.[68] For example, the student's essay referred to the "Zhu-Mao bandit gang" (*Zhu-Mao feibang*) that ruled mainland China. He described being forced to learn Russian, read works on agricultural production, and participate in a

Young Pioneers' team that had its members praise the CCP at every opportunity. After falling sick for two months, he said that he returned to school only to be criticized by his peers for being lazy. That drove him to escape China for the "path of freedom" (ziyou de daolu), which he managed to do because of unspecified sacrifices by his paternal aunt.[69] When KMT ideologues praised the Philippine Chinese as the most ardently pro-Nationalist in the world, such was the kind of cultural production that they had in mind.

Culture, Ceremony, and the Expansion of the PCACL

The civic anticommunism that the PCACL promoted had two interrelated features. First, it was a connective phenomenon that linked Chinese in the islands to each other, to Filipinos, and to global and Nationalist Chinese anticommunist struggles. Second, the PCACL molded its diasporic audiences, youth and students especially, through a shared vocabulary and the techniques of public spectacle, active participation in rituals and performances, and rewards—discursive practices that fused the language of anticommunism with its material and social forms.

High on the list of priorities of the PCACL was ensuring that Chinese beyond Manila were institutionally incorporated into the new organization, much as provincial chambers of commerce and trade associations had been into the Shang Zong. From the jinqiao an to the Cebu reading club arrests, recent events made clear to rightist Chinese that communism was a pan-Philippine problem and that anticommunism had to be similarly broad in geographical scope. Outside the capital, state capacity, border security, and the influence of Shang Zong elites in Manila were weaker. Well into the 1960s, provincial Chinese continued to be involved in transborder smuggling networks, which could be depicted as an ideological problem because of how they connected the Philippines to the Chinese mainland via Hong Kong, the south China coast, and even North Borneo. They could thus serve as channels for the inflow of propaganda, arms, and other subversive elements—including communist agents—into the islands. A delegate from Bacolod City, for instance, urged the PCACL convention to stop Chinese brokers in the provinces from trafficking in communist goods, although the report on his proposal did not specify what sorts of products he was referring to.[70]

To stimulate excitement in the PCACL and pave the way for the formation of chapters in the provinces, the PCACL created a traveling performing arts troupe that toured Northern Luzon during the summer school holidays in 1957 and raised awareness of anticommunism. Enthusiasm for this troupe appears to have come from the bottom up, with the Chinese Students' General Association proposing it to the PCACL shortly after the 1956 convention.[71] Cua Siok Po and six other PCACL members, with logistical support from its secretariat, were responsible for organizing it. More important than what it performed and how it was received was how it mobilized different sectors of the Chinese community in pursuit of a common ideological goal. Active participation in producing—and not just consuming—propaganda was measurable and socially visible and could help inculcate and reinforce the correct ideological dispositions in all those involved. As with Chinese cultural events in general, business leaders financed the troupe to show off their patronage of the arts and ideological credentials; Antonio Roxas Chua's Rice and Sugar Association even provided its members with uniforms. Five of its members were part of the PCACL's secretariat (Cua and others on the organizing committee did not travel with the troupe), and the remaining twenty were performers drawn from the Philippine-Chinese Youth Military Service Fraternity, KMT Artistic Propaganda Troupe, Manila Amateur Dramatic Guild, and Philippine-Chinese Youth Educational Center. With the help of local dramatists and directors, the troupe decided to stage two main items: a skit, "Hell on Earth" (Renjian diyu), and a traditional Hokkien opera. Other items that the troupe prepared included magic acts, harmonica solos, comic dialogues, and the screening of documentary films.[72]

Artistic performances were a staple of PCACL events. Besides encouraging participation in the production of anticommunist discourse and bolstering the attendance, they also allegorized the evils of communism and complemented the speeches and lectures at these events. Although its exact contents are unknown, "hell on earth" was a frequent trope in Nationalist propaganda and a blatant reference to communist rule in China. Its writer, Chu I-Hsiung, taught at Far Eastern University and was a reliable producer of cultural propaganda for the PCACL. The interlude to a February 22, 1958, "Anti-Communist and Salvation Rally" by the PCACL in Manila, for example, was centered on one of his plays, *The Spring Breeze Comes Once Again on the South Bank of the River*, which students and teachers from CKSHS performed in front of Sy En, Fernando Chua, and Pao Shih-tien, the three speakers at the rally. As described in a report on the event: "[The play] tells of the miserable life of Chinese teachers and students who live on the South Bank of the Yangtze River under . . . Communist tyrannical rule. These intelligentsia gradually find themselves unable to endure the suffocating life which is totally different from the life they knew before. Finally, they are able to get away from the Communist occupied area and breathe again the free air in the free land."[73]

On May 8, 1957, the troupe embarked on its sixteen-day tour of Northern Luzon. A day earlier, its members were given a ritualistic send-off at an anti-communist propaganda meeting at the KMT's headquarters in Manila. There, in a gesture that symbolized the conferral of authority by the ROC state on its national subjects, Ambassador Chen presented Fernando Chua with the troupe's flag in a ceremony overseen by the deputy chairman of the KMT Central Committee's Section Three, which handled overseas Chinese affairs. To emphasize the tour's significance, he also gave a lecture, "An Appeal to the Human Race to Save Itself" (Renlei zijiu de huyu), in which he denounced the CCP as being puppets of the Soviets and for using violence and deception to enslave the Chinese people. Warming to a familiar theme in KMT propaganda, he identified three groups of enemies: dictators behind the iron curtain, "hired thugs" (yingquan) from communist states who had infiltrated free societies to do the bidding of these dictators, and indigenous communists.

Civic ceremonies overseen by ROC and KMT officials and the vocabulary of enslavement, thuggery, "hell on earth," "hired thugs," and infiltration on a worldwide scale became increasingly widespread from the late 1950s onward as anticommunism crystallized into a category of Chinese social life. Through these rituals and tropes, the Nationalist state, personified by the likes of Chen Chih-ping and Chen Chih-mai as well as the ubiquitous visages of Chiang Kai-shek and Sun Yat-sen, aimed to bind its overseas subjects more intimately to the Chinese nation and normalize anticommunism as a mode of thinking and feeling. What the performers genuinely thought about Ambassador Chen's lecture, the tour, and its politics is unknowable. Some may have been encouraged to join the troupe by parents, relatives, classmates, teachers, or clan leaders or done so out of an interest in the arts and drama. But above all, they knew the roles they were supposed to perform: those of overseas Chinese participants in a global anticommunist movement spearheaded by the ROC.

The official report on the tour unsurprisingly depicts it as a great success. Stopping in fifteen cities or towns in Northern Luzon with significant Chinese populations, the troupe performed to crowds of, allegedly, over a thousand people each time, including Filipino politicians and military officials.[74] If the performances in themselves were meant partly as entertainment and were no doubt consumed as such by many among the audience, the presence of the troupe and Shang Zong leaders such as Fernando Chua as semiofficial emissaries of the ROC state in the provinces was ultimately about institution building and ideological mobilization. Accordingly, the troupe met with local Chinese leaders to encourage the formation of provincial chapters of the PCACL, with exchanges of anticommunist memorabilia signifying the commitment of all involved—producers, performers, and audience members—to the cause. To encourage such behavior, OCAC presented troupe members on their return to Manila with copies of Chiang Kai-shek's illustrated biography and letters of commendation as tokens of the ROC government's concern for them.[75] Through such symbolically meaningful rewards, the PCACL and similar social institutions incentivized the right ideological behavior among Chinese youth and accorded participation in anticommunist, pro-ROC events prestige and recognition.

In the years following the founding of the PCACL and the troupe's tour of Northern Luzon, anticommunist Chinese periodicals reported on growing public enthusiasm for the PCACL beyond Manila. The October 1957 edition of the English-language *Pacific Review*, for example, described the founding of PCACL chapters in three cities in Northern and Central Luzon: San Fernando, in the province of Pampanga (in July 1957; see figure 5.2), which the troupe had visited; Siain, in Quezon (in August 1957); and Olongapo, in Zambales (in September 1957), with the last becoming the twenty-sixth chapter of the APACL to be re-formed in the past year. Ambassador Chen Chih-mai attended the founding of these chapters as the official ROC representative, presiding over inauguration ceremonies for new members in conference halls that were festooned with ROC and Philippine flags and portraits of Chiang, Garcia, Sun Yat-sen, and Jose Rizal. Accompanying him, to impress on participants the civic-diplomatic nature of these occasions, were PCACL and Shang Zong leaders such as Yu Khe Thai, Shih I-Sheng, and Yao Shiong Shio. To underscore the PCACL's role as a bridge between races, Chinese leaders and students from these cities and Filipino provincial governors and military commanders welcomed and interacted with the visitors from the capital. PCACL leaders presented their provincial and local counterparts with tokens such as their chapters' official seals. Periodicals and special commemorative volumes publicized these chapters, their activities, and those involved in them, registering the presence of the PCACL and its leading figures in the public imagination of Chinese and Filipinos. Congratulatory and hortatory messages from Garcia and ROC and Philippine officials reminded those present that they were performing a vital service to the Philippine nation and also in defense of what Garcia's message to the Zambales PCACL called "the democratic way of life."[76]

FIGURE 5.2.　Inauguration and induction ceremony for officers of the Pampanga Province chapter of the PCACL on July 25, 1957. Image courtesy of the Ateneo de Manila University Library.

The World in the Chinese Anticommunist Imagination

Communism, as framed by the PCACL, its ROC patrons, and anticommunists in general, was a transnational problem: a function of the Soviet Union's imperial designs on "free societies"; its accomplices in China and elsewhere; porous borders; and the lack of vigilance and awareness of communism's depredations. Ideologues inflected this problem differently according to different circumstances. For the ROC and its Philippine supporters, communism was primarily about the fates of China under Mao Zedong's "bandit gang" and of the Chinese nation as a deterritorialized, ethno-cultural community. Similar to the activities they sponsored, the speeches of PCACL leaders explicated how anticommunism was both a global and Chinese movement. At an anticommunist and salvation rally in Manila in February 1958, for example, Pao Shih-tien described the platform of the newly established Overseas Chinese United Salvation Association in Taiwan. Anticommunism, Pao declared, began with "self-salvation" and ended with "saving the whole world." Asia, he said, was a cornerstone for the security of the world and the recovery of China was the "only path towards checking Communist expansion in Asia and rescuing its peoples from enslavement." All Asians had to put aside differences in nationality, religion, and party affiliation, reject neutralism, and lend their full support to the ROC in its campaign to counterattack mainland China. Pao also called for greater solidarity within overseas Chinese societies and higher standards for Chinese education and journalism to promote, he said, "our age-old tradition of character development."[77]

The language of "salvation" here is notable for its historical overtones. National Salvation (Jiuguo) was how the ROC branded the anti-Japanese movement during the War of Resistance, to which overseas Chinese contributed significantly. By casting the post-1949 struggle against communism in comparable terms, the ROC and its overseas Chinese supporters looked to situate anticommunism within a longer genealogy of patriotic movements in defense of the Chinese nation and its legitimate government. Now, imperialistic communism had replaced imperial Japan as China's nemesis. Yet by dropping "national" from "salvation," Pao and other ideologues transformed anticommunism into a less exclusive discursive space that welcomed non-Chinese as well. More than that, by depicting anticommunism as a global movement with Asian and Chinese characteristics, Pao hoped to promote affinity with the ROC among Philippine-Chinese youth through ideological causes that transcended national boundaries and, vice versa, with global anticommunism through the ROC.

Anticommunist movements, the ROC's in particular, consistently emphasized the coming collapse of communism in the hopes of mobilizing peoples against it. In KMT rhetoric, for instance, the "bandit regime" was forever in crisis and the "counterattack" perpetually imminent. With Mao depicted as a puppet of the Soviets, at least until the Sino-Soviet split became too obvious for ROC propagandists to overlook, fissures anywhere in the Soviet imperial edifice could be interpreted as prefiguring the collapse of the entire structure. In 1957, the PCACL seized on the failed Hungarian Revolution against Soviet rule in late 1956 to mobilize Chinese society in opposition to global communism and the PRC. Through the visit of six Hungarian "freedom fighters" to the Philippines, the PCACL hoped to provide Chinese with firsthand accounts of the struggle against communism and channel the resulting social energies toward the fight against Mao.

Demonstrations in support of the uprising and in opposition to the Soviet Union occurred through to September 1957, when the Hungarians' visit took place. In December 1956, for example, twenty-six hundred CKSHS students took part in a mass rally on school grounds to express solidarity with the Hungarian people, during which Pao described the revolution as the death knell for communism and urged all those present to "live up to the spirit of President Chiang and lend determined support to all anti-Communist movements."[78] Hungary quickly became something of a rallying point for anticommunists globally, especially after the pro-Chiang *Time* magazine named the Hungarian freedom fighter its 1956 "Man of the Year," while newspapers in Taiwan provided detailed coverage of events in Hungary.[79] In March 1956, the PCACL sponsored a weeklong series of activities in support of the peoples behind the iron curtain, the Hungarians especially. During that week, the PCACL flooded the Chinese media and civic sphere with special commemorative volumes, cartoons, newspaper articles, slideshows, posters, and pro-Hungary, anti-Soviet speeches; Pao and Fernando Chua held a press conference to publicize these activities. The week culminated in simultaneous mass gatherings across the country; in Manila, some three thousand persons were reported to have shown up to witness, among other presentations, a thousand-student chorus and *Hungary's Mother (Xiongyali de muqin)*. Written specially for the occasion by a local Chinese dramatist and performed by the KMT Propaganda Troupe, this play recounted the "true story of a mother who sacrificed her youngest and only remaining son for the interest and honor of her country" during the revolution.[80]

By September, Chinese youth in the Philippines had been primed to receive the Hungarians and regard the global, Filipino, and Nationalist Chinese anticommunist movements as intertwined. In June, for instance, the PCACL swiftly proclaimed its support for Garcia's Anti-Subversion Act (R.A. No. 1700), which outlawed the Partido Komunista ng Pilipinas (PKP) and similar associations on the grounds that they constituted an "organized conspiracy" to overthrow the Philippine state.[81] The PCACL backed R.A. No. 1700 and intended to help the authorities implement it.[82] A month later, it organized another mobilization week, this time in support of what it called the "mainland antityrannical movement" that had emerged in response to Mao's Hundred Flowers Campaign and that portended the fall of the CCP. As ever, in their speeches to large and enthusiastic crowds, PCACL propagandists were eager to highlight the interconnectedness of different anticommunist struggles. Cua Siok Po, for instance, spoke of an "anti-Communist tide" that had swelled in the preceding five months and "extended from the Danube to the Yellow River," while Jose Ma. Hernandez, an honorary member of the PCACL, cited *Soviet Russia in China* in calling for Taiwan, South Vietnam, and South Korea to unite against their respective communist foes.[83]

Little is known about the visiting Hungarians except their names and occupations and that they arrived from Taiwan. They were moving from one "free" Asian state to another within the anticommunist ecumene. In the Philippines, like foreign heads of state or politicians, they were granted audiences with the president and foreign secretary and accompanied wherever they went by Chen Chih-mai and local Chinese leaders. Chinese anticommunist practices in the Philippines were anything if not repetitive. As we might expect, they visited CKSHS, a hub and symbol of ideological fervor within Chinese society. A rally held on the third and final night of their visit featured a second staging of *Hungary's Mother* and, as was customary, a speech by a Philippine politician. This was Senator Francisco Rodrigo, a member of Catholic Action, the conservative religious organization that Hernandez was president of.[84] It also reinforced the same themes of global ideological identity and the unity of the Chinese and Hungarian struggles that earlier campaigns had promoted. At the rally, for instance, veteran KMT member Chua Lamco invoked human rights as a fundamental principle of anticommunism and said that the ROC and Hungarian peoples were both passengers on the "same storm-tossed ship" (*fengyu tongzhou*). Chen Chih-mai even asserted that the Hungarian Revolution had "inspired and brought about demonstrations, riots, and uprisings all over the mainland of China."[85]

Finally, it was the turn of the three Hungarians to speak. As reported in PCACL propaganda, they not only described their direct experiences of the revolution and denounced communism but also had much to say about Taiwan and the Chinese experience. The nurse Csilla Biro spoke about the high standard of living she had enjoyed during her three-week stay and the "wonderful progress" that Taiwan had made in economic, industrial, and agricultural development. In recounting the revolution, she made it a special point to mention how mainland Chinese students studying in Budapest had joined with Hungarians in their demonstrations. The graduate student Csaba Mezei accused communism of imposing the "evils of materialism" on Hungary and was also full of praise for Taiwan, which he previously thought was "just a military base." After his visit there, Mezei "realized how wrong the conception was" and declared that the "people in Taiwan are now happy in their life of freedom and prosperity." Finally, the writer and musician Jeno Platthy held forth on communism's evils, claiming among other things that the Hungarian "puppet government" had signed a contract to deliver eighty-five hundred Hungarian youths to the Soviet Union and the PRC as forced laborers.[86] As a public spectacle, the Hungarians' visit tripled up as a condemnation of global communism, a call for unity by different national peoples against it, and an advertisement for "Free China." Like the PCACL's many campaigns, it embedded the anticommunist struggle of Taiwan and the overseas Chinese within a wider ideological movement and exploited the gravity of the global state of affairs to drum up *huaqiao* support for Nationalist China.

Over the 1960s, the PCACL flourished, diversifying its activities and expanding into every realm of Chinese cultural life. By 1970, including the other members of the Big Five, the number of provincial chapters and civic organizations that constituted the PCACL was close to two hundred. From 1958 to 1967, fundraising campaigns yielded a total of over three 3 million Philippine pesos (PHP) in support of the league's activities and in response to Taiwan's calls for voluntary contributions by *huaqiao* to the ongoing cause of national salvation. Summer ideological activities were routinized in the form of seminars and workshops on Chinese culture that structured the free time of students and teachers. Such activities organized the calendar of Chinese civic life partly around celebrating the ROC and its leaders, national culture, and ideology, on both regular occasions such as National Day (October 10), Overseas Chinese Day (October 21), and Chiang Kai-shek's birthday (October 31) or special occasions such as Chiang's reelection as ROC president in May 1966 and the one hundredth anniversary of Sun Yat-sen's birthday on November 12 that same year. By ensuring that such events were well publicized, print and radio propaganda helped sustain anticommunism. The PCACL continued to connect like-minded individuals and institutions in the Philippines and Taiwan to each other and to global networks of anticommunism. Under its auspices, organized group visits to Taiwan, which chapter 6 examines, took place regularly, typically in conjunction with recurring or one-off events on what had become a shared civic calendar between the ROC and the Philippine Chinese. Exemplary anticommunist visitors to the Philippines, such as PRC fighter pilots who had defected by flying to Taiwan, remained convenient mouthpieces for the anticommunist cause. In 1961, the PCACL again welcomed the APACL to Manila for its annual meeting; its members continued to be active in regional and global anticommunist organizations such as the APACL's 1967 successor, the World Anti-Communist League (WACL).[87]

By the late 1950s, Chinese society in the Philippines had been restructured in response to Filipino anti-Chinese economic and cultural nationalism and the mass arrests earlier in the decade. Leadership of this society now lay with a small group of elites and five organizations that spanned the country, represented the community, and defined its interests. Anticommunism was one such interest. It transcended national, ethnic, and cultural differences; helped Chinese prove themselves as upstanding residents of their host country; and connected them to Nationalist China, expanding the ROC's sovereignty over them. With Chinese schools such as CKSHS serving as its foundation and the newly formed PCACL as its propagator in chief, anticommunism came to dominate civic life. By expanding across the Philippines and campaigning to support anticommunist causes both locally and globally, the PCACL engaged with Chinese society through public spectacles, rituals, and a shared ideological vocabulary and by encouraging and rewarding participation in anticommunist cultural activities.

In restructuring Chinese society, businessmen such as Yu Khe Thai and intellectuals such as Pao Shih-tien positioned themselves at the forefront of multiple, overlapping institutions with a stake in practicing anticommunism. PCACL events in Manila and the provinces united Chinese and Filipinos against a common enemy. Institutions such as CKSHS and the PCACL were connected not only to Taiwan and the intra-Asian anticommunist ecumene but also to Hungarian "freedom fighters" and a global anticommunist movement. Global anticommunism catalyzed the formation of the PCACL; it supplied broader narratives of ideological solidarity that the PCACL drew on to mobilize support for the struggle against communism in the Philippines, by Nationalist China, and everywhere else.

Partly because of these transformations, the Philippines was the KMT's only unequivocal success story among eight designated "core regions" (*zhongxin diqu*) for overseas anticommunist work in the 1950s. As the former KMT official Yang Jiancheng has written in an overview of these regions from 1950 to 1963, the outlook for the party was less rosy in Japan, South Korea, Hong Kong–Macao, Vietnam, Thailand, Indonesia, and the United States. In the Philippines, party affairs could be "promoted the most smoothly" (*tuizhan zui shunli*). Conversely, Yang assessed that the organizational structure and finances of the KMT in Japan were lacking, noted how the Japanese Communist Party was a legal entity, and believed that one consequence of Japan's democratic system of government was that its Chinese community had become more politically "plural and competitive" (*duoyuanhua jingzheng*), to the detriment of the KMT. In South Korea, the KMT had been prevented from operating openly since 1949 despite Seoul and Taipei's close relationship. Similar constraints inhibited the KMT in Southeast Asia, even in states such as South Korea that were decidedly anticommunist. The Ngô Đình Diệm regime in South Vietnam forced the largest KMT branch in Saigon-Cholon to shut down in 1959, and by 1963, eight years after all Chinese had been legally required to naturalize, 99 percent of them had done so. In Thailand, the KMT's activities had revived in 1954. However, because of intermarriage, restrictions on Chinese education, and a 1955 law on political parties that banned foreigners from engaging in political activities, the party was not in an ideal position there, Yang argued.[88] Around the same time, in the Philippines, the KMT was fortifying its grip on one of the smallest Chinese societies in Southeast Asia.

CHAPTER 6

Experiencing the Nation

Philippine-Chinese Visits to "Free China"

We have returned, bearing
On our shoulders the dust of a drifting life,
A warm longing in our bosom, and
A heart that wants to return home but cannot.

Home, sucked into a black iron curtain, blocking sun
and sky;
Bodies, drifting in the Philippines, haunted by turbid
waves;
Five hundred thousand pairs of teary eyes place their
hopes,
Their hopes on you—free ancestral land, our mother!
You must stand up for freedom and justice!

Retake freedom from the grasp of the devils;
With justice, comfort the people who wander in
foreign lands;
Let tomorrow's timely rain
Fall upon the drought of five hundred million
hearts. . . . . .

We have returned, to breathe in your
Fresh smell, to kiss your
Fragrant soil, we
Shake the dust from our bodies, and with
A rigging of iron, here
Anchor our—
One hope, and
One loyalty!

—Cua Siok Po, "We Have Returned—Arriving
in Taiwan"["Women huilai le—di Tai"] (1950)

In August 1950, Cua Siok Po and forty-five other
Philippine Chinese became part of the very first overseas Chinese delegation
to visit Taiwan since the supposed end of the civil war. There, they met with
the Chiang family and other Republic of China (ROC) leaders (see figure 6.1);

FIGURE 6.1.   The leader of the Philippine-Chinese delegation in 1950 presents Chiang Kai-shek with a gold sculpture of a map of China. Reprinted with permission from Academia Historica.

donated money, radios, and towels to the ROC military; and traveled to Quemoy, the island cluster at the frontline of the Kuomintang's (KMT) ongoing struggle to reclaim the Chinese mainland.[1] A World War II veteran inclined toward literary expression, Cua was so moved that he wrote a series of poems about his experiences in Taiwan and Quemoy and published them in the March 1953 edition of *Wenyi chuangzuo*, a literary magazine established in 1951 by the KMT's Committee on Chinese Literature and Art Awards (Zhonghua Wenyi Jiangjin Weiyuanhui) to promote cultural anticommunism. The first of these eight poems is translated and reproduced above and lays bare the sentimental basis of his anticommunism.[2] In it, the thirty-year-old Cua depicts his visit to Taiwan as that of a Chinese sojourner, "drifting in the Philippines," who has returned to smell and touch the "fragrant soil" of his "free ancestral land, our mother." With "home" having fallen to communist "devils" and behind a "black iron curtain," he sees the ROC as the sole hope for the half a billion Chinese in "foreign lands" seeking "freedom and justice."

While the poem stakes out a seemingly straightforward ideological position, it also betrays tensions over what Taiwan was to its author, at the time a rising young party member in the Philippines. Intentionally or otherwise, Cua grapples with a fundamental challenge that KMT propagandists like him faced in signifying the ROC to the Chinese diaspora after 1949. Cua locates his "home" (*jia*) in mainland China and laments that he wants to return there but cannot. Like most Southeast Asian *huaqiao*, he traced his ancestry not to Taiwan or its offshore islands but to southern Fujian Province, now under communist control. Yet, he also uses a ubiquitous term in anticommunist rhetoric, *ziyou zuguo* ("free ancestral land," "free motherland," or "free homeland") to describe Taiwan. Cua has never previously been to Taiwan. Nonetheless, he says he is "returning" to it and cherishes the sensory and emotional experience of doing so. He invests the visiting of what was not his *jia* with an affective intensity that we typically find in sojourners' descriptions of returning to their native place. His verse makes *jia* and *zuguo* overlap in meaning but cannot make them one and the same thing. If the ROC could not be the former, it could at least represent itself as the latter to Chinese people everywhere.

This and other visits to the ROC were an aspect of the KMT's global contest with the People's Republic of China (PRC) for overseas Chinese capital, remittances, and bodies during the Cold War: a contest to control Chinese transnationalism and press it into the service of the state. Except in several years when the majority ethnic (and questionably "overseas") Chinese societies of Hong Kong and Macao came in first, *huaqiao* groups in the Philippines organized the most "homecoming" (*huiguo*) visits to the ROC annually from 1950 to 1970, whether to "bring greetings and gifts to the troops" (*laojun*), "pay their respects" (*zhijing*) to leaders and officials, "observe and study" (*kaocha*) the development of their *ziyou zuguo*, or participate in "military service" (*junzhong fuwu*) alongside Taiwan's youth.[3] Featuring carefully planned itineraries, sponsored by overseas Chinese civic organizations, and supported by the KMT and government agencies such as the Overseas Chinese Affairs Commission (OCAC) and the Ministry of Foreign Affairs (MOFA), these visits were part of a repertoire of diasporic nation-building strategies that the ROC employed "in the name of legitimacy," as the historian Joan S. H. Wang has put it.[4] From the Big Five to schools and clan, commercial, and veterans' associations, all types of Philippine-Chinese institutions organized them. The average ethnic Chinese person in the Philippines from 1950 onward would likely have gone on these tours or taken part in summer activities in Taiwan at least once, especially if from Manila; both ROC nationals and naturalized Philippine citizens went on them. For the merchants who funded them and the cultural and commercial elites who led them, these visits were a recurring item on their civic calendars and a social, cultural, and political obligation. Like the textbooks that Chinese schools in the Philippines relied on and the graduates of these schools who went on to study in Taiwan, these visits helped constitute the intra-Asian anticommunist ecumene and the dense networks that connected the ROC and its most ardent *huaqiao* supporters in Southeast Asia.

The visits, as my analysis of an OCAC-issued guidebook for visiting *huaq-iao* shows, were a means by which the state projected Taiwan to the world as more than just a province of the ROC. For state propagandists, they were a form of what I call experiential nationalism, whereby *huaqiao* immersed themselves in the culture and traditions of a substitute homeland, beheld firsthand its progress toward modernity and democracy, matched textual and visual descriptions with a well-curated reality, and internalized ways of knowing and feeling about the Chinese nation and its ideological crusade. Like the anticommunist rallies, rituals, and public performances that Chinese staged in the Philippines, these visits were a discursive practice that integrated the vocabulary of ideology and its material forms to shape perceptions of Taiwan, China, and being Chinese.

This chapter also shows that those who organized and went on visits to Taiwan understood the ROC and their support for it in different ways. What, in other words, were the components of their patriotism? As Cua's poem suggests, many visitors truly believed in the Nationalist regime, despite and because of the loss of the mainland. Some, like Cua and other veterans of the anti-Japanese struggle, traced their loyalties back to World War II and imagined the anticommunist crusade as an extension of the KMT's historical mission to unify China against its foreign enemies. For him and others, with mainland China in the grip of a Soviet puppet regime and inaccessible, Taiwan became the object of their affinities for a particular idea of "home." The ROC's promotion of Chinese culture as an ideological bulwark against communism also aligned with simultaneous efforts by Chinese in the Philippines such as Cua to defend their schools and improve Chinese education in response to Filipinization. Yet for some of these educators, Taiwan was less a bastion of anticommunism than a source of professional expertise. For some veterans, patriotism was not reducible to anticommunism. Three specific visits—by the Philippine Chinese Anti-Communist League (PCACL) in 1956, a group of primary school teachers in 1967, and the Chinese Overseas Wartime Hsuehkan Militia (COWHM) Veterans' Association (VA) in 1971—will help us tease out these emotional, practical, and ideological complexities.

Such visits are nothing if not well documented in yearbooks, newsletters, and, in particular, the "special commemorative volumes" (*jinian tekan*) and reports that visiting groups published as souvenirs for participants and to document their experiences. Featuring itineraries, photographs, delegation lists, rules of conduct, advertisements by sponsors, day-by-day narratives, and well-wishes from community leaders and ROC officials, these materials yield valuable insights into the who, when, what, why, and how of these tours. As texts produced by and circulating within two anticommunist societies, they also reproduce the tropes and rhetoric of ROC nationalism. For these reasons, they are vivid examples of nonstate propaganda and the cultural hegemony of *Fangong kang'E* in Taiwan and among the Philippine Chinese. Still, by reading them closely and contextually, we can reconstruct the interests, motivations, and political imaginations of those who organized and went on the tours.

The PRC-ROC Struggle over Chinese Transnationalism

From the late Qing onward, monarchists, reformers, and revolutionaries alike sought not only to stimulate transnational inflows of Chinese people and capital into China for state-building purposes but also to imbue such flows with political meaning in their propaganda. The post-1949 Chinese Communist Party (CCP) and KMT, in this regard, were no different, except that each wished to channel the movement of *huaqiao* and their money toward separate territorial-ideological polities. During the Cold War, the "China" persons of Chinese ancestry traveled to and invested in signaled their political loyalties. By promoting certain forms of Chinese mobility, the PRC and the ROC used Chinese transnationalism to authenticate their claims to represent the Chinese nation.

In terms of investment, neither the PRC nor the ROC could claim much success until the 1960s. Most overseas Chinese capital after 1949, if it did leave Southeast Asia, flowed into Hong Kong, whose free port status, low taxes, and secure colonial legal system gave it an unassailable edge over China and Taiwan until decades later. Moreover, despite restrictions on Chinese economic activity in Indonesia, the Philippines, and Thailand, business opportunities for ethnic Chinese in Malaysia, the country with the largest Chinese population in the region, expanded. China's efforts to attract *huaqiao* capital were also limited by mistrust between its officials and potential investors and the aggressive tactics that the former employed to pressure the latter.[5] These reflected and contributed to growing suspicions of returned overseas Chinese, persons whose foreign and class background rendered them incompatible with demands for continuous revolution. For these reasons, according to one estimate, overseas Chinese investment companies in China may have raised a total of only 100 million US dollars (USD) from the early 1950s until they were disbanded during the Cultural Revolution.[6]

Large-scale capital aside, the CCP was also keen to tap into overseas Chinese remittances, which would help overcome the US-led embargo on trade with China by providing the state with an alternative source of foreign exchange. Its

efforts to nationalize a large and well-organized private remittance sector, however, were never completely successful, with illicit remittance firms continuing
to operate out of Hong Kong well into the late 1950s. Furthermore, many
huaqiao were reluctant to remit money to China, fearing that communist cadres would confiscate it. These fears persisted despite efforts by the state in 1955
to guarantee the right of families to receive and dispose of overseas remittances
as they wished.[7] Perhaps unsurprisingly, only about 30 percent of such remittances that were transferred through Hong Kong after 1949 actually made it
back to mainland China; most simply remained in Hong Kong.[8]

Taiwan's economy, meanwhile, was driven by some USD 100 million in US
nonmilitary aid per year from 1951 to 1964 and had no actual need for foreign
capital until the 1960s.[9] Policies to attract *huaqiao* investment in the 1950s were
thus limited and their effects inhibited by Taiwan's strategy of import-substitution
industrialization. Only in the late 1950s, at the urging of the United States, did
ROC planners embrace export promotion and foreign capital in anticipation of
the end of US aid in 1965. Comprehensive changes to a set of older regulations
for *huaqiao* investment in March 1960 and the enactment of the Statute for the
Encouragement of Investment that September increased the inflow of overseas
Chinese investment from USD 1.13 million in 1960 to USD 8.3 million in 1961.[10]
By the end of 1963, the cumulative value of all 212 *huaqiao* investment projects,
according to official statistics, was USD 60.3 million. Twenty-one of these projects, totaling USD 13.2 million, were from the Philippines; the average value of
each Philippine-Chinese project was over three times that of each Hong Kong–
Chinese project.[11]

Investment and other monetary figures such as the above were frequently
incorporated into publications intended for consumption beyond China and
Taiwan and given an ideological twist. The English-language, bimonthly *Free
China Review* (later renamed the *Taiwan Review*) featured a regular section on
huaqiao affairs that paid increasing attention after 1960 to investment and its
political significance. On November 1, 1961, for example, it not only stated that
overseas Chinese investment in Taiwan since 1951 amounted to an "impressive" USD 66,840,000 but also compared this act of "participating enthusiasti-
cally in the economic buildup of their mother country" with how overseas
Chinese "helped finance Dr. Sun Yat-sen's revolutionary movement to overthrow the Manchus."[12] In this way, state propagandists imagined continuities
between the ROC in 1961 and its founding fifty years earlier and invested the
complex motivations of *huaqiao* merchants with patriotic, historical meaning.

The movement of Chinese persons was also significant to both Chinas. The
PRC's OCAC arranged tours and set up special hotels for visiting overseas

Chinese.[13] In the 1950s, most of these tours originated from Hong Kong and Macao and featured visits to ancestral villages and meetings with officials in Beijing to discuss prospects for trade and investment.[14] On a longer-term or even permanent basis, half a million to six hundred thousand overseas Chinese returned to China from 1950 to 1961, whether because of family ties or patriotism or—particularly in the case of Indonesia—in response to the anti-Chinese policies of Southeast Asian governments. The rubber tycoon Tan Kah Kee, the de facto leader of the Singaporean Chinese community, was the most famous of these *guiqiao*. After returning to China in 1950, he enjoyed a relatively comfortable career in the government and was given a state funeral in 1961 in recognition of his contributions to economic and educational reconstruction in Fujian.[15] Many less prominent *guiqiao* suffered from disillusionment and discrimination and by 1964 around a sixth of them had re-departed the mainland for Southeast Asia via Hong Kong. Still, the CCP spun their initial return journeys as an ideological victory for the New China.[16]

Eager to compete for Chinese bodies, the ROC persisted—albeit selectively—in admitting Chinese into Taiwan despite the threefold increase in its population since 1900 and the influx of just under a million people from the mainland during the final years of the civil war.[17] These included refugees from Hong Kong, around 150,000 of whom were resettled in Taiwan with aid from the United States from 1949 to early 1954; students, welcomed under a program to promote educational opportunities in Taiwan for Southeast Asian Chinese; and, most famously, over fourteen thousand Chinese prisoners of war (POWs) from Korea who were repatriated to Taiwan. This was nearly double the number of those who went back to China.[18] The "return" of these POWs was a propaganda coup for the ROC, which designated January 23, 1954, the day that they arrived in Taiwan, Freedom Day. This was later rebranded World Freedom Day by the World Anti-Communist League (WACL); it is still celebrated today by the WACL's successor, the World League for Freedom and Democracy.

"Free China" as Territory, Text, and Experience

Philippine-Chinese visits to Taiwan were thus one front in the ROC's struggle to politicize the movement of Chinese people to its advantage. These visits and the propaganda associated with them worked on multiple levels to produce the ROC as a territorially sovereign polity and a nation-like *zuguo* for members of a global Chinese nation. To begin with, the very act of regulating the mobility of persons whom the ROC claimed as its nationals consti-

tuted proof of its capacities as a state, despite the chaos that had engulfed it
during the civil war. As Meredith Oyen has shown in her history of US-Chinese
migration diplomacy, the KMT, even after relocating to Taiwan, continued its
postwar policy of investigating and approving all potential emigrants before
granting them a passport, whether or not they resided in Taiwan. This allowed
it to maintain the illusion of control over the transnational communities that
linked their government to that of the United States and improve US opinions of China and the Chinese by ensuring that only the most desirable people
were allowed to emigrate.[19] Similar procedures and logic applied to Chinese
seeking entry into Taiwan. Fearing overpopulation and communist infiltration,
the ROC admitted only a small number of refugees from Hong Kong despite
lobbying on their behalf and a 1954 survey that showed that 70.4 percent of
the 988,545 refugees who were willing to emigrate from Hong Kong hoped
to be resettled in the ROC.[20] It persistently refused to accept the deportation
to Taiwan of the 2,700 Chinese "overstaying temporary visitors" in the Philippines for the same reason.[21]

In the late 1950s, with the situation in Taiwan more stable, the ROC was
willing to simplify bureaucratic procedures for overseas Chinese who wanted
to visit Taiwan. In 1957, the Executive Yuan promulgated a revised series of
"regulations governing entering and exiting the Taiwan region during the period of communist rebellion" (*Kanluan shiqi Taiwan diqu rujing chujing banfa*).
Under these regulations, prospective overseas Chinese visitors from countries
that had diplomatic relations with the ROC (such as the Philippines) filled in
a basic application form and, through their ROC consulate or embassy, submitted it to OCAC together with any supporting documents. OCAC then obtained the approval of various government agencies before requesting that
the MOFA authorize the embassy or consulate to affix a "homecoming endorsement" (*huiguo jiaqian*) to applicants' passports. Ethnic Chinese living in
countries that did not recognize the ROC filled in the same application but
submitted it to OCAC through legal, pro-ROC Chinese organizations, rather
than via a consulate, and received an entry permit, instead of a *huiguo jiaqian*.
Visits fell into seven categories that were based on purpose and the visitors'
places of residence: (1) investment; (2) higher education; (3) "individual" visits by Chinese leaders, schools, and other organizations for business, sightseeing, and *kaocha* and by transit passengers; (4) *kaocha* missions from Hong Kong
or countries without diplomatic ties to the ROC; (5) investment and business
trips from Hong Kong; (6) emigration; and (7) visiting relatives and family.
Most visits by Philippine Chinese belonged to the third category and required
only that four photographs of each applicant be submitted with the basic application form.[22]

Well before the 1950s, such practices of border control and categorization that once worked to exclude Chinese and other Asian peoples from white settler nations such as the United States, Canada, and Australia had been universalized as what Adam McKeown has called the "foundation of sovereignty . . . for all states within the international system."[23] In this regard, the ROC differed only in degree, not in kind, from the white settler nations whose exclusion laws it once vehemently opposed and from postcolonial countries such as the Philippines that placed similar restrictions on Chinese mobility. Ironically, as Oyen has pointed out, common security concerns meant that for Chinese abroad it was just as difficult to gain entry to Taiwan as the United States in the early-mid-1950s.[24] This was doubly ironic given that the ROC legally identified these people as its nationals but did not allow them to enter their supposed *zuguo* freely. For the government, the regulation of overseas Chinese mobility helped protect Taiwan's borders and territorial sovereignty against Red infiltration and avoid overpopulation, thereby projecting the sort of competent governance that the ROC's earlier, corrupt incarnations lacked. They also demonstrated its body-based sovereignty over an ethno-cultural community and highlighted patriotic activities such as investment, attending university, *kaocha* missions, and even visiting one's relatives. In this last respect, the ROC took after its protector, the United States. US immigration laws with respect to the Chinese, as the historian Madeline Y. Hsu writes, functioned not only to exclude undesirable individuals from US soil but also to admit those the state considered assimilable and strategic such as students and intellectuals.[25] The ROC, similarly, welcomed only desirable *huaqiao* into its fold, albeit as visitors, not immigrants.

These legal practices were supplemented by strategies of representation that we find in the ceremonies, rituals, and texts of ROC anticommunism during the Cold War. Sovereignty, as the historians Zvi Ben-Dor Benite and Stefanos Geroulanos and literary theorist Nicole Jerr argue, is "established and maintained as much by aesthetic, artistic, theatrical, and symbolic structures as by political claims" over everyday life, war and peace, life and death, and—in its classic Westphalian form—territory.[26] The workings of what they call a "complex aesthetic scaffold" with respect to overseas Chinese visits are evident in both literary texts such as Cua Siok Po's poem and more prosaic ones such as *A Guidebook for Overseas Compatriots Returning to Taiwan for Sightseeing* (*Qiaobao hui Tai guanguang zhinan*), which OCAC published in 1958.

This guidebook propagandized by organizing factual and practical information in service of the state and filtering such information through the language of ideology. *Huaqiao* looking to visit Taiwan found within this pocket-size volume everything from copies of the basic application form and the rules on permitted and prohibited items in one's hand-carry luggage to the regulations on entering and exiting the ROC for overseas nationals. The last of its eight appendixes implicitly affirmed the ROC's legitimacy in the international order by listing the sixteen foreign consular services in Taipei and their contact details, starting with the most important of them, the US Embassy.[27] To reinforce the aura of sovereignty that such details, forms, and laws helped generate, the guidebook also systematically describes Taiwan's physical and human geography. Its first chapter informs us of the physical dimensions and contours of the island, its climate, industries, special local products, population, administrative divisions, main cities, and transportation infrastructure. Interpolated into these factual data are ideologically charged remarks on Taiwan's "fertile soil" (turang feiwo), "enchanting" (yinren rusheng) natural landscape, "industrious and frugal people" (renmin qinpu), and "favorable foundations" (lianghao jichu) for further industrial growth. The chapter describes Taiwan's local produce as valued by global capitalist markets and the island as connected via sea and air to cities in Asia and the rest of the world. It begins in an empirical reality, takes on board ideological elements as it unfolds, and culminates in the official geopolitical account of Taiwan as a "model province of the Three Principles" (Sanminzhuyi de mofan sheng), the "base of the anticommunist revolution to recover and build the nation" (fangong geming fuguo jianguo de jidi), and the "Free World's protective barrier against communism and invasion" (Ziyou shijie fangong, fanqinlüe de pingzhang).[28] Those who wished to know more about Taiwan could peruse chapters 5–9, which go into greater depth on subjects such as governance, industry, transportation, education, media, and natural scenery.

Like much ROC propaganda, the guidebook depicts Taiwan as a place of modernity, democracy, culture, and natural beauty. Its chapter on governance and politics, for example, makes no mention of martial law and instead emphasizes local county and municipal elections that the KMT had begun implementing in Taiwan from January 1951 onward, calling them "ample evidence of democratic politics and the spirit of the rule of law" (minzhu zhengzhi he fazhi jingshen de chongfen biaoxian).[29] Citizens enjoyed freedom of expression and the press, while overseas Chinese students attending university there were "nurtured in the culture of their motherland and trained intellectually" (zuguo wenhua de xuntao he zhineng de xunlian).[30] Finally, chapter 9, the longest, describes Taiwan's eight natural wonders, including the cloud sea of Alishan, Sun-Moon Lake, and the fishermen's lights of Penghu, and other tourist destinations in cities such as Taipei and Taichung.[31] Besides being of practical use to prospective visitors, therefore, the guidebook also established Taiwan's ontological presence in the world by bombarding readers with lists of places, products, and modes of transportation; data on economic production, *huaqiao* university students, and newspapers; and the measurements of mountains, highways, and forests.

But what was Taiwan supposed to be as a political entity? Like Cua's poem, the text shifts between multiple registers of representation. Its title speaks of "returning to Taiwan" (*hui Tai*). Chapter titles and expressions in it such as "A Short Introduction to Taiwan Province" ("Taiwan sheng jianjie"), "Regulations Governing Entering and Exiting the Taiwan Region," and "model province of the Three Principles of the People" refer to Taiwan as a "province" (*sheng*) or "region" (*diqu*) of the ROC. This narrow, legal understanding of Taiwan reflected the yet incomplete project of retaking the mainland. At all times, however, the guidebook embeds such nomenclature within a broader and more ambiguous discourse on the nation. Terms such as *Ziyou Zhongguo*, *zuguo*, and even *Zhongguo* are frequently employed instead of "Taiwan"; *huaqiao* visits were literally a "return to the nation [motherland or homeland]." Nationalist, ideological, and culturalist conceptions of Taiwan were meant to be more appealing to overseas Chinese visitors and to instill in them a specific set of patriotic affinities. Although Nationalist claims on the Chinese abroad rested on idealized assumptions about how supposed "sojourners" understood their relationship to their so-called homeland, it was politically advantageous after 1949 to keep the terms *huaqiao* and *zuguo* in circulation. Propagandists hoped that the unprecedented levels of overseas Chinese support for the ROC during the Pacific War would carry over into the post-1949 period—that "Free China" would serve as an acceptable substitute for the entire China.

Notably absent in this guidebook and other similar works of propaganda are references to Taiwan as a *jia* for overseas Chinese—it could approximate a "homeland" for them in other words but could not be their "home." In the Chinese sojourning tradition, which Cua's poem draws from, the idea of *jia* was intimately associated with one's native place. One's place of birth was a "critical component of personal identity in traditional China, and geographic origin was generally the first matter of inquiry among strangers, the first characteristic recorded about a person (after name and pseudonyms), and the first fact to be ascertained regarding individuals coming before the law," as the historian Bryna Goodman puts it. "Home" was a specific village or city that sojourners were supposed to return to for marriage, mourning, retirement, and burial and to which they sent their remittances.[32] No amount of propaganda could alter the fact that the vast majority of overseas Chinese were not born in Taiwan, nor could it persuade them to conceive of it as their home; only traces of *jia* could be found there in the form of native-place connections. In fact, the very legitimacy of the post-1949 republic was based on establishing that Taiwan was *not* a home, but a place from which one's native places in China, "sucked into a black iron curtain," could be reclaimed from the CCP.

For ROC supporters and propagandists on both sides of the Luzon Strait, textual strategies were a necessary but insufficient means of producing Taiwan's place in the world. Taiwan had to be experienced directly, not just vicariously, so as to establish a virtuous circle between rhetoric and reality. As the KMT educator Chen Lieh-fu said on the occasion of a visit by Cebu Eastern High School's basketball team to the ROC in May 1968, it was not enough for Philippine-Chinese youth to read about their *zuguo* in textbooks and magazines. Their visit allowed them to "set foot upon the territory [literally, "rivers and mountains"] of their motherland for the first time and appreciate its landscape and famous historical sites" (*chuci tashang zuguo zhi heshan, xinshang fengguang shengji*).[33]

The means by which Philippine Chinese set foot in Taiwan differed. While some visitors traveled by commercial aircraft, the ROC frequently arranged for navy vessels and air force planes to transport large groups of visitors from Manila to Taipei and back.[34] The hundreds of students who "returned" every summer for military training invariably traveled on military transportation. On arriving, delegations adhered to itineraries that reinforced propagandistic depictions of "Free China." While their schedules varied according to the composition and purpose of individual tours, they shared common items. Government and party officials accompanied the tours and answered questions that the participants had about the ROC. Trips also required that their members abide by a written code of conduct. Besides dressing appropriately and being on their best behavior, they also had to remain with the group at all times, except during designated and limited periods of free activity, or unless given special permission to leave the group by their leaders. Even during their free time, socializing with locals was forbidden. Apart from designated spokespersons, no one else was allowed to issue public statements or speak to the media.

Items on their itineraries fell into the very same categories that were used to organize the guidebook. Tours of factories, schools, model villages, military bases, and infrastructural projects such as highways showcased the role of the state in modernizing the island. Some delegations were even given permission to visit Quemoy, which was under military rule because of its proximity to mainland China and its tendency to get shelled by the People's Liberation Army (PLA). Visits to cultural, historical, and scenic locations such as the National Palace Museum, Sun-Moon Lake, and Yangmingshan foregrounded the ROC's role in preserving traditional Chinese culture and Taiwan's natural landscape as an ahistorical, organic embodiment of the Chinese

FIGURE 6.2. Chiang Kai-shek greets a visiting Philippine-Chinese artistic propaganda troupe in Taiwan on May 26, 1959. Reprinted with permission from Academia Historica.

nation. Visiting Philippine Chinese also met with state and party officials, other returning *huaqiao* groups, and even Chiang Kai-shek himself (see figure 6.2)—the flesh-and-blood personification of the ROC. Like factories, mountains, and museums, Chiang gave overseas Chinese something tangible to identify with. Meetings with him were highly ritualized affairs and involved the presentation of gifts or monetary contributions as a gesture of respect and appreciation, followed by photo-taking. After experiencing the Chinese nation, the visitors went back to their country of residence to report favorably on their time in Taiwan, thus reinforcing the relationship between text and experience.

The Philippine Chinese Anti-Communist League in Taiwan in 1958

From 1950 onward, a steady stream of Chinese from across the world, East and Southeast Asia in particular, made their way to Taiwan annually. In October 1952, at a time when the PRC scarcely had an overseas Chinese policy to speak of, the ROC staged a ten-day Overseas Chinese Conference in Taipei that rolled out the blue carpet for 216 *huaqiao* from thirty-four countries or regions, including Alfonso Sycip, Sy En, Chua Lamco, Ong Chuan Seng, Yao

Shiong Shio, and nine others from the Philippines.[35] Organized by OCAC, the conference laid out a broad set of guidelines for *qiaowu* and updated the attendees on the ROC's progress since the formation of the Central Reform Committee two years earlier. October 21, the first day of the conference, soon became Overseas Chinese Day (Huaqiao Jie). The conference overlapped with a visit by members of one of the Philippines' oldest and largest clan associations, the Che, Yong, Cua, and Chua Association. They met with their surname counterparts in cities across Taiwan with the aim of "stimulating the spirit of the nation" (*jifa minzu jingshen*), strengthening anticommunism, and "expanding clan organization" (*kuoda zongqin zuzhi*) in the belief that the "clan is the origin of the nation" (*zongzu shi guozu zhi yuan*).[36] In 1954, summer activities in Taiwan for overseas Chinese students began, with 215 of the 287 visiting *huaqiao* youth coming from the Philippines.[37] The even larger Overseas Chinese Cultural and Educational Conference was held for five days in September 1955 to mobilize educators and journalists against communism.[38] By 1958, these and hundreds of other smaller visits had transformed Taiwan into a cultural and ideological "center" for many overseas Chinese despite its geographical marginality in relation to the mainland.

Two years after its formation, the PCACL coordinated with other members of the Big Five to bring greetings and gifts to the troops and congratulate Chiang Kai-shek on his seventy-second birthday on October 31, 1958. The tour lasted from October 10 to November 3 and became the second of two large-scale visits by the Philippine Chinese that year; the other had been a monthlong, fifty-person educational mission in April and May, led by Pao Shih-tien.[39] October was the most popular month for visits to Taiwan by overseas Chinese, as it encompassed not only Chiang's birthday but also the ROC's National Day on October 10 (Double Tenth) and Overseas Chinese Day. That the PRC's own National Day fell on October 1 meant that the ROC could steal attention from its rival right afterward. In 1958, the October celebrations took on a particular significance, as visitors came immediately after the Second Taiwan Strait Crisis, from late August to late September. The PRC's four-week artillery bombardment of the offshore island chains of Quemoy and Matsu contributed to a sharp increase in "patriotic voluntary contributions" by overseas Chinese to Taiwan, from USD 130,500.52 in 1957 to USD 388,031.87 in 1958 and USD 957,483.52 in 1959—an all-time record. In each of these three years, there were more contributions from the Philippines than anywhere else.[40]

As president of the Federation of Filipino-Chinese Chambers of Commerce and Industry (Shang Zong), Yu Khe Thai was the natural choice to lead the twenty-four-person (twenty-two men and two women) PCACL delegation to

Taiwan. Four out of the five Standing Committee members of the league went on the tour: Yu, vice presidents Chua Lamco and Sy En, and Yao Shiong Shio. The remaining participants represented, in addition to the Shang Zong and General Chamber, branches of the KMT and PCACL in Manila and beyond, the Cantonese Association, the General Association of Chinese Schools (Xiao Zong), the Women's Association, the *Great China Press*, and the Chinese Volunteers in the Philippines (CVP) Fraternity (a veterans' organization). Given the symbolic importance of October and the defense of Quemoy and Matsu to the ROC and its supporters, there was also widespread media coverage of the tour.[41]

Our chief source of information on the trip, a "special volume" published after the occasion by the PCACL, centers the tour on the multiple contributions by the visiting Philippine Chinese to the ROC's defense of its offshore islands. Monetary support amounted to nearly 3 million New Taiwan dollars (NTD) in individual and organizational donations, which Yu and Chua presented to Chiang on the final day of the tour.[42] Tour members, along with other visiting *huaqiao*, also met with and offered comfort and encouragement to wounded soldiers and refugees from Quemoy and Matsu who had been relocated to Taiwan itself; each soldier received NTD 50 from the delegates, while each refugee received NTD 20 and secondhand clothing.[43] Interviews with and speeches to the media also figured frequently on the tour's packed itinerary, as befitting an event whose main purpose was to showcase the ROC to the world and drum up support for the Nationalist regime. A press conference in Taipei allowed Sy, Cua Siok Po, and Fernando Chua to explain the significance of their Quemoy trip and efforts to support ROC troops on the front lines, while also giving one of only two female delegates an opportunity to explicate the activities of the Women's Association.[44] The KMT's China Broadcasting Corporation also invited Yu to deliver a radio address to overseas Chinese and people on the mainland in which he praised the government for bringing about improvements in people's lives, including those of local Taiwanese. Repeating standard KMT talking points, Yu declared that a counterattack against the mainland was inevitable and depended on the morale of their mainland compatriots. He concluded his broadcast on an empathetic note. Despite living abroad, Chinese like him felt the suffering of the Chinese people because of family members and friends on the mainland and the CCP's destruction of ancestral tombs. Separated from their homes and kin, they, like their fellow nationals, ardently wished for the recovery of China.[45] Yu, we must not forget, was a naturalized Philippine citizen and not a KMT member.

The highlight of the tour was a day trip to Quemoy on October 16—ten days after the PRC had announced that it was suspending its bombardment—

by six of the twenty-four delegates: Sy En, Chua Lamco, Fernando Chua, Cua Siok Po, Tang Tack, and the Cantonese Association's vice-chairman, Ren Jiaming. Located only several miles off the coast of Fujian and visible on a clear day from Xiamen, Quemoy, as the historian Michael Szonyi writes in his study of Cold War geopolitics and everyday life there, symbolized the ROC's commitment to anticommunism and its sovereignty over more than just the island of Taiwan.[46] If Taiwan was meant to be a "model province" of the ROC, then Quemoy was a "model county" of that province; it was a microcosm of Taiwan but governed by the military rather than the KMT. Because of its proximity to southern Fujian, native residents of Quemoy also spoke Hokkien. Cua's narrative of the visit, however, made no mention of its social and economic development under military rule. His travelogue opened by contrasting areas of the island that had been shelled by PLA artillery with those that had not. As his jeep wound its way toward the front line, a pastoral landscape of green fields, paved roads, and smiling children receded into a nightmarish one of charred trees, destroyed houses, bomb craters, and unexploded ordinance. Nevertheless, the morale of soldiers and local residents had not been dampened. In striking prose, Cua wrote: "Under the strong sun, the wind and dust blew ever so fiercely and stained our white shirts yellow. Our brothers, topless, were busy digging trenches and constructing fortifications, preparing to welcome a greater battle and victory after this first victorious round."[47]

Accompanied by the chairman of OCAC, officials from the military and county (see figure 6.3), and the media, Cua and the others toured the front lines and met with residents of the villages most affected by the shelling. In what was very likely a prearranged meeting, the delegates "encountered" an old woman in the village of Yangshan who said that she had a son in the Philippines. When Cua asked what she wished to tell her son, she said that she hoped he would send some money to help rebuild their home and maybe come to see it. In her smile, Cua said that he saw his own dear mother, who was living in a state of poverty just across the sea in Jinjiang—his ancestral home, now behind the iron curtain of CCP rule. The tour members also met with a young soldier and presented him with a gift from his father, who was a Standing Committee member of the Philippine KMT. The young man asked them to tell his father that the artillery fire had "tempered" (*molian*) him and made him healthier in mind and body. Cua extolled the act of this son of an overseas Chinese leader fighting on the front lines as having a value greater than any monetary donation. He called shaking hands with him as the "highest honor" (*wushang guangrong*) for the delegates.[48]

Cua's account of the delegation's remaining activities on Quemoy was couched in similar sentimental and ideological terms. He gave a speech to the military radio station there calling on his compatriots in Fujian to rise up against Soviet imperialism and to join ROC troops in retaking the mainland when the time came. The army likely broadcast the speech across the narrow strip of water between Quemoy and Xiamen through large loudspeakers.[49] To complement their monetary contributions, the tour also presented local officials with a book of well-wishes for the soldiers and a compilation of letters for residents of the islands; some may have come from the few Philippine Chinese who traced their ancestry there.[50] Just before they left Quemoy, Cua described Fernando Chua as busy taking photographs and gathering flowers and soil samples as souvenirs; Tang Tack, ROC flag in hand, was deep in conversation with several soldiers in various Chinese dialects; and Ren Jiaming, during his chat with an ROC artilleryman from Guangdong Province, gave a thumbs-up gesture and repeatedly exclaimed "Guangdong spirit!" (*Guangdong jingshen*).[51]

However much the tour was guided by the state and despite media coverage of it, we should not dismiss these melodramatic moments or the emotions expressed in Cua's narrative and poems as utterly contrived and merely for display's sake. For Chinese communities overseas that were historically accustomed to being connected to China, being separated from one's family and native place by a regime that reportedly wrecked ancestral tombs was no trifling matter. When Cua spoke of his mother just across the sea in Jinjiang, or when the *Fookien Times* reporter who accompanied the tour wrote that tour members (figuratively) saw their hometowns from the top of Mashan, the northernmost point of Quemoy, each was expressing the sort of yearning for China that collective and individual memories sustained.[52] Most if not all of the visitors had been born in China and migrated to the Philippines in the first half of the twentieth century. China remained lodged in their imaginaries not despite but because of their separation from it. As Bryna Goodman reminds us, love for one's native place was virtuous because it constituted and strengthened the larger political polity of China.[53] As with affinities between clan and nation that the Che, Yong, Cua, and Chua and other clan associations sought to nurture, love for one's hometown contributed to love for the larger national community.

From the perspective of press coverage and "patriotic voluntary contributions" by overseas Chinese to the ROC, the PCACL's tour of Taiwan and visit to Quemoy were a success for the Nationalist regime. Propaganda and visibility also benefited Philippine-Chinese elites, who were eager to proclaim the record-breaking amount of donations that they helped collect that year. Regular visits to "Free China," on top of efforts to institutionalize Chinese anticommunism and socialize with politicians and officials in the Philippines,

FIGURE 6.3. Cua Siok Po (right) and Sy En (left) on Quemoy with the PCACL in 1958. In the middle is ROC general Ke Yuanfen. Reprinted with permission from Liming Cultural Enterprise.

inoculated them from wayward charges of ideological deviance; it was precisely this institutionalization that enabled their fundraising to be so effective. Yet, as their tour of Quemoy indicates, ideological self-fashioning and self-interest were married to deep-seated and complex affinities for "China." These we must also grasp if we are to understand the motivations of Chinese elites and the intricacies of their support for the ROC.

Philippine-Chinese Primary School Teachers Visit Taiwan

Visits by Chinese in the Philippines to Taiwan clustered around two periods in the calendar year. Commercial elites typically visited in October to join in the festivities surrounding Double Tenth Day, Overseas Chinese Day, and Chiang's birthday, while students, teachers, and principals went during the summer holidays to take part in military training and educational seminars organized by agencies such as OCAC and the China Youth Corps. One such visit involved fifty-seven primary school teachers and principals from May 21 to June 21, 1967, during which they visited schools, met with officials, and took part in an intensive, three-week training program at an educational facility in Panchiao, just outside Taipei. After the end of their stint in Panchiao on June 10, they remained in Taiwan to visit additional schools and government agencies. A close reading of the report that they published after their visit reveals how Chinese education served as a common discursive space for ideological and practical concerns and for the shared interests of the ROC state and Chinese society in the Philippines. The report sheds light on how the Panchiao program disciplined its participants, assimilated them into an idealized national community, and conditioned them against communism. Yet those who went through the program did not necessarily understand their time in Taiwan in relation to ideology. Summer training programs for Chinese teachers in Taiwan were just as much practical as ideological in nature and intended to improve the quality of pedagogy and teaching materials. For many trainees, therefore, culture was less an abstract concept than a means by which they made their professional living.

Sponsored by the ROC Embassy and the Xiao Zong, this visit by the Philippine-Chinese Primary School Teachers' Homecoming, Inspection, and Advanced Study Group (Feilübin Huaqiao Xiaoxue Jiaoshi Huiguo Kaocha Jinxiu Tuan) took place at a time when both Taiwan and the Philippine Chinese were committed to advancing a certain vision of Chinese culture. Over the 1960s, conservative Chinese educators continued the work of strengthening their school system against the Filipinization that had begun with the creation of the Xiao Zong in 1957. For Pao Shih-tien, a long-standing goal since the 1950s had been to establish an institution that offered college-level instruction and teacher training courses. Pao had discussed this matter with Chiang Kai-shek, OCAC, and the ROC Education Ministry in 1955, but legal restrictions and the political climate in the Philippines in the late 1950s prevented him from realizing this vision. Pao persisted, and in 1960 secured permission from Manila to merge Chiang Kai-shek High School (CKSHS) and its affiliated two-year teacher training school next door. After further lobbying, the school was accredited as a four-year, degree-granting institution in 1965 and changed its name to Chiang Kai-shek College (CKSC). CKSC became the only overseas Chinese institution of higher education that had the official backing of both the ROC and the government in its country of residence.[54]

CKSC's founding in 1965 coincided nicely with the launching of the Cultural Renaissance Movement in Taiwan in November 1966, on the centenary of Sun Yat-sen's birth. Writing in 1967, one historian dismissed it a "clear-cut failure" and "either completely ignored by most intellectuals, except for those currying favor, or . . . considered an embarrassing joke."[55] But the Philippine Chinese paid it considerable lip service. One Shang Zong businessman who chaired the Committee for the Promotion of the Cultural Renaissance Movement in the Philippines called Taiwan the "cradle and fortress of Chinese culture at the present time" (*dangqian zhonghua wenhua de yaolan yu baolei*).[56] For him and especially for Pao and Chinese educators, the movement aligned with their own defensive cultural struggle-cum-anticommunist crusade. For example, Pao explained in an essay for the inaugural edition of the *Chiang Kai-shek College Journal* (*Zhongzheng xuebao*) in May 1967 the importance of culture to "extinguishing the evil doctrine of communism" (*xiaomie gongchan xieshuo*). He also argued that only *huaqiao* fully versed in Chinese history and culture, and not those educated at foreign universities, would be able to fully reconstruct mainland China after the KMT had retaken it.[57] Pao and others who were associated with cultural organizations, including the merchants who patronized them, willingly incorporated the movement's ideas into school curricula and the language of cultural renewal into their speeches in support of the ROC.

It was within these contexts that the primary school educators visited Taiwan. More so than tours of Taiwan and Quemoy by Shang Zong and PCACL elites, educational training programs allowed for closer state supervision, a more specialized itinerary, and more meaningful interactions between the visitors and Taiwanese officials. For three weeks, the teachers and principals enrolled in the Panchiao National Schools' Teacher Training Program (Banqiao Guomin Xuexiao Jiaoshi Jiangxi Hui) were subjected to a kind of Foucauldian disciplinary regime within a tightly controlled, panoptical space. At Panchiao, much like the students at the schools they taught in, these educators were not so much explicitly indoctrinated in anticommunism as made to think, feel, act, and speak like exemplary "Chinese" citizens in ways that indirectly fortified them against the ideology of the enemy.[58]

Unusually, for such a large Chinese visit to Taiwan from the Philippines, the members of this particular group were not accompanied by any senior community leaders. This was most likely because the visit itself was planned in haste and had to compete for members with the many other *huiguo* groups that summer. They were, however, given the customary ceremonial send-off by the ROC ambassador and representatives of their sponsoring organization (in this case the Xiao Zong) in Manila.[59] The participants in the training program were instead led by Pan Zhaoying, who was fifty-one years old and the head of moral education at the oldest Chinese school in the country, the Anglo-Chinese School. Of these fifty-seven, only fourteen, including Pan, were male, and only three were naturalized Philippine citizens. Most were in their twenties. Only one was a principal, and the rest were either teachers or department heads like Pan. He was also one of the few to have more than a high school education. In total, they represented thirty-nine schools from across the Philippines, but not CKSC.[60]

Established in May 1956, the Panchiao campus was unremarkable in its layout, consisting of a few buildings clustered around a common area and parade ground. The disciplinary effects of the program lay in its code of conduct for trainees and how their daily schedules, from sunrise to sunset, were organized both within and beyond this space. Codes of conduct for the members of organized visits to Taiwan were commonplace no matter what their age. This particular visit imposed on participants an additional set of twenty-two requirements, in keeping with the broad aims of the Cultural Renaissance and with the regimentation and militarization of Taiwanese society that had taken place since the KMT's declaration of martial law in 1947. Wearing pajamas and slippers outside the residential quarters, smoking, spitting, littering, and speaking loudly were forbidden. Above and beyond these basic expectations, trainees were also supposed to be "sincere and humble" (*chengken xuxin*), to "conscientiously self-evaluate" (*renzhen jiantao*) themselves, and to "accept criticism" (*jieshou piping*). At mealtime, they not only were not to waste food but were to "maintain a cheerful mood" (*baochi yukuai xinqing*) and a "good deportment" (*lianghao yitai*). Conversations had to be in Mandarin.[61]

By the time their training began on May 23, a day after they arrived in Taiwan, participants in the program had been made fully aware of what was expected of them. On the morning of May 21, the trainees gathered at Liberty Hall, the headquarters of the KMT *zongzhibu* in Manila. There, before they made their way to the airport, a Xiao Zong member instructed them to read an article in the *Great China Press* on the meaning of their trip. On arriving in Taipei, they were whisked off to Panchiao by OCAC and divided into groups of around six; each group was then assigned its own living quarters. In the afternoon, OCAC, the KMT Central Committee, and the China Youth Corps hosted them to a reception-cum-symposium on the Cultural Renaissance, during which they swore an oath to the movement and were officially inducted into it. The following day, the director of the Panchiao program, Gao Zi, introduced them to the program, its rules, and the campus facilities.[62]

The training program began on May 23 and ended on June 10, running each day from early in the morning to the evening, except on Saturday afternoons and Sundays, which were designated periods of free activity. Six days a week, the trainees were woken up at 6:00 a.m. by a bell and the sound of martial music, had breakfast, and participated en masse in morning physical exercises (*zaocao*) set to music and lasting for fifty minutes. Usually, this was followed by a "reading and instruction" (*duxun*) session, during which trainees read out loud from their assigned readings or gave speeches. However, on Saturdays, instead of *duxun*, their living quarters were inspected for cleanliness. At 8:00 a.m., an hour before class, the trainees took part in a flag-raising ceremony and sang the ROC national anthem, after which they cleaned their quarters, classrooms, common room, and dining hall. Teachers, staff, and even director Gao joined in this collective labor to order their working and living environments. Educated at Mills College in California and the University of Wisconsin, Gao was a well-known educational reformer in China and an advocate of physical education.[63] A seemingly omnipresent authority figure, she ate with and got to know the trainees, who compared her relationship with them as of a mother to her children. But they also called her a stern lecturer, whom they revered. On one occasion, after some trainees informed her that others were not singing the national anthem loudly enough, Gao reminded the entire delegation at the flag raising the following day of the need to do so as an expression of their "patriotic zeal" (*aiguo rechen*).[64]

From 9:00 a.m. until the late afternoon, the trainees visited schools in the Taipei area that specialized in pedagogical methods such as teaching composition to first graders or the use of music and singing in the classroom; attended small-group classes at Panchiao, taught by instructors from local universities, on teaching everything from mathematics to moral education; and went for lectures on topics such as the foundations of Chinese culture, psychological health, modern history and the spirit of national education, and trends in modern education. Some of these sessions were more overtly ideological than others. On the two Mondays of their program, the trainees participated in a meeting of the entire school to hear guest lectures, "The Three Principles of the People and the Construction of Taiwan" (on May 29) and "An Analysis of the Communist Bandit Situation" (June 5). They also received visitors, whose presence helped to keep them on their best behavior: Pao Shih-tien, for example, stopped by on May 26 to show his support for the program, while ROC journalists did so on June 1. On weekday evenings, the program organized cultural and recreational activities for the trainees and taught them, for instance, Chinese dance.[65]

How did participants in the training program remember their time in the ROC? The report that they published in January 1968, suggests that the teachers' dominant understanding of Taiwan was as a source of pedagogical skills and ideas that they could adopt to become better teachers and educators. Most of them had only a high school education and had received no prior specialized instruction in pedagogy. The report itself is evidence of their pragmatic approach to cultural work. As opposed to shorter *jinian tekan*, this report is one hundred pages long. Besides serving a commemorative purpose, it was meant to be useful. Most of it consists of detailed write-ups on the classes they took, teaching methods they learned, and schools they inspected. Little is said about the foundations of Chinese culture, "the Three Principles of the People and the construction of Taiwan," or "the communist bandit situation." As their afterword to the volume clearly states, they hoped that, through the Xiao Zong and the ROC Embassy, the report would be distributed to Chinese schools across the Philippines to motivate teachers and help raise standards of Chinese education there.[66] Anticommunism and counterattacking the mainland are not explicitly mentioned at all in the report, not even by the ROC ambassador to the Philippines or Gao Zi in their forewords to it.

At another level, the visit was about individual memories of everyday life that had little to do with classes or school visits and that sometimes worked against the ideological messaging and disciplinary techniques of the Panchiao program. In her recollections of the visit that were printed in the report, the forty-six-year old Bai Yueying recalled the complete lack of coordination that she and others displayed during their dance-like *zaocao* regimens. While she dutifully recorded what she had learned about teaching, she also fondly remembered playing badminton with the other trainees, talking with them in the evenings when their classes were over, the scenes of rural life that they observed around them, and listening at night to the wind blowing. Accidents, tragedies, and comic episodes punctuated their weekly routine. A trainee's father passed away. Another was bitten by a dog and had to go for a blood test. On a Sunday sightseeing trip to Wulai, a group of teachers were caught in a torrential downpour while making their way down a mountain and ended up thoroughly soaked. Indeed, if there is a common thread that runs through how different trainees recalled their time in Taiwan, it is not anticommunism, but rain.[67]

None of this is to imply that patriotism, culture, and ideology did not figure into how the trainees understood their time in Taiwan. Indeed, Shi Wenrui, a forty-year-old alumnus of and teacher at Sun Yat-sen High School in Iloilo City, framed his experience of the trip in more orthodox ideological terms. In recollecting the visit, Shi said that he had always wanted to "return to the embrace of his motherland" (*hui dao zuguo de huaibao*) and see for himself its military, economic, and educational progress. The tremendous strides that his homeland had made in education were unimaginable to someone like him living in the Philippines, he said. Children in Taiwan were so fortunate to have their families, schools, and society united in support of them. His only regret was that, because of time constraints, he had not been able to observe Taiwan's military development. A conventional understanding of Chinese culture and the importance of educators to promoting it is also evident in the foreword to the report. Here, the Cultural Renaissance is mentioned by name for the only time in the entire volume. Like Shi's recollections, the foreword draws extensively on stock descriptions of Taiwan and overseas Chinese visits to Taiwan: the "smell of its fragrant soil" (*tudi de xinxiang qiwei*); the sincerity and warmth of their compatriots in the motherland; Taiwan's scenic beauty and all-round development; and hearing, seeing, and feeling their *zuguo*. It is as if the teachers acknowledged the importance of couching their experiences in a common ideological language, irrespective of what Taiwan meant to them individually.

The COWHM Veterans' Association and the ROC

The Philippines was one of multiple countries in Southeast Asia whose Chinese populations organized armed resistance movements against Japanese imperial rule during World War II. As the narratives and monuments constructed by those who joined them remind us, the war has been inscribed in collective and individual Chinese memories in both the Philippines and beyond. For members of KMT-affiliated movements such as Cua Siok Po, Koa Chun-te, and Chua Lamco, the sentiments that their wartime struggle engendered cemented their loyalties to a specific conception of the Chinese nation that their party-state defined; for them, the broad-based struggle against Japan transitioned seamlessly into a more specific crusade against Sino-communism. Yet while anticommunism and patriotism were synonymous with each other in the Cold War political imaginations of these men, they overlapped but were not necessarily one and the same in the worldviews of other veterans.

Among Chinese civic groups in the Philippines, few were as enthusiastic about visiting the ROC than the COWHM VA. That, at least, is how its members hoped to be seen by their public and in particular by the Taiwanese government and media. On the occasion of the ROC's Sixtieth National Day celebrations in October 1971, the VA delegation's deputy leader Wang Tiannian proudly declared that this was the tenth visit by the COWHM to Taiwan since 1954, which made it the champion among all *huaqiao* organizations in the world.[68] By comparison, the CVP Fraternity had made only two visits by that point.[69] ROC officials and journalists who contributed to the VA's "homecoming special issue" (*huiguo tekan*) were full of praise for the organization. One journalist said that the VA enjoyed an "unmatched reputation" (*wubi de shengyu*) among soldiers and civilians in Taiwan for its deeds during World War II, outstanding support for anticommunism, and achievements in "joint service" (*lianhe fuwu*). In 1970, a representative from the ROC's Overseas Chinese News Service hailed the VA not only for meeting with military and government officials and participating in sightseeing (*guanguang*), *zhijing*, and *laojun* activities, as most visiting *huaqiao* did, but also for going out into the countryside of Taiwan to "serve the people" (*wei renmin fuwu*) and contributing their money and labor to nation building.[70]

The COWHM had emerged from World War II as the most decorated of the three KMT-affiliated anti-Japanese groups.[71] Subsequently, it transformed itself into a veterans' organization with branches across the country, joined the Filipino Veterans' Association, and promoted cultural activities and education. To help Chinese youth who had joined the resistance and whose education had been cut short by the war as a result, as well as to prevent communist subversion, COWHM VA members established Loyalty Night School (Danxin Yexiao), an auxiliary educational institution for high schoolers. Through it, a self-governing "student brigade" (*xuesheng dadui*) was formed to sponsor events ranging from music and drama performances to badminton tournaments and anticommunist rallies. Comprising both individuals who had fought the Japanese and students who joined the VA after the war, the brigade also organized regular visits to Taiwan, starting in 1954.[72]

The COWHM VA, a member of the PCACL, was as anticommunist and pro-ROC as any Chinese civic institution in the Philippines at the time.[73] But if it stood within and was emblematic of the ideological mainstream, it was structurally removed from the leading institutions of Chinese society unlike, for example, the CVP, which had been the armed wing of the *zongzhibu* and whose members dominated the leadership of the KMT after the war. Unlike most Chinese civic groups, its visits to Taiwan were not conducted under the auspices of or sponsored by the PCACL, the KMT, the Shang Zong, or similar community organizations. Notably absent from the *tekan* that it published in the late 1960s and early 1970s to commemorate its visits to Taiwan are the well-wishes and exhortations from local Chinese leaders and the ROC ambassador that are typically found in this textual genre. No major community figure is featured on the lists of advisers of the student brigade and editorial board members for these *tekan*. Individual brigade members appear to have financed the printing of these volumes and the trips themselves from their own pockets, bypassing the patronage of local Chinese leaders.[74] The only messages of support in them are from party and state officials and journalists in Taiwan, including Cua Siok Po, who by 1968 had left the Philippines to become deputy chairman of Section Three. Like the absence of direct references to *Fangong kang'E* and counterattacking the mainland in the Panchiao training program report, the absence of the usual community leaders from these volumes, and from the leadership of the VA, is telling. It suggests that COWHM veterans understood and performed their affinity to the ROC in their own ways and that there was more to their support for the ROC than anticommunism. Rather than explicitly practicing anticommunism, they practiced a more general patriotism.

The language of the *tekan* highlights how VA members, in particular those who had fought against the Japanese during the war, saw themselves as participants in a continuous struggle against enemies of the Chinese nation and foreign obstacles standing in the way of a unified China under the KMT's leadership: first the "Japanese invaders" (Rikou) and then the "communist bandits" and "Soviet puppet regime" of Mao. To sustain overseas Chinese support for Nationalist China during the civil war and after, ROC propaganda promoted this long-term historical perspective of *huaqiao* as the "mother of the revolution." But by the 1960s, if not earlier, we find few attempts at drawing such continuities in the civic language of Chinese patriotism in the Philippines. No such references to the War of Resistance can be found in the *tekan* from the PCACL's visit in 1958, for example. The struggle against Japan had receded in popular memory and had been supplanted since 1952 by the Cold War and the restoration of Japan-ROC diplomatic relations. From the Taiwan Strait Crises to the Great Leap Forward to the Cultural Revolution, pro-ROC *huaqiao* did not lack for developments with which to fabricate patriotism and outrage against the CCP. Anticommunism increasingly came to define what it meant to love one's native land, not to mention what it meant to be an ideologically correct alien in the Philippines.

Instead of practicing anticommunism, however, COWHM veterans embraced this ideology as a component of their patriotism and as springing from their earlier service to the nation. Anti-Japanese sentiments remained integral to their worldview. In October 1971, Wang Tiannian wrote grimly that the international situation had worsened. He was not referring primarily to the ROC's loss of its United Nations seat or Nixon's forthcoming visit to China, but to the agreement between the United States and Japan on June 17, in which the former relinquished all rights and interests under Article 3 of the San Francisco Treaty of 1952, transferring sovereignty of Okinawa, the Ryukyu Islands, and the Senkaku or Diaoyu Islands to Japan while retaining its bases on

Okinawa. As both China and Taiwan claimed the Diaoyu Islands as "Chinese" territory, the United States' decision angered ROC partisans. In denouncing this unjust violation of the ROC's sovereignty, Wang resurrected the language of World War II, claiming that the United States and Japan—now allies—were "collaborating to swallow up" (*goujie qintun*) the ROC's "sacred territory" (*shensheng lingtu*).[75] To underscore the emotional resonance of this decision among its members, the VA published two articles on World War II in the *tekan* for that visit. One was a firsthand account of the Japanese military's massacre of around six hundred Chinese in San Pablo, Laguna, in early 1945. The other was a polemic, written under the pseudonym of "old man of the Diaoyu Islands" (*Diao sou*), pledging to protect the islands and warning that in the near future, a unified China would prioritize retaking them from Japan.[76]

In the late 1960s and early 1970s, the VA enacted its affinities to the ROC state differently from other visiting *huaqiao*. In August 1968, responding to the KMT's call for "joint service," nineteen members of the VA headed for Taiwan to "serve the people," spending a month touring rural areas of the island. Appreciative ROC officials-cum-propagandists noted in their well-wishes to the VA that this was an unprecedented act, as most overseas Chinese visitors interacted with ROC officials and soldiers in urban, built, and militarized environments, rather than with ordinary people in the countryside. In total, VA members visited 130 villages and towns in the counties of Taipei, Yilan, Nantou, Tainan, and Kaohsiung, where they donated medicine and household items to farmers and villagers, provided scholarships to schoolchildren, and even helped build houses. To complement and emphasize the broader significance of these activities, the delegation leader Cai Anluo gave speeches on communism, in Mandarin or Hokkien, to various county- and town-level civic associations on each day of the tour. For their contributions to the Chinese nation, the KMT Central Committee's Section Five, which oversaw social movements and associations, presented to them honorary certificates of merit and to the delegation a plaque from Chiang Kai-shek.[77]

Not long after returning to the Philippines, Cai Anluo contacted Section Five and proposed contributing toward a large-scale construction project in Taiwan with some NTD 200,000 that the VA had raised. Working with Cai and the VA, Section Five decided that these funds would go toward the reconstruction of Yuehe, an urban village (*li*) of 144 plains aborigines (*pingdi shanbao*) in the urban township (*zhen*) of Yuli, in Hualien County. A year later, in October 1969, with other VA members in attendance, construction began on new houses for Yuehe's twenty-one indigenous families, whose existing homes were located at the foot of a mountain and were at risk of being destroyed by landslides and flooding. In November 1970, Cai revisited Yuehe to find it a picture of modernity and happiness, according to the director general of Section Five, who accompanied him. Its houses were now made of brick and reinforced by steel, to minimize earthquake damage; modern sanitary facilities and a freshwater reservoir had also been built. On the doors of each home were inscribed the names of Cai and other *huaqiao* who had given back to their nation.[78]

Through the visits made by Philippine Chinese and other overseas Chinese to Taiwan, the ROC fashioned for itself qualities associated with the nation-state as a political form and cultural community in an effort to represent itself as a substitute *zuguo* for overseas Chinese. The visits and textual propaganda on them were constitutive, as this chapter has shown, of a larger struggle between the CCP and the KMT to politicize Chinese transnationalism by channeling Chinese people and capital toward either mainland China or Taiwan. For the KMT, controlling and categorizing the inflow of its nationals were necessary for security purposes and also a way of performing its sovereignty over the ROC's borders and asserting a universally recognized attribute of state-ness. Publications associated with overseas Chinese visits such as *A Guidebook for Overseas Compatriots Returning to Taiwan for Sightseeing* factualized Taiwan's presence in the world as a nation-like polity. While references to Taiwan as a "province" and a "region" may have exposed the ROC's territorial incompleteness and the uncertainty over its geopolitical future, propagandists retained the use of terms such as *Zhongguo* and *zuguo* to appeal to overseas Chinese visitors and legitimize the KMT-ROC party-state. These texts and the direct experience of visiting Taiwan were meant to be mutually reinforcing so that the returning overseas Chinese internalized certain ideological and cultural dispositions toward the nation.

The three groups of Philippine-Chinese visitors that we have examined experienced "Free China" in ways that deepen and challenge official understandings of the visits. For many of the PCACL's leaders who traveled to Taiwan and Quemoy in October and November 1958, shortly after the Second Taiwan Strait Crisis, native-place sentiment and nostalgia for their home on the mainland underpinned their support for their *zuguo*. For the primary school educators who spent a month in the summer of 1967 attending a teacher training program at Panchiao and visiting schools across Taiwan, the ROC was a provider of educational expertise and professional training, which they lacked. In the contexts of the Cultural Renaissance Movement and efforts by Philippine-Chinese leaders to defend their schools against further Filipinization, Chinese education became a common ground for both ideological and practical interests. Finally, members of the COWHM VA understood anticommunism in relation to their services to the ROC during World War II and as an aspect of their patriotism. This patriotism expressed itself not in anticommunist practices alone, but also in the forms of anti-Japanese attitudes and "joint service" to the people of Taiwan.

CHAPTER 7

Dissent and Its Discontents

The *Chinese Commercial News* Affair

On the evening of May 4, 1970, immigration agents detained Quintin and Rizal Yuyitung, respectively the publisher and editor of the *Chinese Commercial News* (*CCN*), at the Manila Overseas Press Club. At the time, the *CCN* was probably the most widely read Chinese newspaper in the Philippines.[1] The Yuyitungs had been, since March 24, on trial by the Deportation Board for having purportedly published pro-communist articles in their newspaper and were then out on bail. Eight years earlier, in March 1962, they and ten other *CCN* employees had been arrested and charged with comparable offenses. On May 14, 1968, the Yuyitungs published an apology and retraction, and the board dropped its case against them, placing them on probation instead. In March 1970, however, President Ferdinand Marcos resurrected these charges, claiming that they had reverted to their former ways (see figure 7.1). This time, they would not escape the two regimes that opposed them. With their hearings ongoing, and without their being allowed to contact their lawyers or family members or gather their personal belongings, Marcos had them bundled onto a Philippine Air Force plane in the early hours of May 5 and deported to Taiwan as "Chinese nationals." On August 14, after a hearing that lasted only three and a half hours and was covered by the international media, a military court found them guilty. Quintin was sentenced to two years of reformatory education and Rizal to three years.

Similar to the cases of Co Pak in 1951, the *jinqiao* in 1952, and the Cebu students in 1954, the Yuyitung affair involved the arrest and deportation of Chinese associated with communism. Like the Yuyitungs, Co fell afoul of the Kuomintang (KMT). But the evidence of his connections to the Chinese left, compared to the Yuyitungs', was substantial. Unlike with the *jinqiao* and the Cebu students, the Philippine military twice acted against the Yuyitungs with the full support of the Republic of China (ROC) Embassy and the KMT, which had long sought their deportation. For many Filipino journalists, Quintin and Rizal's persecution signaled nothing less than de facto and de jure Taiwanese encroachment on Philippine sovereignty. On April 27, 1970, for example, Ernesto Granada of the *Manila Chronicle* denounced the KMT as "practically a government within a government in this country."[2] The day after they were deported, Napoleon G. Rama of the *Philippines Free Press* denounced his country for having "degenerated into a puppet of a puppet."[3]

While the Cold War rhetoric of puppetry goes overboard by denying the Philippines agency in its relationship of shared sovereignty with Taiwan, the assertions of ROC involvement are broadly true. No episode in Philippines-Taiwan relations illustrates more vividly how Nationalist China asserted its extraterritorial claims on the Philippine Chinese through its overseas networks and how it colluded with the Philippines against "Chinese communism." Indeed, despite passing resemblance to the *China Daily News* (*CDN*) saga in the United States in the 1950s, the *CCN* affair was without exact precedent anywhere in the world. It is also a rich case study with which to analyze the ideological texture of Philippine-Chinese society, the institutions that sustained it, and the nature and extent of dissent from the status quo. The paper's nonconformist approach to reporting news on China and its support for political and cultural integration indirectly challenged the KMT's hold on Chinese society and the hegemony of anticommunism. At the same time, the affair shows how representatives of the status quo thought and acted in response to what they considered and constructed as heterodoxy.

Scholarship examining the campaign against the *CCN* is virtually nonexistent.[4] Most of what we know about the affair comes from journalists and political activists in the Philippines and beyond who defended the Yuyitungs in the name of press freedom, denounced the Marcos and Chiang regimes, and lobbied for the brothers to be released from Taiwan. Years later, Rizal Yuyitung compiled a selection of articles into *The Case of the Yuyitung Brothers: Philippine Press Freedom under Siege*. This volume, together with his own recollections, as told in a series of interviews to scholars from the Institute of Modern History (IMH) at Academia Sinica in 1993, are our two main published sources on the Yuyitung affair today.[5] But they do not explain the anti-*CCN* side of the story:

how, for instance, the KMT, embassy, and military worked together behind the scenes to persecute the brothers. It is here that the largely untapped records of the Ministry of Foreign Affairs (MOFA) Archives in Taiwan become invaluable—their own gaps and prejudices notwithstanding.

This chapter explains how and why KMT officials and ROC diplomats in both countries—which I refer to collectively as a "Nationalist Chinese bloc"—colluded with the Philippine military, Marcos, and his cronies, against the *CCN*. Drawing on the published sources mentioned above and archival materials from Taiwan and the United States, I examine how this bloc gathered, forged, and interpreted evidence to assist the military in making a case for deportation in 1962 and 1970. It supplied the linguistic and cultural resources needed for the Yuyitungs to be identified as pro-communist Chinese and pressured Philippine officials and politicians such as Marcos from behind the scenes. The military, on its part, fronted the campaign and supplied the coercive means and legal justification needed to bring the brothers into the fold of the state. In December 1952, the absence of such collaboration destabilized Chinese society and threatened the legitimacy of institutions such as the ROC Embassy and the KMT that claimed to defend its interests. The anti-*CCN* campaign showed that by the 1960s, these institutions had re-arrogated to themselves the power to determine the ideological guilt of Chinese in the Philippines. In this sense, the KMT was indeed a "government within a government."

The Nationalist Chinese bloc and the Philippine state acted against the *CCN* for reasons that are not always explicit or easy to discern. The *CCN*'s support for integration and its criticisms of Chinese education were at odds with the chauvinistic worldview of intellectuals such as Cua Siok Po and his former colleague at the *Great China Press*, Hsin Kwan-chue. Personal vendettas and factional politics likely drove some to seek the destruction of the paper. And, in the context of the political crisis that engulfed the Philippines in early 1970 and the declaration of martial law that followed two years later in 1972, Marcos may have ordered the Yuyitungs' deportation to assess how repressive measures against the press would be received. These are the motivations that Rizal Yuyitung and *CCN* supporters have cited to explain the conspiracy against them. Evidence from the MOFA Archives, however, shows that those involved focused exclusively on exposing the paper as a pro-communist mouthpiece or even a communist organ; nothing in these hundreds of pages of documentation suggests that factors such as cultural integration mattered at all. Most anti-*CCN* actors, therefore, not only employed anticommunism as a strategy but also genuinely believed that it supported communism. Individuals associated with the paper had been deported as communist suspects. Most of all, the KMT perceived the *CCN*'s self-proclaimed independent, centrist editorial policy

FIGURE 7.1.   Philippine immigration commissioner Edmundo Reyes (right) reads out the charges against Quintin Yuyitung (left) and Rizal Yuyitung (center) in 1970. A portrait of President Ferdinand Marcos hangs on the wall in the background. Reprinted with permission from the *Commercial News* (*Shangbao*).

as pro-Beijing because of how conservative and pro-KMT the Chinese mediascape was in general. By reprinting articles on China from foreign wire agencies that cited the official People's Republic of China (PRC) news agencies and their ideologically incorrect language, for example, the *CCN* was seen as reporting favorably on the PRC. A common, often a priori, conviction in the *CCN*'s communist sympathies sustained opposition to it across the years and the factions that constituted the anti-*CCN* coalition. Its members saw themselves not as framing the innocent, but as prosecuting the guilty through any means necessary, including the manipulation of intelligence to make a more persuasive case for deportation.

Party and Papers, 1937–1954

The *CCN* was founded in October 1919 as the monthly journal of the General Chamber of Commerce and edited by Yu Yi-tung, a teacher from China who had become the General Chamber's secretary-general. In 1922, with the financial backing of lumber magnate and chamber president Dee C. Chuan, it became a daily, independent paper. Except during the war and despite the campaign against it in the 1960s, it remained in circulation for half a century, until martial law in 1972; in 1986, it resumed publication. Yu Yi-tung did not survive the Japanese occupation. For refusing to propagandize on behalf of Japan, he was executed and the newspaper closed in early 1942. In April 1945, his four children, including Quintin and Rizal, resurrected the paper. By the 1960s, the *CCN* had become the largest of the four Chinese dailies in the country, and it remains a staple of the Chinese community today.[6]

The political scientist James Roland Blaker, in his 1965 study of Chinese newspapers in the Philippines, described the *CCN* as a prototypically "Type II," or "internal-political," paper that was established in response to developments not in China, but in the countries where *huaqiao* lived—in the *CCN*'s case, less the May Fourth Movement and more the Bookkeeping Act.[7] By the 1960s, long after the pre-1949 heyday of Chinese print journalism in the country, it was the only such paper of its type remaining. Unlike "Type I," or "external-political," papers that focused on China such as the KMT's mouthpieces, the *Great China Press* and *Kong Li Po*, the *CCN* adopted what it considered to be a nonpartisan approach to reporting the news. Like the General Chamber that it sprung from and was affiliated with, the paper was in many respects, to use Blaker's term, a "traditionalist" outfit. Rizal, in recalling his life, attributed the *CCN*'s apolitical editorial policy to his family's unusual ethnic background. Born in Manila, the Yuyitungs were also not Han Chinese, but Manchus. "Our background and family history," he said, "would not allow us to take extreme positions. We were unenthusiastic about politics, especially Quintin. Once, when angry, he said to me that the CCN should simply not publish front page international news or supplements."[8]

By the late 1930s, the *CCN*'s purported objectivity and nonpartisanship had fallen out of step with a polarized political climate in China and among Chinese nationalist circles in Southeast Asia. During the Second Sino-Japanese

War, Rizal recalled, while the *Fookien Times* reported only that Chinese troops were victorious, the *CCN* reported both Japan's victories and defeats and relied on news dispatches from both the ROC's Central News Agency (Zhongyang Tongxunshe, or CNA) and the Associated Press. If the latter cited Japanese government sources, the *CCN* translated them without modifying their original language, however derogatory toward the ROC it might be, and maintained the same policy of indirectly quoting PRC news agencies. Consequently, even though it supported the War of Resistance, the *CCN* became a "traitorous" newspaper to KMT loyalists in the Philippines.[9] After World War II, the *CCN*'s determination to avoid taking sides in the civil war saw it caught in the middle of a vicious war of words between leftist and right-wing Chinese newspapers. Pro-communist outlets such as the *Chinese Guide* regarded it as a "running dog of the rightists," while to the *Kong Li Po*, *Chung Cheng Daily News*, *Great China Press*, and *Chungking Times*, it was insufficiently pro-KMT.[10] With the collapse of the radical Chinese left and its media organs by the late 1940s, Chinese public opinion in the Philippines shifted rightward and the *CCN* assumed its position at the leftmost extreme of a narrow political spectrum. Thus, well before 1962, the paper had antagonized ideological extremists. In a 1962 interview with the *Philippines Free Press*, shortly after the first round of arrests, Quintin Yuyitung said: "There is a Chinese group that has tried for years, even before the war, to undercut my family and our newspaper." "For upholding the policy of truthful reporting my paper has offended many in the Chinese community," he claimed, in a thinly veiled reference to the KMT.[11]

Over the course of the KMT's long war with the Japanese and the communists from the 1930s onward, therefore, the *CCN* acquired a reputation for ideological unreliability that informed how a generation of KMT partisans perceived it. The *CCN*'s "objective" journalism ran contrary to the policies of a censorious, state-controlled media regime, the fascistic cult of personality surrounding Chiang Kai-shek, and institutions such as the Jiangxi Political School in Nanchang and the Central Military Academy in Nanjing and Chengdu that trained and indoctrinated party cadres.[12] Had the paper circulated in China during the 1930s, it would have been shut down by the Nationalist state for propagating ideas "discordant with the Three Principles of the People and People's Revolution" and subjected to violent attacks by the Blue Shirts.[13] These illiberal attitudes toward the press and the institutions that fostered such illiberalism were transplanted to Taiwan. There, after 1949, they found fertile ground in a society under martial law that was being mobilized to counterattack the mainland. Their enemy's modus operandi involved propagating ideologies such as neutralism and "peaceful coexistence," which hard-line anticommunists found intolerable.

The *CCN's* first postwar encounter with the authorities appears to have taken place in mid-1950, when Quintin Yuyitung left Manila on a cruise ship for a two-week tour of Hong Kong and Tokyo. On returning to the Philippines on June 12, he was interrogated by the Military Intelligence Service (MIS) and his luggage searched. According to a US Air Force intelligence agent present at the interrogation, Quintin said that he had traveled to Hong Kong to buy typecasting equipment for the newspaper. The search of his belongings yielded nothing of note. British intelligence had subjected him to similar procedures on his arrival in Hong Kong and had shadowed him. US agents who trailed him in Japan said that he was on a sightseeing tour organized by the Japan Travel Bureau and also found nothing suspicious about his behavior. The US Air Force agent who reported on him called him the "suspected head of the Chinese Communist Party [CCP] in Manila." His source was Chow Shu-kai, a counselor at the ROC Embassy (and future foreign minister), who asserted that Quintin was planning to meet with high-ranking communist leaders in Hong Kong and Tokyo to exchange documents with them. Chow's informant was a "highly reliable person in the Chinese Nationalist Party organization in Manila."[14]

Several months after Quintin returned from his cruise and following Ramon Magsaysay's appointment as secretary of national defense in August 1950, three men associated with the *CCN* were arrested by the military as part of a fresh wave of crackdowns on Chinese undesirables in the country. Lim Hua Sin had worked for the *CCN* as a translator after the war and had been attached to the ROC Consulate and Embassy; Ma Piao Ping was then the *CCN's* circulation manager; and Pao Kee Tung was Ma's business partner and a writer for the paper.[15] All three were charged with being communist propagandists. Rizal Yuyitung blamed the KMT for these arrests. Over forty years later, he insisted that Lim's only crime, according to a conversation that he had with Immigration Commissioner Engracio Fabre, was to translate an article for the newspaper reflecting on Eleanor Roosevelt's plans to visit Moscow.[16] The actual offending evidence consisted, first, of an article by Lim in the *CCN* in 1946 ironically titled "I Became Left-Leaning," in which he declared that he had no connections with any political parties and claimed, prophetically, that anyone at the time who identified as a centrist risked being called a communist. Lim's diary, however, revealed that he was in financial difficulty and thus had sought to sell arms and ammunition to the Huks.[17] The deportation case against Ma was based on a master list of communists that the KMT had provided to the military and on sworn statements that he was an active communist. Pao owned a bookstore at Ongpin Street that sold communist propaganda and testified that Ma had knowledge of all the books and magazines stocked there. The

KMT and embassy further believed that Pao's "habitual words and actions" (*pingsu yanxing*) made him suspect.[18] Lim, Ma, Pao, and a few other Chinese were deported to Taiwan in early 1951 as the anti-Chinese Red scare in the Philippines escalated. In January 1952, Taiwan sentenced Lim to an undisclosed period of political reeducation; Ma was tried in July 1953 and found innocent, while Pao was sentenced to seven years in jail.[19]

What is interesting here is that Taiwan's Public Security Bureau (Guojia Anquan Ju), in its profile of Lim Hua Sin, described the *CCN* as a centrist paper that had been attacked by the *Chinese Guide* and the *Great China Press*. It concluded that Lim had not joined any illegal organizations but that "his thinking was clearly biased" (*sixiang xian you pianpo*) because he had considered selling materiel to the communists.[20] The Nationalist state in Taiwan, as distinct from the KMT and ROC officials in the Philippines, was evidently skeptical of claims from its diasporic periphery that the *CCN* was a communist publication, even if it was within its power to find persons who had worked or written for the paper ideologically suspect according to the standards of martial law. If Rizal Yuyitung is to be believed, all three men and not just Ma were released shortly after being deported. They then started families and businesses in Taiwan instead of returning to the Philippines.[21] While ROC sources do not reveal if Lim and Pao were released, it is clear from them that a handful within the government were concerned that the ROC had erred in acceding to their repatriation. At this time, a critical mass of evidence needed to prove that the Yuyitungs and the paper in general were ideologically undesirable did not yet exist.

Around the same time that Quintin Yuyitung, Ma, Lim, and Pao were getting into trouble with the Philippine authorities, the New York–based *CDN* became an early victim of the post-1949 KMT's Cold War against the overseas Chinese media. The *CDN* was the newspaper of the Chinese Hand Laundry Association in the city and in 1950, like the *CCN* in 1962 and 1970, incurred the wrath of the KMT for its editorial policy. In December that year, the party-controlled Chinese Consolidated Benevolent Association called for a boycott of the *CDN*. Two years later, after a federal investigation, the US attorney general charged the paper with crimes ranging from illegally remitting money to China to extortion, murder, and robbery. In 1954, in what Meredith Oyen calls a "foregone conclusion," the editor Eugene Moy and two others were found guilty of extortion. Moy was sentenced to two years in jail and the *CDN* was fined 25,000 US dollars (USD).[22]

The *CDN* affair gives us a sampling of the KMT's fondness for persecuting dissent among Chinese communities globally, but in several key respects it differs from the *CCN* case. For one, the *CDN* was clearly a left-wing paper, albeit an independent one that was not directly controlled by the CCP. Unlike the *CCN*, it was openly critical of the KMT and pro-CCP. The court case, unlike the Yuyitungs' deportation trials, revolved around the issue of extortion rather than ideology; the presiding judge said that he did not care what the political leanings of the paper were. Moy was only jailed, not deported. Finally, although *CDN* staff and Hand Laundry Association members were convinced that the court case was a "conspiracy" by the KMT and "American reactionaries" against them, we have no direct evidence of how exactly the KMT and the US government colluded against the *CDN*.[23]

By contrast, we know much more about the KMT's plot against the *CCN*. Over the 1950s and particularly from 1960 to 1962, ROC partisans became convinced that the *CCN* was pro-communist. The basis for the conviction expanded from guilt by association with specific persons to include what they considered the heterodox ideas and bad faith of the paper itself. For instance, the known fact that Koa Chian had worked for the *CCN* before and after World War II does not appear to have mattered much. Opposition to the *CCN*, rather, was directed toward the content of the paper. In September 1956, at the first Philippine Chinese Anti-Communist League (PCACL) convention, among the items on the agenda was a proposal by a representative of the Co clan association to censure the paper for "pro-communist opinions and attitudes and confusing what Chinese saw and heard" (*tangong yanlun taidu raoluan huaqiao shiting*). After some discussion, the motion passed.[24] Two years later, an anticommunist working group in the Philippines, convened by the ROC ambassador, adopted similar language in discussing how best to persuade the paper to change its "communist-leaning opinions" (*qinfei yanlun*).[25]

Undermining "Chineseness"?

Anticommunism was one of two related reasons for opposition to the *CCN* among Chinese conservatives; the other concerned the paper's provocative stance on Chineseness as a legal and cultural identity in the Philippines. In June 1952, the *CCN* published a two-part article, "The Road Ahead for Chinese Society" ("Huaqiao shehui de luxiang"), in its Sunday supplement, the *Chinese Weekly* (*Huaqiao zhoukan*). Written under a pseudonym by the literary editor Go Eng Guan, the article criticized the China-oriented "provincialism" (*xiangtu zhuyi*) of his ethno-cultural compatriots. In a not especially subtle reference to the KMT's newspaper, Go said that Chinese paid lip service to Sino-Filipino friendship in the presence of Filipinos but, when their backs were turned, reverted to a "Great China" (*Da Zhongguo*) mentality. Returning to

China was not realistic. Instead, Go called on Chinese to contribute their skills and talents to the Philippines and for the weaving of cultural Chineseness into the multiethnic fabric of the Philippine nation.[26]

A steady stream of such pieces followed in the years to come. While critical of Manila's discriminatory economic policies, the CCN established itself as one of the most outspoken critics of Chinese education from within the community. From August 31 to October 19, 1958, the CCN published an eight-part series, "The Bankruptcy of Chauvinistic Education" ("Pochan de shawen zhuyi de jiaoyu"), which attacked Chinese schools' inattention to English instruction and dogmatic adherence to an outmoded form of nationalist education, calling for a complete overhaul of the system to meet the needs of a rapidly changing society.[27] Starting in 1960, usually under a pseudonym, Rizal Yuyitung took to the *Chinese Weekly* to promote the "metamorphosis" (*tuibian*) of Chinese into Filipinos. This did not only entail acquiring citizenship, for one's legal status as a citizen did not necessarily entail a sense of cultural belonging. More importantly, it also involved the "hybridization" (*hunhua*) of Chinese and Filipino cultures through, for instance, the widespread adoption of Filipino languages by Chinese and the relegation of Chinese to a secondary tongue.[28]

The liberal, multiculturalist outlook of the CCN slowly gained currency among a younger, college-educated generation of ethnic Chinese who had been born and grown up in the Philippines, spoke better Tagalog than Chinese, and saw themselves as culturally Filipino as much as Chinese. In the late 1960s, they took up the Yuyitungs' cause by organizing in support of jus soli citizenship and the Filipinization of Chinese schools; ironically, they achieved their aims under martial law. But in the 1950s and early 1960s, the CCN, at least among most Chinese, was ahead of its time. Unsurprisingly, its advocacy angered those affiliated with the KMT who had appointed themselves the arbiters of Chinese culture in the country and the Cold War world. Foremost among them was the editor in chief of the *Great China Press*, Hsin Kwan-chue. Like his colleagues Koa Chun-te and Cua Siok Po, Hsin was a transnational Chinese conservative whose travels had taken him to the Philippines. Born in Jiangsu, he first arrived in 1946 as the editorial director for the CNA, having earlier worked in China as a journalist and propagandist for the KMT. Over the course of a long career in China, the Philippines, and Taiwan, Hsin published dozens of volumes of poems and literary criticism in praise of an essentialized Chinese tradition.[29] He wrote frequently for the *Great China Press* under the suitably conservative pen name Sima Guang and condemned the Yuyitungs for "forgetting their roots" (*shu dian wang zu*) in calling for cultural integration.[30]

Hsin and other KMT cultural warriors in the Philippines such as Cua had many reasons for resenting the *CCN*. By branding Chinese schools as malintegrative and chauvinistic, the paper was effectively siding with the Philippine government in the ongoing debate over the future of Chinese education and "betraying" its own people. Leading party members were not implacably opposed to legal naturalization and some, such as Antonio Roxas Chua, came around to supporting it by the end of the 1960s. But cultural Filipinization was a more serious threat because it would erode a particular form of Chineseness and threaten the party's raison d'être and institutional foundations. As identities underwent *hunhua*, the logic of cultural chauvinism went, so too did identification with the ROC—the self-appointed guardian of Chinese "traditions"—diminish, depriving Taiwan of diasporic support. To compound the Yuyitungs' fraught relationship with the KMT, from the mid-1950s onward, supporting the integration of Southeast Asia's Chinese became the official policy of the PRC as it sought to win over nonaligned countries and allay their fears of Chinese populations as potential fifth columnists. In December 1956, PRC Premier and Foreign Minister Zhou Enlai gave a speech in Burma making it clear that all Chinese living abroad could unilaterally renounce their PRC citizenship. By the end of 1957, the PRC had shifted from merely giving them this choice to actively encouraging them to naturalize, limit their pro-PRC advocacy, and practice cultural integration through intermarriage and other activities.[31] There is nothing to suggest that the *CCN*'s stance on integration was influenced by the PRC, or if the KMT believed that such influence existed, but the KMT cannot have failed to notice broad similarities between the *CCN*'s position and the PRC's. Advocating cultural integration was thus a "communist-leaning opinion" because it threatened to sever the link between cultural and political identity that the KMT had forged and on which its ideological project depended.

Rizal, Quintin, and their lawyers were adamant that the *CCN*'s support for integration was a crucial reason for the Philippine KMT's and the ROC's hostility toward the paper, and we have no reason to doubt them. Beyond their own statements, however, there is no evidence from the ROC archives to show that the Nationalist Chinese bloc used integration to oppose the Yuyitungs during the Deportation Board trials in 1962 or 1970 or at the military tribunal in Taipei in 1970.[32] The ROC's stance on integration, as opposed to the views of individual KMT ideologues, was never explicitly articulated. While the ROC neither modified its 1929 Nationality Law nor relinquished its cultural claims over Chinese abroad, as the PRC did, it did not officially regard support for integration as anti-ROC and pro-communist behavior. A legal argument against the *CCN* on such grounds would not have persuaded Taiwan to accept the Yuyitungs as deportees, and nor would the Deportation Board have entertained it. Integration, after all, was pro-Filipino. "Undesirability" had to be located elsewhere.

Furthermore, while opposition to integration may have driven ideologues such as Hsin to oppose the *CCN*, it cannot explain the Philippine military's and the ROC Embassy's involvement in the anti-*CCN* conspiracy. This campaign was centered on anticommunism. As an ideological lens through which they apprehended social reality and the justification and strategy for persecuting the brothers, anticommunism united these factions. The *CCN*'s balanced reporting on mainland China evinced pro-communist tendencies in their eyes and became the evidentiary basis for the case against the paper.

Undermining Anticommunism?

In the 1950s and 1960s, as the KMT solidified its control over diasporic cultural and civic life, practicing anticommunism was normalized and articulating positions contrary to the status quo became increasingly difficult and perilous. Dissent lay just beneath the surface of ideological hegemony, as the examples of Koa Chian and the Cebu students suggest. But, in many respects, they are the exceptions that prove the rule. For the most part, dissent did not clothe itself in the robes of communism and support for the PRC, in direct and explicit infringement of *Fangong kang'E*. Rather, it obliquely counterposed the ideology du jour. Support for cultural integration was one such manifestation of what we might call anti-anticommunism or non-anticommunism.

Dissent could also take the form of comparable attempts to depoliticize mainland China by distinguishing one's affinities for China as a cultural homeland, on the one hand, from support for the CCP and enthusiasm for communism, on the other. We know that the Chinese in the Philippines persisted, via third-party brokers in Hong Kong, in remitting money to family members in China; this was despite Manila's ban on such transactions and the KMT's efforts to depict them as aiding and abetting Mao. A rare concrete example of this particular expression of dissent can be found in the memoirs of the ex–Philippine-Chinese Anti-Japanese and Anti-Puppets League (Kang Fan) guerrilla and Nanyang High School (NHS) alumnus Santos Ong. Despite his affiliation with the Kang Fan during the occupation, Ong was branded a KMT agent and threatened by his former comrades in 1946 for refusing to include an article on Marxism in a school publication that he was editing. Forced to carry a gun to protect himself, he ended up being publicly defended by the KMT. Ong then returned to China for a year, but he became disillusioned with the corruption and chaos that had engulfed his homeland and before long was back in the Philippines—where he wrote regularly for the *Kong Li Po*.[33]

In his autobiography, which was published in Beijing in 1989, Ong represents himself as a patriotic overseas Chinese who was above ideology and keen to promote cross-strait dialogue. For not being an anticommunist and for seeking to cultivate cultural ties with the mainland, he became politically suspect to the KMT. At a 1969 meeting of the Xibian native-place association, Ong and three others proposed a fundraising campaign for a school in their home village. Incensed, a KMT member who was present launched into an anticommunist tirade against them. Ong waited patiently for him to finish before explaining that their fundraising had nothing to do with political affiliation. Regardless of which regime controlled Xibian, their elder kinsmen were still their elder kinsmen and deserved their support. Several months later, the ROC ambassador summoned Ong for a meeting and informed him that the National Bureau of Investigation had produced a receipt for 120,000 Philippine pesos (PHP) issued by the Xibian association. Fortunately, the ambassador was not willing to pursue the matter further, fearing that this "small spark could set the entire plains on fire" (*xingxing zhi huo, keyi liaoyuan*) and adversely affect all of Chinese society. He thus persuaded the bureau to destroy the receipt. Ong acknowledged their donation drive but denied that it was about aiding the communists. He said that the school in Xibian was old and dilapidated and that village elders had written to their overseas kinsmen on multiple occasions for aid. Ong had been prepared to wait for the KMT's counterattack, but unfortunately, twenty years had passed without that happening. What would the ambassador do if he were in Ong's position, Ong asked. The ambassador thought for some time before responding that while the "ethical ideas" (*lunli guannian*) underlying Ong's actions were excusable, one should never remit money to the mainland.[34] While Ong never shook off the KMT's suspicions of him, he was also never punished for his transgressions—unlike the Yuyitungs.

This episode from Ong's memoirs offers unusually detailed insights into how non- or anti-anticommunists positioned themselves in relation to the ideological mainstream and negotiated the structures of power of Chinese society. Ong and the Yuyitungs make for an excellent comparison in this regard. Each contested the Cold War ideological binary that Nationalist China's organs and partisans sought to impose on civic life and discourse. Ong fashioned a thoroughly China-centered cultural subjecthood and patriotism that he believed transcended ideology entirely. The Yuyitungs turned away from a certain version of cultural Chineseness as defined by the KMT but, like Ong, questioned the polarization inherent in *Fangong kang'E*. Out of principle, they gravitated toward what they considered the political center, only to find this space full of peril.

The *CCN* did not practice anticommunism. Rizal Yuyitung, in his IMH interviews, explained that the *CCN* was neither a left-wing nor a right-wing newspaper and was chiefly interested in reporting on issues of interest to local Chinese merchants. He stated that it encouraged integration, for instance, as the most realistic solution to anti-Chinese economic nationalism. Not being a KMT organ, unlike the *Great China Press* or *Kong Li Po*, the paper cherished its independence and felt no compulsion to toe the party line. Politically, the *CCN* also differed from the *Fookien Times*, which was independently run, but whose founder and publisher, Go Puan Seng, was a committed anticommunist. International news tended to receive less attention than local news, but it increased in proportion to the latter during the 1950s as the *CCN* sought to boost its readership.[35] In reporting on China, it did so in the belief that, regardless of the KMT-CCP divide, readers had the right to know what was truly happening there because they had relatives on the mainland and many had been born there. At the time, however, neither English nor Chinese newspapers in the Philippines had direct access to the PRC's official news agency, Xinhua. Chinese papers, including the *CCN*, obtained most of their news on China from the CNA, while English-language papers also relied on international news agencies such as Reuters, Agence France-Presse (AFP), United Press International (UPI), and the Associated Press, all of which subscribed to Xinhua. Unlike the other three Chinese dailies, with which it competed for readers, the *CCN* translated and published these agencies' articles verbatim to offer a diversity of perspectives on China, similar to how it had reported on Japan before the occupation.[36] It also covered the public visits by Filipinos to mainland China that started during the Marcos presidency. Rizal recalled that when a group of Filipino journalists traveled to the PRC (he did not say exactly when), the *CCN* translated their report, which provided both favorable and critical views of the communist regime.[37]

Although unremarkable by the standards of English-language papers in the Philippines, the *CCN*'s balanced coverage of developments in mainland China and indirect reproduction of official PRC sources was unacceptable to the KMT. The party considered a news item titled "Red China Navy Rated Strongest in the Far East" "pro-communist" simply because it reported positively on the PRC. Provenance was unimportant. The frame of reference for Nationalist ideologues was the tightly regulated media scene in martial-law Taiwan, where "balanced" reporting on China was nonexistent. Neutralism, as PCACL propagandists reminded local Chinese, was a Trojan horse for communism. By the end of the 1940s and certainly by the mid-1950s, Nationalist organs such as the KMT, the PCACL, Chiang Kai-shek High School (CKSHS), and the embassy had largely succeeded in creating a Chinese public sphere that approximated Taiwan's—with one notable exception.

A constant and prominent obstacle to the ideological monopoly of anti-communism was the country's most widely read Chinese newspaper. The *CCN* did not merely print news on China not from the CNA. It also violated the linguistic-ideological guidelines that the central KMT imposed on the media in Taiwan and required all organs of the state and party at home and abroad to adopt. In July 1947, the KMT stipulated that all official correspondence, press releases, and newspapers refer to the CCP as "communist bandits" (*gongfei*), an announcement that the ROC consolidated into a comprehensive set of guidelines for "rectifying names" (*zhengming*) to delegitimize and reflect the "true" nature of the CCP, the PRC, the Soviet Union, and their leaders. For instance, "*fei*" was to be attached as a suffix to the family names of Mao and other CCP leaders, while the PRC was always supposed to be the "communist bandit regime" (*gongfei zhengquan*), never the "People's Republic of China" (*Zhonghua renmin gongheguo*).[38] In the Philippines, the KMT, party newspapers, the *Fookien Times*, and Chinese organizations in general adhered strictly to this naming policy, blanketing Chinese public discourse with KMT-approved ideological signifiers. The *CCN* did not observe these strictures. As a matter of principle, it retained the original language of any news dispatches that it reprinted, including that of the KMT and the CNA. Thus, in translating and publishing articles from AFP and other international wire agencies, it did not employ the rhetoric of banditry. Mao was simply Mao and Beijing was Beijing (Northern Capital), which Taiwan persisted in naming Beiping (Northern Peace) to maintain the fiction that Nanjing (Southern Capital) remained the true capital. The KMT did not accept this, Rizal said: "It believed that you had to use 'Beiping.' If you used 'Beijing,' you were recognizing the CCP; if you did not employ 'Mao-bandit,' 'Mao-traitor' [*zei*], and similar language, you were a leftist, a communist."[39] To make matters worse, in indirectly citing PRC news sources, the *CCN* often published pejorative descriptions of Chiang Kai-shek, whom the PRC denounced as a "bandit" in exactly the same way that the ROC disparaged Mao.[40] For example, it republished a UPI article in May 1962 that quoted a PRC news release attacking Chiang Kai-shek's "bandit gang" (*feibang*) in Taiwan and Chiang as a "cruel bandit" (*canfei*).[41]

To maintain its editorial independence, the *CCN* also refused to allow the KMT to dictate how it should publish the party's news items. Rizal explained that in the late 1940s and early 1950s, the Philippine *zongzhibu* and Section Three of the KMT Central Committee regularly issued press releases to the *CCN* with instructions on which page to print them on, how much space they should take up, and the size of the headline. When the Yuyitungs persistently refused to comply with the KMT, the party stopped issuing the *CCN* with its news releases in the late 1950s and pressured the CNA into canceling the *CCN*'s subscription to it in 1969.[42] This forced the *CCN*, according to Rizal, to rely only on international wire agencies for its news on mainland China.[43]

Ironically, evidence from the PRC corroborates Rizal Yuyitung's claims about the *CCN*'s editorial policies and political neutrality, even as it also shows that he was not being entirely forthright about the paper's reporting on China. From 1960, the *CCN* began receiving news items from the PRC's second-largest news agency after Xinhua, the China News Service (Zhongguo Xinwen She, or Zhongxin), which targeted Hong Kong and the overseas Chinese and was keen on breaking through the "news blockade" (*xinwen fengsuo*) that the Philippines had erected between itself and the PRC. In 1961, Zhongxin officials in Fujian reported that they had sent fifty-three dispatches to the *CCN* in 1960, mostly on topics unrelated to current affairs such as sojourners' villages, local historical figures, and an "introduction to the puppetry arts of Quanzhou." The *CCN* published twenty of these pieces, mostly in the *Chinese Weekly*. Analysis of the paper by the communist authorities suggests that they understood the *CCN*'s politics far better than the KMT did. They regarded the *CCN* as a "centrist" (*zhongjian xing*) paper in 1959 and, in 1960, "center-left" (*zhong zuo*) compared to the "center-right" (*zhong you*) *Fookien Times* and the "reactionary" (*fandong*) *Kong Li Po* and *Great China Press*. In 1963, the Fujian government even allowed the *CCN* to circulate in Jinjiang for a year.[44] We do not know if the KMT was aware of any of this.

The 1962 Arrests and Deportation Board Hearings

In condemning the KMT, Rizal Yuyitung's reminiscences reveal the gulf in attitudes between the *CCN* and the KMT toward the role of the media in society and how "China" should be represented in print. A good liberal, Rizal was committed to fairness and balance in reporting the news and to a free and independent press. He had only scorn for what he considered the servility of other Chinese papers toward the KMT government and their meddlesome pursuit of ideological uniformity: he and his brother approached the news as Filipino journalists might. Yet he also acknowledged that his enemies' belief in the *CCN*'s guilt was genuine, however much his paper was innocent. KMT ideologues not only were intolerant of deviations from official naming policy but also had been trained to ascribe such deviations to bad faith and communist scheming. In the Cold War that they imagined, *gongfei* were ubiquitous and constantly seeking to subvert overseas Chinese societies. In the Philippines, the *jinqiao an* and the absence of an active Chinese communist movement since the late 1940s only heightened right-wing Chinese and Filipinos' fears of a hidden Red menace—whose outward signs they were convinced they had identified in the early 1960s.

Quintin and Rizal Yuyitung were arrested for the first time in the early hours of March 8, 1962, together with ten *CCN* staffers; two additional *CCN* employees on the military's wanted list of fourteen names were never caught. Quintin, Rizal recalled, was dragged out of bed at home and taken to the offices of the *CCN*, which the military ransacked. Finding nothing of note, they returned the following evening and "found" a letter to Quintin from Li Weihan, head of the United Work Front Department of the CCP. Rizal's house was also raided. In recalling what happened, Rizal remembered that the Filipino officer in charge of the raid was "very polite" but "did not understand a thing about communism": "They confiscated several hundred of my books, because they believed that so long as someone's last name ended with 'ski,' he was a communist. What a joke!" Most of the people arrested were released the following day, but Rizal was detained for two weeks and Quintin for six months. Even after both were freed, they had to remain within a ten-mile radius of Manila and report to a police station once a week.[45]

The operation against the *CCN* in March 1962 originated with the military, with the KMT playing a vital supporting role. In the year before the arrests, MIS started gathering evidence and shadowing major figures associated with the paper.[46] In August and September 1961, it formed a special working group to accelerate its operation and invited four senior members of the KMT in the Philippines to join it: Cua Siok Po, the KMT *zongzhibu*'s secretary-general; Lim Soo Chan, Cua's deputy; Cheng Kim Tiao, the *Kong Li Po*'s general manager; and Koa Chun-te, the publisher of the *Great China Press*. Several months later, the ROC Embassy came on board at MIS's request. It formed its own internal working group to discuss how local Chinese and ROC diplomats should cooperate with MIS and how to represent the arrests to the media and the Chinese public. Cua and Lim were also members of this second group.[47]

All involved took it as a given that the *CCN* was pro-communist; if there were dissenting views, they are not to be found in the archives. MIS believed that the *CCN* directly subscribed to Xinhua and was willfully publishing CCP propaganda, as its arrest warrant for the Yuyitungs and their employees shows.[48] The *CCN* merely pretended that its Xinhua pieces were secondhand by attributing them to AFP.[49] The ROC ambassador admitted in a private conversation with Alfonso Sycip that while he did not read the paper closely every day, his general impression was that it inclined toward the communists.[50] On February 3, 1962, the embassy's working group stated emphatically that cooperating with the Philippine authorities to eliminate the *CCN* was the "most concrete and important work" (*zui shiji er you zhongda de gongzuo*) against the CCP overseas. For the Nationalist Chinese bloc, the issue was not whether the *CCN* was guilty, but the optics and legality of the case and its ramifications for Chinese society. It was essential, party and embassy agreed, that they work closely with MIS to avoid implicating innocent Chinese and any repeat of the *jinqiao an*.[51] Equally vital was ensuring that the Philippines take the initiative and act legally; that Nationalist Chinese assistance be rendered in secret so as to avoid accusations of meddling in the Philippines' internal affairs; and—in the closest we come to an admission that considerations other than national security were at play—that the arrests be framed as an anticommunist operation and nothing more.[52]

In the months before March 8, 1962, the embassy's working group provided four forms of assistance to MIS. First, it vetted the original list of twenty-seven suspects that MIS drew up and advised it to cut the list down to fourteen names, lest the arrests be seen as targeting Chinese society in general as opposed to key figures in the *CCN*. Second, the embassy secured the approval of the ROC to have the suspects deported to Taiwan. Third, in January 1962, the working group covered the *Kong Li Po*'s subscription to AFP so that the military could cross-reference its dispatches with *CCN* articles. Fourth, to make up for MIS's lack of manpower and translators, embassy staffers helped translate three years' worth of the *CCN*'s "pro-communist" articles, which later served as evidence for the prosecution.[53]

Also working against the *CCN* behind the scenes was Hsin Kwan-chue, whom MIS invited to serve as its principal translator before the embassy joined the campaign. Ideological and cultural differences aside, Hsin nursed a grudge against the paper for running stories about his opera singer wife and exposing him as a plagiarist, according to Rizal Yuyitung.[54] Besides writing propaganda and literary criticism, Hsin was also involved in intelligence work. In early to mid-1960, Hsin turned over to Narciso Ramos, the Philippines' ambassador to the ROC, a cache of documents purportedly detailing the activities and structure of the CCP in the Philippines from 1926 to the late 1950s. At Ramos's request, Hsin wrote a summary of these documents that circulated widely and was highly regarded within the intelligence community. How Hsin obtained—if, indeed, he simply "obtained"—these materials and their contents is unknown, but, according to Ramos, he sought no material reward for handing them over. Nor was Hsin financially compensated for translating thousands of *CCN* news items in the three months leading up to March 8 or for sorting through and translating *CCN* staffers' books and documents that were seized.[55]

To make its case for deportation, the military submitted a total of 1,916 items of evidence to the Deportation Board, most of which consisted of articles that Hsin and embassy staffers had translated. Also included as evidence were several "anti-Filipino" cartoons and poems; books and periodicals that MIS had confiscated; *Kong Li Po* editorials; a report by Narciso Ramos; and the December 15, 1961, letter from Li Weihan that MIS "found" in Quintin's study.[56] The anti-*CCN* conspirators evidently felt the need to produce as wide a range of evidence as possible in the hope that some, if not all, of it would prove persuasive. Li Weihan's letter was key, because it was the only direct "proof" of ties between the CCP and the *CCN*. In this letter, Li addressed Quintin as "Comrade Chang-Chen" and praised him, Rizal, and twenty-one other persons (mostly *CCN* employees) for working hard over the previous year, before criticizing them for not keeping pace with changing times. It stated that "reactionary forces [had] been greatly expanding" with the Liberal Party's victory in the November 1961 presidential elections and the growing strength of the "Chiang Kai-shek clique" in the Philippines. The letter, which was written largely in simplified Chinese, ended with Li instructing Quintin and the rest to "discuss humbly the reasons why [they could not] keep pace with [the] change of environs" and to submit a plan for 1962 to Li for endorsement.[57] Quintin denied having ever seen the letter and knowing its origins.[58]

The letter was almost certainly a forgery, given how it was "discovered" a day after Quintin was arrested, when he had been removed from his home. Rizal was certain that it was the product of collaboration between the KMT and the military. That twenty-three names were squeezed onto a one-page letter suggests that it was fabricated and planted specifically to incriminate the entire *CCN* staff, he argued.[59] Whoever forged it must have had knowledge of the CCP's organizational structure and propaganda. It resembled internal CCP missives and propaganda in style and content, and its use of simplified Chinese characters further "proved" that it originated in the PRC. Hsin was likely behind it. With his background as a propagandist and counterintelligence agent, recent record of "obtaining" such documents, and enmity toward the *CCN*, he had both the motivation and means to forge the letter.

Hsin himself was a witness for the prosecution, but he appears not to have commented on the Li Weihan letter. Instead, he was introduced as a specialist on the Chinese language and tasked with explaining to the Deportation Board why the *CCN*'s published output was pro-communist. According to Rizal, Hsin indicted the *CCN* for using simplified Chinese in its news items and publishing news items from Xinhua. But, Rizal said in response to Hsin, the *CCN* did not use simplified characters, because the type for its printers consisted only of traditional characters. The only character it used that could even be considered simplified was *yi* ("art" or "talent"), which it printed in its cursive form because of how complex its traditional form was. Hsin insisted that this was a simplified character, despite clear differences between its simplified and cursive forms.[60] Quintin and his lawyer, none other than Alexander Sycip (ironically, the ROC Embassy's legal adviser until he was compelled to resign from the position during the trial because of a conflict of interest), deftly handled Hsin's accusation that the *CCN* printed CCP propaganda, explaining that it was an independent paper that published news on mainland China because its readers were interested in developments there. The *CCN* did so through foreign wire agencies rather than the CNA because it did not want to publish anything that had previously been vetted by any government. Commenting on the news item "Red China Navy Rated Strongest in the Far East," Quintin explained that "a reporter is not on the side of A in a basketball game against B simply because he reported that A won the game."[61]

Instead of Hsin, the prosecution leveraged its ties to the larger intra-Asian anticommunist ecumene by calling on a Hong Kong–based "authority" on communism, Chao Ching Win, to analyze Li Weihan's letter and testify against the *CCN*. The ROC Embassy's working group had recommended Chao as an expert witness and also paid for his two visits to the Philippines and his living expenses. Chao had no formal affiliation with the KMT or the ROC state and had never traveled to the Philippines previously, which explains why the prosecution felt that he would be a more credible witness. Born in Liaoning and educated in Tokyo, Ann Arbor (Michigan), and London, Chao was a founder of the China Democratic League, a coalition of political parties that sought a "third way" between the KMT and the CCP, in 1941. In December 1956, having attended the first and second People's Political Consultative Conferences in the PRC, he defected to Hong Kong. There, he wrote a best-selling critique of the CCP, *Ten Stormy Years* (*Fengbao shinian*), which was translated into English, Japanese, and Korean; refounded, in 1958, the journal *Modern Critique*; and, in 1960, established the Mainland Research Institute, which published an intelligence digest in English on the PRC and employed refugee intellectuals like him.[62]

Chao testified to the Deportation Board that, while part of the Democratic League, he had met Li Weihan and that Li was indeed head of the United Work Front Department. Li had either penned the letter personally or directed someone else to write it for him. Everything about it—its letterhead, seal, use of simplified characters, and style—was identical to CCP documents.[63] Chao was adamant that the *CCN* was a Red organ, despite having no previous history with the paper. But he had different standards of proof from the board, which remained skeptical of his interpretation of the evidence. Chao quickly grew frustrated with his limited influence over proceedings. During his second visit to the Philippines, Chao lectured the military on the CCP's united front activities. He also complained about the prosecution's poor preparation, the board's limited understanding of the case, Filipinos' general lack of understanding of communism, and his minimal contact with Philippine KMT members and local Chinese. After testifying, an exasperated Chao told Koa Chun-te that Koa had to find someone from Taiwan who was knowledgeable about the CCP to continue Chao's work. "This case must be won" (*ci an bixu dasheng*), he declared, as a loss would have a huge impact on the overseas Chinese in the future. Ironically, he believed that it was acceptable to "make up a little evidence" (*zao dian zhengju*) and "treat [the Yuyitungs] a little unfairly" (*yuanqu tamen yidian*). In other countries, on the basis of evidence such as Li Weihan's letter, they would have been found guilty much earlier. Chao said much the same to a Philippine military official and warned him not to release the brothers. Before returning to Hong Kong, Chao accused one of the three Deportation Board members (he did not say who) as well as the English-language media, which had reported sympathetically on the *CCN*, of having been bribed by communists.[64]

In late 1962, the Deportation Board concluded its hearings and found the Yuyitungs guilty of "printing communistic news items and offensive cartoons and articles" from 1949 to 1962.[65] It rejected the other evidence and arguments, including Li Weihan's letter. However, instead of simply recommending that President Diosdado Macapagal deport the Yuyitungs, it suggested that if they apologized for their actions, they be allowed to remain in the Philippines after a five-year probation period. The deportation order never came, despite persistent lobbying efforts by the ROC bloc and MIS. From what we can tell, Macapagal was concerned that the Yuyitungs might be sentenced to death in Taiwan and that his complicity in their deportation would affect his own popularity.[66] But in February 1965, Macapagal seems to have indicated a willingness to deport the Yuyitungs on the condition that the ROC pay PHP 2 million and send an airplane to pick up the brothers.[67] This money was not forthcoming. Either too distracted by the impending elections or afraid of how any decision of his would play out with the electorate and the opposition Nacionalistas, Macapagal was quite happy to stymie the anti-*CCN* bloc even further. After his defeat in November, the case passed into the hands of his successor.

Marcos, like Macapagal, did not prioritize the Yuyitung case, at least during his first term in office. His inaction, the ROC Embassy conjectured, was down to an unwillingness to offend the English-language media—among whom the Yuyitungs had many friends and supporters—and be seen as violating freedom of the press.[68] When Marcos eventually acted in 1968, he went with the recommendation of the Deportation Board and insisted that the Yuyitungs apologize for and retract the offending articles, so that they might be put on probation. Although they were at first unwilling to apologize because they had done nothing wrong, their friends persuaded them to, so that they could get on with their lives.[69] The *CCN* published their apology in English and Chinese on May 14, 1968. The Nationalist Chinese bloc treated that as proof of the *CCN*'s guilt and stepped up its surveillance of the paper in the hopes of finding fresh opportunities to act against it.[70]

The Thunderbolt Plan and the First Quarter Storm

In early 1970, leftist opposition to the once popular Marcos administration surged. After lying dormant for many years since the end of the Huk Rebellion, Filipino communism found a new lease of life with the establishment of the Communist Party of the Philippines (CPP), along Maoist lines, in December 1968, and the creation of its armed wing, the New People's Army (NPA), in March 1969. In November 1969, Marcos was reelected by a substantial margin after what the historian Alfred W. McCoy calls "an exceptional surge in violence and blatant vote buying."[71] In early 1970, Marcos's popularity, especially among younger Filipinos, nose-dived in response to a postelection financial crisis and austerity measures. In what became known as the First Quarter Storm, leftist student demonstrations erupted in Manila against Marcos and his US patrons, starting with the visit of US vice president Spiro Agnew in December 1969 and continuing beyond then. On January 30, violent clashes between protesters and the police near Malacañang Palace resulted in six students being killed and hundreds more injured.[72] For the first time in the history of the Philippines as an independent country, anti-Chinese sentiment manifested itself on the streets. On February 27, some two hundred protesters massed in front the ROC Embassy on Dewey Boulevard, waving huge portraits of Mao Zedong and Che Guevara and calling on Taipei to resolve the "irritants" in its diplomatic relationship with Manila.[73] Before the police arrived, they banged on the front doors of the embassy building and stoned its windows, including those of Ambassador Patrick Pichi Sun's office. During this period, there were also minor occurrences of vandalism against businesses and cars in Chinatown.[74]

Everyone—from Marcos to members of the Philippine political and military establishment to right-wing Chinese and Filipinos—was convinced that a Maoist plot against the Philippine and other Asian governments was under way, especially after January 30. The journalist Jose F. Lacaba reported that a police officer had called the events of that day an "insurrection," while the president had labeled them "a revolt by local Maoist Communists" and an "act of rebellion and subversion."[75] Fanning the flames of hysteria, the Philippine Anti-Communist Movement declared that Congress, the University of the Philippines (UP), and "practically all government offices had been infiltrated by subversive elements."[76] For the ROC, social instability, left-wing anti-Chinese populism, and the emergence of the CPP would all help it press its case against the Yuyitungs and ingratiate itself with Marcos and the military. As Chao Ching Win's comments from 1962 indicate, Chinese anticommunists long believed that Filipinos did not comprehend the magnitude of the threat that they were facing. This was evident in what Taiwanese officials believed was the Manila police's sluggish and excessively tolerant response to the embassy protests. The police not only arrived forty-five minutes after being contacted, but also made no attempt to disperse the demonstrators or stop them from waving Mao's and Che's portraits. In lodging an official complaint with the Department of Foreign Affairs, the embassy said that the ROC would never allow Chinese protesters to wave portraits of Filipino communist leaders in front of the Philippine embassy in Taipei.[77] Taiwan's expertise was therefore needed to help the Philippines come to terms with this resurgent Maoist menace.

The anti-*CCN* campaign had in fact restarted prior to the First Quarter Storm, which proved to be as unexpectedly beneficial to Marcos's political ambitions as it was to the ROC's long-term goal of purging Chinese public discourse of ideological heterodoxy. As the case dragged on during the 1960s, a handful of state and party officials in Taiwan and the Philippines came increasingly to view the paper as a threat that had to be dealt with in such a way that it had "no way of continuing to exist" (*wufa jixu shengcun*).[78] Half a year after the Yuyitungs apologized, the Nationalist Chinese bloc sprang into action again, prompted by what it saw as continuing textual evidence of the *CCN*'s pro-communist tendencies and the paper's violation of the conditions of its probation. Unlike in the early 1960s, when it is unclear precisely what or whose actions prompted the Philippine military to launch its operation against the *CCN*, the initiative this time can clearly be attributed to the KMT. In January 1969, it launched what it called the Thunderbolt Plan (Leiting Jihua) and, together with the embassy and the *Great China Press*, resumed compiling and translating articles from the *CCN*.[79]

The Thunderbolt Plan unfolded on multiple fronts in early 1970 as part of a multifaceted campaign by the embassy and local Chinese leaders to protect Chinese property, clarify the ROC's efforts to resolve problems in the diplomatic relationship, and strengthen ROC-Philippine relations on the basis of a shared commitment to anticommunism. Officially, Ambassador Sun was tasked with meeting Marcos and offering ROC and Philippine-Chinese aid in combating the Maoist problem. The first recorded meeting between Sun and Marcos on this issue took place on February 6, during which Sun briefly mentioned the CCN's role in fanning the flames of antigovernment unrest. In response, Marcos said that he had "also heard about this."[80] By then, the Thunderbolt planners had likely nearly completed their translation of the CCN's articles for the benefit of the military.

Thunderbolt was a transnational conspiracy made possible by the KMT's institutional and personal networks that connected Taiwan and the Philippines. It was instigated at the highest levels of the party in Taipei by Section Three, whose chairman was none other than Mah Soo-Lay and deputy chairman was Cua Siok Po. Mah had led an eventful and peripatetic life since helping to found the Mutual Aid Society in Manila in 1936. After remaining in China during the Pacific War and the civil war, he traveled to Indonesia in 1950 to launch a newspaper, taking advantage of Jakarta's short-lived tolerance of the KMT as a political organization despite its diplomatic ties with the PRC.[81] In 1960, Mah, the highest-ranking KMT member in Indonesia, was thrown out of the country because of Taipei's clandestine support for antigovernment rebellions in Sumatra and Sulawesi. Taiwan's meddling triggered mass deportations and confiscations of Chinese property and brought about the destruction of the party there.[82] Caught up in this crisis, Mah went back to Taiwan to helm Section Three and through his friendship with Koa Chun-te stayed abreast of the CCN case.[83] Cua Siok Po had assumed his appointment in Section Three in November 1967.[84] In early 1970, Cua revisited the Philippines to rally party members and "patriotic Chinese" behind the Thunderbolt Plan. Joining him there from Taiwan was Hsin Kwan-chue, who had left his position at the Great China Press in 1968 to become a visiting professor of foreign languages and literature at the Political Warfare Cadres Academy in Taipei. Because of his ties to MIS, Hsin was given the task of encouraging the Philippine military to restart its operation against the Yuyitungs and assist it in doing so.[85] According to Rizal, four Philippine KMT members were also involved in the plan: Lim Soo Chan, who had become secretary-general of the zongzhibu; Cheng Kim Tiao of the Kong Li Po; Billy Chan, a journalist for the Great China Press; and the Press's new editor in chief, Jose Lim Chua, who was a CKSHS alumnus and also the secretary of the PCACL.[86] Rizal believed that Lim Chua, like

Hsin, bore a grudge against the *CCN*. This was because its international affairs editor had supposedly attacked Lim Chua in print over the latter's personal life.[87]

Cultural conservatives associated with the KMT were thus the driving force against the *CCN* in both 1962 and 1970. The business community appears to have played a supporting role and had its own reasons for disliking the paper. In 1960, a war of words erupted between the Federation of Filipino-Chinese Chambers of Commerce and Industry (Shang Zong) and the *CCN* following Rizal Yuyitung's criticism of its lackluster response to Filipinization. The Shang Zong proceeded to censure the *CCN* at its annual meeting. Two years later, several Shang Zong members appeared before the Deportation Board as witnesses for the prosecution and accused the *CCN* of being pro-communist.[88] Rizal also accused Antonio Roxas Chua, president of the Shang Zong from 1970 to 1974, of actively seeking the Yuyitungs' deportation, but this is difficult to corroborate given the absence of any references to him in MOFA records.[89]

Marcos ordered the arrest of the Yuyitungs on March 23, 1970. In his interviews with IMH, Rizal stated that the newly appointed secretary of national defense Juan Ponce Enrile wrote a report to the president, who then had Enrile act against them.[90] But in his notoriously unreliable memoirs, Enrile said that an intelligence report from the military had prompted Marcos to have him "revive the deportation case against Quintin and Rizal."[91] The president's rationale for arresting them is not hard to grasp. Excerpts from Marcos's diaries show that he had given serious consideration to declaring martial law during the First Quarter Storm, particularly after January 30. On February 17, he wrote: "I have that feeling of certainty that I will end up with dictatorial powers if the situation continues—and the situation will continue." Seeing himself surrounded by enemies, he was especially hostile to liberal Filipino journalists. They were "busy placing the government in disrepute and holding it in contempt before the people" by blaming it for the unrest and criticizing its policies toward the protesters. Marcos did not seem to think that the CPP was receiving external military aid (i.e., from China), but he was quite willing to believe that communists and their fellow travelers in the Philippine media were lending rhetorical aid and legitimacy to "rebellion and subversion."[92] His was a very similar conspiratorial logic to the KMT's. Moreover, acting against the *CCN* allowed him not only to rid the Philippines of supposed subversives but also to test the waters before declaring martial law. A lawyer for the *CCN* argued that Marcos's persecution of the brothers was one of the "principal conditioning methods" with which he prepared the people to accept authoritarianism. While he did not believe that he could directly assault the Filipino media, he reckoned that no one would care if he arrested and deported two

Chinese journalists whose newspaper was read only by a small fraction of the country's population.[93]

The 1970 Deportation Board Hearings

The evidence presented by the prosecution at the Deportation Board hearings consisted of the military's intelligence report and sixty-eight articles from the paper from November 9, 1968, to March 6, 1970, that Thunderbolt's conspirators had collected and translated.[94] Forty-seven of them were from foreign wire services and twenty-one from the Philippine News Service.[95] The report combined previous evidence against the CCN (such as Li Weihan's letter, which Rizal remembers was dredged up again) with an assortment of fresh charges, among them that Quintin had used a lecture series at the UP Asian Center to spread Maoism, that the Yuyitungs had secretly funded Maoist student leaders at UP, and that they had remitted money illegally to mainland China. Quintin, in fact, had not lectured at UP, but had merely attended the lectures of Antonio Araneta Jr. Araneta and several Asian Center students confirmed this as witnesses before the board. Other UP students whom the brothers were said to have financed testified that they did not know them at all, had met them only once and not received money from them, or had never visited the Manila Overseas Press Club, where they were reported to have met the Yuyitungs.[96] The illegal remittances charge proved to be just as unfounded. As Rizal recalled: "A person whose last name was 'Lee' said we had helped him send money to his children in China. In other words, we had violated the law. But this Mr. Lee, when questioned, did not dare to say his parents' names and could not describe the surroundings of his residence in Manila. I remember a Western newspaper jokingly referring to him as 'the worst KMT special agent.'"[97]

Neither of the two "expert" witnesses for the prosecution provided persuasive arguments for deportation. The first was Captain Romualdo Dizon, a "specialist on China," who admitted during his cross-examination to not knowing Chinese and who also said that he had nothing to do with the intelligence report that he was supposed to testify about.[98] The second was Hsin Kwan-chue, who reprised his role as interpreter in chief of the CCN. Engaging in a close reading of the articles that Thunderbolt had gathered, Hsin indicted the CCN for using "leftist" terms such as "fascism," "imperialism," "feudalism," "protracted struggle," "serving the people," "Beijing," and "People's Republic of China," dismissing as irrelevant the origins of these terms in foreign news dispatches and factual reports on China's domestic affairs.[99] The journalists present at the hearings recorded an extraordinary exchange between Hsin and one of the Yuyitungs' lawyers, ostensibly about press freedom in Taiwan, but which quickly devolved into a remarkable act of self-sabotage by Hsin:

"You will agree with me," [said] Attorney [Juan] Quijano on cross-examination, "that in Taipeh [*sic*], in Taiwan, your newspapers do not enjoy the full freedom of the press."

"We enjoy fullest freedom of press," replied Professor Hsin, "so much as you enjoy right here. The only thing. . . .you see, we do it not upon the censorship of the government but upon the agreement of the editors."

> QUIJANO: "Can you publish in Taipeh an article severely or savagely criticizing General Chiang Kai-shek?"
>
> HSIN: "This is. . . . this belongs to a different tradition. We Chinese. . . ."
>
> QUIJANO: "No, no, just answer my question."
>
> HSIN: "We never do that."
>
> QUIJANO: "You never do that. That's the answer there."
>
> HSIN: "Simply because our tradition is different."
>
> QUIJANO: "You never do that."
>
> HSIN: "How would we do that? You see, I hate these people who do that."
>
> QUIJANO: "Now, suppose there is an editor in Taipeh whose sentiment is different from yours, whose guts or courage is different from yours, will he be free to criticize General Chiang Kai-shek savagely, the way our newspapers criticize our President?"
>
> HSIN: "Mr. Attorney, your question is hypothetical, you see. I don't want to . . ."
>
> QUIJANO: "No, my question is not hypothetical . . ."
>
> HSIN: "There is nothing wrong with President Chiang Kai-shek! Why should the people start attacking him? There's no reason!"[100]

To ensure that the board recommended deportation and that he would simply be seen as adhering to its verdict, Marcos had instructed that only Immigration Commissioner Edmundo Reyes, who was his appointee, conduct the hearings, as opposed to a conventional three-person panel.[101] But even Reyes acknowledged the poverty of Dizon's and Hsin's testimonies. Quijano and other members of the Yuyitungs' legal team succeeded at having the witnesses' testimonies discarded.[102]

The evidentiary basis for prosecution thus narrowed to the MIS intelligence report and the sixty-eight *CCN* articles. On the question of press freedom, the prosecution argued that Quintin and Rizal, as ROC citizens, did not possess the same rights as Philippine journalists, but the defense countered that there was nothing in the constitution that limited such freedom to only Philippine citizens.[103] The urgent need to deliver a guilty verdict was compounded by the

FIGURE 7.2.   Immigration Commissioner Reyes (left), Quintin Yuyitung (center), and Juan David (right), one of the Yuyitungs' lawyers, during the deportation hearings in 1970. Reprinted with permission from the *Commercial News* (*Shangbao*).

brothers' declarations on April 25 and 26 that they were renouncing their "Chinese" citizenship to protest their persecution by the ROC. But to escape the shackles of nationality and become legally stateless, they needed Taipei's approval first.[104] By then, their guilt was fait accompli. Taiwan had already agreed to accept them, and the logistics of deportation were already being discussed. The Department of National Defense (DND) had originally hoped to deport them on April 21, but Rizal had fallen sick on April 18, and the trial had not ended as early as hoped because of the Yuyitungs' legal team's efforts before the Deportation Board (see figure 7.2).[105] Marcos, fed up with the delays and confident of being able to defend his decision, ordered the Yuyitungs rearrested on May 4 and deported the morning after.

The Yuyitungs in Taiwan and Taiwan in the World, 1970–1973

The outcome of the August 14 trial of the Yuyitungs in Taipei, like that of the Deportation Board's hearings, was a foregone conclusion. Fully aware of this, the Yuyitungs admitted in writing to knowing beforehand that all the materials that they published were "for the benefit of Chinese Communist propaganda," while at the same time seeking to secure a more lenient sentence.

Rizal, for example, said that because he had grown up in the Philippines, he was "not aware of the situation of his fatherland and might have committed mistakes." Despite having read some of Mao's works, he asserted that his thinking had not been affected by them and that he had published news from CCP-controlled regions of China solely to sustain and expand the *CCN*'s readership. After three months in Taipei, he had a "better understanding of the situation of his mother country now" and hoped that the ROC would "forgive him for his past mistakes." His brother similarly contended that he had no intention of aiding the CCP and that the *CCN* published what it did for the sake of "professional competition," in view of how English-language papers in the Philippines published articles by foreign wire services that quoted official PRC sources.[106] Their legal strategy succeeded. The military tribunal found that, in 1968, the brothers had "redoubled their efforts in propaganda articles for the benefit of the Chinese Communist rebels" and that "prominent spaces were devoted to false and over exaggerated reports on Peiping's military, political, economic, cultural, scientific and industrial activities." The accused had admitted that their publications "[had] been 100 per cent pro-Peiping in the last few years." Therefore, as ROC nationals, they were guilty of violating the Statute for the Punishment of Seditious Acts even though they had committed their offenses abroad. However, as the brothers "lacked knowledge of Chinese Communist schemes and atrocities" and had "shown signs of sincere repentance since their arrest and deportation to Taiwan," they were to be "given an opportunity to reform themselves."[107]

The deportation and Taiwan's verdict met with widespread and near universal condemnation. Six days after the Yuyitungs were deported, the CPP's youth arm issued a manifesto, "The Moving Finger of Imperialist Diktat: The Yuyitung Case," which denounced Marcos for enacting a "hitlerite [*sic*] policy of repression" and colluding with the "KMT pirates" before pivoting to a full-throated attack on US imperialism—"the No. 1 enemy of the Filipino people" and the prime mover of what had happened.[108] Liberals, both in the Philippines and globally, denounced the deportation in the name of press freedom and human rights. Amnesty International mobilized persons from the global North into bombarding Chiang Kai-shek with postcards and letters calling for the brothers' release and, in 1971, chose them as its prisoners of conscience for the year. The only organized and sustained campaign in defense of the Yuyitungs, however, came from the Zurich-based International Press Institute (IPI), a nongovernmental organization of journalists that the ROC had only just joined in 1969. Working with the Yuyitungs' lawyers and the founder and owner of the *United Daily News* (*Lianhe bao*) in Taiwan, the IPI attempted to secure the early release of the brothers, in return for which the *CCN* would self-censor its reporting on the ROC.[109] When they were not released early, the ROC was expelled from the IPI on October 22, 1971, just three days before it was also expelled from the United Nations.[110]

Ironically, right-wingers as much as liberals resented Taiwan's decision to mete out *ganhua* to the Yuyitungs. The chief of the National Bureau of Investigation expressed the views of many within the Philippine military and intelligence community when he said that the lenient sentence encouraged communist activity. Echoing him, an unnamed member of MIS's working group on the *CCN* said that the verdict "disheartened" them and wondered why the tribunal had not adhered strictly to the letter of the law by sentencing the Yuyitungs to jail for at least seven years.[111] The KMT was likewise unhappy for these same reasons. Far from cowing the *CCN* into toeing the line, the deportation of its owners only emboldened it further and solidified its anti-ROC stance. On January 11, 1971, for example, the *CCN* published a cartoon depicting the ROC's ambassadors to Italy, Chile, and Canada dejectedly carrying their embassies' signs on their backs and returning to Taiwan, as if to mock the ROC's loss of diplomatic recognition.[112] On January 17, an article in the *Chinese Weekly* substituted the character *min* (people) in the Three Principles of the People with *mian* (sleep), outraging Mah Soo-Lay.[113]

In the end, the Yuyitungs were not released ahead of schedule—even though, if Rizal is to be believed, the ROC state came to discover that they were innocent and that the Philippine KMT had deceived Taipei. "When our case reached the highest levels of government, they had to collect intelligence from different sources, and from this they came to realize that we were not communists," Rizal asserted in 1993. "The Taiwan Garrison–General Headquarters also sent agents to Manila to infiltrate the newspaper and found nothing. It decided we had been the victim of a malicious plot and were completely innocent."[114] There is no evidence to corroborate these claims or to shed light on many of the discussions that took place behind closed doors in Taipei, unfortunately, so we can but deduce the political logic at work. In early 1970, the diplomatic tides were turning against the ROC. The number of countries that recognized the PRC had been steadily increasing. Chiang Kai-shek would have been aware of secret exchanges taking place between Washington and Beijing.[115] With its legitimacy in the world under scrutiny, the ROC could not afford to cave to pressure from the likes of Amnesty International and the IPI and thus be seen as erring fundamentally in its legal judgment. Like the Philippine military before the *jinqiao an* in 1952, the ROC needed a communist threat to justify its existence, even if it had to invent or exaggerate one and even though reclaiming mainland China had long ceased to be a viable military or mobilizational strategy. It needed, finally, to

sustain the fiction of its body-based sovereignty over "Chinese nationals" overseas, such as the Yuyitungs.

For these reasons, ROC leaders abided by the military court's August 1970
verdict while ensuring that the Yuyitungs were as well treated as possible during *ganhua*. Quintin and Rizal ended up in an air-conditioned detention facility in Panchiao. Rizal recalled that they had a personal cook and could watch
television and listen to wireless radio and that he could even tune into PRC
broadcasts if he tried to. They were supposed to have been subjected to anticommunist indoctrination but were the only ones in the facility who did not
have to attend classes. Instead, lecturers visited their quarters to instruct them.
To pass the time, Rizal read the Three Principles, Chiang Kai-shek's speeches,
all of Shakespeare, and—twice—the Bible.[116]

Controversy erupted one last time in 1972, when Quintin's two-year period
of reformatory education was coming to an end. After much discussion, state
and party officials agreed that Quintin would be permitted to leave Taiwan
after being released, obtain a ROC passport, and travel to the United States at
the invitation of the US committee of the IPI. The Philippine KMT, already
unhappy at what it perceived was the ROC's excessively lenient treatment of
the brothers and weakness in the face of pressure from the IPI, reacted by
threatening to secede from the Central Committee. In its view, the ROC had
disregarded the rule of law. Based on how the *CCN* continued to report on the
ROC, party hard-liners also believed that the paper's pro-communist attitudes
had intensified and that it was incapable of reforming itself. Were Quintin to
return to the Philippines at some point, he would no doubt resume propagandizing on behalf of the CCP. All in all, KMT members in the Philippines felt
that Taipei's management of the Yuyitung affair was having a dispiriting effect on their anticommunist efforts.

The KMT Central Committee responded to this crisis in intraparty, center-
periphery relations by dispatching Cua Siok Po to the Philippines on September
5–10, 1972, shortly after Quintin had been released from Panchiao, but before
he left Taiwan, to explain Taipei's thinking. Along with the ROC ambassador
and a handful of party elders who accepted the decision, such as Koa Chun-te
and Pao Shih-tien, Cua spent his first three days there meeting with disgruntled
party members individually. On September 8, he addressed a meeting of about
forty KMT members in Manila. After praising the Philippine KMT for its "reso-
lute fighting spirit" (*douzhi jianqiang*) and "firm stance" (*lichang jianjue*), Cua explained that Taipei had decided to allow Quintin to leave Taiwan because of the
"current international environment" (*dangqian guoji huanjing*) and to snuff out
a plot against the ROC by leftist IPI members. He assured them that Quintin

would not be allowed to return to the Philippines. Cua was successful, and the Philippine KMT withdrew its threat to secede. In a written response to Cua, the *zongzhibu* called for improved cooperation between the Central Committee and its Philippine branches at this uncertain time for the ROC, particularly in areas such as propaganda, the media, and outreach to Filipinos. Party members expressed doubts that two years of reformatory education had changed Quintin's political beliefs and said that they deeply regretted how international public opinion had decisively influenced his release. Looking ahead, they urged Taipei to ignore public pressure when handling Rizal. They hoped that if Rizal remained obstinate in his political views in a year's time, he would continue undergoing *ganhua* and Taipei would consult closely with them. Not doing so, it hyperbolically threatened, would precipitate the "complete disintegration" (*quanmian wajie*) of the KMT in the Philippines.[117]

Following his release from Panchiao, Quintin remained in Taiwan for several months to obtain a passport and a visa to the United States through the US Embassy in Taipei. On November 11, Chiang Ching-kuo authorized Quintin's departure, and on December 8, Quintin left Taipei for San Francisco.[118] A year later, Rizal was released from detention with little fanfare and joined his brother in the United States. There were no protests from the Philippine KMT this time. Rizal eventually settled down in Toronto. He and Quintin returned to the Philippines to reestablish the *CCN* after Marcos was overthrown in 1986. Quintin died in San Francisco in 1990, and Rizal in Toronto in 2007.

The Yuyitung affair, which brings our narrative of the Philippine Chinese as Cold Warriors to a close, encapsulates the major concerns of this book. Through institutions such as the PCACL and individual ideologues such as Mah Soo-Lay, the KMT sustained its diasporic networks in the Philippines and asserted Nationalist China's extraterritorial sovereignty over the Chinese. Decades after Mah and others had implanted the KMT in the country, these networks reached deep into the Chinese community and the Philippine state. They facilitated the spread of a stifling ideological orthodoxy and, failing that, the identification and persecution of the few open dissenters from the status quo such as Quintin and Rizal. The Yuyitungs were not communists; most of those who were, like Co Keng Sing, had long since left the islands. Their persecutors from within Chinese society were more constitutive of its ideological mainstream. In many ways, then, the KMT achieved with regard to the Philippine Chinese, and with Manila's consent and support, a degree of dominance second only to what it managed in martial law Taiwan.

The Yuyitungs and other non- or anti-anticommunists aside, *Fangong kang'E* proliferated among the Philippine Chinese: indeed, this book argues that anticommunism became part of their identity as ethnic minorities. The reasons for that, as the *CCN* case reveals, are many and difficult to disentangle from each other. Mah, Hsin Kwan-chue, Koa Chun-te, Cua Siok Po, and others had been indoctrinated in the ideology of the party, and some had fought for it during the War of Resistance. We have little reason to doubt that they genuinely despised communism and remained steadfast in their commitment to the KMT's cause. At the same time, however, an unknowable portion of their opposition to the *CCN* stemmed from petty self-interest: Hsin's bitterness toward it for publishing stories about his wife, for example. Elsewhere in this book, the stories of men like Alfonso Sycip, Shih I-Sheng, and Antonio Chua Cruz further highlight the nonideological and adaptive aspects of anticommunism. Opposing communism benefited their reputations within Chinese society and could be profitable: there may not have been actual communists to oppose, but there were wealthy Chinese to accuse of heterodoxy and blackmail. For them and other, more ordinary Chinese, the consequences of such heterodoxy, even perceived, could be dire. To become part of Cold War and postcolonial Philippine society as aliens, many Philippine Chinese performed their conformity to the ideology du jour. The right ideology, in short, helped mitigate the "wrong" ethnicity.

Such was the Cold War for the KMT and the Philippine Chinese. The Yuyitungs, tethered to Taiwan by their "nationality" and the KMT's networks, experienced this conflict principally in terms of Taiwanese, not US, intervention in their lives. The United States was not unaware of what was going on among the Philippine Chinese, for sure, but its considerable energies in the country were directed elsewhere and not toward a small, unproblematic Chinese community. Besides, the KMT had things well under control within its sovereign, diasporic space—as its campaign against the *CCN* and penetration of civic life suggest. For the Nationalist regime, which lacked territorial control over the mainland, claiming, maintaining, and multiplying these spaces mattered greatly in its post-1949 struggle against the CCP for legitimacy. Thus, the region where most overseas Chinese lived was crucial to the KMT's Cold War—as it had always been to the diasporically oriented party.

Conclusion: Rethinking "China," the Overseas Chinese, and the Cold War

In hindsight, the Yuyitungs' deportation to Taiwan represented the apogee of Nationalist China's ideological hegemony over and among the Philippine Chinese. In the five years following the brothers' show trial in Taipei, the Republic of China's (ROC) influence in what was once one of its staunchest allies in Asia declined considerably. Sino-US rapprochement and the People's Republic of China's (PRC) admission into the United Nations in 1971 and 1972 delegitimized the ROC in the world. During the first three years of the martial law era in the Philippines, from 1972 to 1975, a series of far-reaching executive decisions and generational changes within Philippine-Chinese society intersected with each other to cripple the Kuomintang (KMT) in the country. Chinese schools were at last Filipinized. In a move that younger Chinese social activists also welcomed and had fought for, the naturalization process for foreign nationals was vastly simplified. Finally, immediately afterward, Manila recognized Beijing. Ironically, the same person who had greenlighted the deportation of the Yuyitungs in anticipation of authoritarian rule also helped realize their integrationist aims under authoritarian rule. All this brought about not an immediate end to the Cold War for the Philippine Chinese and the Philippine KMT, but rather, in the anthropologist Heonik Kwon's words, its "decomposition."[1] Taiwan did not go quietly in the Philippines. The institutional remnants of the KMT can be found even today, and some individuals remain committed to it still.

The first pillar of KMT influence in the Philippines to crumble was its control over Chinese education. The state's previous efforts in the mid-1950s to supervise Chinese schools had left their Chinese-language curriculum and the ROC's all-important role in shaping it basically untouched (chapter 5). Nationalization, however, remained on the political agenda and was raised again during the 1971–1972 constitutional convention that Marcos convened to extend his presidency beyond its two-term constitutional limit.[2] During the convention, thirty-eight resolutions recommended provisions to Filipinize or incapacitate Chinese schools. After much debate, the proposed constitution was amended to reflect widespread support for educational Filipinization within the political establishment.[3] In April 1973, seven months into martial law, Marcos issued Presidential Decree No. 176, instructing the Department of Education to implement Article XV, Section 8, of the new constitution. Henceforth, all educational institutions not only were placed under government supervision but also had to be owned solely by Filipinos or corporations that were controlled by a 60 percent Filipino majority. No schools were to be established exclusively for aliens or any school to offer a curriculum exclusively for aliens.[4] The Chinese curriculum, patterned after Taiwan's, was canceled and the teaching of Chinese made optional and only as a foreign language. All Chinese schools were given until the end of the 1976–1977 school year to meet these requirements.[5] With the stroke of a pen, Marcos had unilaterally abrogated the ROC's "liberty to establish schools for the education of their children," which the Treaty of Amity had spelled out in 1947.

The severing of diplomatic ties between Taiwan and the Philippines and the establishment of Philippine-China relations soon followed in 1975; the groundwork for that had been laid during the preceding decade. After he entered office, Marcos, in the hope of diversifying his country's trade relations, almost immediately lifted a ban on Philippine citizens traveling to socialist countries. By March 1974, the Philippines had normalized relations with Bulgaria, Poland, Czechoslovakia, East Germany, Hungary, and Mongolia. Trade between the Philippines and these states, along with the Soviet Union and the PRC, had reached some 80 million US dollars (USD), with China accounting for nearly half the total volume. The PRC, which had recently discovered large deposits of oil in Heilongjiang, was a potential source of discounted oil imports at a time of volatility in global energy markets; Marcos also feared that the Organization of Petroleum Exporting Countries would curb oil exports to the Philippines in retaliation for the military's armed operations against the Moro Islamic Liberation Front in Mindanao. Apart from economic concerns, Marcos also believed that opening up relations with China would end its provision of weapons to and rhetorical support for the Maoist Communist Party of the Philippines (CPP) and the New People's Army (NPA).[6]

Marcos adopted a consultative approach toward normalization, which became linked to the citizenship question. Three of the officials whom he turned to first, including the former ambassador to the ROC Narciso Ramos, cautioned against establishing relations with the PRC, believing that it would allow the PRC to expand its influence in Chinese society. Unconvinced by their arguments, Marcos sought the opinion of Benito Lim, a lecturer in contemporary China at the University of the Philippines (UP). Marcos asked Lim for his views on mass naturalization, which the president believed had to be part of any plan to establish relations with the PRC to prevent it from laying claim to the Philippine Chinese. Lim, who had previously failed in his application for citizenship because he could not afford to pay the bribe that the presiding judge had demanded, advocated this policy. With Marcos's backing, Lim surveyed Chinese attitudes toward citizenship, the PRC, and schools. The results dispelled any fears that the Chinese could be vulnerable to the PRC's influence. Of those surveyed, 85 percent expressed fears of communism and 90 percent preferred to become Philippine, not PRC, nationals. On April 11, 1975, acting on these results, Marcos simplified the previously cumbersome and expensive naturalization process for aliens by empowering a special committee chaired by the solicitor general to approve all applications for naturalization.[7] Within five years, this committee received 43,180 applications in comparison to the 579 petitions for citizenship that were filed via the courts from 1969 to 1974.[8] On June 7, 1975, Marcos went on a five-day official visit to China, and on June 9, the PRC and the Philippines recognized each other. During his visit, posters of Mao and PRC flags were prominently displayed in some establishments in Chinatown.[9] That would not have been possible five years earlier.

This shift away from Nationalist China in the 1970s—the unsharing of sovereignty between Manila and Taipei—was driven by longer-term social changes and, ironically, the partial success of the KMT's ideological mobilization. Having been exposed to KMT propaganda and lived in a highly anticommunist country for decades, most Philippine Chinese were either noncommunist or anticommunist and were unlikely to gravitate en masse toward the PRC. Where the ROC and its loyalists failed was in hindering cultural integration into Filipino society and in maintaining identification between the Nationalist state and younger Chinese. The rearguard action of Pao Shih-tien and other conservative educators from the mid-1950s onward, educational and military service trips to the "homeland," textbooks and teachers from Taiwan, Philippine Chinese Anti-Communist League (PCACL) rallies, Chinese elites' promotion of the Cultural

Renaissance Movement—none could sustain the ethnocentrism that ROC influence depended on. The US political scientist Robert O. Tilman found in 1970 that many Chinese high school students had difficulty reading and writing Chinese characters and few read Chinese papers or periodicals except those prescribed in school.[10] Even among those fluent in Chinese, attitudes were changing. In that same year, taking up the Yuyitungs' cause, young ethnic Chinese university graduates—including a few who had studied at Chiang Kai-shek College (CKSC)—formed the civic organization Pagkakaisa sa Pag-unlad to advocate for jus soli citizenship and the Filipinization of Chinese schools at the constitutional convention.[11] If the *Chinese Commercial News*' (*CCN*) calls for "metamorphosis" and "hybridization" seemed out of place previously, they were now becoming increasingly accepted. Born and having lived their entire lives in the Philippines, these younger ethnic Chinese did not perceive their cultural Chineseness as inextricably linked to a China-centered national identity and political project.

A further challenge to the established ideological order emerged from among the relatively few and hitherto marginalized members of the Federation of Filipino-Chinese Chambers of Commerce and Industry (Shang Zong) who favored closer relations with the PRC, whether for political or cultural reasons. As the example of Santos Ong (chapter 7) shows us, there were always those within the organization who dissented from its pro-Taiwan line and were willing to articulate their views cautiously and in private. In 1970, as the political winds began to shift direction, several Shang Zong businessmen came out into the open by founding the Filipino-Chinese Amity Club (Feihua Lianyi Hui). This pro-PRC organization soon had branches across the country, as Chinese merchants gradually began to distance themselves from Taiwan. After 1975, the Amity Club was able to operate more openly and cultivated as one of its patrons the First Lady, Imelda Marcos. This undermined the Shang Zong's previously exclusive access to Malacañang Palace, ushering in the sort of ideological competition between rival Chinas that Chinese society had not witnessed since the early years after World War II.[12]

Despite and because of these shifts, the conservatives fought back. Although Pagkakaisa's calls for citizenship based on jus soli were backed by a few Shang Zong members, its support for the Filipinization of Chinese schools proved highly unpopular. Pagkakaisa founding member and civic activist Teresita Ang See recalls that when her late husband, Chinben See, gave a lecture on educational Filipinization at CKSC, he was "almost literally thrown out" of the school.[13] Marcos's decision to establish diplomatic ties with Beijing proved just as controversial. Officially, the Shang Zong supported the move, fearing retribution from Malacañang. But when its newly emboldened but still small pro-PRC faction, including Amity Club members, insisted on replacing the ROC flag inside the Shang Zong's headquarters with a PRC one, the dominant pro-Taiwan leadership held a special meeting, dug in their heels, and decided that only the Philippine flag was to be displayed. The Shang Zong's president, KMT stalwart Yao Shiong Shio, and four vice presidents threatened to resign if this gesture of defiance did not carry the day. With the dispute roiling Chinatown, Marcos personally intervened and urged the warring factions to resolve their differences amicably. He indicated that while he would respect the decision to display the Philippine and PRC flags inside the building, only the former ought to be flown outside it. One of the most outspoken members of the pro-PRC faction was eventually suspended from the Shang Zong after launching a campaign in the Chinese-language media calling for the federation to treat both flags equally. In another era, he might have been reported to the military and deported to Taiwan. The Amity Club, although patronized by the First Lady, was not supported by the new PRC Embassy, which—unlike its predecessor—was careful not to become involved in local Chinese politics. Pro-Beijing views needed time to gain currency. The Shang Zong held out against recognizing the PRC for almost two decades, until 1994, when fifty-five of its members officially visited China as part of a larger Northeast Asian trade mission. Immediately after leaving China, they proceeded to Taipei, where they assured ROC officials that the close ties between them, built up over the previous four decades, would persist. Ever attentive to symbolism, they spent ten days each in Taiwan and China.[14] It was only after then that the Shang Zong gravitated toward the mainland; it is thoroughly pro-Beijing today.

And what of the KMT? Taiwan persisted in courting the overseas Chinese; for having lost its United Nations seat, it was in greater need of allies and sympathizers than ever. The institutions that it relied on for diasporic mobilization were not completely shut down, and instead many were simply renamed to reflect Taiwan's diminished status and lower profile in international society. In the Philippines, just as the ROC Embassy became the Pacific Economic and Cultural Center in 1975 and the Taipei Economic and Cultural Office in 1989, the KMT was transformed into the Filipino-Chinese Cultural and Economic Association (Feihua Wenhua Jingji Zonghui, or Wen Zong).[15] Its two newspapers, the *Great China Press* and *Kong Li Po*, were forced to merge in 1973 and scale back on supporting Taiwan. In 1975, the PCACL was dissolved.[16] Over time, even its antagonistic relations with the CCN dissipated. In 1980, the ROC jettisoned anticommunism as its basic national policy.

Old attitudes die hard, however, and for some, the party's goals endured. One was to "win the hearts of overseas compatriots" (*zhengqu qiaobao xiangxin*) by promoting Chinese culture, and the other was to champion democracy.

This was how Lim Soo Chan, the *zongzhibu*'s longtime secretary-general and unindicted coconspirator against the Yuyitungs, put it to interviewers from Taiwan in 1993. Party stalwarts like him held fast to the belief that most Philippine Chinese were lovers of freedom and democracy and thus steadfast supporters of Taiwan. On their part, Lim and others proved far more conservative than Taiwan's leaders in their attitudes toward the PRC. The *zongzhibu* disapproved of high-level visits by Taiwanese officials to mainland China, for example, and for a time, local KMT members holding committee appointments who wished to do so had to inform the party first. While the KMT's distinctive Cold War vocabulary of "communist banditry" and "counterattacking the mainland" was soon abandoned, anticommunism remained, in practice if not in discourse, the organization's raison d'être. We must maintain our anticommunist posture, Lim insisted, and oppose the application of the communist system to China; this was something, he said, that "we could not give up" (*buneng fangqi*), regardless of what other Philippine Chinese believed in.[17] In late 2019, aged ninety-five, Lim was interviewed by a Chinese-language correspondent for the British Broadcasting Corporation. "I am not Taiwanese" (Wo bushi Taiwan ren), he declared; "I am an ROC national" (Wo shi Zhonghua minguo de guomin). His lifelong wish is for a unified China under the ROC. For him, the PRC "fundamentally does not exist" (*genben bu cunzai*).[18] The Cold War is not over for him.

Today, relations between the PRC and the Philippines are closer than they have ever been, with President Rodrigo Duterte having steered Manila toward Beijing and away from Washington since he came into power in 2016. But as Chinese foreign investment and the number of mainland Chinese in the Philippines have grown, so too has disquiet among many Filipinos toward China. Beijing refuses to recognize Manila's sovereignty over the "West Philippine Sea," despite the Permanent Court of Arbitration's July 2016 ruling in favor of the latter. Numerous PRC Chinese currently work in the country for online betting websites—what are known as Philippine offshore gaming operators (POGOs)—that cater mostly to customers in China. Many Filipinos resent these new Chinese migrants and blame them for an upsurge in crime and prostitution. Tsinoys, consequently, find themselves in an awkward position. Although they identify themselves as Filipinos, their fellow citizens are not above conflating them with mainland Chinese and leveling accusations of disloyalty against them. Sinophobia, never far below the surface of Filipino life, is bubbling up again as China "rises."

Where can we turn to for historical perspectives on contemporary relations between the Philippines, China, and the Philippine Chinese? Rather than focusing on Chinese migration to the Philippines, the origins of Chinese society in the archipelago, and the Spanish and US colonial periods, as most prior scholarship has done, this book emphasizes the mid-twentieth century history of the Philippine Chinese and their ties to the KMT-ROC party-state. Of course, a great many Taiwanese today would reject any attempt to equate Taiwan and China, in the same way that Tsinoys resent charges of being loyal to the PRC. But neither of these contemporary assertions of national identity changes the fact that the KMT and many Philippine Chinese from different walks of life perceived and produced the ROC as "China" not long ago.

Indeed, no better example illustrates the agency and appeal of this "China" in the Cold War diasporic world than the Philippines. *Diasporic Cold Warriors* examines how and why so many members of one of the smallest Chinese societies in Southeast Asia threw their weight behind the KMT and actively supported its crusade against Chinese communism, especially from the 1950s to the 1970s. As with elsewhere in the region, the KMT established a foothold in the Philippines in the early twentieth century and came into conflict with the Chinese left in the 1930s. But only in the first three years after the Japanese occupation was the KMT able to drive this adversary from the country with the support of the Philippine state. Mere fragments of a once small but vibrant Sino-communist movement survived. By contrast, the governments of Malaya, Thailand, and Indochina, despite their anticommunism, were as wary of or downright opposed to the KMT's designs on their significantly larger Chinese populations. Indonesia, although diplomatically aligned with the PRC, tolerated both the KMT (until 1958) and communist Chinese activism. In the Philippines, the state was allied to Taiwan, accommodated the KMT as a "local" civic organization, and was implacably hostile toward Sino-communism.

As fears of this particular strain of communism intensified in the Philippines and beyond from the late 1940s onward, the KMT entered into an informal relationship of convenience with the coercive organs of its host state. Many Chinese, regardless of their ideological affinities, found it expedient and beneficial to practice anticommunism. Designated as foreigners and discriminated against as racial others, they integrated into the Philippines by fashioning the right civic identities. Starting in the mid-1950s, in response to Manila's interventions in Chinese economic activity and education, the mass arrests of alleged Sino-communists in December 1952, and the Cebu reading club affair in July 1954, Chinese leaders reorganized the institutions of community governance. In doing so, they recommitted themselves to *Fangong kang'E*. Chiang Kai-shek High School (CKSHS) and the PCACL led the way in propagating this ideology. The multiple annual visits to "Free China" that they and other Chinese civic groups organized strengthened the community's ties to Taiwan and the KMT's networks.

With Sinocentric anticommunism having become overwhelmingly normative, the KMT worked assiduously to extirpate what it considered to be the remaining traces of dissent within Chinese society. Chief among its targets was the *CCN*. As an advocate of Chinese integration into Filipino society and the sole provider of balanced news coverage on China within the community, it was the preeminent non- or anti-anticommunist Chinese media outlet in the Philippines. First in 1962 and again in 1970, the KMT leveraged its networks and colluded with the Philippine state to brand the liberal *CCN* a pro-communist organ and have Quintin and Rizal Yuyitung deported to Taiwan. The second time, they succeeded. The KMT achieved with regard to the Philippine Chinese, with Manila's active participation, a degree of social and cultural dominance second only to what it managed in martial law Taiwan.

From this narrative flow the book's three principal arguments. It argues, first, that the ROC-KMT party-state, which historians of modern China and Taiwan have predominantly imagined in territorialized terms, can and should be understood diasporically. Through mobile nationalists such as Mah Soo-Lay, Cua Siok Po, Shih I-Sheng, and Koa Chun-te; diplomats such as Chen Chih-ping; and organizations such as party branches, schools, and the PCACL, Nationalist China sought to mobilize what it considered a global Chinese nation against communism. Second, the book argues that in sanctioning the KMT's extraterritorial nationalism and collaborating with the party against Sino-communism, the Philippines entered into a relationship of shared sovereignty with the ROC and helped construct an intra-Asian anticommunist ecumene. I approach the Cold War, in other words, from the perspective of Asian state and nonstate actors and investigate the connections between them, rather than between them and the United States. Third, and finally, the book contends that because of the KMT's involvement in Philippine-Chinese society, Chinese identity formation and practices of belonging were imbricated with ideology. Instead of viewing Chinese integration into the nation-state solely in ethno-cultural terms or focusing narrowly on the business community, I explain how anticommunism became a means for different Chinese actors to perform conformity to Filipino civic nationalist values—as ethnic minorities.

Diasporic Cold Warriors, in sum, uses the particular experiences of the Philippine Chinese to historicize the KMT, the Chinese diaspora, sovereignty, and the Cold War in relation to each other. In framing it as such, I hope that it will speak to a diverse range of scholars, help chart future research directions, and enable us to think more imaginatively about our fields. By linking overseas Chinese identity and integration to ideology; explaining how the state's attitudes toward the KMT and Sino-communism, among other factors, were critical to the KMT's flourishing in the Philippines; and occasionally venturing beyond the islands to survey the rest of the region, this book can serve as a heuristic for investigating "China" and the "Chinese" elsewhere in Southeast Asia. Mine is not a comparative history, but it supplies concepts and narratives that translate across borders and illuminate aspects of the KMT in post-1945 Malaya and Malaysia, Singapore, Thailand, Vietnam, and Indonesia.[19] Scholarship on these places would be able to draw on regional and colonial archives and libraries and also the Ministry of Foreign Affairs (MOFA) Archives and other underutilized source collections in Taiwan that teem with information on *huaqiao* communities. It would expand the surprisingly limited historiography on postcolonial Southeast Asian Chinese societies' and states' approaches to the Chinese question. Finally, it would add significantly to the study of an organization that has become unfashionable because of Taiwanization and democratization and to the study of a small, increasingly marginalized state that has been overshadowed by the "rise of China." Yet, as we have seen, the KMT was capable of exercising significant extraterritorial influence despite its declining international status after 1949. Far from being irrelevant to the present, the KMT's historical interventions in postcolonial Southeast Asia are antecedents of the PRC's involvement in the region in our time. We cannot study one without the other. Michael Szonyi points out that the Chinese Communist Party (CCP) and the KMT, as Leninist parties with an entangled history, consistently exchanged disciplinary and repressive techniques despite their equally strenuous efforts to define themselves in opposition to each other.[20] These synchronic cross-strait comparisons invite diachronic and interregional analogizing between the historical KMT and the contemporary CCP. In light of the resurgence of Sinophilia and Sinophobia across the region, we might compare, for example, the KMT's and the CCP's shared commitment to promoting "Chineseness" in Southeast Asia and their attempts at Sinicizing and re-Sinicizing the region's Chinese, then and today. It is telling that a current *CCN* employee whose father also worked for the paper said to me once that the PRC's cultural diplomacy among the Philippine Chinese today resembles what Taiwan was doing half a century earlier.[21]

Even more broadly, I hope that *Diasporic Cold Warriors* will help practitioners of modern Chinese history, particularly in North American academia, reflect on its relationship to the study of Chinese migration and diaspora. As the intellectual product of Cold War–era area studies, the opening up of archives in the PRC since the 1980s, and traditional Sinology, this burgeoning field remains very much centered on mainland China as a territorialized space for the unfolding of the "Chinese" past; the "rise of China" has only reinforced such centrism. This is despite "turns" within the field that have enriched our understanding of relations between China proper and inner Asia and of China in global history. The historians Shelly Chan's and Wayne Soon's excellent monographs, for example, focus on how the diaspora shaped developments in China (and, in the latter case, Taiwan) such as socialist nation-building and modern medicine, rather than on overseas Chinese societies themselves.[22] While Chan floats the notion of a composite body of knowledge called "global Chinese history" that comprises overseas Chinese history, modern Chinese history (in the conventional, territorialized sense), and Chinese American history, the "diasporic moments" that she uses to connect these literatures are fundamentally about how Chinese migration affected China at certain temporal junctures. She rightly notes that scholarship on how China affected the diaspora and on the Chinese "elsewhere" predominates.[23]

Rather than figuratively "returning" to mainland China, this book—to use another diasporic metaphor—sows the seeds of an alternative, nonexclusive, and constructivist approach to global Chinese history. In addition to Chan's and Soon's works, I draw inspiration from Philip A. Kuhn's argument that Chinese migration overseas and migration within China are comparable processes, from critical Han studies, and especially from Sinophone studies, which calls attention to Chinese-language literary and cultural production beyond mainland China.[24] Building on their insights, this approach might also be considered "Sinophone history," in that it emphasizes the experiences of and connections between persons, societies, and states in different settings that saw themselves, or were seen and produced by others, as "Chinese," while not limiting itself to literary and cultural texts. It encompasses the historical study of overseas Chinese communities and Han Chinese migration to, and settlement in, frontier regions of China. It treats Sinicization and de-Sinicization in mainland China, Taiwan, Hong Kong, and Southeast Asia, and in relation to Manchus, Uyghurs, the indigenous peoples of Taiwan, Tsinoys, Hong Kongers, and ethnic Chinese Singaporeans, for instance, as comparable processes that span geographies and are enmeshed in distinct historical contexts and political processes. Such an approach can facilitate productive intellectual exchanges between different groups of "Chinese" historians, and between "Chinese" historians and historians of Southeast Asia; it is meant to complement, not supplant, existing fields. More than that, it has political and ethical ramifications. As numerous scholars have pointed out, the term "Chinese" is an ambiguous, contested, and powerful signifier.[25] In the hands of racists, demagogues, and states such as the PRC, the KMT-ROC, and New Order Indonesia, it is and has been able to inflict great harm when used to categorize and essentialize peoples. For such reasons, we owe it to our peers and publics to problematize and pluralize "Chineseness" and "Chinese" history. Perhaps, in its own small way, *Diasporic Cold Warriors* can contribute to this conversation.

NOTES

Abbreviations Used in the Notes

AH	Academia Historica
AHC	American Historical Collection
CCN	*Chinese Commercial News*
CNBKSY	National Index to Chinese Newspapers and Periodicals
CREST	Central Intelligence Agency Records Search Tool
FHL	Filipinas Heritage Library
HILA	Hoover Institution Library and Archives
IMH	Institute of Modern History
ISEAS	Institute of Southeast Asian Studies–Yusof Ishak Institute
KHC	Kaisa Heritage Center
KMT	Kuomintang
LOC	Library of Congress
MSLP	Mah Soo-Lay Papers
NARA	National Archives and Records Administration
NCL	National Central Library
OCCD	Overseas Chinese Clippings Database
RG	record group
UARD	University Archives and Records Depository

Introduction

1. "Information Work among Overseas Chinese of Southeast Asia," record group (RG) 84, Series: Classified General Records, 1949–1961, box 31, folder: 350 South East Asia, National Archives and Records Administration (NARA), College Park, MD.

2. Li Pusheng, *Wo ke pei de huaqiao pengyou* (Taipei: Zhengzhong shuju, 1958), 34.

3. "The Overseas Chinese and U.S. Policy," RG 59, Series: Subject and Country Files, 1952–1958, box 32, folder: China—Overseas Chinese, NARA.

4. *Qiaowu tongji* (Taipei: Qiaowu weiyuanhui tongjishi, 1964), 68–69.

5. G. William Skinner, "Overseas Chinese in Southeast Asia," *Annals of the American Academy of Political and Social Science* 321 (January 1959): 137.

6. Kuan-Hsing Chen, *Asia as Method: Toward Deimperialization* (Durham, NC: Duke University Press, 2010), 154.

7. Jacques Amyot, *The Manila Chinese: Familism in the Philippine Environment* (Quezon City: Institute of Philippine Culture, Ateneo de Manila University, 1973), 1; Richard T.

Chu, *Chinese and Chinese Mestizos of Manila: Family, Identity, and Culture, 1860s–1930s* (Leiden: Brill, 2010), 4.

8. I take the term "self-identification" from Frederick Cooper, *Colonialism in Question: Theory, Knowledge, History* (Berkeley: University of California Press, 2005), 71.

9. "Tsinoy" is an amalgam of the Spanish term "Tsino" / "Chino" and the colloquial term for Filipino, "Pinoy." Caroline S. Hau, *The Chinese Question: Ethnicity, Nation, and Region in and beyond the Philippines* (Singapore: NUS Press, 2014), 12–13.

10. Chinben See, "Chinese Clanship in the Philippine Setting," *Journal of Southeast Asian Studies* 12, no. 1 (March 1981): 225. These figures correspond closely with those in Edgar Wickberg, *The Chinese in Philippine Life, 1850–1898* (Quezon City: Ateneo de Manila University Press, 2000), 172.

11. See G. William Skinner, "Report on the Chinese in Southeast Asia" (Southeast Asia Program, Department of Far Eastern Studies, Cornell University, Ithaca, NY, December 1950), 80. Skinner places the number of Philippine Chinese in 1950 who were from Fujian Province at only 70 percent, but this figure is still the highest among all dialect groups in different countries in the region. The 1996 *Quanzhou City Overseas Chinese Gazetteer* has the proportion of Philippine Chinese from Fujian in 1939 at 80 percent and from Quanzhou at 75 percent. Quanzhou shi huaqiao zhi bianzuan weiyuanhui, ed., *Quanzhou shi huaqiao zhi* (Beijing: Zhongguo shehui chubanshe, 1996), 11.

12. Amyot, *Manila Chinese*, 54.

13. For a summary of the debate over the term *sangley*, see Hau, *Chinese Question*, 9.

14. Hau, *Chinese Question*, 7.

15. Wickberg, *Chinese in Philippine Life*, 147, 204.

16. Filomeno V. Aguilar Jr., "Between the Letter and Spirit of the Law: Ethnic Chinese and Philippine Citizenship by Jus Soli, 1899–1947," *Southeast Asian Studies* 49, no. 3 (December 2011): 433; Hau, *Chinese Question*, 26.

17. For example, see Zwia Lipkin, *Useless to the State: "Social Problems" and Social Engineering in Nationalist Nanjing, 1927–1937* (Cambridge, MA: Harvard University Asia Center, 2006); Maggie Clinton, *Revolutionary Nativism: Fascism and Culture in China, 1925–1937* (Durham, NC: Duke University Press, 2017); Brian Tsui, *China's Conservative Revolution: The Quest for a New Order, 1927–1949* (Cambridge: Cambridge University Press, 2018); and J. Megan Greene, *The Origins of the Developmental State in Taiwan: Science Policy and the Quest for Modernization* (Cambridge, MA: Harvard University Press, 2008).

18. The sole English-language history on the KMT in Southeast Asia remains C. F. Yong and R. B. McKenna, *The Kuomintang Movement in British Malaya 1912–1949* (Singapore: Singapore University Press, 1990). There is coverage of the party, though, in books such as G. William Skinner, *Leadership and Power in the Chinese Community of Thailand* (Ithaca, NY: Cornell University Press, 1958); and Taomo Zhou, *Migration in the Time of Revolution: China, Indonesia, and the Cold War* (Ithaca, NY: Cornell University Press, 2019). On the KMT in the United States, see Charlotte Brooks, *Between Mao and McCarthy: Chinese American Politics in the Cold War Years* (Chicago: University of Chicago Press, 2015); Him Mark Lai, *Chinese American Transnational Politics* (Urbana: University of Illinois Press, 2010); and Renqiu Yu, *To Save China, to Save Ourselves: The Chinese Hand Laundry Alliance of New York* (Philadelphia: Temple University Press, 1992). For the Americas and Australasia, see Judith Brett and Mei-fen Kuo, *Unlocking the History of the Australasian Kuo Min Tang, 1911–2013* (North Melbourne: Australian Schol-

arly Publishing, 2013); and Fredy González, *Paisanos Chinos: Transpacific Politics among Chinese Immigrants in Mexico* (Oakland: University of California Press, 2017).

19. See, for example, *Zhongguo Guomindang zai haiwai yibai nian* (Taipei: Haiwai chubanshe, 1994), 56–102.

20. Jianli Huang argues that Sun likely never uttered the exact phrase *"huaqiao wei geming zhi mu."* See Jianli Huang, "Umbilical Ties: The Framing of the Overseas Chinese as the Mother of the Revolution," *Frontiers of History in China* 6, no. 2 (June 2011): 183–228.

21. Andrew R. Wilson, *Ambition and Identity: Chinese Merchant Elites in Colonial Manila, 1880–1916* (Honolulu: University of Hawai'i Press, 2004), 4.

22. L. Ling-chi Wang, "The Structure of Dual Domination: Toward a Paradigm for the Study of the Chinese Diaspora in the United States," *Amerasia Journal* 21, nos. 1–2 (1995): 155.

23. Prasenjit Duara, "Transnationalism and the Predicament of Sovereignty: China, 1900–1945," *American Historical Review* 102, no. 4 (October 1997): 1032.

24. Nicole Phelps, "State Sovereignty in a Transnational World: US Consular Expansion and the Problem of Naturalized Migrants in the Habsburg Empire, 1880–1914," *German Historical Institute Bulletin Supplement* 5 (2008): 41–42. I thank Madeline Y. Hsu for sending me this article.

25. Dan Shao, "Chinese by Definition: Nationality Law, Jus Sanguinis, and State Succession, 1909–1980," *Twentieth-Century China* 35, no. 1 (November 2009): 5.

26. On the functioning of these migrant networks, see Adam McKeown, "Conceptualizing Chinese Diasporas, 1840 to 1949," *Journal of Asian Studies* 58, no. 2 (May 1999): 306–337.

27. The highest governing body of the KMT was the Central Executive Committee, from 1925 to 1950; the Central Reform Committee, from 1950 to 1952; and the Central Committee, from 1952 onward.

28. Shao, "Chinese by Definition," 5.

29. Stephen Fitzgerald, *China and the Overseas Chinese: A Study of Peking's Changing Policy, 1949–1970* (Cambridge: Cambridge University Press, 1972), 135, 141–143.

30. Zhuang Guotu, *Huaqiao huaren yu zhongguo de guanxi* (Guangzhou: Guangdong gaodeng jiaoyu chubanshe, 2001), 251–252.

31. For a discussion of *huaqiao*, *huaren*, and *huayi*, see Wang Gungwu, "The Chinese Revolution and the Overseas Chinese," in *Diasporic Chinese Ventures: The Life and Work of Wang Gungwu*, ed. Gregor Benton and Liu Hong (London: Routledge, 2000), 196–209.

32. Stephen D. Krasner, "Building Democracy after Conflict: The Case for Shared Sovereignty," *Journal of Democracy* 16, no. 1 (January 2005): 70.

33. Stephen Rosskamm Shalom, *The United States and the Philippines: A Study of Neocolonialism* (Philadelphia: Institute for the Study of Human Issues, 1981), xiv. For a revisionist view, see Nick Cullather, *Illusions of Influence: The Political Economy of United States–Philippine Relations, 1942–1960* (Stanford, CA: Stanford University Press, 1994).

34. For an analysis that questions the applicability of the colonialism versus nationalism framework, see Steven E. Phillips, *Between Assimilation and Independence: The Taiwanese Encounter Nationalist China, 1945–1950* (Stanford, CA: Stanford University Press, 2003).

35. Ang Cheng Guan, *Southeast Asia's Cold War: An Interpretive History* (Honolulu: University of Hawai'i Press, 2018), 54.

36. *Zhongguo Guomindang zai haiwai: Jiushi nian lai de fendou licheng* (Taipei: Haiwai chubanshe, 1984), 118.

37. *Gongfei dui huaqiao zhi yinmou* (Taipei: Haiwai chubanshe, 1954), 3.

38. *Zhongguo Guomindang zai haiwai*, 71.

39. That Southeast Asia's Cold War was a victory for anticommunism is a central argument in Wen-Qing Ngoei, *Arc of Containment: Britain, the United States, and Anti-communism in Southeast Asia* (Ithaca, NY: Cornell University Press, 2019).

40. Susan Bayly, *Asian Voices in a Post-Colonial Age: Vietnam, India and Beyond* (Cambridge: Cambridge University Press, 2007), 9.

41. On US-Taiwan Cold War relations, see Stephen G. Craft, *American Justice in Taiwan: The 1957 Riots and Cold War Foreign Policy* (Lexington: University Press of Kentucky, 2016); Hsiao-ting Lin, *Accidental State: Chiang Kai-shek, the United States, and the Making of Taiwan* (Cambridge, MA: Harvard University Press, 2016); and Nancy Bernkopf Tucker, *Strait Talk: United States–Taiwan Relations and the Crisis with China* (Cambridge, MA: Harvard University Press, 2009). On the Philippines, see Cullather, *Illusions of Influence*; Alfred W. McCoy, *Policing America's Empire: The United States, the Philippines, and the Rise of the Surveillance State* (Madison: University of Wisconsin Press, 2009); and Colleen Woods, *Freedom Incorporated: Anticommunism and Philippine Independence in the Age of Decolonization* (Ithaca, NY: Cornell University Press, 2020). More generally, see Daniel Fineman, *A Special Relationship: The United States and Military Government in Thailand, 1947–1958* (Honolulu: University of Hawai'i Press, 1997); Edward Miller, *Misalliance: Ngo Dinh Diem, the United States, and the Fate of South Vietnam* (Cambridge, MA: Harvard University Press, 2013); Ngoei, *Arc of Containment*; and Bradley R. Simpson, *Economists with Guns: Authoritarian Development and U.S.-Indonesian Relations, 1960–1968* (Stanford, CA: Stanford University Press, 2008).

42. Qiang Zhai, *China and the Vietnam Wars, 1950–1975* (Chapel Hill: University of North Carolina Press, 2001); Hong Liu, *China and the Shaping of Indonesia, 1949–1965* (Singapore: NUS Press, 2011); Zhou, *Migration in the Time of Revolution*.

43. On right-wing transnationalism in general, see Martin Durham and Margaret Power, eds., *New Perspectives on the Transnational Right* (New York: Palgrave Macmillan, 2010).

44. Notable scholarship on intra-Asian Cold War anticommunism includes Hao Chen, "Resisting Bandung? Taiwan's Struggle for 'Representational Legitimacy' in the Rise of the Asian Peoples' Anti-Communist League, 1954–57," *International History Review* 43, no. 2 (2021): 244–263; Reto Hofmann, "What's Left of the Right: Nabeyama Sadachika and Anti-Communism in Transwar Japan, 1930–1960," *Journal of Asian Studies* 79, no. 2 (June 2020): 403–427; and Mitchell Tan, "Spiritual Fraternities: The Transnational Networks of Ngô Đình Diệm's Personalist Revolution and the Republic of Vietnam," *Journal of Vietnamese Studies* 14, no. 2 (May 2019): 1–67.

45. Zhou, *Migration in the Time of Revolution*; Meredith Oyen, *The Diplomacy of Migration: Transnational Lives and the Making of U.S.-Chinese Relations in the Cold War* (Ithaca, NY: Cornell University Press, 2015).

46. My work draws extensively on scholarship in Cold War social and cultural history, especially Masuda Hajimu, *Cold War Crucible: The Korean Conflict and the Postwar World* (Cambridge, MA: Harvard University Press, 2015); Heonik Kwon, *The Other Cold War* (New York: Columbia University Press, 2010); Tuong Vu and Wasana Wongsurawat,

eds., *Dynamics of the Cold War in Asia: Ideology, Identity, and Culture* (New York: Palgrave Macmillan, 2009); and Zheng Yangwen, Hong Liu, and Michael Szonyi, eds., *The Cold War in Asia: The Battle for Hearts and Minds* (Leiden: Brill, 2010).

47. Teresita Ang See, Go Bon Juan, Doreen Go Yu, and Yvonne Chua, eds., *Tsinoy: The Story of the Chinese in Philippine Life* (Manila: Kaisa Para sa Kaunlaran, 2005).

48. The goals of the organization are introduced in Charles J. McCarthy, ed., *Philippine-Chinese Profile: Essays & Studies* (Manila: Pagkakaisa sa Pag-unlad, 1974).

49. Kaisa Para sa Kaunlaran, "About Kaisa," accessed February 20, 2021, https://www.kaisa.org.ph/?page_id=2.

50. Ang See et al., *Tsinoy*, 5.

51. McKeown, "Conceptualizing Chinese Diasporas," 327.

52. For example, Teresita Ang See and Lily T. Chua, eds., *Crossroads: Short Essays on the Chinese Filipinos* (Manila: Kaisa Para sa Kaunlaran, 1988); and Teresita Ang See, ed., *The Chinese in the Philippines: Problems and Perspectives* (Manila: Kaisa Para sa Kaunlaran, 1997–2004), vols. 1–3. See also Richard T. Chu, ed., *More Tsinoy than We Admit: Chinese-Filipino Interactions over the Centuries* (Quezon City: Vibal Foundation, 2015); and Juliet Lee Uytanlet, *The Hybrid Tsinoys: Challenges of Hybridity and Homogeneity as Sociocultural Constructs among the Chinese in the Philippines* (Eugene, OR: Pickwick Publications, 2016).

53. Ang See et al., *Tsinoy*, 184–185.

54. For example, John T. Omohundro, *Chinese Merchant Families in Iloilo: Commerce and Kin in a Central Philippine City* (Quezon City: Ateneo de Manila University Press, 1981); Wilson, *Ambition and Identity*; Theresa Chong Carino, *Chinese Big Business in the Philippines: Political Leadership and Change* (Singapore: Times Academic Press, 1998); Zhu Dongqin, *Chongtu yu ronghe: Feihua shanglian zonghui yu zhanhou Feihua shehui de fazhan* (Xiamen: Xiamen daxue chubanshe, 2005); and Chang Tsun-wu [Zhang Cunwu] and Ong Kok-Chung [Wang Guozhang], *Feihua shanglian zonghui zhi xingshuai yu yanbian* (Taipei: Zhongyang yanjiuyuan yatai yanjiu jishu, 2002).

55. González, *Paisanos Chinos*, 4.

56. Caroline S. Hau, *Necessary Fictions: Philippine Literature and the Nation, 1946–1980* (Quezon City: Ateneo de Manila University Press, 2000), 140.

57. Jacques Amyot, *The Chinese and the National Integration in Southeast Asia* (Bangkok: Institute of Asian Studies, Faculty of Political Science, Chulalongkorn University, October 1972), 40.

58. Terry Eagleton, *Ideology: An Introduction* (London: Verso, 1991), 29.

59. Michel de Certeau, *The Practice of Everyday Life*, trans. Steven Randall (Berkeley: University of California Press, 1984), xix.

60. Judith Farquhar and Qicheng Zhang, "Biopolitical Beijing: Pleasure, Sovereignty, and Self-Cultivation in China's Capital," *Cultural Anthropology* 20, no. 3 (August 2005): 310.

1. The KMT, Chinese Society, and Chinese Communism in the Philippines before 1942

1. "Zongzhibu xin dangsuo luocheng," *Chungking Times*, March 4, 1947, 4, Hoover Institution Library and Archives (HILA), Stanford, CA.

2. Fitzgerald, *China and the Overseas Chinese*, 11.

3. Zhongping Chen, *Modern China's Network Revolution: Chambers of Commerce and Sociopolitical Change in the Early Twentieth Century* (Stanford, CA: Stanford University Press, 2011), 7.

4. McKeown, "Conceptualizing Chinese Diasporas," 317.

5. *Zhongguo Guomindang zai haiwai*, 15.

6. *Zhongguo Guomindang zai haiwai*, 18.

7. Yong and McKenna, *Kuomintang Movement in British Malaya*, 31.

8. *Zhongguo Guomindang zai haiwai*, 18.

9. *Wang guxiaozhang Quansheng shishi wushi zhounian jinian teji* (Manila: Purity Printers, 2006), 5–6.

10. *Zhongguo Guomindang zai haiwai*, 2.

11. Yong and McKenna, *Kuomintang Movement in British Malaya*, 38.

12. *Zhongguo Guomindang zai haiwai*, 22; Philip A. Kuhn, *Chinese among Others: Emigration in Modern Times* (Lanham, MD: Rowman & Littlefield, 2009), 267.

13. *Zhongguo Guomindang zai haiwai*, 22–23.

14. Yoji Akashi, *The Nanyang Chinese National Salvation Movement, 1937–1941* (Lawrence: Center for East Asian Studies, University of Kansas, 1970), 6.

15. *Zhongguo Guomindang zai haiwai*, 24.

16. "Zhongguo Guomindang haiwai zongzhibu zhixing weiyuanhui zuzhi tiaoli," "Zhongguo Guomindang haiwai zongzhibu zhixing weiyuanhui zuzhi xize," "Zhongguo Guomindang haiwai zhibu zhixing weiyuanhui zuzhi tiaoli," "Zhongguo Guomindang haiwai zhibu zhixing weiyuanhui zuzhi xize," and "Zhongguo Guomindang haiwai fenbu zhixing weiyuanhui zuzhi tiaoli," *Zhongyang zhoubao* 24 (1928): 14–16, National Index to Chinese Newspapers and Periodicals (CNBKSY). Not all *zhibu* and *fenbu* were subordinate to *zongzhibu*. In many parts of the world with sparser Chinese populations, *zhibu* or *fenbu* were directly subordinate (*zhishu*) to the center in the absence of *zongzhibu*.

17. Akashi, *Nanyang Chinese National Salvation Movement*, 6.

18. Kuhn, *Chinese among Others*, 267–268.

19. Clinton, *Revolutionary Nativism*, 36–37. For a detailed study of the Blue Shirts, see Frederic Wakeman Jr., "A Revisionist View of the Nanjing Decade: Confucian Fascism," *China Quarterly* 150 (June 1997): 395–432.

20. Fitzgerald, *China and the Overseas Chinese*, 76.

21. Lloyd Eastman, *The Abortive Revolution: China under Nationalist Rule, 1927–1937* (Cambridge, MA: Harvard University Press, 1974); Hung-mao Tien, *Government and Politics in Kuomintang China, 1927–1937* (Stanford, CA: Stanford University Press, 1972).

22. Yang Jiancheng, ed., *Zhongguo Guomindang yu huaqiao wenxian chubian, 1908–1945* (Taipei: Zhonghua xueshuyuan Nanyang yanjiusuo, 1984), 7.

23. Wilson, *Ambition and Identity*, 176–177.

24. Wong Kwok-chu, *The Chinese in the Philippine Economy, 1898–1941* (Quezon City: Ateneo de Manila University Press, 1999), 58–59.

25. Wong, *Chinese in the Philippine Economy*, 2.

26. Clark L. Alejandrino, "The Population History of the Chinese in the Philippines: An Evaluative Historiography," *Philippine Population Review* 9, no. 1 (December 2010): 94–95.

27. Wong, *Chinese in the Philippine Economy*, 14.

28. Amyot, *Manila Chinese*, 15.

29. Yung Li Yuk-wai, *The Huaqiao Warriors: Chinese Resistance Movement in the Philippines, 1942–1945* (Quezon City: Ateneo de Manila University Press, 1996), 63–64.

30. Weber employs "elective affinity" (*Wahlverwandtschaft*), originally from Goethe, to imply an internal but not deterministic connection between two different phenomena rooted in a shared feature and / or clear historical linkage (such as certain religious beliefs and a vocational ethic). See Max Weber, *The Protestant Ethic and the Spirit of Capitalism*, trans. Stephen Kalberg (London: Routledge, 2001), lxxvii, 49–50.

31. Wilson, *Ambition and Identity*, 180.

32. Wilson, *Ambition and Identity*, 5–6, 10, 135, 163, 178, 184.

33. Antonio S. Tan, *The Chinese in the Philippines, 1898–1935: A Study of Their National Awakening* (Quezon City: R. P. Garcia Publishing, 1972), 255–256.

34. Wong, *Chinese in the Philippine Economy*, 85.

35. Chu, *Chinese and Chinese Mestizos*, 323–324, 329.

36. Tan, *Chinese in the Philippines, 1898–1935*.

37. Wilson, *Ambition and Identity*, 225.

38. Chu, *Chinese and Chinese Mestizos*, 288–291.

39. Wilson, *Ambition and Identity*, 225.

40. Yong and McKenna, *Kuomintang Movement in British Malaya*, 76, 117.

41. Anuson Chinvanno, *Thailand's Policies towards China, 1949–54* (Basingstoke: Macmillan, 1992), 35–37.

42. In 1929, the Philippine KMT had 3,834 members, according to Yang Jiancheng, *Zhongguo Guomindang haiwai gongzuo de lilun yu shijian,1924–1991* ([Taipei], 2001), 10.

43. Yang, *Zhongguo Guomindang haiwai gongzuo*, 64.

44. Chinben See, "Education and Ethnic Identity among the Chinese in the Philippines," in *Chinese in the Philippines*, ed. Theresa Chong Carino (Manila: China Studies Program, De La Salle University, 1985), 33–34.

45. See the list of Chinese schools in Tan, *Chinese in the Philippines, 1898–1935*, 157–159.

46. James Roland Blaker, "The Chinese in the Philippines: A Study of Power and Change" (PhD diss., Ohio State University, 1970), 111.

47. *Dai Kuisheng huiyi lu* ([Taipei], 1980), 54–56.

48. "Wang Quansheng deng zhi wu quanda mishuchu han," Records of the Fifth National Party Congress, 1935, 5.1 reel 16, file ID: 34.12, November 14, 1935, Zhongguo Guomindang Records (KMT Records), HILA.

49. Shen Fushui, "Feilübin huaqiao ge laogong tuanti lianhehui de zhanmen licheng," *Guangdong wenshi ziliao* 54 (1988): 100–101; Hau, *Chinese Question*, 174.

50. Liu Haoran, ed., *Xu Li tongzhi zhuisi jinian kan 1905–1995* (Quanzhou: Feilübin Xushi zongqin zonghui, 1995), 6–7.

51. Hau, *Chinese Question*, 175.

52. Ken Fuller, *Forcing the Pace: The Partido Komunista ng Pilipinas; From Foundation to Armed Struggle* (Diliman: University of the Philippines Press, 2007), 39n49.

53. *Communism in the Philippines: The PKP* (Quezon City: Historical Commission, Partido Komunista ng Pilipinas, 1996), 1:114–115.

54. Anna Belogurova, *The Nanyang Revolution: The Comintern and Chinese Networks in Southeast Asia, 1890–1957* (Cambridge: Cambridge University Press, 2019), 73–74.

55. Renato Constantino and Letizia R. Constantino, *The History of the Philippines: From the Spanish Colonization to the Second World War* (New York: Monthly Review Press, 1975), 362.

56. Tan, *Chinese in the Philippines, 1898–1935*, 258.

57. Shen, "Feilübin huaqiao ge laogong tuanti lianhehui," 103.

58. Yung Li, *Huaqiao Warriors*, 65. On the lack of direct evidence linking the CCP in China to the Philippines, see Hau, *Chinese Question*, 199n9.

59. Yang, *Zhongguo Guomindang haiwai gongzuo*, 13.

60. Hau, *Chinese Question*, 177–179.

61. Shen, "Feilübin huaqiao ge laogong tuanti lianhehui," 107–112.

62. Liu, *Xu Li tongzhi zhuisi jinian kan*, 6–9.

63. Liang Shang Wan [Leong Siong Yuen] and Cai Jian Hua [Chua Kian Hua], *The Wha Chi Memoirs*, trans. Joaquin Sy (Manila: Kaisa Para sa Kaunlaran, 1998), 2.

64. Yung Li, *Huaqiao Warriors*, 79.

65. Caroline S. Hau and Kasian Tejapira, eds., *Traveling Nation-Makers: Transnational Flows and Movements in the Making of Modern Southeast Asia* (Kyoto: Kyoto University Press, 2011).

66. For a list of the *zongzhibu*'s ranking members in 1953, see *Philippine-Chinese Business Guide and Pictorial Directory* (Cebu City: Philippine Konghooy Publication, 1953), M-96.

67. Fang Chih-chou [Fang Zhizhou], "Benshe zhi guoqu xianzai yu weilai," *Huaqiao huji she Feilübin zhishe Minlila fenshe yuandan tekan*, January 1948, 34–35, CNBKSY; Lin Gangqiang, "Lizhi fenshe de renwu," *Huaqiao huji she Feilübin zhishe Minlila fenshe yuandan tekan*, January 1948, 59, CNBKSY.

68. Wu Tiecheng, "Xinsui xianci," *Huaqiao huji she Feilübin zhishe Minlila fenshe yuandan tekan*, January 1948, 28–29, CNBKSY.

69. Lee Hai-jo [Li Hairuo], "Kanyan de hua," *Huaqiao huji she Feilübin zhishe Minlila fenshe yuandan tekan*, January 1948, 16, CNBKSY.

70. Mah's unpublished autobiography, which I date to around 1969 on the basis of the official appointments listed in it, can be found in box 18, Mah Soo-Lay Papers (MSLP), HILA. The materials in these sixty boxes of papers are not indexed.

71. Akashi, *Nanyang Chinese National Salvation Movement*, 90.

72. Yung Li, *Huaqiao Warriors*, 59, 135.

73. Julia C. Strauss, "The Evolution of Republican Government," *China Quarterly* 150 (June 1997): 347; Zhang Yougao, "Zhongyang xunlian tuan," *Minguo dang'an* 2 (1994): 141–143.

74. Yung Li, *Huaqiao Warriors*, 22.

75. Akashi, *Nanyang Chinese National Salvation Movement*, 43.

76. Yang, *Zhongguo Guomindang haiwai gongzuo*, 48–49.

77. Wong, *Chinese in the Philippine Economy*, 99.

78. Akashi, *Nanyang Chinese National Salvation Movement*, 44–48.

79. Akashi, *Nanyang Chinese National Salvation Movement*, 177n139.

80. Akashi, *Nanyang Chinese National Salvation Movement*, 90.

81. A fourth, nominally right-wing, organization, the Pekek Squadron, or Poji Tuan, split from the Chinese Overseas Wartime Hsuehkan Militia (COWHM) in mid-1943 and later worked with the communist Wha Chi, but we know little about this rather

small group and will not discuss it here. For more on the Pekek Squadron, see Yung Li, *Huaqiao Warriors*, 126–129.

82. Jennifer Liu, "Indoctrinating the Youth: Guomindang Policy on Secondary Education in Wartime China and Postwar Taiwan, 1937–1960" (PhD diss., University of California, Irvine, 2010), 62.

83. Yung Li, *Huaqiao Warriors*, 117–118, 129.

84. Yung Li, *Huaqiao Warriors*, 117–125; "Brief History—the Development of the COWHM," Series IV, box 6, folder: Guerrillas, Chinese, Manuel A. Roxas Papers, University Archives and Records Depository (UARD), University of the Philippines Diliman.

85. Shi Youtu, *Dahan hun zhuanji: Huaqiao kangri yiyongjun dixia zuozhan fendou shilüe* (Manila: Feilübin huaqiao yiyong hui tongzhi hui, 1995), 8.

86. Yung Li, *Huaqiao Warriors*, 135.

87. Chang Tsun-wu, Chu Hong-yuan, Dory Poa, and Lin Shu-hui, eds., *The Reminiscences of the Chinese in the Philippines* (Taipei: Institute of Modern History, Academia Sinica, 1996), 29–30; Yung Li, *Huaqiao Warriors*, 12, 29–30.

88. "Jun weihui weiyuanzhang shi sanchu zhi waijiaobu han," TE 5 Special Archives of the KMT Party Affairs, TE 5 reel 1, file ID: 1.1, April 8, 1940; "Zhongyang haiwaibu zhi waijiaobu han," TE 5 Special Archives of the KMT Party Affairs, TE 5 reel 1, file ID: 1.3, May 15, 1940, KMT Records, HILA.

89. "Zhu Fei zongzhibu zhiweihui shang zhongyang haiwaibu cheng," TE 5 Special Archives of the KMT Party Affairs, TE 5 reel 1, file ID: 1.4, April 30, 1940, KMT Records, HILA.

90. "Zhu Fei zongzhibu zhiweihui shang zhongyang haiwaibu cheng," TE 5 Special Archives of the KMT Party Affairs, TE 5 reel 1, file ID: 1.4, April 30, 1940, KMT Records, HILA.

91. "Zhu Manila zongling shiguan shang waijiaobu cheng," TE 5 Special Archives of the KMT Party Affairs, TE 5 reel 1, file ID: 1.9, August 6, 1940, KMT Records, HILA.

92. "Zhu Manila zongling shiguan shang waijiaobu cheng," TE 5 Special Archives of the KMT Party Affairs, TE 5 reel 1, file ID: 1.11, August 24, 1940, KMT Records, HILA.

93. "Moudang zai Fei shouyao fenzi Xu Jingcheng deng huodong qingxing biao," TE 5 Special Archives of the KMT Party Affairs, TE 5 reel 1, file ID: 1.12, September 10, 1940, KMT Records, HILA.

94. Liang and Cai, *Wha Chi Memoirs*, 9.

95. Shen, "Feilübin huaqiao ge laogong tuanti lianhehui," 112–113.

96. Shen, "Feilübin huaqiao ge laogong tuanti lianhehui," 113–115.

97. Santos Ong [Wang Wenhan], *Fengchen wushinian* (Beijing: Zhongguo youyi chuban gongsi, 1989), 27.

98. Gong Taoyi, ed., *Feilübin huaqiao guiqiao aiguo danxin lu* (Beijing: Huawen chubanshe, 2002), 36.

99. Fang, "Benshe zhi guoqu xianzai yu weilai," 34, CNBKSY. Mah's autobiography mentions that he taught at three schools: Philippine-Chinese High School, Anglo-Chinese School, and Nanyang High School. See box 18, MSLP, HILA.

100. Gong, *Feilübin huaqiao guiqiao aiguo danxin lu*, 64–69.

101. Yung Li, *Huaqiao Warriors*, 75–152.

2. A "Period of Bloody Struggle"

1. Liu, *Xu Li tongzhi zhuisi jinian kan*, 107.

2. Gong, *Feilübin huaqiao guiqiao aiguo danxin lu*, 106–108.

3. Antonio S. Tan, *The Chinese in the Philippines during the Japanese Occupation, 1942–1945* (Quezon City: University of the Philippines Press, 1981), 52–62.

4. Tee's membership of the *zongzhibu* in the 1930s is noted in "Han zhongyang zuzhibu (fu mingdan)—Zhu Feilübin zongzhibu diwu jie zhijian weiyuan zhunyu beian, qing zhuanzhi," *Zhongyang dangwu yuekan* 39 (1931): 40–41, CNBKSY. On Go's death, see Tan, *Chinese in the Philippines during the Japanese Occupation*, 63–64; Chang et al., *Reminiscences*, 116.

5. Tan, *Chinese in the Philippines during the Japanese Occupation*, 68.

6. "Zhu Fei zongzhibu muqian renshi zuzhi ji gongzuo qingxing qingbao," June 19, 1945, Te 19/1.10, Kuomintang (KMT) Archives, Taipei.

7. Chen Hsiao-yu [Chen Xiaoyu], ed., *Philippine Chinese Chronicle* (Manila: Philippine Chinese Chronicle Publisher, 1948), vol. 2, *chu* 5–6.

8. Good examples of scholarship on collaboration with the Japanese include Timothy Brook, *Collaboration: Japanese Agents and Local Elites in Wartime China* (Cambridge, MA: Harvard University Press, 2005); and Yumi Moon, *Populist Collaborators: The Ilchinhoe and the Japanese Colonization of Korea, 1896–1910* (Ithaca, NY: Cornell University Press, 2013).

9. Tan, *Chinese in the Philippines during the Japanese Occupation*, 65.

10. Brook, *Collaboration*, 5.

11. *Zhongguo Guomindang diqi jie quanguo daibiao da hui dangwu baogao* (Taipei: Zhongyang gaizao weiyuanhui, 1952), 1:53.

12. Shi, *Dahan hun zhuanji*, 8.

13. Lin spent most of the next three decades in Taiwan but returned to the Philippines following his retirement in 1974 to work in Davao, first as a Taiji teacher and then as a principal. See Chang et al., *Reminiscences*, 80.

14. "Feilübin zhengli weiyuan mingdan," June 14, 1945, Hui 6.3/4.15, KMT Archives.

15. Lee Hai-jo [Li Hairuo], "Kanyan de hua," *Huaqiao huji she Feilübin zhishe Minlila fenshe yuandan tekan*, January 1948, 16, CNBKSY; Fang Chih-chou [Fang Zhizhou], "Benshe zhi guoqu xianzai yu weilai," *Huaqiao huji she Feilübin zhishe Minlila fenshe yuandan tekan*, January 1948, 35, CNBKSY.

16. Liu, *Xu Li tongzhi zhuisi jinian kan*, 106.

17. "Zhu Feilübin zongzhibu dangwu gongzuo baogaoshu," Records of the Seventh National Party Congress, 7.1 reel 3, file ID: 71, October 1952, KMT Records, HILA.

18. Cua Siok Po [Ke Shubao], *Fendou rensheng* (Taipei: Liming wenhua shiye gufen youxian gongsi, 1982), 60.

19. Tan, *Chinese in the Philippines during the Japanese Occupation*, 39.

20. Yun Xia, *Down with Traitors: Justice and Nationalism in Wartime China* (Seattle: University of Washington Press, 2017), 46.

21. Tan, *Chinese in the Philippines during the Japanese Occupation*, 101.

22. McCoy, *Policing America's Empire*, 373.

23. "What We Have Done after the Surrender of the Japanese (July–November 1945)," RG 407: Records of the Adjutant General's Office, 1917–, Series: Guerrilla Unit Recogni-

tion Files, 1941–1948, box 323, folder: 105 Phil Chinese Anti-Japanese Vol Corps (Wa-Chi Unit), NARA.

24. Wong, *Chinese in the Philippine Economy*, 62.

25. Yung Li, *Huaqiao Warriors*, 159.

26. Tan, *Chinese in the Philippines during the Japanese Occupation*, 96–97, 101.

27. Chang et al., *Reminiscences*, 165.

28. Moon, *Populist Collaborators*, 7.

29. Chu-Pei Chen, "Chinese and the War in the Philippines," manuscript submitted to Institute of Pacific Relations (ca. 1948), 51, Library of Congress (LOC), Washington, DC.

30. "Wang Quansheng zhi Wu Tiecheng han," April 15, 1945, Te 31/43.75, KMT Archives.

31. *Wang guxiaozhang Quansheng shishi wushi zhounian jinian teji*, 5–6.

32. The entry on Yu in a two-volume biographical dictionary of prominent Southeast Asian Chinese does not mention his participation in the CA, but states only that he was given amnesty by Japan in 1943 before skipping to the end of World War II. Teresita Ang See, "Yu Khe Thai," in *Southeast Asian Personalities of Chinese Descent: A Biographical Dictionary*, ed. Leo Suryadinata (Singapore: Institute of Southeast Asian Studies, 2012), 1:1378–1380.

33. "Zhu Feilübin zongzhibu dangwu gongzuo baogaoshu," KMT Records, HILA; Shi, *Dahan hun zhuanji*, 132. In 1948, after merging with the *Chiang Kai-shek Daily News* (*Zhongzheng ribao*), the *Great China Press*'s Chinese name became the *Da zhonghua ribao*.

34. Gong Taoyi, ed., *Feilübin huaqiao kangri aiguo yinghun lu* (Beijing: Huawen chubanshe, 2001), 217.

35. "Monthly Situation Report No. 2, July 1945," RG 496: Records of General Headquarters, Southwest Pacific Area and United States Army Forces, Pacific (World War II), Series: Monthly Reports of Counter-Intelligence Corps Area #1 1945, box 445, folder: July 1945, NARA.

36. "Monthly Situation Report No. 3, August 1945," RG 496, Series: Monthly Reports of Counter-Intelligence Corps Area #1 1945, box 445, folder: August 1945, NARA.

37. Dy Sun is mentioned in Mah Soo-Lay's unpublished autobiography. See box 18, MSLP, HILA. On the threatening letter from the Anti-Collaboration Commission, see "United States of America vs. Masao Tachibana, Asao Namiki, Volume III," 223–224, RG 331: Records of Allied Operational and Occupation Headquarters, World War II, Series: USA versus Japanese War Criminals Case File, 1945–1949, box 1554, folder 22, NARA.

38. Tan, *Chinese in the Philippines during the Japanese Occupation*, 101, 104.

39. David Joel Steinberg, *Philippine Collaboration in World War II* (Ann Arbor: University of Michigan Press, 1967), 107.

40. Steinberg, *Philippine Collaboration*, 115, 126–127.

41. Luis Taruc, *Born of the People* (New York: International Publishers, 1953), 76; Hau, *Chinese Question*, 190.

42. Luis Taruc, *He Who Rides the Tiger: The Story of an Asian Guerrilla Leader* (New York: Praeger, 1967), 34.

43. Benedict J. Kerkvliet, *The Huk Rebellion: A Study of Peasant Revolt in the Philippines* (Lanham, MD: Rowman & Littlefield, 2002), 112.

44. Remigio E. Agpalo, *The Political Process and the Nationalization of the Retail Trade in the Philippines* (Diliman: University of the Philippines, Office of Coordinator of Research, 1962), 35–38.

45. Liu, *Xu Li tongzhi zhuisi jinian kan*, 105; Yung Li, *Huaqiao Warriors*, 157.

46. "Feidao zhi Wu Tiecheng han bao," October 10, 1945, Te 5/1.29, KMT Archives; "1,000 Chinese in Huk Parade," *Daily News*, September 25, 1945, 1, LOC. Taruc, who was released on September 30, mentions the September 23 protests in his memoir and estimates the number of protesters at fifty thousand. See Taruc, *Born of the People*, 211.

47. Co Keng Sing, "We Demand Justice," *New China Review* 1, no. 2 (October 1, 1945): 10, 12, HILA.

48. "1,000 Chinese in Huk Parade," *Daily News*, September 25, 1945, 1–2, LOC.

49. "By His Actions, Osmena Is Chinese Puppet Leader Here," editorial, *Daily News*, September 26, 1945, 1–2, LOC.

50. "Zhu Manila zong lingshiguan shang waijiaobu cheng," November 19, 1945, Te 5/1.32, KMT Archives.

51. Agpalo, *Nationalization of the Retail Trade*, 38.

52. Kerkvliet, *Huk Rebellion*, 141.

53. "Big Head of the Chinese Communist Party," October 29, 1945, Series IV, box 8, folder: Chinese Communists 1945–1946, Roxas Papers, UARD.

54. "Deport Undesirable Chinese," 1945, Series IV, box 8, folder: Chinese Communists 1945–1946, Roxas Papers, UARD.

55. "Nobody Safe," *Philippines Free Press* 37, no. 2 (March 2, 1946): 18.

56. "Cai Yunqin bei bang sha busui," *Dahan hun yuekan* 1, no. 1 (October 15, 1946): 20, CNBKSY; "Zhu Feilübin zongzhibu dangwu gongzuo baogaoshu," KMT Records, HILA.

57. "35 Unsolved Murder Mysteries," *Philippines Free Press* 37, no. 12 (May 11, 1946): 7.

58. "Zhu Feilübin zongzhibu dangwu gongzuo baogaoshu," KMT Records, HILA.

59. "Feidao gongdang zuzhi jigou ji huodong diaocha zhuanbao," April 1946, Te 5/1.36; "Zhongyang haiwaibu zhi waijiaobu han," April 11, 1946, Te 5/1.33, KMT Archives.

60. Koa Chun-te [Ke Junzhi], "Fakan ci," *Dahan hun yuekan* 1, no. 1 (October 15, 1946): 1, CNBKSY.

61. Chiang employed the term in a 1951 tract titled "Why *Hanjian* Will Perish and the Invasion Will be Defeated" (*Weihe hanjian biwang qinlüe bibai*). See Xia, *Down with Traitors*, 180.

62. On the KMT's use of *fei* to describe the CCP, see Hui-Ching Chang and Richard Holt, *Language, Politics and Identity in Taiwan: Naming China* (London: Routledge, 2015), 15–56. For a genealogy and analysis of the term *hanjian*, see Xia, *Down with Traitors*.

63. "Xuegan tuan huo fei hou suo zaoyu de bozhe," *Dahan hun yuekan* 1, no. 1 (October 15, 1946): 19; "Cai Yunqin bei bang sha busui," 20.

64. "Sotto Stresses Chinese Menace," *Manila Times*, September 5, 1946, 12; "Sotto Denounces Illegal Entry," *Manila Times*, September 15, 1946, 1, 15.

65. Gong, *Feilübin huaqiao kangri aiguo yinghun lu*, 191.

66. "Zhu Feilübin zongzhibu dangwu gongzuo baogaoshu," KMT Records, HILA.

67. "Wei Daoming shang waijiaobu dian," May 14, 1946, Te 5/1.34, KMT Archives; telegram from Ambassador in the Philippines (McNutt) to the Secretary of State, Sep-

tember 8, 1946, in *Foreign Relations of the United States, 1946*, vol. 8, *The Far East* (Washington, DC: Government Printing Office, 1947), 909–910.

68. Kerkvliet, *Huk Rebellion*, 189.

69. "Palace Orders MPs to Stop Chinese Raids," *Manila Times*, September 7, 1946, 16; Tan, *Chinese in the Philippines during the Japanese Occupation*, 110.

70. Tan, *Chinese in the Philippines during the Japanese Occupation*, 110.

71. "Palace Orders MPs to Stop Chinese Raids," 16.

72. "Feidao huaqiao yu gongdang baozhi zaoyao zhongshang Shi Yisheng fouren yu souchashi youguan," *Jiaotongbu Jinpuqu tielu guanliju ribao* 164 (September 10, 1946): 3, CNBKSY.

73. "Zhu Feilübin zongzhibu dangwu gongzuo baogaoshu," KMT Records, HILA.

74. Gong, *Feilübin huaqiao kangri aiguo yinghun lu*, 191.

75. Shen, "Feilübin huaqiao ge laogong tuanti lianhehui," 124–126.

76. "Zhu Feilübin zongzhibu dangwu gongzuo baogaoshu," KMT Records, HILA.

77. "Zhu Feilübin zongzhibu dangwu gongzuo baogaoshu," KMT Records, HILA.

78. "Zhu Feilübin zongzhibu dangwu gongzuo baogaoshu," KMT Records, HILA.

79. Commonwealth Act No. 613, August 26, 1940, *Official Gazette*, https://www.officialgazette.gov.ph/1940/08/26/commonwealth-act-no-613/.

80. Unless otherwise stated, my analysis of this case is based primarily on the Supreme Court's decision, which can be read in full online. See G.R. No. L-1673, October 22, 1948, Chan Robles Virtual Law Library, https://www.chanrobles.com/cralaw/1948octoberdecisions.php?id=194.

81. Charge d'Affaires Thomas H. Lockett to Secretary of State, October 25, 1948, RG 84, Series: Classified General Records, 1946–1961, box 6, folder: 800.B Bolshevism—Activities, NARA.

82. File 005: Spot Intelligence Report, Subject: Arms Smuggling in the Philippines (September 26, 1949), box 5, folder 7: National Intelligence Coordinating Agency (1948), Elpidio Quirino Papers, Filipinas Heritage Library (FHL), Ayala Museum, Manila.

83. Shen, "Feilübin huaqiao ge laogong tuanti lianhehui," 127.

84. Lockett to Secretary of State, October 25, 1948, NARA.

85. Shen, "Feilübin huaqiao ge laogong tuanti lianhehui," 127–130.

86. Liang and Cai, *Wha Chi Memoirs*, 98; Hau, *Chinese Question*, 177.

87. Gong, *Feilübin huaqiao guiqiao aiguo danxin lu*, 255.

88. "Zhu Feilübin zongzhibu dangwu gongzuo baogaoshu," KMT Records, HILA.

89. "Feilübin Xu Zhibei you bufa huodong an," 21, 062.6/0011, December 1950–April 1956, Institute of Modern History (IMH) Archives, Academia Sinica, Taipei.

90. On the origins of the Hongmen, see Dian H. Murray and Qin Baoqi, *The Origins of the Tiandihui: The Chinese Triads in Legend and History* (Stanford, CA: Stanford University Press, 1994).

91. Liu, *Xu Li tongzhi zhuisi jinian kan*, 155.

92. "Feilübin Xu Zhibei you bufa huodong an," 16–20, 125–127, IMH Archives.

93. "Fei huaqiao Xu Zhibei panchu wuqi tuxing," *United Daily News*, September 21, 1952, 1.

94. "Feilübin Xu Zhibei you bufa huodong an," 108, IMH Archives.

95. "Feilübin Xu Zhibei you bufa huodong an," 129, IMH Archives.

96. "Feilübin Xu Zhibei you bufa huodong an," 126, 128, IMH Archives.

97. "Feilübin Xu Zhibei you bufa huodong an," 17–18, 106, IMH Archives.

98. "Feilübin Xu Zhibei you bufa huodong an," 21, IMH Archives.

99. Hsiao Shi-ching, *Chinese-Philippine Diplomatic Relations, 1946–1975* (Quezon City: Bookman Printing House, 1975), 14.

100. Manuel Roxas and Chen Chih-ping, "Sino-Philippine Treaty of Amity, April 1947," *International Law Quarterly* 2, no. 1 (Spring 1948): 132–134.

101. For a detailed analysis of the Jose Tan Chong case and the shift from jus soli to jus sanguinis citizenship in the Philippines, see Aguilar, "Letter and Spirit of the Law." The Supreme Court's verdict on the case can be read at G.R. No. 47616, September 16, 1947, Chan Robles Virtual Law Library, https://www.chanrobles.com/cralaw/1947september decisions.php?id=125.

102. Charles J. McCarthy, "The Chinese in the Philippines," in *Philippine-Chinese Profile: Essays & Studies*, ed. Charles J. McCarthy (Manila: Pagkakaisa sa Pag-unlad, 1974), 25; Commonwealth Act No. 473, June 17, 1939, the Lawphil Project, https://www.lawphil.net/statutes/comacts/ca_473_1939.html.

103. Anuson, *Thailand's Policies towards China*, 42. On the Yaowarat Incident, see Wasana Wongsurawat, *The Crown and the Capitalists: The Ethnic Chinese and the Founding of the Thai Nation* (Seattle: University of Washington Press, 2019), 141–145.

104. Skinner, "Report on the Chinese in Southeast Asia," 3, 73.

105. Anuson, *Thailand's Policies towards China*, 63.

106. Fineman, *Special Relationship*, 75.

107. Fineman, *Special Relationship*, 99.

108. Skinner estimated in 1950 that Vietnam's Chinese population was 750,000, Singapore's was 790,000, and the rest of peninsula Malaya's was 2,008,000. Skinner, "Report on the Chinese in Southeast Asia," 19, 30, 40.

109. Thomas Engelbert, "Vietnamese-Chinese Relations in Southern Vietnam during the First Indochina Conflict," *Journal of Vietnamese Studies* 3, no. 3 (October 2008): 198.

110. Engelbert, "Vietnamese-Chinese Relations," 206–207.

111. Engelbert, "Vietnamese-Chinese Relations," 199.

112. Cheah Boon Kheng, *Red Star over Malaya: Resistance and Social Conflict during and after the Japanese Occupation* (Singapore: NUS Press, 2012), 167–168.

113. Yong and McKenna, *Kuomintang Movement in British Malaya*, 217–219.

114. Yong and McKenna, *Kuomintang Movement in British Malaya*, 220.

115. Fujio Hara, *Malayan Chinese and China: Conversion in Identity Consciousness, 1945–1957* (Singapore: Singapore University Press, 2003), 23.

116. Zhou, *Migration in the Time of Revolution*, 25.

117. Chang Pao-min, *Beijing, Hanoi, and the Overseas Chinese* (Berkeley: Institute of East Asian Studies, University of California, Berkeley, Center for Chinese Studies, 1982), 12–15.

118. Barbara Watson Andaya and Leonard Y. Andaya, *A History of Malaysia* (Basingstoke: Palgrave, 2001), 276.

3. Practicing Anticommunism

1. "Dear Mr. President," *The Bullseye*, January 28, 1954, in Ramon Magsaysay Scrapbook, vol. 2 (January 22–February 19, 1954), 168, Asian Library, Ramon Magsaysay

Center, Manila. The propaganda materials that Lim says were received through the mail were titled "Appeal of Philippine Overseas Chinese Communist Party to All Chinese in the Philippines for Unity in Opposing U.S.-Sino-Philippine Reactionaries and for Fight of Liberation," December 28, 1953, and "Further Statement of Philippine Overseas Chinese Communist Party to All Chinese People Recommendation [*sic*] for Chinese Investment in National Construction," January 1, 1954. See "Chinese Communist Party Propaganda Documents," February 4, 1954, CIA-RDP80-00810A003500700009-7, Central Intelligence Agency Records Search Tool (CREST), NARA. There is no indication in this brief report as to whether the materials were authentic or forgeries.

2. "Deport Undesirable Chinese," 1945, Series IV, box 8, folder: Chinese Communists 1945–1946, Roxas Papers, UARD.

3. Certeau, *Practice of Everyday Life*, xix.

4. The ACM's official English name was the Philippine-Chinese United Organization in Support of Anti-Communist Movement. A more literal translation of Feilübin Huaqiao Fangong Kang'E Houyuanhui is Philippine-Chinese Association in Support of Anticommunism and Resistance to Russia.

5. Scholarship on the subject suggests that no such instructions were forthcoming. See Larissa Efimova, "Did the Soviet Union Instruct Southeast Asian Communists to Revolt? New Russian Evidence on the Calcutta Youth Conference of February 1948," *Journal of Southeast Asian Studies* 40, no. 3 (October 2009): 449–469.

6. See Cheung Shing Kit, "Immigrating Visitors: The Case of Overstaying Chinese in the Philippines, 1947–75" (MPhil thesis, University of Hong Kong, 1997).

7. Chargé d'Affaires Thomas H. Lockett to Secretary of State, October 21, 1948, RG 84, Series: Classified General Records, 1946–1961, box 6, folder: 800.B Bolshevism—Activities, NARA. On CUFA and how it was modeled after the notorious House Un-American Activities Committee in the United States, see Colleen Woods, *Freedom Incorporated: Anticommunism and Philippine Independence in the Age of Decolonization* (Ithaca, NY: Cornell University Press, 2020), 107–108.

8. File 002, box 14, folder 6: Interior, Department of the (Philippine Constabulary), Quirino Papers, FHL.

9. File 007, box 5, folder 7: National Intelligence Coordinating Agency (1948), Quirino Papers, FHL.

10. "Lü Fei buliang huaqiao," vol. 4, 21, 020-010708-0019, May 30–November 27, 1951, Academia Historica (AH), Taipei.

11. Chu, *Chinese and Chinese Mestizos*, 330.

12. File 006, box 5, folder 7, Quirino Papers, FHL.

13. File 007, box 5, folder 7, Quirino Papers, FHL.

14. Kuhn, *Chinese among Others*, 300.

15. Agpalo, *Nationalization of the Retail Trade*, 39–54.

16. Political Secretary Edward E. Rice to Chargé d'Affaires Vinton Chapin, November 24, 1950, RG 84, Series: Classified General Records, 1946–1961, box 33, folder: 370 Public Order and Safety, NARA.

17. "Lü Fei buliang huaqiao," vol. 3, 98, 020-010708-0018, March 5–May 27, 1951, AH.

18. Amyot, *Manila Chinese*, 46; Konrad Bekker and Charles Wolf Jr., "The Philippine Balance of Payments," *Far Eastern Survey* 19, no. 4 (February 22, 1950): 41–43.

19. On this letter-writing campaign, see Glen Peterson, *Overseas Chinese in the People's Republic of China* (London: Routledge, 2012), 33.

20. R. A. Spruance to State Department, April 1, 1952, RG 84, Series: Classified General Records, 1946–1961, box 32, folder: 350.21 Chinese Communists, NARA.

21. Blaker, "Chinese in the Philippines," 195.

22. Blaker, "Chinese in the Philippines," 131.

23. Wilson, *Ambition and Identity*, 6.

24. David W. Mabon, "Elusive Agreements: The Pacific Pact Proposals of 1949–1951," *Pacific Historical Review* 57, no. 2 (May 1988): 144–177.

25. Blaker, "Chinese in the Philippines," 206–209.

26. Party membership figures from 1950 can be found in Yang, *Zhongguo Guomindang haiwai gongzuo*, 26, and from October 1952 in "Zhu Feilübin zongzhibu dangwu gongzuo baogaoshu," Records of the Seventh National Party Congress, 7.1 reel 3, file ID: 71, October 1952, KMT Records, HILA.

27. "Zhu Feilübin zongzhibu dangwu gongzuo baogaoshu," KMT Records, HILA.

28. Philippine Chinese General Chamber of Commerce, *Golden Book 1955: Commercial Almanac and Yearbook 1904–1954* [Feilübin Minlila zhonghua shanghui wushi zhounian jinian kan] (Manila: Fookien Times Publishing Company, 1955), Chinese section, Jia (8).

29. Ellen D. Wu, *The Color of Success: Asian Americans and the Origins of the Model Minority* (Princeton, NJ: Princeton University Press, 2014), 116.

30. *Zhongguo Guomindang diqi jie quanguo daibiao da hui dangwu baogao*, 2:95–96.

31. "Bendang cedong Feilübin huaqiao huiguo weilao jingguo," Central Reform Committee Archive, 6.4-1 reel 8, file ID: 215, September 14, 1950, KMT Records, HILA.

32. On the reforms to transform the KMT, see Ramon Myers and Hsiao-ting Lin, *Breaking with the Past: The Kuomintang Central Reform Committee on Taiwan, 1950–52* (Stanford, CA: Hoover Institution Press, 2007).

33. "Feihua fangong kang'E zonghui," vol. 1, 7, 062.2/0004, December 1950–December 1959, IMH Archives.

34. "Feihua fangong kang'E zonghui," vol. 1, 25, IMH Archives; Charter of the Philippine-Chinese United Organization in Support of Anti-Communist Movement, RG 84, Series: Classified General Records, 1946–1961, box 32, folder: 350.21 Communism in the Philippines, January 1950–June 1951, NARA.

35. Philippine Chinese General Chamber of Commerce, *Golden Book 1955*, Chinese section, 24.

36. Philippine Chinese General Chamber of Commerce, *Golden Book 1955*, Chinese section, Jia (11).

37. "Lü Fei buliang huaqiao," vol. 6, 23, 020-010708-0021, September 19, 1952–December 13, 1954, AH.

38. "Re: attached A-192, 11 / 27 / 1956 to Taipei concerning acknowledgement to be made to Alfonso Z. Sy Cip," December 4, 1956, RG 59, Series: Decimal Files, 1954–1957, box 21, folder: 010 Correspondences with Public, NARA.

39. Akashi, *Nanyang Chinese National Salvation Movement*, 92.

40. "Zhongyang haiwaibu zhi waijiaobu han," TE 5 Special Archives of the KMT Party Affairs, TE 5 reel 1, file ID: 1.14, January 29, 1941, KMT Records, HILA.

41. "Zhu Manila zongling shiguan shang waijiaobu cheng," TE 5 Special Archives of the KMT Party Affairs, TE 5 reel 1, file ID: 1.19, May 13, 1941, KMT Records, HILA.

42. "Feihua fangong kang'E zonghui," vol. 1, 13–14, IMH Archives.

43. "Feihua fangong kang'E zonghui," vol. 1, 53, IMH Archives.

44. Myron M. Cowen, "The 'Philippine-Chinese United Organization in Support of Anti-Communist Movement,'" RG 84, Series: Classified General Records, 1946–1961, box 32, folder: 350.21 Communism in the Philippines, January 1950–June 1951, NARA.

45. "Feihua fangong kang'E zonghui," vol. 1, 37, IMH Archives.

46. "Feihua fangong kang'E zonghui," vol. 1, 81–82, IMH Archives.

47. *Qiaowu tongji*, 68.

48. Alfonso Z. Sycip, "The Role of the Overseas Chinese in the Worldwide Struggle against Communism," *Fookien Times Yearbook*, September 1952, 73, 75.

49. Alfonso Z. Sycip, "An Appeal to the People of Free Nations," *Fookien Times Yearbook*, September 1953, 81.

50. Tan, *Chinese in the Philippines*, 73, 112.

51. "Feihua fangong kang'E zonghui," vol. 1, 115–118, IMH Archives.

52. "Businessman Chosen to Represent Local Chinese in China's Assembly," *Manila Times*, April 22, 1946, 1.

53. "Shi Yisheng huanqiu lüxing," *United Daily News*, October 18, 1951, 1; "Shi Yisheng fan Fei," *United Daily News*, April 8, 1952.

54. "Feidao dangwu ji qingnian yundong," 5–9, 11, 020-010799-0081, July 19, 1950–February 7, 1952, AH; Assistant Chief of Staff, G-2, Headquarters Philippine Command Clifford L. Sawyer to US Military Attaché, January 29, 1949, RG 165: Records of the War Department General and Special Staffs, Series: Security Classified Correspondence Relating to Military Attachés, 1938–1949, box 189, folder: MA Philippines: 080, Philippine China Cultural Association, NARA.

55. In October 1952, 60.5 percent of Philippine KMT members were in commerce, according to the party's report that month to the Seventh National Party Congress in Taipei. "Zhu Feilübin zongzhibu dangwu gongzuo baogaoshu," KMT Records, HILA.

56. Cowen, "'Philippine-Chinese United Organization in Support of Anti-Communist Movement,'" NARA; 1135th Counter-Intelligence Corps Detachment to Assistant Chief of Staff, G-2, January 29, 1948, RG 165, Series: Security Classified Correspondence Relating to Military Attachés, 1938–1949, box 189, folder: MA Philippines: 080, Philippine China Cultural Association, NARA.

57. "Feidao dangwu ji qingnian yundong," 185–187, AH.

58. *Free China Magazine* 1, no. 2 (October 10, 1951): 13, American Historical Collection (AHC), Ateneo de Manila University, Manila.

59. *Free China Magazine* 1, no. 2 (October 10, 1951): 6, AHC. "Double Tenth" is October 10, the ROC's National Day.

60. "Feidao dangwu ji qingnian yundong," 25–28, 186, AH.

61. Shih I-Sheng to First Secretary Edward Earl Rice, June 5, 1950, and Edward Lim to Rice, June 9, 1950, RG 84, Series: Classified General Records, 1946–1961, box 32, folder: 350.21 Communism in the Philippines, January 1950–June 1951, NARA.

62. "Feidao dangwu ji qingnian yundong," 186, AH.

63. "Feidao dangwu ji qingnian yundong," 186–187, 205, AH.

64. "Zhonggaihui di erjiuqi ci huiyi jilu," Minutes of the Central Reform Committee Meetings, 6.4-2 reel 7, file ID: 31.7, February 19, 1952, KMT Records, HILA.

65. Chen Lieh-fu [Chen Liefu], *Feiyou guangan ji* (Xiamen: Nanyang tongxunshe, 1948), 47.

66. Sawyer to US Military Attaché, January 29, 1949, NARA.

67. *Philippines-China Cultural Journal*, vol. 1 (1947), RG 165, Series: Security Classified Correspondence Relating to Military Attachés, 1938–1949, box 189, folder: MA Philippines: 080, Philippine China Cultural Association, NARA.

68. "Feidao dangwu ji qingnian yundong," 71, AH.

69. File 001, box 6, folder 3: National Intelligence Coordinating Agency (January 1951), Quirino Papers, FHL.

70. "Feidao dangwu ji qingnian yundong," 211–212, 215, AH.

71. "Lü Fei buliang huaqiao," vol. 5, 70–71, 020-010708-0020, November 18, 1951–August 13, 1952, AH; "Lü Fei buliang huaqiao," vol. 6, 58–59, AH.

72. "Lü Fei buliang huaqiao," vol. 5, 71–75, AH; "Continued Intervention of Ranking Philippine Officials in Case of Chinese Gangsters Held for Deportation," January 21, 1952, CIA-RDP82-00457R010000290003-0, CREST, NARA.

73. "Lü Fei buliang huaqiao," vol. 5, 73, AH.

74. "Cai Binqing ni fadong Fei jizhetuan lai Tai," 10–12, 020-010702-0021, May 3–July 6, 1951, AH.

75. "Lü Fei buliang huaqiao," vol. 5, 75, AH.

76. "Lü Fei buliang huaqiao," vol. 6, 96–97, AH.

4. Anticommunism in Question

1. Zhou, *Migration in the Time of Revolution*, 55.

2. Anuson, *Thailand's Policies towards China*, 80. Daniel Fineman has the number of Thai Chinese arrested at seven hundred. Fineman, *Special Relationship*, 165.

3. "Lü Fei huaqiao gongxian," vol. 1, 39, 062.6/0002, December 1952–May 1953, IMH Archives. The exact number of Chinese arrested varies from source to source. Chen Chihping's memorandum on January 29, 1953, in the file cited at the beginning of this note, has it at 309, but the *Philippines Free Press* put the number at 347. See "347 Chinese Red Suspects Nabbed in Surprise Raid," *Philippines Free Press* 44, no. 1 (January 3, 1953): 26. Later reports cite figures of 297 and 315. See, respectively, "Lü Fei huaqiao gongxian," vol. 2, 17, 062.6/0006, December 1952–November 1962, IMH Archives; and "Lü Fei huaqiao gongxian," vol. 3, 6, 062.6/0007, December 1952–November 1962, IMH Archives.

4. "347 Chinese Red Suspects Nabbed," 26.

5. "Mass Roundup of Dangerous Aliens," *Philippines Free Press* 44, no. 2 (January 10, 1953): 5.

6. "Lü Fei buliang huaqiao," vol. 8, 84, 020-010708-0023, April 18, 1958–September 9, 1961, AH.

7. "Lü Fei huaqiao gongxian," vol. 3, 74, IMH Archives.

8. "Lü Fei buliang huaqiao," vol. 8, 84, AH.

9. "Lü Fei huaqiao gongxian," vol. 3, 74–87, IMH Archives; "Lü Fei buliang huaqiao," vol. 8, 84, AH. This may have been the same organization that Lim Tian Seng was referring to in chapter 3.

10. "Lü Fei huaqiao gongxian," vol. 3, 74–87, IMH Archives; "Lü Fei buliang huaqiao," vol. 8, 84, AH.

11. "Relationship of Philippine Communist Party with Chinese Communists in the Philippines," May 18, 1951, CIA-RDP82-00457R007400100007-6, CREST, NARA.

12. "347 Chinese Red Suspects Nabbed," 26.

13. "Lü Fei huaqiao gongxian," vol. 3, 104–105, IMH Archives.

14. "Relationship of Philippine Communist Party with Chinese Communists in the Philippines," CREST, NARA; "Lü Fei huaqiao gongxian," vol. 3, 105, IMH Archives.

15. "Relationship of Philippine Communist Party with Chinese Communists in the Philippines," CREST, NARA.

16. "Document Containing March 1951 Resolution of Philippine Communist Party Political Bureau on Chinese Bureau," November 14, 1951, CIA-RDP82-00457R00920 011001-0, CREST, NARA.

17. "Lü Fei huaqiao gongxian," vol. 3, 84, 112, IMH Archives.

18. "Lü Fei huaqiao gongxian," vol. 3, 99–100, IMH Archives.

19. "Lü Fei huaqiao gongxian," vol. 3, 103–104, 106, IMH Archives.

20. "Lü Fei huaqiao gongxian," vol. 3, 103–104, IMH Archives.

21. "Lü Fei huaqiao gongxian," vol. 3, 80–81, IMH Archives.

22. "Lü Fei huaqiao gongxian," vol. 3, 110–111, 114, IMH Archives; "Lü Fei huaqiao gongxian," vol. 5, 231, 062.6/0003, May–August 1953, IMH Archives.

23. "Lü Fei huaqiao gongxian," vol. 3, 80, IMH Archives.

24. "Lü Fei huaqiao gongxian," vol. 3, 75, IMH Archives.

25. "Lü Fei huaqiao gongxian," vol. 3, 115–120, IMH Archives.

26. "Lü Fei huaqiao gongxian," vol. 3, 89, IMH Archives.

27. "Lü Fei huaqiao gongxian," vol. 3, 71–72, 95, IMH Archives.

28. "Lü Fei huaqiao gongxian," vol. 1, 41–42, IMH Archives.

29. "Lü Fei huaqiao gongxian," vol. 1, 40–41, IMH Archives.

30. "Lü Fei huaqiao gongxian," vol. 1, 39, IMH Archives.

31. "Wu Wenbin deng qianpei," 15, 020-010708-0015, October 25, 1952–September 2, 1957, AH.

32. Hau, *Chinese Question*, 25.

33. "347 Chinese Red Suspects Nabbed," 26; *In Re Chin Sang, et als., Respondents, Case No. R-489: Motion to Dismiss and Memorandum* (Manila: Quisumbing, Sycip, Quisumbing, and Salazar, January 4, 1954), 6, 26–28, 38–39, 69, AHC.

34. "Lü Fei huaqiao gongxian," vol. 1, 41–42, IMH Archives.

35. "Lü Fei buliang huaqiao," vol. 6, 76, 020-010708-0021, September 19, 1952–December 13, 1954, AH.

36. "Lü Fei huaqiao gongxian," vol. 5, 231, IMH Archives.

37. "Lü Fei buliang huaqiao," vol. 8, 85, AH.

38. On the "paper sons" strategy, see Madeline Y. Hsu, *Dreaming of Gold, Dreaming of Home: Transnationalism and Migration between the United States and South China, 1882–1943* (Stanford, CA: Stanford University Press, 2000), 74.

39. See "347 Chinese Red Suspects Nabbed," 26; and *In Re Chin Sang, et als., Respondents, Case No. R-489*, AHC.

40. "Lü Fei huaqiao gongxian," vol. 5, 209, IMH Archives.

41. "Lü Fei huaqiao gongxian," vol. 5, 202–204, 209–210, 239, IMH Archives.

42. "Lü Fei buliang huaqiao," vol. 8, 86, AH.

43. "Lü Fei buliang huaqiao," vol. 8, 86–90, AH; "Fei pohuo huaqiao xuesheng feidie zuzhi," vol. 1, 114, 005.8/0001, August 1954–May 1958, IMH Archives.

44. "Lü Fei buliang huaqiao," vol. 8, 86, AH.

45. "Lü Fei huaqiao gongxian," vol. 3, 176, IMH Archives.

46. "Qijie zhongweihui gongzuo huiyi di 96 ci huiyi jilu," Records of the Seventh National Working Committee, 7.4 reel 6, file ID: 96, September 3, 1954, KMT Records, HILA; "Lü Fei huaqiao gongxian," vol. 3, 169–170, IMH Archives.

47. "Lü Fei buliang huaqiao," vol. 8, 86, AH.

48. "Lü Fei huaqiao gongxian," vol. 3, 168, IMH Archives.

49. "Lü Fei huaqiao gongxian," vol. 3, 254–255, IMH Archives.

50. "Lü Fei huaqiao gongxian," vol. 3, 156, IMH Archives.

51. "Qijie zhongweihui gongzuo huiyi di 96 ci huiyi jilu," KMT Records, HILA.

52. "Qijie zhongweihui gongzuo huiyi di 96 ci huiyi jilu," KMT Records, HILA; "Lü Fei huaqiao gongxian," vol. 3, 158–166, IMH Archives.

53. "Fei pohuo huaqiao xuesheng feidie zuzhi," vol. 1, 39–40, IMH Archives.

54. "Lü Fei huaqiao gongxian," vol. 3, 172, IMH Archives.

55. "Lü Fei huaqiao gongxian," vol. 3, 155–156, IMH Archives.

56. "Lü Fei huaqiao gongxian," vol. 3, 130–144, IMH Archives; "Fei pohuo huaqiao xuesheng feidie zuzhi," vol. 1, 19–21, IMH Archives; "Lü Fei buliang huaqiao," vol. 8, 90–91, AH.

57. "Lü Fei huaqiao gongxian," vol. 3, 183, IMH Archives.

58. "Lü Fei huaqiao gongxian," vol. 3, 159, IMH Archives.

59. "Chengzhi panluan tiaoli," Laws and Regulations Database of the Republic of China (Quanguo Fagui Ziliaoku), accessed February 20, 2021, https://law.moj.gov.tw /LawClass/LawAll.aspx?pcode=C0000010.

60. "Lü Fei buliang huaqiao," vol. 8, 155–157, AH.

61. "Lü Fei buliang huaqiao," vol. 8, 87, 90–91, AH.

62. "Lü Fei buliang huaqiao," vol. 8, 153–157, 200–203, AH.

63. Oyen, *Diplomacy of Migration*, 101.

64. On South Vietnam, see Chang, *Beijing, Hanoi, and the Overseas Chinese*, 12–15. On the anti-Chinese crisis in Indonesia, see Zhou, *Migration in the Time of Revolution*, 115–131; and on the targeting of the KMT during this crisis, see V. Hanssens, "The Campaign against Nationalist Chinese," in *Indonesia's Struggle, 1957–1958*, ed. B. H. M. Vlekke (The Hague: Netherlands Institute of International Affairs, 1959), 56–76.

65. Oyen, *Diplomacy of Migration*, 112–113.

66. "Lü Fei huaqiao gongxian," vol. 1, 70, IMH Archives.

67. "Lü Fei huaqiao gongxian," vol. 1, 44, IMH Archives; *In Re Chin Sang, et als., Respondents*, Case No. R-489, 2, AHC.

68. "Lü Fei huaqiao gongxian," vol. 1, 52, IMH Archives.

69. "Lü Fei huaqiao gongxian," vol. 1, 41–45, IMH Archives.

70. "Lü Fei huaqiao gongxian," vol. 1, 54, 105–106, IMH Archives.

71. Tang Tack [Deng Yingda], *Wo zai Shang Zong sanshinian: Deng Yingda huiyi lu* (Manila, 1988), 80.

72. "Lü Fei huaqiao gongxian," vol. 2, 11, IMH Archives.

73. "Lü Fei huaqiao gongxian," vol. 2, 93, IMH Archives.

74. "Feilübin qiaoqing baogao," March 1954, Yiban 556.1/276, KMT Archives.

75. Most narratives, including Tang Tack's, Liu Chi-tien's, and Chang Tsun-wu and Ong Kok-Chung's, have the number of *jinqiao* who were put on trial at 152 and who were released on bail at 99, but if we add this number to the 34 who were released and the 13 who remained in custody, the total is only 146. See Tang, *Wo zai Shang Zong sanshinian*, 80; Liu Chi-tien [Liu Zhitian], *Zhong Fei guanxi shi* (Taipei: Zhengzhong

shuju, 1964), 732–733; and Chang and Ong, *Feihua shanglian zonghui zhi xingshuai yu yanbian*, 29. The only archival evidence to account for the remaining six individuals is the first of two executive orders from President Carlos Garcia in December 1961, in which charges against five of them are said to have been "disposed of," while one is said to have passed away. See "Lü Fei huaqiao gongxian," vol. 4, 145, 062.6/0008, December 1952–November 1962, IMH Archives. This document does not specify when the five were "disposed of" or when the other person passed away.

76. "Lü Fei huaqiao gongxian," vol. 2, 110, IMH Archives.

77. "Lü Fei huaqiao gongxian," vol. 1, 53, IMH Archives.

78. "Feilübin qiaoqing baogao," KMT Archives.

79. "Lü Fei huaqiao gongxian," vol. 2, 10–14, IMH Archives.

80. "Fei pohuo huaqiao xuesheng feidie zuzhi," vol. 1, 176–177, IMH Archives.

81. "Lü Fei huaqiao gongxian," vol. 3, 7–8, IMH Archives; Tang, *Wo zai Shang Zong sanshinian*, 81.

82. "Lü Fei huaqiao gongxian," vol. 3, 13, IMH Archives.

83. "Lü Fei huaqiao gongxian," vol. 3, 14–15, IMH Archives.

84. "Lü Fei huaqiao gongxian," vol. 3, 9–10, IMH Archives.

85. "Lü Fei huaqiao gongxian," vol. 3, 205–206, IMH Archives.

86. "Lü Fei huaqiao gongxian," vol. 4, 21, IMH Archives; Tang, *Wo zai Shang Zong sanshinian*, 82–83.

87. "Lü Fei huaqiao gongxian," vol. 4, 145–148, IMH Archives. A more detailed and firsthand account of how they were released can be found in Tang, *Wo zai Shang Zong sanshinian*, 83–85.

88. "Fei pohuo huaqiao xuesheng feidie zuzhi," vol. 2, 4–5, 005.8/0002, November 1958–March 1962, IMH Archives.

89. "Fei pohuo huaqiao xuesheng feidie zuzhi," vol. 2, 42, IMH Archives.

90. "Fei pohuo huaqiao xuesheng feidie zuzhi," vol. 2, 82–83, IMH Archives.

91. "Lü Fei huaqiao gongxian," vol. 3, 228, IMH Archives; "Lü Fei buliang huaqiao," vol. 8, 168–169, AH.

92. "Lü Fei huaqiao gongxian," vol. 3, 252, IMH Archives.

93. "Lü Fei buliang huaqiao," vol. 8, 176–177, AH.

94. "Lü Fei buliang huaqiao," vol. 8, 161–165, AH.

95. "Gongfei zai geguo huodong qingxing zhuanti baogao," 116, 020-010110-0122, August 12, 1964–March 16, 1966, AH.

96. I am grateful to one of my interviewees for introducing me to the Sy Gaisano family member who revealed what happened to Sy Yan Wan.

5. Networking Ideology

1. All the pieces were featured in *Shijie qingnian* 6 (January 21, 1972), Chinben See Memorial Library, Kaisa Heritage Center (KHC), Manila.

2. Cited in Joseph Scalice, "Crisis of Revolutionary Leadership: Martial Law and the Communist Parties of the Philippines, 1959–1974" (PhD diss., University of California, Berkeley, 2017), 271.

3. Zhou, *Migration in the Time of Revolution*, 77.

4. Yang, *Zhongguo Guomindang haiwai gongzuo*, 40.

5. Brooks, *Between Mao and McCarthy*, 123, 148, 178.

6. Belogurova, *Nanyang Revolution*; Tim Harper, *Underground Asia: Global Revolutionaries and the Assault on Empire* (London: Allen Lane, 2020).

7. Agpalo, *Nationalization of the Retail Trade*, 93–133. R.A. No. 1180 was repealed only in 2000 with the passing of R.A. No. 8762, the Retail Trade Liberalization Law.

8. Carino, *Chinese Big Business in the Philippines*, 33; Agpalo, *Nationalization of the Retail Trade*, 224–255.

9. Jesus E. Perpiñan, "New Controversy over Chinese Schools," in *Chinese Participation in Philippine Culture and Economy*, ed. Shubert S. C. Liao (Manila, 1964), 334–335.

10. Jiang Xingshan, *Zhanhou Feilübin huawen jiaoyu yanjiu (1945–1976)* (Guangzhou: Jinan daxue chubanshe, 2013), 146.

11. Eufronio M. Alip, *Ten Centuries of Philippine-Chinese Relations (Historical, Political, Social, Economic)* (Manila: Alip & Sons, 1959), 130–135.

12. Sheldon Appleton, "Communism and the Chinese in the Philippines," *Pacific Affairs* 32, no. 4 (December 1959): 384; Perpiñan, "New Controversy over Chinese Schools," 334.

13. Robert O. Tilman, "Philippine Chinese Students" (unpublished manuscript, n.d.), chap. 4, 4–5, KHC.

14. Tang, *Wo zai Shang Zong sanshinian*, 8–9.

15. Philippine Chinese General Chamber of Commerce, *Golden Book 1955*, Chinese section, Jia (9).

16. Tang, *Wo zai Shang Zong sanshinian*, 4; Federation of Filipino-Chinese Chambers of Commerce and Industry, *The Philippine Chinese Decennial Book 1954–1974* [Shang Zong ershi nian: Feihua shanglian zonghui chengli ershi zhounian jinian tekan] (Manila, 1974), Chinese section, 90–94.

17. Carino, *Chinese Big Business in the Philippines*, 79–82.

18. "Huashang zonghui," vol. 1, 180, 062.2/0001, October 1953–October 1954, IMH Archives.

19. Carino, *Chinese Big Business in the Philippines*, 23–28; Zhu, *Chongtu yu ronghe*, 48–49.

20. See, for example, Gerald A. McBeath, *Political Integration of the Philippine Chinese* (Berkeley: Center for South and Southeast Asian Studies, University of California, 1973), 60; Blaker, "Chinese in the Philippines," 215; and Zhu, *Chongtu yu ronghe*, 48.

21. Chang et al., *Reminiscences*, 373.

22. "Feilübin Xu Zhibei you bufa huodong an," 130, 062.6/0011, December 1950–April 1956, IMH Archives.

23. Address of President Magsaysay to the Convention of Chinese Chambers of Commerce Chinese Trade Associations in the Philippines, March 26, 1954, *Official Gazette*, https://www.officialgazette.gov.ph/1954/03/26/address-of-president-magsaysay-to-the-convention-of-chinese-chambers-of-commerce-chinese-trade-associations-in-the-philippines/.

24. "Huashang zonghui," vol. 1, 185–189, IMH Archives.

25. "Huashang zonghui," vol. 1, 194–195, IMH Archives.

26. Chang et al., *Reminiscences*, 190–194.

27. Pao Shih-tien, "Chinese Schools in the Philippines," *Fookien Times Yearbook*, September 1961, 185.

28. Pao, "Should the Chinese Schools Be Abolished?," *Chinese Participation in Philippine Culture and Economy*, 342–350.

29. Pao, "Chinese Schools in the Philippines," 186; Pao Shih-tien [Bao Shitian], *Yang hao ji* (Manila: Feilübin Zhongzheng xueyuan Shitian wenjiao jijin hui, 1996), 55.

30. Pao, *Yang hao ji*, 61.

31. Jiang, *Zhanhou Feilübin huawen jiaoyu yanjiu*, 150.

32. *Feilübin huaqiao xuexiao diyi ci daibiao dahui zhuankan*, 1957, 1, National Central Library (NCL), Taipei.

33. "Lü Fei huaqiao gongxian," vol. 1, 53, 062.6/0002, December 1952–May 1953, IMH Archives.

34. "Materials from the Asian Peoples' Anti-Communist League Conference, Manila," March 9, 1955, 5, History and Public Policy Program Digital Archive, B-392-001, Documents Related to the Asian Anti-Communist League Conference, Papers Related to Treaty-Making and International Conferences, Syngman Rhee Institute, Yonsei University, Wilson Center Digital Archive, https://digitalarchive.wilsoncenter.org/document/118346.

35. Tang, *Wo zai Shang Zong sanshinian*, 4.

36. "Feihua fangong kang'E zonghui," vol. 1, 182, 062.2/0004, December 1950–December 1959, IMH Archives.

37. "Feihua fangong kang'E zonghui," vol. 1, 132, IMH Archives; *Shang Zong yuebao* 1, no. 9 (September 1956): 75, KHC.

38. Carino, *Chinese Big Business in the Philippines*, 78.

39. "Feihua fangong kang'E zonghui," vol. 1, 123, IMH Archives.

40. Liang Ziheng, *Huaqiao shehui yanjiu* (Hong Kong: Haichao chubanshe, 1958), 74, 80.

41. Amyot, *Manila Chinese*, 77.

42. *Anti-Communist Movement: A Chinese-Filipino Joint Endeavour* (Manila, 1957), chap. 1, "Organization of the Philippine-Chinese Anti-Communist League," Institute of Southeast Asian Studies–Yusof Ishak Institute (ISEAS) Library, Singapore. The document is unpaginated.

43. "Feihua fangong kang'E zonghui," vol. 1, 183, IMH Archives.

44. "Feihua fangong kang'E zonghui," vol. 1, 185, IMH Archives.

45. *Zhongguo Guomindang zai haiwai*, 98.

46. Napoleon G. Rama, "Spotlight on the Kuomintang," *Philippines Free Press* 63, no. 20 (July 25, 1970): 18.

47. Myers and Lin, *Breaking with the Past*, 7.

48. Yun-han Chu and Jih-wen Lin, "Political Development in 20th-Century Taiwan: State-Building, Regime Transformation and the Construction of National Identity," *China Quarterly* 165 (March 2001): 113–115.

49. Arif Dirlik, "The Ideological Foundations of the New Life Movement: A Study in Counterrevolution," *Journal of Asian Studies* 34, no. 4 (August 1975): 976.

50. Tsui, *China's Conservative Revolution*, 4, 6–7.

51. Allen Chun, "From Nationalism to Nationalizing: Cultural Imagination and State Formation in Postwar Taiwan," *Australian Journal of Chinese Affairs* 31 (January 1994): 56–58.

52. See McBeath, *Political Integration of the Philippine Chinese*, 103; McCarthy, "Chinese in the Philippines," 19; and Teresita Ang See and Carmelea Ang See, "Navigating Cultures, Forming Identities," *Kritika Kultura*, no. 21/22 (2013/2014): 363.

53. Chen Lieh-fu [Chen Liefu], *Feilübin huaqiao jiaoyu* (Taipei: Haiwai chubanshe, 1958), 1, 4–5.

54. Yang, *Zhongguo Guomindang yu huaqiao wenxian chubian*, 23.

55. "Tai (44) zhongmishi zi di 0367 hao Zhang Qiyun, Zheng Yanfen cheng," October 5, 1953, Zongcai piqian 42/0272, KMT Archives.

56. George Henry Weightman, "The Philippine Chinese: A Cultural History of a Marginal Trading Community" (PhD diss., Cornell University, 1960), 379.

57. Tilman, "Philippine Chinese Students," chap. 4, 19–20; Philippine Chinese General Chamber of Commerce, *Golden Book 1955*, English section, 89–90.

58. Jiang, *Zhanhou Feilübin huawen jiaoyu yanjiu*, 77.

59. Tilman, "Philippine Chinese Students," chap. 4, 23–27.

60. McBeath, *Political Integration of the Philippine Chinese*, 86–88, 99–100; Jiang, *Zhanhou Feilübin huawen jiaoyu yanjiu*, 77.

61. Thomas A. Marks, *Counterrevolution in China: Wang Sheng and the Kuomintang* (London: Frank Cass Publishers, 1998), 136.

62. "Tai (44) zhongmishi dengzi di 203 hao Zhang Lisheng, Zheng Yanfen cheng," July 15, 1955, Zongcai piqian 44/0136, KMT Archives.

63. Chiang Kai-shek, *Soviet Russia in China: A Summing-Up at Seventy* (New York: Farrar, Straus, and Cudahy, 1957).

64. *Anti-Communist Movement*, chap. 9, "Philippine Chinese Reaction to President Chiang's Book," ISEAS Library.

65. *Zhongzheng xuesheng* no. 66 (October 1957), Chinese section, 33, KHC; *Anti-Communist Movement*, chap. 9, ISEAS Library.

66. *Zhongzheng xuesheng* no. 66 (October 1957), Chinese section, 33–35, KHC.

67. "Statistical table of both old and new OC students in the different departments of universities and colleges for the first semester of FY 1957," box P-96, folder—Education—General 1956–1960, Asia Foundation Records 1951–1996, HILA.

68. *Gongfei huoqiao shilu* (Taipei: Haiwai chubanshe, 1955); *Zhonggong zenyang duidai qiaosheng* (Taipei: Haiwai chubanshe, 1956).

69. *Zhongzheng xuesheng* no. 66 (October 1957), Chinese section, 28, KHC.

70. "Feihua fangong kang'E zonghui," vol. 1, 185, IMH Archives.

71. *Anti-Communist Movement*, chap. 3, "Youth Participation in the Anti-Communist Movement," ISEAS Library.

72. *Anti-Communist Movement*, chap. 4, "The League's Initial Efforts in Support of Mainland People," ISEAS Library.

73. "Philippine Chinese Anti-Communist and Salvation Rally Held in Manila," *Pacific Review*, April 1958, 31–32, AHC.

74. The fifteen stops were Tarlac, Dagupan, San Fernando (in La Union Province), Vigan, Laoag, Aparri, Tuguegarao, Ilagan, Cauayan, Cabatuan, Santiago (Isabela), Solano (Nueva Vizcaya), Cabanatuan, Baguio, and San Fernando (Pampanga). See *Anti-Communist Movement*, chap. 4, ISEAS Library.

75. *Anti-Communist Movement*, chap. 4, ISEAS Library; "Feihua fangong kang'E zonghui," vol. 1, 194–196, IMH Archives.

76. "PCACL, Pampanga Chapter, Inaugurated in San Fernando," "Ambassador Chen Attends Inauguration of PCACL, Quezon Chapter," and "PCACL Chapter in Zambales Inaugurated," *Pacific Review*, October 1957, 19–23, 33, AHC.

77. "Philippine Chinese Anti-Communist and Salvation Rally Held in Manila," 31–32, AHC.

78. *Anti-Communist Movement*, chap. 6, "The Hungarian Revolution," ISEAS Library.

79. See the cover of *Time* 69, no. 1 (January 7, 1957), and especially the article inside, "Freedom's Choice."

80. *Anti-Communist Movement*, chap. 11, "Other Activities in Support of Hungary's Freedom Movement," ISEAS Library; "Feihua fangong kang'E zonghui," vol. 1, 191–192, IMH Archives.

81. *Anti-Communist Movement*, chap. 8, "The Anti-Subversion Act," ISEAS Library; Republic Act No. 1700, June 20, 1957, the Lawphil Project, https://www.lawphil.net /statutes/repacts/ra1957/ra_1700_1957.html.

82. Chen Chih-mai, "The Philippines: Further Impressions," *Fookien Times Yearbook*, September 1957, 55.

83. *Anti-Communist Movement*, chap. 10, "The Farce of Communist Democratization," ISEAS Library.

84. Rodrigo and Hernandez had "fought, tooth and nail, against the imposition of [Jose Rizal's novels] *Noli Me Tangere* and *El Filibusterismo* in all schools and colleges in the Philippines without a Catholic commentary on the incidents and characteristics presented by Rizal." See Jose Ma. Hernandez, *And the Day but One: An Autobiography* (Manila: Aljun Printing Press, 2000), 102.

85. "Feihua fangong kang'E zonghui," vol. 1, 192–193, IMH Archives; "Local Chinese Hold Big Rally in Honor of the Hungarian Freedom Fighters," *Pacific Review*, October 1957, 33–34, AHC.

86. "Feihua fangong kang'E zonghui," vol. 1, 192–193, IMH Archives; "Local Chinese Hold Big Rally in Honor of the Hungarian Freedom Fighters," *Pacific Review*, October 1957, 33–34, AHC.

87. See, for example, "Feihua fangong kang'E zonghui," vol. 2, 062.2/0005, February 1963–July 1964, IMH Archives; "Feihua fangong kang'E zonghui disi ci quan Fei daibiao dahui gongzuo baogaoshu," October 1964–May 1968, KHC; "Feihua fangong kang'E zonghui diwu ci quan Fei daibiao dahui gongzuo baogaoshu," June 1968– September 1970, KHC.

88. Yang, *Zhongguo Guomindang haiwai gongzuo*, 25–28.

6. Experiencing the Nation

1. "Bendang cedong Feilübin huaqiao huiguo weilao jingguo," Central Reform Committee Archive, 6.4-1 reel 8, file ID: 215, September 14, 1950, KMT Records, HILA.

2. Cua Siok Po [Ke Shubao], *Song dahan hun: Ke Shubao lü Fei shiwen cun* (Taipei: Liming wenhua shiye gufen youxian gongsi, 1980), 5, 6–8.

3. *Qiaowu tongji*, 22–25.

4. Joan S. H. Wang, "In the Name of Legitimacy: Taiwan and Overseas Chinese during the Cold War," *China Review* 11, no. 2 (Fall 2011): 65–90. Wang, who focuses primarily on Chinese Americans, is one of the few scholars to have written about overseas Chinese visits to Taiwan. Another is Ellen D. Wu, author of "Chinese-American Transnationalism aboard the Love Boat: The Overseas Chinese Youth Language Training and Study Tour to the Republic of China," *Chinese America: History and Perspectives* 19 (2005): 51–64.

5. Peterson, *Overseas Chinese*, 97–99.

6. J. Paul Bolt, *China and Southeast Asia's Ethnic Chinese: State and Diaspora in Contemporary Asia* (Westport, CT: Praeger, 2000), 47.

7. Peterson, *Overseas Chinese*, 70–73, 77.

8. Chun-hsi Wu, *Dollars, Dependents, and Dogma: Overseas Chinese Remittances to Communist China* (Stanford, CA: Hoover Institution on War, Revolution, and Peace, 1967), 85.

9. Peter Chen-main Wang, "A Bastion Created, a Regime Reformed, an Economy Reengineered, 1949–1970," in *Taiwan: A New History*, ed. Murray Rubinstein (Armonk, NY: M. E. Sharpe, 1999), 325.

10. Wang, "Bastion Created," 332; Pan Meizhi, "1960 niandai Feilübin huaqiao lai Tai touzi baoxianye zhi yanjiu—Yi Shi Xingshui ji Yang Yinglin wei li" (master's thesis, National Taiwan Normal University, 1991), 33–35.

11. *Qiaowu tongji*, 66.

12. "Overseas Chinese," *Free China Review*, November 1, 1961. This and other issues of the publication are available online at https://taiwantoday.tw/.

13. Meredith Oyen, "Communism, Containment, and the Chinese Overseas," in *The Cold War in Asia: The Battle for Hearts and Minds*, ed. Zheng Yangwen, Hong Liu, and Michael Szonyi (Leiden: Brill, 2010), 75.

14. Peterson, *Overseas Chinese*, 96.

15. C. F. Yong, *Tan Kah Kee: The Making of an Overseas Chinese Legend* (Singapore: World Scientific Publishing, 2013), 348–353.

16. Peterson, *Overseas Chinese*, 102–103, 107, 137–138.

17. Taiwan's population figures are taken from Te-Tsui Chang, "Land Utilization on Taiwan," *Land Economics* 28, no. 4 (November 1952): 362. The number of persons from the mainland who fled to Taiwan is taken from Dominic Meng-Hsuan Yang, *The Great Exodus from China: Trauma, Memory, and Identity in Modern Taiwan* (Cambridge: Cambridge University Press, 2020), 63.

18. Oyen, *Diplomacy of Migration*, 165. The "return" of these POWs is covered in David Cheng Chang, *The Hijacked War: The Story of Chinese POWs in the Korean War* (Stanford, CA: Stanford University Press, 2020).

19. Oyen, *Diplomacy of Migration*, 105–106.

20. This 988,545 figure represented 39.8 percent of the total refugee population in Hong Kong at the time; 52.5 percent of this population hoped to settle permanently in Hong Kong, 0.4 percent were willing to return to China, and 7.3 percent claimed to be indifferent. Oyen, *Diplomacy of Migration*, 162–163.

21. Cheung, "Immigrating Visitors," 10–15. The case dragged on for decades despite continuous efforts by both governments to resolve the issue. It was finally resolved following Marcos's decision to simplify the Philippines' naturalization laws by decree in 1975, a move that allowed the overstayers (and the many other Chinese who were legally ROC nationals) to acquire Philippine citizenship.

22. *Qiaobao hui Tai guanguang zhinan* (Taipei: Qiaowu weiyuanhui, September 1958), 3–7.

23. Adam McKeown, *Melancholy Order: Asian Migration and the Globalization of Borders* (New York: Columbia University Press, 2008), 3.

24. Oyen, *Diplomacy of Migration*, 106.

25. Madeline Y. Hsu, *The Good Immigrants: How the Yellow Peril Became the Model Minority* (Princeton, NJ: Princeton University Press, 2015), 8.

26. Zvi Ben-Dor Benite, Stefanos Geroulanos, and Nicole Jerr, "Editors' Introduction," in *The Scaffolding of Sovereignty: Global and Aesthetic Perspectives on the History of a Concept*, ed. Zvi Ben-Dor Benite, Stefanos Geroulanos, and Nicole Jerr (New York: Columbia University Press, 2017), 3–5.

27. The sixteen were the US Embassy, Apostolic Internunciature Legation, Belgian Consulate, Brazilian Embassy, British Vice-Consulate, Dominican Embassy, French Embassy, Japanese Embassy, Korean Embassy, Panamanian Embassy, Philippine Embassy, Spanish Embassy, Royal Thai Embassy, Turkish Embassy, Venezuela Legation, and Vietnam Embassy.

28. *Qiaobao hui Tai guanguang zhinan*, 1–2.

29. Myers and Lin, *Breaking with the Past*, 14; *Qiaobao hui Tai guanguang zhinan*, 17.

30. *Qiaobao hui Tai guanguang zhinan*, 29–30.

31. *Qiaobao hui Tai guanguang zhinan*, 30–36.

32. Bryna Goodman, *Native Place, City, and Nation: Regional Networks and Identities in Shanghai, 1853–1937* (Berkeley: University of California Press, 1995), 4–5.

33. "Feilübin Suwu dongfang lanqiudui huiguo laojun bisai jinian tekan," May 1968, unpaginated, KHC.

34. "Feiji qiaosheng lai Tai shou xunlian jiufen," 110, 020-010708-0103, August 13–October 31, 1959, AH; "Feilübin huaqiao qingnian huiguo junzhong fuwu," 256, 061.2/0002, February 1954–May 1960, IMH Archives.

35. *Qiaowu huiyi shilu* (Taipei: Haiwai chubanshe, 1953), 21.

36. "Lü Fei Ji Yang Ke Cai zongqin zonghui wushier nian jinian tekan" [Che, Yong, Cua, & Chua Association Fiftieth Anniversary Golden Book], September 1960, L1, KHC.

37. *Qiaowu tongji*, 39.

38. "Overseas Chinese Conference," *Free China Review*, October 1, 1955.

39. "Feilübin huaqiao jiaoyu jie huiguo jiaoyu kaocha tuan baogaoshu," 1959, 1, KHC.

40. *Qiaowu tongji*, 68–69.

41. "Feilübin huaqiao gejie huiguo laojun tuan zhushou laojun tekan," January 1959, 6, KHC.

42. "Feilübin huaqiao gejie huiguo laojun tuan zhushou laojun tekan," 21, KHC. NTD 3 million was around USD 75,000 at the time. The approximately 40 to 1 NTD-USD exchange rate in the late 1950s is from Michael Szonyi, *Cold War Island: Quemoy on the Front Line* (Cambridge: Cambridge University Press, 2008), xiv.

43. "Feilübin huaqiao gejie huiguo laojun tuan zhushou laojun tekan," 14, 17, KHC.

44. "Feilübin huaqiao gejie huiguo laojun tuan zhushou laojun tekan," 15, KHC.

45. "Feilübin huaqiao gejie huiguo laojun tuan zhushou laojun tekan," 4–5, KHC.

46. Szonyi, *Cold War Island*, 26.

47. "Feilübin huaqiao gejie huiguo laojun tuan zhushou laojun tekan," 10–11, KHC.

48. "Feilübin huaqiao gejie huiguo laojun tuan zhushou laojun tekan," 10–11, KHC.

49. On the ROC's propaganda techniques on Quemoy, see Szonyi, *Cold War Island*, 95.

50. On overseas Chinese connections with Quemoy, see Chiang Bo-wei, "A Special Intermittence and Continuity in Local History: The Chinese Diaspora and Their Hometown in Battlefield Quemoy during 1949–1960s," *Journal of Chinese Overseas* 7, no. 2 (May 2011): 169–186.

51. "Feilübin huaqiao gejie huiguo laojun tuan zhushou laojun tekan," 12, KHC.

52. "Jinmen laojun ji," *Fookien Times*, October 28, 1958, Overseas Chinese Clippings Database (OCCD), Hong Kong Baptist University.

53. Goodman, *Native Place, City, and Nation*, 13.

54. Pao Shih-tien [Bao Shitian], "Wenhua fuxing yu Zhongzheng xueyuan," *Zhongzheng xuebao* 1 (May 1967): 3–4, KHC.

55. Stephen Uhalley Jr., "Taiwan's Response to the Cultural Revolution," *Asian Survey* 7, no. 11 (November 1967): 827.

56. "Qiaowu weiyuanhui Zhonghua hanshou xuexiao Feilübin xueyuan huiguo guanguang zhijingtuan jinian tekan" [Philippine Chinese Youth Goodwill Mission to Free China—1967], KHC. The entire document is unpaginated.

57. Pao, "Wenhua fuxing yu Zhongzheng xueyuan," 2, KHC.

58. On the KMT's use of Foucauldian methods of disciplining the native Taiwanese population, see Ketty W. Chen, "Disciplining Taiwan: The Kuomintang's Methods of Control during the White Terror Era (1947–1987)," *Taiwan International Studies Quarterly* 4, no. 4 (Winter 2008): 185–210.

59. "Feilübin huaqiao xiaoxue jiaoshi huiguo kaocha jinxiu tuan baogaoshu," 1968, 8, KHC.

60. "Feilübin huaqiao xiaoxue jiaoshi huiguo kaocha jinxiu tuan baogaoshu," 32–36, KHC.

61. "Feilübin huaqiao xiaoxue jiaoshi huiguo kaocha jinxiu tuan baogaoshu," 31, KHC.

62. "Feilübin huaqiao xiaoxue jiaoshi huiguo kaocha jinxiu tuan baogaoshu," 89, KHC.

63. "Guojiao zhi mu, Gao Zi gongji," *Central Daily News*, October 22, 1997, 16.

64. "Feilübin huaqiao xiaoxue jiaoshi huiguo kaocha jinxiu tuan baogaoshu," 4, 40, 88, 90, KHC.

65. "Feilübin huaqiao xiaoxue jiaoshi huiguo kaocha jinxiu tuan baogaoshu," 37–40, 91–92, KHC.

66. "Feilübin huaqiao xiaoxue jiaoshi huiguo kaocha jinxiu tuan baogaoshu," 100, KHC.

67. "Feilübin huaqiao xiaoxue jiaoshi huiguo kaocha jinxiu tuan baogaoshu," 38, 88, 91, KHC.

68. "Feilübin Xuegan tuan di shisi fenbu huiguo zhijing tuan tekan" [COWHM Veterans' Association 14th Branch Goodwill Troupe], October 1971, 21, KHC.

69. Shi, *Dahan hun zhuanji*, 146.

70. "Feilübin Xuegan tuan di shisan fenbu erdu huiguo fuwu tuan jinian tekan" [COWHM Veterans' Association, 13th Branch Souvenir Issue], April 1970, A-6, A-7, KHC.

71. Yung Li, *Huaqiao Warriors*, 125.

72. "Feilübin Xuegan tuan di shisi fenbu huiguo zhijing tuan tekan," 7–8, KHC.

73. "Feihua fangong kang'E zonghui diwu ci quan Fei daibiao dahui gongzuo baogaoshu," 10, June 1968–September 1970, 21 [page is unnumbered, but comes after page 20], KHC.

74. "Feilübin Xuegan tuan di shisi fenbu huiguo zhijing tuan tekan," 10, 44, KHC; "Feilübin Xuegan tuan di shisan fenbu erdu huiguo fuwu tuan jinian tekan," A-21, A-22, KHC; "Feilübin Xuegan tuan di shisan fenbu huiguo minzhong fuwu laojun tuan jinian tekan" [COWHM Veterans' Association, 13th Branch Souvenir Issue], July 1968, 15, 27–28, KHC. Note that the second and third of these volumes have the same given English title.

75. "Feilübin Xuegan tuan di shisi fenbu huiguo zhijing tuan tekan," 21, KHC.

76. "Feilübin Xuegan tuan di shisi fenbu huiguo zhijing tuan tekan," 27–29, KHC.

77. "Fei Xuegan tuan fenbu laojun tuan zuo fanguo," *United Daily News*, August 1, 1968, 2; "Feilübin Xuegan tuan di shisan fenbu erdu huiguo fuwu tuan jinian tekan," A-3, A-8, A-9, A-10, KHC.

78. "Feilübin Xuegan tuan di shisan fenbu erdu huiguo fuwu tuan jinian tekan," A-2, A-3, A-4, KHC.

7. Dissent and Its Discontents

1. Zhao Zhenxiang, Yan Lifeng, Jiang Xiding, Hou Peishui, Wu Jiansheng, and Chen Huayue, *Feilübin huawen baoshi gao* (Beijing: Shijie zhishi chubanshe, 2006), 130.

2. Rizal Yuyitung, ed., *The Case of the Yuyitung Brothers: Philippine Press Freedom under Siege* (Manila: Yuyitung Foundation, 2000), 104.

3. Yuyitung, *Case of the Yuyitung Brothers*, 258.

4. There are two exceptions: one, which focuses on the *CCN* affair as it relates to the issue of press freedom in Taiwan, is Yang Hsiu-chin [Yang Xiujing], "Feilübin 'Huaqiao shangbao' an yu xinwen ziyou wenti," *Zhengda shicui* 9 (December 2005): 145–179; the other is Zhao et al., *Feilübin huawen baoshi gao*. Other monographs have examined the affair in relation to questions of citizenship and identity among the Chinese overseas, but without probing the ROC's and the Philippine KMT's involvement in it. See Shao, "Chinese by Definition"; and Hau, *Chinese Question*, 91–136.

5. Yuyitung, *Case of the Yuyitung Brothers*; Chang et al., *Reminiscences*.

6. "History of Chinese Commercial News," *Chinese Commercial News*, accessed January 20, 2021, https://web.archive.org/web/20050503203257/http://www.siongpo.com/history2.htm; James Roland Blaker, "The Chinese Newspaper in the Philippines: Toward the Definition of a Tool," *Asian Studies* 3, no. 2 (1965): 251. For a more comprehensive history of Chinese newspapers in the Philippines, see Zhao et al., *Feilübin huawen baoshi gao*.

7. Blaker, "Chinese Newspaper in the Philippines," 246, 251–253.

8. Chang et al., *Reminiscences*, 317.

9. Yuyitung, *Case of the Yuyitung Brothers*, ii.

10. Chang et al., *Reminiscences*, 313.

11. The interview is reproduced in "Huaqiao shangbao an," vol. 1, 35–36, 020-010708-0067, February 15–May 3, 1962, AH.

12. On KMT censorship of the press in China, see Stephen R. MacKinnon, "Toward a History of the Chinese Press in the Republican Period," *Modern China* 23, no. 1 (January 1997): 15–19. On the Chiang personality cult, see Jeremy E. Taylor, "The Production of the Chiang Kai-shek Personality Cult, 1929–1975," *China Quarterly* 185 (March 2006): 96–110.

13. Clinton, *Revolutionary Nativism*, 43, 181–187.

14. RG 319: Records of the Army Staff, 1903–2009, Series: Intelligence and Investigative Dossiers Personal Files, ca. 1977–ca. 2004, box 877, folder: YU, Yi Tung Quin Tin—XA544488, NARA.

15. Chang et al., *Reminiscences*, 321.

16. Chang et al., *Reminiscences*, 321. Rizal's recollections here are inaccurate, as Eleanor Roosevelt's visit to Moscow took place in 1957.

17. "Lü Fei buliang huaqiao," vol. 4, 128, 020-010708-0019, May 30–November 27, 1951, AH; "Lü Fei buliang huaqiao," vol. 5, 173–174, 020-010708-0020, November 18, 1951–August 13, 1952, AH.

18. "Lü Fei buliang huaqiao," vol. 6, 23, 020-010708-0021, September 19, 1952–December 13, 1954, AH.

19. "Lü Fei buliang huaqiao," vol. 6, 140–142, AH.

20. "Lü Fei buliang huaqiao," vol. 6, 140–142, AH; "Lü Fei buliang huaqiao," vol. 5, 173–174, AH.

21. Chang et al., *Reminiscences*, 321.

22. Oyen, *Diplomacy of Migration*, 147–150. On the Chinese Hand Laundry Association, see Yu, *To Save China, to Save Ourselves*.

23. Oyen, *Diplomacy of Migration*, 147; Yu, *To Save China, to Save Ourselves*, 188.

24. "Feihua fangong kang'E zonghui," vol. 1, 185, 062.2/0004, December 1950–December 1959, IMH Archives.

25. "Tai (48) yang mizi di 001 hao Zhang Lisheng, Zheng Yanfen cheng," Zongcai piqian 48/0001, December 31, 1958, KMT Archives.

26. *Huaqiao shehui de luxiang: Shangbao yanlun xuanji* (Manila: Yitong chubanshe, 1961), 35–49.

27. The articles are summarized in McBeath, *Political Integration of the Philippine Chinese*, 100–103.

28. Zhao et al., *Feilübin huawen baoshi gao*, 172–174. See, for example, "Shi tuibian de shihou le," *CCN*, November 27, 1960, 3; and "Hunhua er bushi tonghua," *CCN*, March 12, 1961, 3.

29. Hsin Kwan-chue [Xing Guangzu], *Jingli de rensheng* (Taipei: Great Han Publishing Company, 1976), 243–245.

30. Zhao et al., *Feilübin huawen baoshi gao*, 171. Sima Guang was a conservative scholar-official during the Song Dynasty and the author of the monumental *Comprehensive Mirror to Aid in Government (Zizhi Tongjian)*.

31. Fitzgerald, *China and the Overseas Chinese*, 135, 141–143.

32. The Taiwanese historian Yang Hsiu-chin, the only other scholar to have done work on the Yuyitung affair using ROC MOFA sources, arrives at the same conclusion in "Feilübin 'Huaqiao shangbao' an yu xinwen ziyou wenti," 155–156. The Yuyitungs' attorney during their 1962 Deportation Board trial, Alexander Sycip, argued that the *CCN*'s support for integration explained ROC and KMT hostility toward the paper, but this claim received no further attention. See "Huaqiao shangbao an," vol. 3, 60, 020-010708-0069, May 8–August 27, 1962, AH.

33. Ong, *Fengchen wushinian*, 29–38.

34. Ong, *Fengchen wushinian*, 63–66.

35. Zhao et al., *Feilübin huawen baoshi gao*, 167.

36. On the *CCN*'s news coverage of the PRC, see Chang et al., *Reminiscences*, 316.

37. Chang et al., *Reminiscences*, 327. Two such visits took place, once in 1964 and the other in 1967, during the Cultural Revolution. See Zhao et al., *Feilübin huawen baoshi gao*, 155–156.

38. Chang and Holt, *Language, Politics and Identity in Taiwan*, 19–22.

39. Chang et al., *Reminiscences*, 326.

40. "Huaqiao shangbao an," vol. 3, 60, AH.

41. "Meiguo junji luzhan dui luxu jiangluo yu Taiguo," *CCN*, May 17, 1962, 1.

42. "Yu shi xiongdi qianpei (jianbao ziliao)," vol. 1, 91, 020-010710-0007, August 6, 1966–September 27, 1970, AH.

43. Chang et al., *Reminiscences*, 322.

44. Zhonggong Fujian sheng qiaowei dang zu, "Qing xiezhu sheng zhong fenshe jinxing dui Fei Huaqiao shangbao fagao gongzuo," March 17, 1959; Zhongxin she Fujian fenshe, "1960 nian dui Fei Huaqiao shangbao fagao qingkuang," January 1961; Fujian sheng xinwen chuban she, "Zhun yu jinkou 'Xingzhou ribao,' 'Huaqiao shangbao' ji 'Nanyang shangbao' shi," July 18, 1960, Jianguo hou dang'an, Fujian Provincial Archives, Fuzhou.

45. Chang et al., *Reminiscences*, 324–325.

46. "Huaqiao shangbao an," vol. 1, 135, 020-010710-0007, August 6, 1966–September 27, 1970, AH.

47. "Huaqiao shangbao an," vol. 1, 82, AH.

48. "Huaqiao shangbao an," vol. 1, 99–100, AH.

49. "Huaqiao shangbao an," vol. 1, 82, AH.

50. "Huaqiao shangbao an," vol. 1, 55, AH.

51. "Huaqiao shangbao an," vol. 1, 137, AH.

52. "Huaqiao shangbao an," vol. 1, 82–85, 173, AH.

53. "Huaqiao shangbao an," vol. 1, 55, 84–87, 136, AH.

54. Chang et al., *Reminiscences*, 328; Zhao et al., *Feilübin huawen baoshi gao*, 183–184.

55. "Huaqiao shangbao an," vol. 4, 26–28, 020-010708-0070, April 1, 1963–August 26, 1964, AH.

56. "Huaqiao shangbao an," vol. 3, 84–85.

57. "Huaqiao shangbao an," vol. 1, 60–61, AH.

58. "Huaqiao shangbao an," vol. 3, 58, 60–63, AH.

59. Chang et al., *Reminiscences*, 324.

60. Chang et al., *Reminiscences*, 326.

61. "Huaqiao shangbao an," vol. 2, 70, 020-010708-0068, March 17, 1961–June 27, 1962, AH; "Huaqiao shangbao an," vol. 3, 60, AH.

62. "Huaqiao shangbao an," vol. 3, 11, AH; Chao Ching Win, *Fengbao shinian: Zhongguo hongse zhengquan de zhen mianmao* (Hong Kong: Shidai pinglun she, 1959), available in full at Marxists Internet Archive, https://www.marxists.org/chinese/reference-books/zjw1959.

63. "Huaqiao shangbao an," vol. 1, 9, AH; "Zhou Jingwen zi Gang fu Fei wei Yu Changcheng an zuozheng," *United Daily News*, April 24, 1962, 4.

64. "Huaqiao shangbao an," vol. 3, 218–222, AH.

65. "Mageshi tongzong weihe qianpei Yu shi xiongdi," 2, undated manuscript, KHC.

66. "Huaqiao shangbao an," vol. 5, 194, 020-010708-0071, July 20, 1962–February 15, 1965, AH.

67. "Huaqiao shangbao an," vol. 5, 210, AH.

68. "Yu shi xiongdi qianpei (jianbao ziliao)," vol. 1, 12–14, AH.

69. Chang et al., *Reminiscences*, 327; Yuyitung, *Case of the Yuyitung Brothers*, vi.

70. "Yu shi xiongdi qianpei (jianbao ziliao)," vol. 1, 12–14, AH.

71. McCoy, *Policing America's Empire*, 390.

72. Robert O. Tilman, "The Philippines in 1970: A Difficult Decade Begins," *Asian Survey* 11, no. 2 (February 1971): 140–141.

73. According to the manifesto of Makabansa sa Pugad Lawin, one of the protesting groups, these irritants were Taiwan's refusal to accept the deportation of 109 ethnic Chinese detainees who were being held on Engineering Island at the time; its

tolerance of illegal fishing by Taiwanese fishermen in Philippine waters; and the long-standing problem of the "overstaying temporary visitors." See "Feiguo xuesheng shi-wei," vol. 1, 113, 020-010709-0013, February 2, 1970–July 16, 1971, AH. As for the 109 Chinese detained on Engineering Island, they were deported in mid-March. See "Yu shi xiongdi qianpei (jianbao ziliao)," vol. 1, 122, AH.

74. "Feiguo xuesheng shiwei," vol. 1, 110–112, AH.

75. Jose F. Lacaba, "And the January 30 Insurrection," *Philippines Free Press*, February 7, 1970, https://philippinesfreepress.wordpress.com/1970/02/07/and-the-january-30-insurrection-february-7-1970/.

76. "Feiguo xuesheng shiwei," vol. 2, 49, 020-010709-0014, February 3, 1970–April 14, 1971, AH.

77. "Feiguo xuesheng shiwei," vol. 1, 110–112, AH.

78. "Huaqiao shangbao an," vol. 4, 59, AH.

79. Copies of the April 29, 1970, report on the Thunderbolt Plan can be found in the first of two files on "demonstrations by Filipino students" at Academia Historica and in Mah Soo-Lay's papers at the Hoover Institution. See "Feiguo xuesheng shiwei," vol. 1, 192–200, AH; Mah Soo-Lay, "Feilübin shiwei baoluan fazhan zhong Huaqiao shangbao an zhi zhixing ji jinhou zai Fei gongzuo fangzhen," April 29, 1970, box 20, MSLP, HILA.

80. "Yu shi xiongdi qianpei (jianbao ziliao)," vol. 1, 106, AH.

81. Unpublished autobiography of Mah Soo-Lay, box 18, MSLP, HILA.

82. Yang, *Zhongguo Guomindang haiwai gongzuo*, 40; Hanssens, "Campaign against Nationalist Chinese."

83. Handwritten letter from Mah Soo-Lay to Koa Chun-te, undated, box 22, MSLP, HILA; handwritten letter from Mah Soo-Lay to Koa Chun-te, undated, box 25, MSLP, HILA.

84. "Ke Shubao jieren Guomindang zhongyang san zu fu zhuren," *United Daily News*, November 30, 1967, 2.

85. "Feiguo xuesheng shiwei," vol. 1, 192–200, AH; Mah, "Feilübin shiwei baoluan fazhan zhong Huaqiao shangbao an," MSLP, HILA.

86. Jose Lim Chua [Cai Jingfu], *Liuzai Zhong Fei menghuan jian* (Taipei: Zhaoming chubanshe, 1978), 259.

87. Chang et al., *Reminiscences*, 337. Rizal's recollections here are corroborated by documents that the CCN obtained detailing the meetings of a "Joint Operational Committee" from July 1969 to January 1970. This committee comprised Lim Soo Chan, Jose Lim Chua, Billy Chan, Cheng Kim Tiao, and two Philippine military intelligence officers. I thank one of my interviewees for providing me with these documents.

88. Zhao et al., *Feilübin huawen baoshi gao*, 151–152.

89. On Rizal Yuyitung's accusation against Antonio Roxas Chua, see Chang et al., *Reminiscences*, 337.

90. Chang et al., *Reminiscences*, 336.

91. Nelson A. Navarro, ed., *Juan Ponce Enrile: A Memoir* (Quezon City: ABS CBN Publishing, 2012), 287–288. I am grateful to Joseph Scalice for pointing out to me the unreliability of Enrile's memoirs.

92. See the relevant entries for January 30, 1970 and February 17, 1970 from Marcos's diaries at the Philippine Diary Project, https://philippinediaryproject.wordpress.com/1970/01/ and https://philippinediaryproject.wordpress.com/1970/02/.

93. Yuyitung, *Case of the Yuyitung Brothers*, xvi.

94. Yuyitung, *Case of the Yuyitung Brothers*, 35.

95. Yuyitung, *Case of the Yuyitung Brothers*, xxiv.

96. Yuyitung, *Case of the Yuyitung Brothers*, 32–33.

97. Chang et al., *Reminiscences*, 327.

98. Chang et al., *Reminiscences*, 336; Yuyitung, *Case of the Yuyitung Brothers*, 29–30.

99. Yuyitung, *Case of the Yuyitung Brothers*, xxv.

100. Yuyitung, *Case of the Yuyitung Brothers*, 30–31.

101. Yuyitung, *Case of the Yuyitung Brothers*, 28.

102. Yuyitung, *Case of the Yuyitung Brothers*, xxv.

103. Yuyitung, *Case of the Yuyitung Brothers*, 36.

104. "Benbao bianji Yu Changgeng zuo gongzheng zhengqu mingnian xiuxian jie-shou tusheng huaren cheng Fei gongmin," *CCN*, April 25, 1970, 7; "Yu Changcheng gongbu fangqi Zhonghua minguo de guoji," *CCN*, Apr 26, 1970, 7.

105. "Yu shi xiongdi qianpei (jianbao ziliao)," vol. 1, 35, 48–50, AH.

106. "Yu shi xiongdi," vol. 2, 020-091300-0020, 1970–1971, AH.

107. "Yu shi xiongdi," vol. 1, 020-091300-0019, 1970–1971, AH.

108. "Feiguo xuesheng shiwei," vol. 1, 204, AH.

109. "Yu shi xiongdi," vol. 2, AH.

110. "Recognition Suspended," *IPI Report: Monthly Bulletin of the International Press Institute* 20 (November 1971): 1.

111. "Yu shi xiongdi qianpei (jianbao ziliao)," vol. 1, 200–201, AH.

112. *CCN*, January 11, 1971, 2.

113. "Si jiao ba jiao shier jiao," *CCN*, January 17, 1971, 2.

114. Chang et al., *Reminiscences*, 350, 354–355.

115. Jay Taylor, *The Generalissimo: Chiang Kai-shek and the Struggle for Modern China* (Cambridge, MA: Belknap Press of Harvard University Press, 2009), 548.

116. Chang et al., *Reminiscences*, 350–351.

117. "Yu shi xiongdi qianpei (jianbao ziliao)," vol. 2, 278, 020-010710-0008, May 7, 1970–April 4, 1973, AH.

118. "Yu shi xiongdi," vol. 4, 020-091300-0022, 1971, AH; "Yu Changgeng fu Mei," *United Daily News*, December 9, 1972.

Conclusion

1. Kwon, *Other Cold War*, 8.

2. Albert F. Celoza, *Ferdinand Marcos and the Philippines: The Political Economy of Authoritarianism* (Westport, CT: Praeger, 1997), 43.

3. Charles J. McCarthy, "The Chinese Schools 1899–1972," in *Philippine-Chinese Profile: Essays and Studies*, ed. Charles J. McCarthy (Manila: Pagkakaisa sa Pag-unlad, 1974), 176.

4. Presidential Decree No. 176, April 16, 1973, the Lawphil Project, https://www.lawphil.net/statutes/presdecs/pd1973/pd_176_1973.html.

5. Antonio S. Tan, "The Philippine Chinese, 1946–1984," in *Changing Identities of the Southeast Asian Chinese since World War II*, ed. Jennifer Cushman and Wang Gungwu (Hong Kong: Hong Kong University Press, 1986), 190.

6. Benito Lim, "The Political Economy of Philippines-China Relations," PASCN Discussion Paper 99-16 (Philippine APEC Study Center Network, Manila, September 1999),

8–9; Filomeno V. Aguilar Jr., "Interview with Benito Lim: Philippine Citizenship through Mass Naturalization, a Dictator's Largesse?," *Philippine Studies* 60, no. 3 (September 2012): 393–395.

7. Aguilar, "Interview with Benito Lim," 396–405.

8. Carino, *Chinese Big Business in the Philippines*, 56; Purificacion C. Valera Quisumbing, *Beijing-Manila Détente, Major Issues: A Study in China-ASEAN Relations* (Quezon City: Bookman Printing House, 1983), 140.

9. Carino, *Chinese Big Business in the Philippines*, 57.

10. Cited in Tan, "Philippine Chinese," 190.

11. Carino, *Chinese Big Business in the Philippines*, 64–65.

12. Carino, *Chinese Big Business in the Philippines*, 59–60, 69.

13. Teresita Ang See, interview by Reynard Hing, September 13, 2016, 4, https://www.china-studies.taipei/comm2/Teresita Ang See2.pdf.

14. Carino, *Chinese Big Business in the Philippines*, 57–58, 91–92.

15. The Facebook page of the Wen Zong is, tellingly, https://www.facebook.com/kuomintang.ph. As of writing, the organization's official website, https://www.fccea.org.ph, is down.

16. *Zhongguo Guomindang zai haiwai*, 151.

17. Chang et al., *Reminiscences*, 373–374.

18. "Feilübin jiu xun huaqiao: Rentong 'Minguo' he 'Gongheguo' de liangzhong qunti," BBC News, October 2, 2019, https://www.bbc.com/zhongwen/simp/chinese-news-48443934.

19. On the KMT in postcolonial Indonesia, see Zhou, *Migration in the Time of Revolution*. On Malaysia, see Toh Jin-xuan [Du Jinxuan], *Xuetong de yuanzui: Bei qian wang de baise kongbu dongnanya shounanzhe* (Taipei: Taiwan shangwu yinshu guan, 2020). Toh's book narrates the experiences of Malaysian-Chinese victims of the White Terror in martial law Taiwan.

20. Szonyi, *Cold War Island*, 7–8.

21. I am grateful to one of my interviewees for this insight.

22. Shelly Chan, *Diaspora's Homeland: Modern China in the Age of Global Migration* (Durham, NC: Duke University Press, 2018); Wayne Soon, *Global Medicine in China: A Diasporic History* (Stanford, CA: Stanford University Press, 2020).

23. Chan, *Diaspora's Homeland*, 1, 3, 12–13.

24. Philip A. Kuhn, "Why China Historians Should Study the Chinese Diaspora, and Vice-Versa," *Journal of Chinese Overseas* 2, no. 2 (November 2006): 163–172. On critical Han studies, see Thomas Mullaney, James Patrick Leibold, Stéphane Gros, and Eric Vanden Bussche, eds., *Critical Han Studies: The History, Representation, and Identity of China's Majority* (Berkeley: University of California Press, 2012). On Sinophone studies, see Shu-mei Shih, "Introduction: What Is Sinophone Studies?," in *Sinophone Studies: A Critical Reader*, ed. Shu-mei Shih, Chien-tsin Tsai, and Brian Bernards (New York: Columbia University Press, 2012), 1–16.

25. See, for example, Allen Chun, "Fuck Chineseness: On the Ambiguities of Ethnicity as Culture as Identity," *boundary 2* 23, no. 2 (Summer 1996): 111–138.

GLOSSARY OF SELECTED CHINESE NAMES

Name/Term	Chinese Characters
Act for the Control and Punishment of Rebellion	懲治叛亂條例
Ang Giok Lun	洪玉润
Anglo-Chinese School	中西學校
"Anticommunism and resist Russia"	反共抗俄
Anti-Communist and Resist Russia League of Chinese Youth	中國青年反共抗俄聯合會
Blue Shirts	藍衣社
Bonaobra, Felix	吳天從
Cabo Chan, Justo	曾廷泉
Cai Anluo	蔡安洛
Cai Jian Hua	蔡建華
Cai Liyi	蔡麗意
Cai Yunqin	蔡云欽
case of the five Chinese communists	五華共案
Cebu Eastern High School	宿務東方中學
Central Executive Committee	中央執行委員會
Central News Agency	中央通訊社
Chan, Billy	陳瑞時
Chang, Smin	張思明
Chao Ching Win	周鯨文
Chen Chih-mai	陳之邁
Chen Chih-ping	陳質平
Chen Lieh-fu	陳烈甫
Cheng Chung Book Company	正中書局
Cheng Kim Tiao	莊金朝
Chiang Kai-shek High School	中正中學
Chiang Kai-shek College	中正學院
Chinese Association	華僑協會
Chinese Commercial Bulletin	僑商公報
Chinese Commercial News	華僑商報
Chinese Bureau	中國共產黨菲律賓華僑局
Chinese Communist Youth League	中國共產主義青年團
Chinese Freemasons	洪門

Chinese Guide	華僑導報
Chinese Overseas Wartime Hsuehkan Militia	華僑戰時血幹團
Chinese Revolutionary Party	中國革命黨
Chinese Volunteers in the Philippines	菲律賓華僑義勇軍
Chinese Weekly	華僑周刊
Chow Shu-kai	周書楷
Chu I-Hsiung	朱一雄
Chua, Fernando	蔡顯祖
Chua Lamco	蔡功南
Chuan, Dee C.	李清泉
Co Chi Meng	許志猛
Co Keng Sing	許敬誠
Co Pak	許志北
Cruz, Antonio Chua	蔡彬慶
Cua Siok Po	柯叔寶
Cultural Renaissance Movement	中華文化復興運動
Dy Eng Hao	李永孝
Dy Huan Chay	李煥彩
Dy Sun, Vicente	李峻峰
Fang Chih-chou	方稚周
Federation of Filipino-Chinese Chambers of Commerce and Industry	菲華商聯總會
Forceful Action Society	力行社
Gao Zi	高梓
Garrison–General Headquarters	警備總司令部
Gawhok, Gonzalo	吳金聘
General Association of Chinese Schools	菲律賓華僑學校聯合總會
Go Chi Kok	吳志國
Go Co-Lay	吳筍來
Go Eng Guan	吳永源
Go Puan Seng	吳重生
Gong Taoyi	龔陶怡
Grand Family Association	菲律賓各宗親聯合會
Great China Press	大華日報 / 大中華日報
Hsin Kwan-chue	邢光祖
Huang He-de	黃和德
Huang Wei	黃薇
Kipsi Primary School	及時小學
Koa Chian ("Benito")	柯千
Koa Chun-te	柯俊智
Kong Li Po	公理報
Ku Cheng-kang	谷正綱
Lao Han Keng	劉漢卿
Lao Kiat	劉賢吉
Lee Hai-jo	李海若
Li Weihan	李維漢

Liang Shang Wan	梁上苑
Liberty Hall	自由大廈
Lim, Edward	林應彬
Lim, Peter	林為白
Lim Chua, Jose	蔡景福
Lim Hua Sin	林華新
Lim Soo Chan	林樹燦
Lim Yan Yan	林燕燕
Lin Tso-mei	林作梅
Liu Chi-tien	劉芝田
Loyal Soul Fraternity	華僑忠魂社
Loyalty Night School	丹心夜校
Ma Piao Ping	馬飄萍
Mah Soo-Lay	馬樹禮
Ong, Santos	王文漢
Ong Chuan Seng	王泉笙
Overseas Chinese Affairs Commission	僑務委員會
Overseas Party Affairs Committee	海外黨務委員會
Pan Zhaoying	潘肇英
Pao Kee Tung	鮑居東
Pao Shih-tien	鮑事天
Philippine Chinese Anti-Communist League	菲律賓華僑反共抗俄總會
Philippine-Chinese Anti-Japanese and Anti-Puppets League	菲律賓抗日反奸大同盟
Philippine-Chinese Anti-Japanese Force	菲律賓華僑抗日支隊
Philippine-Chinese Anti-Japanese Volunteer Corps	菲律賓華僑抗日鋤奸義勇軍
Philippine-Chinese Democratic League	菲律賓華僑民主大同盟
Philippine Chinese General Chamber of Commerce in Manila	菲律賓岷里拉中華商會
Philippine-Chinese Labor Association	菲律賓華僑總工會
Philippine-Chinese Labor Federation	菲律賓華僑各老公團體
Philippine-Chinese Mutual Aid Society	菲律賓華僑互濟社
Philippine-Chinese Resist-the-Enemy Committee	菲律賓華僑抗敵後援會
Philippine-Chinese Students' Anti-Japanese and Anti-Traitors Association	菲律賓華僑學生抗日反奸大同盟
Philippine-Chinese United Organization in Support of Anti-Communist Movement	菲律賓華僑反共抗俄後援會
Philippine-Chinese United Workers Union	菲律賓各勞工團體聯合會
Philippine Chinese Youth Wartime Special Services Corps	菲律賓華僑青年戰時特別工作總隊
Philippines-China Cultural Association	中菲文化協會
Political Warfare Cadres Academy	政工幹部學校
Pua Chin Tao	潘行素

Qua Chi Peng	柯子冰
Que, Profiteza ("Baby Zenaida")	郭珠寶 / 郭秀治
Ren Jiaming	任家銘
Renaissance Society	復興社
Roxas Chua, Antonio	蔡文華
Say Kok Chuan	史國銓
Shen Fushui	沈福水
Shi Wenrui	施文瑞
Shih I-Sheng	施逸生
Soul of the Great Han	大漢魂
Sun, Patrick Pichi	孫碧奇
Sun Yat-sen High School, Iloilo	怡朗中山中學
Sy Bun Chiong	施文章
Sy En	施性水
Sy Yan Wan	施燕婉
Sycip, Albino	薛敏老
Sycip, Alfonso	薛芬士
Tan Kah Kee	陳嘉庚
Tang Tack	鄧英達
Tee Han Kee	鄭漢祺
Three Principles' Youth Corps	三民主義青年團
United Daily News	聯合報
United Work Front Department	統一戰線工作部
Uy Bee Siong	黃美嫦
Uy Ting Bing	黃鼎銘
Wang Jiawai	王家外
Wang Sheng	王昇
Wang Tiannian	王天年
Wong Kiat	黃杰
Workers' Association	工人協會
World Book Company	世界書局
Wu Tiecheng	吳鐵城
Yao Shiong Shio	姚迺崑
Young Ching-tong	楊靜桐
Youth World	世界青年
Yu Khe Thai	楊啟泰
Yu Yi-tung	于以同
Yuyitung, Quintin	于長城
Yuyitung, Rizal	于長庚
Zheng Tingting	鄭婷婷

BIBLIOGRAPHY

Archives and Libraries

China

Fujian Provincial Archives, Fuzhou

Hong Kong

Overseas Chinese Clippings Database, Hong Kong Baptist University

Philippines

American Historical Collection, Ateneo de Manila University, Manila
Asian Library, Ramon Magsaysay Center, Manila
Chinben See Memorial Library, Kaisa Heritage Center, Manila
Filipinas Heritage Library, Ayala Museum, Manila
National Library, Manila
University Archives and Records Depository, University of the Philippines Diliman,
Manila

Taiwan

Academia Historica, Taipei
Institute of Modern History Archives, Academia Sinica, Taipei
Kuomintang Archives, Taipei
National Central Library, Taipei

Singapore

Institute of Southeast Asian Studies–Yusof Ishak Institute Library

United States

Hoover Institution Library and Archives, Stanford, California
Library of Congress, Washington, District of Columbia
National Archives and Records Administration, College Park, Maryland

Digital

Chan Robles Virtual Law Library, https://lawlibrary.chanrobles.com
The Lawphil Project, https://www.lawphil.net

Laws and Regulations Database of the Republic of China (Quanguo Fagui Zilia-oku), https://law.moj.gov.tw

National Index to Chinese Newspapers and Periodicals (Quanguo Baokan Suoyin), http://www.cnbksy.com

Official Gazette, https://www.officialgazette.gov.ph

Philippine Diary Project, https://philippinediaryproject.wordpress.com

Philippines Free Press, https://philippinesfreepress.wordpress.com

Taiwan Review (formerly *Free China Review*), https://taiwantoday.tw

Wilson Center Digital Archive, https://digitalarchive.wilsoncenter.org

Newspapers and Periodicals

China

Dahan hun yuekan
Huaqiao hujishe Feilübin zhishe Minlila fenshe yuandan tekan
Jiaotongbu Jinpuqu tielu guanliju ribao
Zhongyang dangwu yuekan
Zhongyang zhoubao

Philippines

The Bullseye
Chinese Commercial News (Huaqiao shangbao)
Chungking Times (Chongqing ribao)
Daily News
Fookien Times (Xinmin ribao)
Great China Press (Da zhonghua ribao)
Kong Li Po (Gongli bao)
Manila Times
Philippines Free Press

Taiwan

Central Daily News (Zhongyang ribao)
United Daily News (Lianhe bao)

Published Primary Sources

Aguilar, Filomeno V., Jr. "Interview with Benito Lim: Philippine Citizenship through Mass Naturalization, a Dictator's Largesse?" *Philippine Studies* 60, no. 3 (September 2012): 391–415.

Ang See, Teresita. Interview by Reynard Hing. September 13, 2016. https://www.china-studies.taipei/comm2/Teresita Ang See2.pdf.

Ang See, Teresita, and Carmelea Ang See. "Navigating Cultures, Forming Identities." *Kritika Kultura*, no. 21 / 22 (2013 / 2014): 353–372.

Cai Wenhua xiansheng jinian ji. Taipei: Zhonghua caise yinshua gufen youxian gongsi, 1980.

Chang Tsun-wu, Chu Hong-yuan, Dory Poa, and Lin Shu-hui, eds. *The Reminiscences of the Chinese in the Philippines*. Taipei: Institute of Modern History, Academia Sinica, 1996.

Chao Ching Win [Zhou Jingwen]. *Fengbao shinian: Zhongguo hongse zhengquan de zhen mianmao*. Hong Kong: Shidai pinglun she, 1959.

Chen Chih-mai. "The Philippines: Further Impressions." *Fookien Times Yearbook*, September 1957.

Chen Hsiao-yu [Chen Xiaoyu], ed. *Philippine Chinese Chronicle*. Vols. 1–2. Manila: Philippine Chinese Chronicle Publisher, 1948.

Chen Lieh-fu [Chen Liefu]. *Feilübin huaqiao jiaoyu*. Taipei: Haiwai chubanshe, 1958.

———. *Feiyou guangan ji*. Xiamen: Nanyang tongxunshe, 1948.

Chiang Kai-shek. *Soviet Russia in China: A Summing-Up at Seventy*. New York: Farrar, Straus, and Cudahy, 1957.

Chinese Commercial News. "History of Chinese Commercial News." Accessed January 20, 2021. https://web.archive.org/web/20050503203257 /http://www.siongpo.com/history2.htm.

Commission of the Census, Commonwealth of the Philippines. *Census of the Philippines: 1939*, Vol. 2, *Summary for the Philippines and General Report for the Censuses of Population and Agriculture*. Manila: Bureau of Printing, 1941.

Communism in the Philippines: The PKP. Vol. 1. Quezon City: Historical Commission, Partido Komunista ng Pilipinas, 1996.

Cua Siok Po [Ke Shubao]. *Fendou rensheng*. Taipei: Liming wenhua shiye gufen youxian gongsi, 1982.

———. *Song dahan hun: Ke Shubao lü Fei shiwen cun*. Taipei: Liming wenhua shiye gufen youxian gongsi, 1980.

Dai Kuisheng. *Dai Kuisheng huiyi lu*. [Taipei], 1980.

Du Ai. *Fengyu Taipingyang*. Vol. 1. Guangzhou: Huacheng chubanshe, 1985.

———. *Fengyu Taipingyang*. Vol. 2. Guangzhou: Huacheng chubanshe, 1988.

———. *Fengyu Taipingyang*. Vol. 3. Zhuhai: Zhuhai chubanshe, 2002.

Dy Sun, Vicente [Li Junfeng]. *Li Junfeng liushi huiyi*. Taipei: Kenye Co., [1976].

Federation of Filipino-Chinese Chambers of Commerce and Industry. *The Philippine Chinese Decennial Book 1954–1974* [Shang Zong ershi nian: Feihua shanglian zonghui chengli ershi zhounian jinian tekan]. Manila, 1974.

Foreign Relations of the United States, 1946. Vol. 8, *The Far East*. Washington, DC: Government Printing Office, 1947.

Gong Taoyi, ed. *Feilübin huaqiao guiqiao aiguo danxin lu*. Beijing: Huawen chubanshe, 2002.

———, ed. *Feilübin huaqiao kangri aiguo yinghun lu*. Beijing: Huawen chubanshe, 2001.

———, ed. *Feilübin huaqiao kangri douzheng jishi*. Beijing: Zhongguo guoji guangbo chubanshe, 1997.

Gongfei dui huaqiao zhi yinmou. Taipei: Haiwai chubanshe, 1954.

Gongfei huoqiao shilu. Taipei: Haiwai chubanshe, 1955.

Hernandez, Jose Ma. *And the Day but One: An Autobiography*. Manila: Aljun Printing Press, 2000.

Hsin Kwan-chue [Xing Guangzu]. *Jingli de rensheng*. Taipei: Great Han Publishing Company, 1976.

Huang Wei and Gong Taoyi. *Fengyu rensheng*. Beijing: Zhongguo wenshi chubanshe, 2000.

Huaqiao shehui de luxiang: Shangbao yanlun xuanji. Manila: Yitong chubanshe, 1961.

Kaisa Para sa Kaunlaran. "About Kaisa." Accessed February 20, 2021. https://www .kaisa.org.ph/?page_id=2.

Li Pusheng. *Wo ke pei de huaqiao pengyou*. Taipei: Zhengzhong shuju, 1958.

Liang Shang Wan [Leong Siong Yuen] and Cai Jian Hua [Chua Kian Hua]. *The Wha Chi Memoirs*. Translated by Joaquin Sy. Manila: Kaisa Para sa Kaunlaran, 1998.

Lim Chua, Jose [Cai Jingfu]. *Liuzai Zhong Fei menghuan jian*. Taipei: Zhaoming chubanshe, 1978.

Liu Haoran, ed. *Xu Li tongzhi zhuisi jinian kan 1905–1995*. Quanzhou: Feilübin Xushi zongqin zonghui, 1995.

Navarro, Nelson A., ed. *Juan Ponce Enrile: A Memoir*. Quezon City: ABS CBN Publishing, 2012.

Ong, Santos [Wang Wenhan]. *Fengchen wushinian*. Beijing: Zhongguo youyi chuban gongsi, 1989.

Pao Shih-tien. "Chinese Schools in the Philippines." *Fookien Times Yearbook*, September 1961.

Pao Shih-tien [Bao Shitian]. *Yang hao ji*. Manila: Feilübin Zhongzheng xueyuan Shitian wenjiao jijin hui, 1996.

Philippine-Chinese Business Guide and Pictorial Directory. Cebu City: Philippine Konghooy Publication, 1953.

Philippine Chinese General Chamber of Commerce. *Golden Book 1955: Commercial Almanac and Yearbook 1904–1954* [Feilübin Minlila zhonghua shanghui wushi zhounian jinian kan]. Manila: Fookien Times Publishing Company, 1955.

Qiao zi gongchang zai Ziyou Zhongguo. Taipei: Haiwai chubanshe, 1958.

Qiaobao hui Tai guanguang zhinan. Taipei: Qiaowu weiyuanhui, September 1958.

Qiaowu huiyi shilu. Taipei: Haiwai chubanshe, 1953.

Qiaowu tongji. Taipei: Qiaowu weiyuanhui tongjishi, 1964.

"Recognition Suspended." *IPI Report: Monthly Bulletin of the International Press Institute* 20 (November 1971): 1.

Roxas, Manuel, and Chen Chih-ping. "Sino-Philippine Treaty of Amity, April 1947." *International Law Quarterly* 2, no. 1 (Spring 1948): 132–134.

Shen Fushui. "Feilübin huaqiao ge laogong tuanti lianhehui de zhanmen licheng." *Guangdong wenshi ziliao* 54 (1988): 100–133.

Shi Youtu. *Dahan hun zhuanji: Huaqiao kangri yiyongjun dixia zuozhan fendou shilüe*. Manila: Feilübin huaqiao yiyong hui tongzhi hui, 1995.

Sycip, Alfonso Z. "An Appeal to the People of Free Nations." *Fookien Times Yearbook*, September 1953.

——. "The Role of the Overseas Chinese in the Worldwide Struggle against Communism." *Fookien Times Yearbook*, September 1952.

Tang Tack [Deng Yingda]. *Wo zai Shang Zong sanshinian: Deng Yingda huiyi lu*. Manila, 1988.

Taruc, Luis. *Born of the People*. New York: International Publishers, 1953.

——. *He Who Rides the Tiger: The Story of an Asian Guerrilla Leader*. New York: Praeger, 1967.

Wang guxiaozhang Quansheng shishi wushi zhounian jinian teji. Manila: Purity Printers, 2006.

Yang Jiancheng, ed. *Zhongguo Guomindang yu huaqiao wenxian chubian, 1908–1945*. Taipei: Zhonghua xueshuyuan Nanyang yanjiusuo, 1984.

Yuyitung, Rizal, ed. *The Case of the Yuyitung Brothers: Philippine Press Freedom under Siege*. Manila: Yuyitung Foundation, 2000.

——, ed. *Zhong hun yi po: Yu Yitong lieshi yu Huaqiao shangbao*. Manila: Yu Yitong jijinhui, 1997.

Yuyitung, Rizal [Yu Changgeng], ed. *Liangdi yuanyu: Yu Changcheng Changgeng qianpei an huibian*. Manila: Yu Yitong jijinhui, 2000.

Zhonggong zenyang duidai qiaosheng. Taipei: Haiwai chubanshe, 1956.

Zhongguo Guomindang diqi jie quanguo daibiao da hui dangwu baogao. Vols. 1–2. Taipei: Zhongyang gaizao weiyuanhui, 1952.

Zhongguo Guomindang zai haiwai: Jiushi nian lai de fendou licheng. Taipei: Haiwai chubanshe, 1984.

Zhongguo Guomindang zai haiwai yibai nian. Taipei: Haiwai chubanshe, 1994.

Ziyou Zhongguo da zhong xuexiao jianjie. Taipei: Haiwai chubanshe, 1957.

Secondary Sources

Abinales, Patricio N., and Donna J. Amoroso. *State and Society in the Philippines*. Lanham, MD: Rowman & Littlefield, 2005.

Agpalo, Remigio E. *The Political Process and the Nationalization of the Retail Trade in the Philippines*. Diliman: University of the Philippines, Office of Coordinator of Research, 1962.

Aguilar, Filomeno V., Jr. "Between the Letter and Spirit of the Law: Ethnic Chinese and Philippine Citizenship by Jus Soli, 1899–1947." *Southeast Asian Studies* 49, no. 3 (December 2011): 431–463.

Akashi, Yoji. *The Nanyang Chinese National Salvation Movement, 1937–1941*. Lawrence: Center for East Asian Studies, University of Kansas, 1970.

Alejandrino, Clark L. "The Population History of the Chinese in the Philippines: An Evaluative Historiography." *Philippine Population Review* 9, no. 1 (December 2010): 85–108.

Alip, Eufronio M. *Ten Centuries of Philippine-Chinese Relations (Historical, Political, Social, Economic)*. Manila: Alip & Sons, 1959.

Amyot, Jacques. *The Chinese and the National Integration in Southeast Asia*. Bangkok: Institute of Asian Studies, Faculty of Political Science, Chulalongkorn University, October 1972.

——. *The Manila Chinese: Familism in the Philippine Environment*. Quezon City: Institute of Philippine Culture, Ateneo de Manila University, 1973.

Andaya, Barbara Watson, and Leonard Y. Andaya. *A History of Malaysia*. Basingstoke: Palgrave, 2001.

Ang Cheng Guan. *Southeast Asia's Cold War: An Interpretive History*. Honolulu: University of Hawai'i Press, 2018.

Ang See, Teresita, ed. *The Chinese in the Philippines: Problems and Perspectives*. Vols. 1–3. Manila: Kaisa Para sa Kaunlaran, 1997–2004.

——. "Yu Khe Thai." In *Southeast Asian Personalities of Chinese Descent: A Biographical Dictionary*, edited by Leo Suryadinata, 1:1378–1380. Singapore: Institute of Southeast Asian Studies, 2012.

Ang See, Teresita, and Lily T. Chua, eds. *Crossroads: Short Essays on the Chinese Filipinos*. Manila: Kaisa Para sa Kaunlaran, 1988.

Ang See, Teresita, Go Bon Juan, Doreen Go Yu, and Yvonne Chua, eds. *Tsinoy: The Story of the Chinese in Philippine Life*. Manila: Kaisa Para sa Kaunlaran, 2005.

Anuson Chinvanno. *Thailand's Policies towards China, 1949–54*. Basingstoke: Macmillan, 1992.

Appleton, Sheldon. "Communism and the Chinese in the Philippines." *Pacific Affairs* 32, no. 4 (December 1959): 376–391.

Bachrack, Stanley K. *The Committee of One Million: "China Lobby" Politics, 1953–1971*. New York: Columbia University Press, 1976.

Barrett, Tracy C. *The Chinese Diaspora in South-East Asia: The Overseas Chinese in Indochina*. London: I. B. Tauris, 2012.

Bayly, Susan. *Asian Voices in a Post-Colonial Age: Vietnam, India and Beyond*. Cambridge: Cambridge University Press, 2007.

BBC News. "Feilübin jiu xun huaqiao: Rentong 'Minguo' he 'Gongheguo' de liangzhong qunti." October 2, 2019. https://www.bbc.com/zhongwen/simp/chinese-news-48443934.

Bekker, Konrad, and Charles Wolf Jr. "The Philippine Balance of Payments." *Far Eastern Survey* 19, no. 4 (February 22, 1950): 41–43.

Belogurova, Anna. *The Nanyang Revolution: The Comintern and Chinese Networks in Southeast Asia, 1890–1957*. Cambridge: Cambridge University Press, 2019.

Benite, Zvi Ben-Dor, Stefanos Geroulanos, and Nicole Jerr. "Editors' Introduction." In *The Scaffolding of Sovereignty: Global and Aesthetic Perspectives on the History of a Concept*, edited by Zvi Ben-Dor Benite, Stefanos Geroulanos, and Nicole Jerr, 1–49. New York: Columbia University Press, 2017.

——, eds. *The Scaffolding of Sovereignty: Global and Aesthetic Perspectives on the History of a Concept*. New York: Columbia University Press, 2017.

Blaker, James Roland. "The Chinese in the Philippines: A Study of Power and Change." PhD diss., Ohio State University, 1970.

——. "The Chinese Newspaper in the Philippines: Toward the Definition of a Tool." *Asian Studies* 3, no. 2 (1965): 243–261.

Bolt, J. Paul. *China and Southeast Asia's Ethnic Chinese: State and Diaspora in Contemporary Asia*. Westport, CT: Praeger, 2000.

Brett, Judith, and Mei-fen Kuo. *Unlocking the History of the Australasian Kuo Min Tang, 1911–2013*. North Melbourne: Australian Scholarly Publishing, 2013.

Brook, Timothy. *Collaboration: Japanese Agents and Local Elites in Wartime China*. Cambridge, MA: Harvard University Press, 2005.

Brooks, Charlotte. *Between Mao and McCarthy: Chinese American Politics in the Cold War Years*. Chicago: University of Chicago Press, 2015.

Bullard, Monte R. *The Soldier and the Citizen: The Role of the Military in Taiwan's Development*. Armonk, NY: M. E. Sharpe, 1997.

Carino, Theresa Chong. *Chinese Big Business in the Philippines: Political Leadership and Change*. Singapore: Times Academic Press, 1998.

——, ed. *Chinese in the Philippines*. Manila: China Studies Program, De La Salle University, 1985.

Celoza, Albert F. *Ferdinand Marcos and the Philippines: The Political Economy of Authoritarianism*. Westport, CT: Praeger, 1997.

Certeau, Michel de. *The Practice of Everyday Life*. Translated by Steven Randall. Berkeley: University of California Press, 1984.

Chan, Shelly. *Diaspora's Homeland: Modern China in the Age of Global Migration*. Durham, NC: Duke University Press, 2018.

Chang, David Cheng. *The Hijacked War: The Story of Chinese POWs in the Korean War*. Stanford, CA: Stanford University Press, 2020.

Chang, Hui-Ching, and Richard Holt. *Language, Politics and Identity in Taiwan: Naming China*. London: Routledge, 2015.

Chang, Pao-min. *Beijing, Hanoi, and the Overseas Chinese*. Berkeley: Institute of East Asian Studies, University of California, Berkeley, Center for Chinese Studies, 1982.

Chang, Te-Tsui. "Land Utilization on Taiwan." *Land Economics* 28, no. 4 (November 1952): 362–368.

Chang Tsun-wu [Zhang Cunwu] and Ong Kok-Chung [Wang Guozhang]. *Feihua shanglian zonghui zhi xingshuai yu yanbian*. Taipei: Zhongyang yanjiuyuan yatai yanjiu jishu, 2002.

Cheah Boon Kheng. *Red Star over Malaya: Resistance and Social Conflict during and after the Japanese Occupation*. Singapore: NUS Press, 2012.

Chen, Hao. "Resisting Bandung? Taiwan's Struggle for 'Representational Legitimacy' in the Rise of the Asian Peoples' Anti-Communist League, 1954–57." *International History Review* 43, no. 2 (2021): 244–263.

Chen, Ketty W. "Disciplining Taiwan: The Kuomintang's Methods of Control during the White Terror Era (1947–1987)." *Taiwan International Studies Quarterly* 4, no. 4 (Winter 2008): 185–210.

Chen, Kuan-Hsing. *Asia as Method: Toward Deimperialization*. Durham, NC: Duke University Press, 2010.

Chen, Zhongping. *Modern China's Network Revolution: Chambers of Commerce and Sociopolitical Change in the Early Twentieth Century*. Stanford, CA: Stanford University Press, 2011.

Chen Horng-Yu. *Zhonghua minguo yu dongnanya geguo waijiao guanxi shi, 1912–2000*. Taipei: Dingwen shuju, 2004.

Chen Jian. *Mao's China and the Cold War*. Chapel Hill: University of North Carolina Press, 2001.

Cheung Shing Kit. "Immigrating Visitors: The Case of Overstaying Chinese in the Philippines, 1947–75." MPhil thesis, University of Hong Kong, 1997.

Chiang Bo-wei. "A Special Intermittence and Continuity in Local History: The Chinese Diaspora and Their Hometown in Battlefield Quemoy during 1949–1960s." *Journal of Chinese Overseas* 7, no. 2 (May 2011): 169–186.

Chirot, Daniel, and Anthony Reid, eds. *Essential Outsiders: Chinese and Jews in the Modern Transformation of Southeast Asia and Central Europe*. Seattle: University of Washington Press, 1997.

Chu, Richard T. *Chinese and Chinese Mestizos of Manila: Family, Identity, and Culture, 1860s–1930s*. Leiden: Brill, 2010.

——, ed. *More Tsinoy than We Admit: Chinese-Filipino Interactions over the Centuries.* Quezon City: Vibal Foundation, 2015.

Chu, Yun-han, and Jih-wen Lin. "Political Development in 20th-Century Taiwan: State-Building, Regime Transformation and the Construction of National Identity." *China Quarterly* 165 (March 2001): 102–129.

Chun, Allen. "From Nationalism to Nationalizing: Cultural Imagination and State Formation in Postwar Taiwan." *Australian Journal of Chinese Affairs* 31 (January 1994): 49–69.

——. "Fuck Chineseness: On the Ambiguities of Ethnicity as Culture as Identity." *boundary 2* 23, no. 2 (Summer 1996): 111–138.

Clinton, Maggie. *Revolutionary Nativism: Fascism and Culture in China, 1925–1937.* Durham, NC: Duke University Press, 2017.

Constantino, Renato, and Letizia R. Constantino. *The History of the Philippines: From the Spanish Colonization to the Second World War.* New York: Monthly Review Press, 1975.

Cooper, Frederick. *Colonialism in Question: Theory, Knowledge, History.* Berkeley: University of California Press, 2005.

Copper, John. *Taiwan: Nation-State or Province?* Boulder, CO: Westview Press, 2009.

Craft, Stephen G. *American Justice in Taiwan: The 1957 Riots and Cold War Foreign Policy.* Lexington: University Press of Kentucky, 2016.

Cullather, Nick. *Illusions of Influence: The Political Economy of United States–Philippine Relations, 1942–1960.* Stanford, CA: Stanford University Press, 1994.

Cushman, Jennifer, and Wang Gungwu, eds. *Changing Identities of the Southeast Asian Chinese since World War II.* Hong Kong: Hong Kong University Press, 1986.

Dirlik, Arif. "The Ideological Foundations of the New Life Movement: A Study in Counterrevolution." *Journal of Asian Studies* 34, no. 4 (August 1975): 945–980.

Doronila, Amando. *The State, Economic Transformation, and Political Change in the Philippines, 1946–1972.* Singapore: Oxford University Press, 1992.

Duara, Prasenjit. "Nationalists among Transnationalists: Overseas Chinese and the Idea of China, 1900–1911." In *Ungrounded Empires: The Cultural Politics of Modern Chinese Transnationalism*, edited by Aihwa Ong and Donald M. Nonini, 39–60. New York: Routledge, 1997.

——. "Transnationalism and the Predicament of Sovereignty: China, 1900–1945." *American Historical Review* 102, no. 4 (October 1997): 1030–1051.

Durham, Martin, and Margaret Power, eds. *New Perspectives on the Transnational Right.* New York: Palgrave Macmillan, 2010.

Eagleton, Terry. *Ideology: An Introduction.* London: Verso Books, 1991.

Eastman, Lloyd. *The Abortive Revolution: China under Nationalist Rule, 1927–1937.* Cambridge, MA: Harvard University Press, 1974.

Efimova, Larissa. "Did the Soviet Union Instruct Southeast Asian Communists to Revolt? New Russian Evidence on the Calcutta Youth Conference of February 1948." *Journal of Southeast Asian Studies* 40, no. 3 (October 2009): 449–469.

Engelbert, Thomas. "Vietnamese-Chinese Relations in Southern Vietnam during the First Indochina Conflict." *Journal of Vietnamese Studies* 3, no. 3 (October 2008): 191–230.

Farquhar, Judith, and Qicheng Zhang. "Biopolitical Beijing: Pleasure, Sovereignty, and Self-Cultivation in China's Capital." *Cultural Anthropology* 20, no. 3 (August 2005): 303–327.

Felix, Alfonso, ed. *The Chinese in the Philippines*. Vol. 2. Manila: Solidaridad Publishing House, 1969.

Fineman, Daniel. *A Special Relationship: The United States and Military Government in Thailand, 1947–1958*. Honolulu: University of Hawai'i Press, 1997.

Fitzgerald, Stephen. *China and the Overseas Chinese: A Study of Peking's Changing Policy, 1949–1970*. Cambridge: Cambridge University Press, 1972.

Fuller, Ken. *Forcing the Pace: The Partido Komunista ng Pilipinas; From Foundation to Armed Struggle*. Diliman: University of the Philippines Press, 2007.

González, Fredy. *Paisanos Chinos: Transpacific Politics among Chinese Immigrants in Mexico*. Oakland: University of California Press, 2017.

Goodman, Bryna. *Native Place, City, and Nation: Regional Networks and Identities in Shanghai, 1853–1937*. Berkeley: University of California Press, 1995.

Goscha, Christopher. *Thailand and the Southeast Asian Networks of the Vietnamese Revolution, 1885–1954*. London: Curzon Press, 1999.

Greene, J. Megan. *The Origins of the Developmental State in Taiwan: Science Policy and the Quest for Modernization*. Cambridge, MA: Harvard University Press, 2008.

Guingona, Phillip B. "The Sundry Acquaintances of Dr. Albino Z. Sycip: Exploring the Shanghai-Manila Connection, circa 1910–1940." *Journal of World History* 27, no. 1 (March 2016): 27–52.

Hanssens, V. "The Campaign against Nationalist Chinese." In *Indonesia's Struggle, 1957–1958*, edited by B. H. M. Vlekke, 56–76. The Hague: Netherlands Institute of International Affairs, 1959.

Hara, Fujio. *Malayan Chinese and China: Conversion in Identity Consciousness, 1945–1957*. Singapore: Singapore University Press, 2003.

Harper, Tim. *Underground Asia: Global Revolutionaries and the Assault on Empire*. London: Allen Lane, 2020.

Hau, Caroline S. "Becoming 'Chinese' in Southeast Asia." In *Sinicization and the Rise of China: Civilizational Processes beyond East and West*, edited by Peter J. Katzenstein, 175–206. London: Routledge, 2012.

———. *The Chinese Question: Ethnicity, Nation, and Region in and beyond the Philippines*. Singapore: NUS Press, 2014.

———. *Necessary Fictions: Philippine Literature and the Nation, 1946–1980*. Quezon City: Ateneo de Manila University Press, 2000.

Hau, Caroline S., and Kasian Tejapira, eds. *Traveling Nation-Makers: Transnational Flows and Movements in the Making of Modern Southeast Asia*. Kyoto: Kyoto University Press, 2011.

Hernandez, Eduardo F., and Oscar A. Domingo. *Philippine Immigration Law and Procedure*. Mandaluyong, Rizal: SMA Printing Company, 1970.

Hofmann, Reto. "What's Left of the Right: Nabeyama Sadachika and Anti-Communism in Transwar Japan, 1930–1960." *Journal of Asian Studies* 79, no. 2 (June 2020): 403–427.

Hsia Chen-hwa [Xia Chenghua]. *Feihua zhengce dui huaqiao jingji zhi yingxiang*. Taipei: Zhonghua minguo haiwai huaren yanjiu xuehui, 2003.

——. *Minguo yilai de qiaowu yu huaqiao jiaoyu yanjiu (1912–2004)*. Hsinchu: Xuanzang daxue haiwai huaren yanjiu zhongxin, 2005.

Hsiao Shi-ching. *Chinese-Philippine Diplomatic Relations, 1946–1975*. Quezon City: Bookman Printing House, 1975.

Hsiao Shi-ching [Xiao Xiqing]. *Zhong Fei waijiao shi*. Taipei: Zhengzhong shuju, 1995.

Hsu, Madeline Y. *Dreaming of Gold, Dreaming of Home: Transnationalism and Migration between the United States and South China, 1882–1943*. Stanford, CA: Stanford University Press, 2000.

——. *The Good Immigrants: How the Yellow Peril Became the Model Minority*. Princeton, NJ: Princeton University Press, 2015.

Huang, Ching-Yi. "Performing an Absent China: Cultural Propaganda in Anti-Communist Taiwan in the 1950's and 1960's." PhD diss., University of Washington, 2013.

Huang, Jianli. "Umbilical Ties: The Framing of the Overseas Chinese as the Mother of the Revolution." *Frontiers of History in China* 6, no. 2 (June 2011): 183–228.

Jiang Xingshan. *Zhanhou Feilübin huawen jiaoyu yanjiu (1945–1976)*. Guangzhou: Jinan daxue chubanshe, 2013.

Kerkvliet, Benedict J. *The Huk Rebellion: A Study of Peasant Revolt in the Philippines*. Lanham, MD: Rowman & Littlefield, 2002.

Khin Khin Myint Jensen. "The Chinese in the Philippines during the American Regime, 1898–1946." PhD diss., University of Wisconsin, 1956.

Koen, Ross Y. *The China Lobby in American Politics*. New York: Harper & Row, 1974.

Kramer, Paul A. *The Blood of Government: Race, Empire, the United States, and the Philippines*. Chapel Hill: University of North Carolina Press, 2006.

Krasner, Stephen D. "Building Democracy after Conflict: The Case for Shared Sovereignty." *Journal of Democracy* 16, no. 1 (January 2005): 69–83.

Kuhn, Philip A. *Chinese among Others: Emigration in Modern Times*. Lanham, MD: Rowman & Littlefield, 2009.

——. "Why China Historians Should Study the Chinese Diaspora, and Vice-Versa." *Journal of Chinese Overseas* 2, no. 2 (November 2006): 163–172.

Kwon, Heonik. *The Other Cold War*. New York: Columbia University Press, 2010.

Lai, Him Mark. *Chinese American Transnational Politics*. Urbana: University of Illinois Press, 2010.

——. "The Kuomintang in Chinese American Communities before World War II." In *Entry Denied: Exclusion and the Chinese Community in America, 1882–1943*, edited by Sucheng Chan, 170–212. Philadelphia: Temple University Press, 1991.

Lary, Diana. *China's Civil War: A Social History, 1945–1949*. Cambridge: Cambridge University Press, 2015.

Liang Ziheng. *Huaqiao shehui yanjiu*. Hong Kong: Haichao chubanshe, 1958.

Liao, Shubert S. C., ed. *Chinese Participation in Philippine Culture and Economy*. Manila, 1964.

Lim, Benito. "The Political Economy of Philippines-China Relations." PASCN Discussion Paper 99-16. Philippine APEC Study Center Network, Manila, September 1999.

Lin, Hsiao-ting. *Accidental State: Chiang Kai-shek, the United States, and the Making of Taiwan*. Cambridge, MA: Harvard University Press, 2016.

Lipkin, Zwia. *Useless to the State: "Social Problems" and Social Engineering in Nationalist Nanjing, 1927–1937.* Cambridge, MA: Harvard University Asia Center, 2006.

Liu, Hong. *China and the Shaping of Indonesia, 1949–1965.* Singapore: NUS Press, 2011.

Liu, Jennifer. "Indoctrinating the Youth: Guomindang Policy on Secondary Education in Wartime China and Postwar Taiwan, 1937–1960." PhD diss., University of California, Irvine, 2010.

Liu Chi-tien [Liu Zhitian]. *Zhong Fei guanxi shi.* Taipei: Zhengzhong shuju, 1964.

Mabon, David W. "Elusive Agreements: The Pacific Pact Proposals of 1949–1951." *Pacific Historical Review* 57, no. 2 (May 1988): 144–177.

MacKinnon, Stephen R. "Toward a History of the Chinese Press in the Republican Period." *Modern China* 23, no. 1 (January 1997): 3–32.

Marks, Thomas A. *Counterrevolution in China: Wang Sheng and the Kuomintang.* London: Frank Cass Publishers, 1998.

Masuda Hajimu. *Cold War Crucible: The Korean Conflict and the Postwar World.* Cambridge, MA: Harvard University Press, 2015.

McBeath, Gerald A. *Political Integration of the Philippine Chinese.* Berkeley: Center for South and Southeast Asian Studies, University of California, 1973.

McCarthy, Charles J. "The Chinese in the Philippines." In *Philippine-Chinese Profile: Essays and Studies,* edited by Charles J. McCarthy, 1–32. Manila: Pagkakaisa sa Pag-unlad, 1974.

——. "The Chinese Schools 1899–1972." In *Philippine-Chinese Profile: Essays and Studies,* edited by Charles J. McCarthy, 168–183. Manila: Pagkakaisa sa Pag-unlad, 1974.

——, ed. *Philippine-Chinese Profile: Essays and Studies.* Manila: Pagkakaisa sa Pag-unlad, 1974.

McCoy, Alfred W. *Policing America's Empire: The United States, the Philippines, and the Rise of the Surveillance State.* Madison: University of Wisconsin Press, 2009.

McKeown, Adam. "Conceptualizing Chinese Diasporas, 1840 to 1949." *Journal of Asian Studies* 58, no. 2 (May 1999): 306–337.

——. *Melancholy Order: Asian Migration and the Globalization of Borders.* New York: Columbia University Press, 2008.

Miller, Edward. *Misalliance: Ngo Dinh Diem, the United States, and the Fate of South Vietnam.* Cambridge, MA: Harvard University Press, 2013.

Moon, Yumi. *Populist Collaborators: The Ilchinhoe and the Japanese Colonization of Korea, 1896–1910.* Ithaca, NY: Cornell University Press, 2013.

Mullaney, Thomas, James Patrick Leibold, Stéphane Gros, and Eric Vanden Bussche, eds. *Critical Han Studies: The History, Representation, and Identity of China's Majority.* Berkeley: University of California Press, 2012.

Murray, Dian H., and Qin Baoqi. *The Origins of the Tiandihui: The Chinese Triads in Legend and History.* Stanford, CA: Stanford University Press, 1994.

Murray, Douglas P. "Chinese Education in South-East Asia." *China Quarterly* 20 (1964): 67–95.

Myers, Ramon, and Hsiao-ting Lin. *Breaking with the Past: The Kuomintang Central Reform Committee on Taiwan, 1950–52.* Stanford, CA: Hoover Institution Press, 2007.

Ngoei, Wen-Qing. *Arc of Containment: Britain, the United States, and Anticommunism in Southeast Asia.* Ithaca, NY: Cornell University Press, 2019.

Nonini, Donald M. *"Getting By": Class and State Formation among Chinese in Malaysia*. Ithaca: Cornell University Press, 2015.

Omohundro, John T. *Chinese Merchant Families in Iloilo: Commerce and Kin in a Central Philippine City*. Quezon City: Ateneo de Manila University Press, 1981.

Oyen, Meredith. "Communism, Containment, and the Chinese Overseas." In *The Cold War in Asia: The Battle for Hearts and Minds*, edited by Zheng Yangwen, Hong Liu, and Michael Szonyi, 59–94. Leiden: Brill, 2010.

——. *The Diplomacy of Migration: Transnational Lives and the Making of U.S.-Chinese Relations in the Cold War*. Ithaca, NY: Cornell University Press, 2015.

Pan Meizhi. "1960 niandai Feilübin huaqiao lai Tai touzi baoxianye zhi yanjiu—Yi Shi Xingshui ji Yang Yinglin wei li." Master's thesis, National Taiwan Normal University, 1991.

Perpiñan, Jesus E. "New Controversy over Chinese Schools." In *Chinese Participation in Philippine Culture and Economy*, edited by Shubert S. C. Liao, 331–337. Manila, 1964.

Peterson, Glen. *Overseas Chinese in the People's Republic of China*. London: Routledge, 2012.

Phelps, Nicole. "State Sovereignty in a Transnational World: US Consular Expansion and the Problem of Naturalized Migrants in the Habsburg Empire, 1880–1914." *German Historical Institute Bulletin Supplement* 5 (2008): 41–59.

Phillips, Steven E. *Between Assimilation and Independence: The Taiwanese Encounter Nationalist China, 1945–1950*. Stanford, CA: Stanford University Press, 2003.

Png Poh Seng. "The Kuomintang in Malaya, 1912–1941." *Journal of Southeast Asian History* 2, no. 1 (March 1961): 1–32.

Purcell, Victor. *The Chinese in Southeast Asia*. Kuala Lumpur: Oxford University Press, 1980.

Quanzhou shi huaqiao zhi bianzuan weiyuanhui, ed. *Quanzhou shi huaqiao zhi*. Beijing: Zhongguo shehui chubanshe, 1996.

Quisumbing, Purificacion C. Valera. *Beijing-Manila Détente, Major Issues: A Study in China-ASEAN Relations*. Quezon City: Bookman Printing House, 1983.

Ren Na. *Feilübin shehui shenghuo zhong de huaren (1935–1965): Cong zuji guanxi de jiaodu suo zuo de tansuo*. Guizhou: Guizhou renmin chubanshe, 2004.

Rubinstein, Murray, ed. *Taiwan: A New History*. Armonk, NY: M. E. Sharpe, 1999.

Scalice, Joseph. "Crisis of Revolutionary Leadership: Martial Law and the Communist Parties of the Philippines, 1959–1974." PhD diss., University of California, Berkeley, 2017.

See, Chinben. "Chinese Clanship in the Philippine Setting." *Journal of Southeast Asian Studies* 12, no. 1 (March 1981): 224–247.

——. "Chinese Organizations and Ethnic Identity in the Philippines." In *Changing Identities of the Southeast Asian Chinese since World War II*, edited by Jennifer Cushman and Wang Gungwu, 303–318. Hong Kong: Hong Kong University Press, 1986.

——. "Education and Ethnic Identity among the Chinese in the Philippines." In *Chinese in the Philippines*, edited by Theresa Chong Carino, 32–49. Manila: China Studies Program, De La Salle University, 1985.

——. "The Ethnic Chinese in the Philippines." In *The Ethnic Chinese in the ASEAN States: Bibliographic Essays*, edited by Leo Suryadinata, 203–220. Singapore: Institute of Southeast Asian Studies, 1989.

See, Chinben, and Teresita Ang See. *Chinese in the Philippines: A Bibliography*. Manila: Chinese Studies Program, De La Salle University, 1990.

Shalom, Stephen Rosskamm. *The United States and the Philippines: A Study of Neocolonialism*. Philadelphia: Institute for the Study of Human Issues, 1981.

Shao, Dan. "Chinese by Definition: Nationality Law, Jus Sanguinis, and State Succession, 1909–1980." *Twentieth-Century China* 35, no. 1 (November 2009): 4–28.

Shih, Shu-mei. "Introduction: What Is Sinophone Studies?" In *Sinophone Studies: A Critical Reader*, edited by Shu-mei Shih, Chien-tsin Tsai, and Brian Bernards, 1–16. New York: Columbia University Press, 2012.

Sidel, John T. *Capital, Coercion, and Crime: Bossism in the Philippines*. Stanford, CA: Stanford University Press, 1999.

Simpson, Bradley R. *Economists with Guns: Authoritarian Development and U.S.-Indonesian Relations, 1960–1968*. Stanford, CA: Stanford University Press, 2008.

Skinner, G. William. *Leadership and Power in the Chinese Community of Thailand*. Ithaca, NY: Cornell University Press, 1958.

——. "Overseas Chinese in Southeast Asia." *Annals of the American Academy of Political and Social Science* 321 (January 1959): 136–147.

——. "Report on the Chinese in Southeast Asia." Southeast Asia Program, Department of Far Eastern Studies, Cornell University, Ithaca, NY, December 1950.

Song Ping. *Chengji yu shanbian: Dangdai Feilübin huaren shetuan bijiao yanjiu*. Xiamen: Xiamen daxue chubanshe, 1995.

Soon, Wayne. *Global Medicine in China: A Diasporic History*. Stanford, CA: Stanford University Press, 2020.

Steinberg, David Joel. *Philippine Collaboration in World War II*. Ann Arbor: University of Michigan Press, 1967.

Strauss, Julia C. "The Evolution of Republican Government." *China Quarterly* 150 (June 1997): 329–351.

Suryadinata, Leo, ed. *Southeast Asian Personalities of Chinese Descent: A Biographical Dictionary*. 2 vols. Singapore: Institute of Southeast Asian Studies, 2012.

Szonyi, Michael. *Cold War Island: Quemoy on the Front Line*. Cambridge: Cambridge University Press, 2008.

Tan, Antonio S. *The Chinese in the Philippines, 1898–1935: A Study of Their National Awakening*. Quezon City: R. P. Garcia Publishing, 1972.

——. *The Chinese in the Philippines during the Japanese Occupation, 1942–1945*. Quezon City: University of the Philippines Press, 1981.

——. "The Philippine Chinese, 1946–1984." In *Changing Identities of the Southeast Asian Chinese since World War II*, edited by Jennifer Cushman and Wang Gungwu, 177–203. Hong Kong: Hong Kong University Press, 1986.

Tan, Mitchell. "Spiritual Fraternities: The Transnational Networks of Ngô Đình Diệm's Personalist Revolution and the Republic of Vietnam." *Journal of Vietnamese Studies* 14, no. 2 (May 2019): 1–67.

Taylor, Jay. *The Generalissimo: Chiang Kai-shek and the Struggle for Modern China.* Cambridge, MA: Belknap Press of Harvard University Press, 2009.

Taylor, Jeremy E. "The Production of the Chiang Kai-shek Personality Cult, 1929–1975." *China Quarterly* 185 (March 2006): 96–110.

Tien, Hung-mao. *Government and Politics in Kuomintang China, 1927–1937.* Stanford, CA: Stanford University Press, 1972.

Tilman, Robert O. "Philippine Chinese Students." Unpublished manuscript, n.d.

——. "The Philippines in 1970: A Difficult Decade Begins." *Asian Survey* 11, no. 2 (February 1971): 139–148.

To, James Jiann Hua. *Qiaowu: Extra-Territorial Policies for the Overseas Chinese.* Leiden: Brill, 2014.

Toh Jin-xuan [Du Jinxuan]. *Xuetong de yuanzui: Bei qian wang de baise kongbu dong-nanya shounanzhe.* Taipei: Taiwan shangwu yinshu guan, 2020.

Tsui, Brian. *China's Conservative Revolution: The Quest for a New Order, 1927–1949.* Cambridge: Cambridge University Press, 2018.

Tucker, Nancy Bernkopf. *Strait Talk: United States–Taiwan Relations and the Crisis with China.* Cambridge, MA: Harvard University Press, 2009.

Uhalley, Stephen, Jr. "Taiwan's Response to the Cultural Revolution." *Asian Survey* 7, no. 11 (November 1967): 824–829.

Uytanlet, Juliet Lee. *The Hybrid Tsinoys: Challenges of Hybridity and Homogeneity as Sociocultural Constructs among the Chinese in the Philippines.* Eugene, OR: Pickwick Publications, 2016.

Van der Kroef, Justus M. "Philippine Communism and the Chinese." *China Quarterly* 30 (1967): 115–148.

Vu, Tuong, and Wasana Wongsurawat, eds. *Dynamics of the Cold War in Asia: Ideology, Identity, and Culture.* New York: Palgrave Macmillan, 2009.

Wakeman, Frederic, Jr. "A Revisionist View of the Nanjing Decade: Confucian Fascism." *China Quarterly* 150 (June 1997): 395–432.

Wang, Joan S. H. "In the Name of Legitimacy: Taiwan and Overseas Chinese during the Cold War Era." *China Review* 11, no. 2 (Fall 2011): 65–90.

Wang, L. Ling-chi. "The Structure of Dual Domination: Toward a Paradigm for the Study of the Chinese Diaspora in the United States." *Amerasia Journal* 21, no. 1–2 (1995): 145–165.

Wang, Peter Chen-main. "A Bastion Created, a Regime Reformed, an Economy Reengineered, 1949–1970." In *Taiwan: A New History*, edited by Murray Rubinstein, 320–338. Armonk, NY: M. E. Sharpe, 1999.

Wang Gungwu. *China and the Chinese Overseas.* Singapore: Eastern Universities Press, 2003.

——. "The Chinese Revolution and the Overseas Chinese." In *Diasporic Chinese Ventures: The Life and Work of Wang Gungwu*, edited by Gregor Benton and Liu Hong, 196–209. London: Routledge, 2000.

——. *Community and Nation: Essays on Southeast Asia and the Chinese.* Kuala Lumpur: Heinemann Educational Books, 1981.

Weber, Max. *The Protestant Ethic and the Spirit of Capitalism.* Translated by Stephen Kalberg. London: Routledge, 2001.

Weightman, George Henry. "The Philippine Chinese: A Cultural History of a Marginal Trading Community." PhD diss., Cornell University, 1960.

Wickberg, Edgar. "Anti-Sinicism and Chinese Identity Options in the Philippines." In *Essential Outsiders: Chinese and Jews in the Modern Transformation of Southeast Asia and Central Europe*, edited by Daniel Chirot and Anthony Reid, 153–186. Seattle: University of Washington Press, 1997.

———. *The Chinese in Philippine Life, 1850–1898*. Quezon City: Ateneo de Manila University Press, 2000.

———. "Notes on Contemporary Chinese Organizations in Manila Chinese Society." In *China, across the Seas: The Chinese as Filipinos*, edited by Aileen S. P. Baviera and Teresita Ang See, 43–66. Quezon City: Philippine Association of Chinese Studies, 1992.

Wilson, Andrew R. *Ambition and Identity: Chinese Merchant Elites in Colonial Manila, 1880–1916*. Honolulu: University of Hawai'i Press, 2004.

Wong Kwok-chu. *The Chinese in the Philippine Economy, 1898–1941*. Quezon City: Ateneo de Manila University Press, 1999.

Wongsurawat, Wasana. *The Crown and the Capitalists: The Ethnic Chinese and the Founding of the Thai Nation*. Seattle: University of Washington Press, 2019.

Woods, Colleen. *Freedom Incorporated: Anticommunism and Philippine Independence in the Age of Decolonization*. Ithaca, NY: Cornell University Press, 2020.

Wu, Chun-hsi. *Dollars, Dependents, and Dogma: Overseas Chinese Remittances to Communist China*. Stanford, CA: Hoover Institution on War, Revolution, and Peace, 1967.

Wu, Ellen D. "Chinese-American Transnationalism aboard the Love Boat: The Overseas Chinese Youth Language Training and Study Tour to the Republic of China." *Chinese America: History and Perspectives* 19 (2005): 51–64.

———. *The Color of Success: Asian Americans and the Origins of the Model Minority*. Princeton, NJ: Princeton University Press, 2014.

Xia, Yun. *Down with Traitors: Justice and Nationalism in Wartime China*. Seattle: University of Washington Press, 2017.

Yang, Dominic Meng-Hsuan. *The Great Exodus from China: Trauma, Memory, and Identity in Modern Taiwan*. Cambridge: Cambridge University Press, 2020.

Yang Hsiu-chin [Yang Xiujing]. "Feilübin 'Huaqiao shangbao' an yu xinwen ziyou wenti." *Zhengda shicui* 9 (December 2005): 145–179.

———. *Taiwan jieyan shiqi de xinwen guanzhi zhengce*. Taipei: Guoli bianyi guan, 2005.

Yang Jiancheng. *Zhongguo Guomindang haiwai gongzuo de lilun yu shijian, 1924–1991*. [Taipei], 2001.

Yen Ching-hwang. *The Chinese in Southeast Asia and Beyond: Socioeconomic and Political Dimensions*. Singapore: World Scientific Publishing, 2008.

Yong, C. F. *Tan Kah Kee: The Making of an Overseas Chinese Legend*. Singapore: World Scientific Publishing, 2013.

Yong, C. F., and R. B. McKenna. *The Kuomintang Movement in British Malaya 1912–1949*. Singapore: Singapore University Press, 1990.

Yu, Renqiu. *To Save China, to Save Ourselves: The Chinese Hand Laundry Alliance of New York*. Philadelphia: Temple University Press, 1992.

Yung Li Yuk-wai. *The Huaqiao Warriors: Chinese Resistance Movement in the Philippines, 1942–1945*. Quezon City: Ateneo de Manila University Press, 1996.

Zhai, Qiang. *China and the Vietnam Wars, 1950–1975*. Chapel Hill: University of North Carolina Press, 2001.

Zhang Yougao. "Zhongyang xunlian tuan." *Minguo dang'an* 2 (1994): 141–143.

Zhao Zhenxiang, Yan Lifeng, Jiang Xiding, Hou Peishui, Wu Jiansheng, and Chen Huayue. *Feilübin huawen baoshi gao.* Beijing: Shijie zhishi chubanshe, 2006.

Zheng Yangwen, Hong Liu, and Michael Szonyi, eds. *The Cold War in Asia: The Battle for Hearts and Minds.* Leiden: Brill, 2010.

Zhou, Taomo. *Migration in the Time of Revolution: China, Indonesia, and the Cold War.* Ithaca, NY: Cornell University Press, 2019.

Zhu Dongqin. *Chongtu yu ronghe: Feihua shanglian zonghui yu zhanhou Feihua shehui de fazhan.* Xiamen: Xiamen daxue chubanshe, 2005.

Zhuang Guotu. *Huaqiao huaren yu zhongguo de guanxi.* Guangzhou: Guangdong gaodeng jiaoyu chubanshe, 2001.

Index

Page numbers in italics indicate figures; those with a t indicate tables.

National Taiwan Normal University, 141
"national values," 76, 81, 138, 221
nationalism, 17, 114, 135, 155; Chinese, 4,
  22, 28, 37, 156; cultural, 114, 136, 150;
  economic, 114, 150, 194; extraterritorial,
  221; Filipino, 4, 79, 81; "national
  bloodline," 137; territorial, 6
"Nationalist China," 2, 6, 8, 11, 17, 69–70,
  82, 102, 114, 119, 120, 130, 135, 136, 138,
  149–151, 177, 182, 193, 212, 214, 216, 221.
  See also Republic of China
nationality, 3, 5, 77, 79, 125, 147, 208, 213
nationality law: China, 7, 8, 26, 70, 191;
  Philippines, 29, 79
nationalization, 17, 54, 60, 69, 73, 114, 114,
  125, 127, 157, 215
native place, 4, 22, 28, 67, 154, 162–163, 168,
  179
native-place associations, 25, 28, 192; Xibian
  Native-Place Association, 193
naturalization, 17, 73, 130, 191, 214, 216;
  naturalization law (1939), 5, 71
Negros Occidental, 35
networks, 8, 80, 124, 125, 142, 150;
  commercial, 22, 33; kinship, 22, 34;
  migration, 7, 22; native-place, 67; party, 2,
  7, 9, 11, 12, 17, 21, 22, 26, 30, 45, 48, 84,
  136, 137, 182, 204, 212, 213, 220, 221
"neutralism," 131, 147, 186, 194
New England Hotel and Restaurant, 52
New Fourth Army, 40, 41, 43
New Life Movement, 94, 135–136, 138
New People's Army (NPA), 202, 216
New York, 114, 188
Ng Bun Ho, 62, 64
Ng Le Chiao, 105, 108, 109, 109t, 116
Ngô Đình Diệm, 73, 114, 151
Nixon, Richard M., 122, 177
nonterritorial sovereignty, 2, 212
North Atlantic Treaty Organization
  (NATO), 82
North Korea, 131
Northern Expedition, 24

Office of the President (Philippines), 61
Okinawa, 177–178
Ong Chuan Seng, 19–21, 20, 22, 23, 28, 31,
  34–36, 39, 42, 50–51, 82, 86, 90, 130, 164
Ong, Santos, 41, 192–193, 217
Operation Chopsuy, 106–107, 116
opium, 4, 68, 79
Organization of Petroleum Exporting
  Countries, 215
Osmeña, Sergio, 53–54, 55

"overseas Chinese affairs" (qiaowu), 7, 8, 42,
  114, 117, 136, 144, 157
Overseas Chinese Affairs Commission
  (OCAC, Qiaowu Weiyuanhui), ROC, 1,
  24, 25, 87, 133, 155; as the "Overseas
  Community Affairs Council," 8
Overseas Chinese Conference, 115, 164
Overseas Chinese Cultural and Educational
  Conference, 165
Overseas Chinese Day (Huaqiao Jie), 150,
  165, 170
Overseas Chinese News Service, 176
Overseas Chinese United Salvation
  Association, 146
Overseas Department (Haiwaibu), 24
Overseas Party Affairs Committee (Haiwai
  Dangwu Weiyuanhui, OPAC), 24, 25, 33,
  35, 37–38, 48
Overseas Series (Haiwai wenku), 138
Oyen, Meredith, 11, 114, 159, 160, 188

Pacific Economic and Cultural Center, 218
Pacific Pact, 82
Pacific Review, 145
Pacific War, 42, 51, 69, 73, 82, 162, 204.
  See also World War II
Pagkakaisa sa Pag-unlad (Unity in Progress),
  14, 217
Pampanga, 54, 62; San Fernando, 54, 145
Panay Island, 90
Pan Zhaoying, 172
Panchiao, 170, 171, 211, 212
Panchiao National Schools' Teacher
  Training Program (Banqiao Guomin
  Xuexiao Jiaoshi Jiangxi Hui), 171–174,
  177, 179
Pao Kee Tung, 187–188
Pao Shih-tien, 130–133, 137, 138, 143,
  146–148, 151, 165, 170–171, 173, 211, 216
paramilitary groups, 26, 37, 72
Partido Komunista ng Pilipinas (PKP),
  32–34, 45, 54, 103–105, 110, 120, 148;
  Chinese Branch, 103; Politburo, 32
party-state (dangguo), 2, 5, 8, 21, 24, 26, 68,
  135, 136, 137, 175, 179, 220, 221;
  "partification" (danghua), 135; Soviet
  model for, 6
passports, 89, 96, 159, 211, 212; "homecoming
  endorsement," 159
"patriotic voluntary contributions" (aiguo
  zidong juanxian), 1, 87, 165, 168
Patriotism, 17, 29, 36, 41, 65, 77, 98, 147,
  154–155, 158, 160, 162, 173, 174, 175, 177,
  180, 193, 204

corruption, 27, 75, 77, 78, 79, 80, 92; economy of, 27; independence (1946), 9, 29, 69; international trade, 215; Japanese occupation, 15, 21, 22, 38, 40, 41, 43, 44, 46–49, 50, 51, 60, 81, 90, 130, 185, 192, 220; "period of bloody struggle," 15–16, 49, 62, 67, 74, 82; population of Chinese in, 1, 27, 131; PRC embassy, 218; recognition of the PRC, 17; ROC embassy, 67, 77, 82, 90, 93–95, 96–97, 101–102, 108, 110, 115–120, 129, 131, 133, 138, 159, 170, 174, 182, 183, 187–188, 192, 195, 197–199, 200, 201, 202–204, 218; Second Philippine Republic (1943–1945), 46, 53; US embassy, 63, 80, 85, 86, 92, 95, 161; US colonial rule (1898–1946), 4, 26, 42, 219

Philippines-China Cultural Association (Zhong Fei Wenhua Xiehui, PCCA), 93–94, 96, 98, 99

Philippines-China Cultural Journal, 94, 98

Philippines Free Press, 57, 67, 109, 123, 182, 186

Platthy, Jeno, 149

pluralism, 12

Poland, 215

Political Warfare Cadres Academy (Zhenggong Ganbu Xuexiao), 139, 204

populism, 5, 60, 70, 79, 125, 203

Presidential Decree No. 176, 215

prisoners of war (POWs), 158

professions: retailing, 4, 54, 60, 79, 81, 126; wholesaling, 4

profiteering, 62

propaganda, 10, 24, *25*, 25t, 37, 47, 58, 76, 78, 91, 98, 103, 104, 111, 112, 123, 124, 131, 132, 134, 142–144, 149, 150, 156, 158, 161–162, 168, 177, 179, 187, 197, 199–200, 208, 211, 216; "Propaganda Warfare," 139

prostitution, 62, 68, 107, 219

Provost Marshal's Office (Manila), 52

"Psychological Warfare," 139

Pua Chin Tao, 92, 93

Pyongyang, 89

qiaoling ("leader"), 93, 98

Qing dynasty, 7, 19, 23, 28, 156; anti-Qing societies 6, 19, 22–23

Qua Chi Peng, 115, 116

Que, Profiteza (Baby Zenaida), 105–106, 107, 108, 116, 118

Quemoy (Jinmen), 84, 153, 163, 165–169, 171, 179; Mashan, 168; military rule, 167; Yangshan village, 167

Quezon Province, 112; Siain, 145

Quirino, Elpidio, 82, 84, 86, 88, 98, 106

Quisumbing, Sycip, Quisumbing, and Salazar (law firm), 115–116

racketeering, 76

radio broadcasting, 104, 134, 150, 168

Rama, Napoleon G., 182

Ramos, Narciso, 198, 199, 216

"Red imperialism," 131

"reformatory education" (*ganhua*), 113, 119, 181

reformers: Chinese, 5, 124, 156, 173

refugees 158, 159, 166, 200

remittances, 73, 80, 98, 154, 156–157, 162, 192, 206

Ren Jiaming, 167, 168

Renaissance Society (Fuxingshe), 26, 35, 38

Republic Act (R.A.) No. 1180 (Retail Trade Nationalization Act), 79, 126

Republic of China (ROC): "communist infiltration," 159, 160; consulate in Manila, 21–22, 37, 38, 39–40, 48, 49, 62, 65, 72; diplomatic relations with Japan, 177; emigration from, 159; Executive Yuan, 24, *25*, 67, 159; First National Assembly (Taiwan), 117; "Freedom Day," 158; Legislative Yuan, 51, 69, 130; militarization of society, 36, 172; Ministry of Defense, 119; National Assembly (1946), 89; Public Security Bureau (Guojia Anquan Ju), 188; "overpopulation," 159

retail trade, 4, 54, 60, 79, 81, 125–126

"returned overseas Chinese" (*guiqiao*), 66, 156

Reuters, 194

Revive China Society (Xingzhonghui), 19, 22–23

revolutions: Chinese nationalist, 22, 138, 139, 186; Xinhai (1911), 19, 23, 28

revolutionaries: Chinese, 5, 22, 45, 124, 156; CCP, 28; KMT, 22

Revolutionary Alliance (Tongmenghui), 19–20, 23; overseas branches, 23, 46

Reyes, Edmundo, *184*, 207, *208*

Rice and Sugar Association, 127, 143

Riots, 71, 149; anti-Chinese, 29

Rizal, Jose, 4, 145

robbery, 56, 188

Rodrigo, Francisco, 149

Roosevelt, Eleanor, 187

Roxas City, 30

Roxas Chua, Antonio, 127–128, 143, 191, 205

STUDIES OF THE WEATHERHEAD EAST ASIAN INSTITUTE

COLUMBIA UNIVERSITY

Selected Titles
(Complete list at: weai.columbia.edu/content/publications)

Middlemen of Modernity: Local Elites and Agricultural Development in Modern Japan, by Christopher Craig. University of Hawai'i Press, 2021.

Isolating the Enemy: Diplomatic Strategy in China and the United States, 1953–1956, by Tao Wang. Columbia University Press, 2021.

A Medicated Empire: The Pharmaceutical Industry and Modern Japan, by Timothy M. Yang. Cornell University Press, 2021.

Dwelling in the World: Family, House, and Home in Tianjin, China, 1860–1960, by Elizabeth LaCouture. Columbia University Press, 2021.

Disunion: Anticommunist Nationalism and the Making of the Republic of Vietnam, 1954–1963, by Nu-Anh Tran. University of Hawai'i Press, 2021.

Made in Hong Kong: Transpacific Networks and a New History of Globalization, by Peter Hamilton. Columbia University Press, 2021.

China's Influence and the Center-Periphery Tug of War in Hong Kong, Taiwan and Indo-Pacific, by Brian C. H. Fong, Wu Jieh-min, and Andrew J. Nathan. Routledge, 2020.

The Power of the Brush: Epistolary Practices in Chosŏn Korea, by Hwisang Cho. University of Washington Press, 2020.

On Our Own Strength: The Self-Reliant Literary Group and Cosmopolitan Nationalism in Late Colonial Vietnam, by Martina Thucnhi Nguyen. University of Hawai'i Press, 2020.

A Third Way: The Origins of China's Current Economic Development Strategy, by Lawrence C. Reardon. Harvard University Asia Center, 2020.

Disruptions of Daily Life: Japanese Literary Modernism in the World, by Arthur M. Mitchell. Cornell University Press, 2020.

Recovering Histories: Life and Labor after Heroin in Reform-Era China, by Nicholas Bartlett. University of California Press, 2020.

Figures of the World: The Naturalist Novel and Transnational Form, by Christopher Laing Hill. Northwestern University Press, 2020.

Arbiters of Patriotism: Right-Wing Scholars in Imperial Japan, by John Person. University of Hawai'i Press, 2020.

The Chinese Revolution on the Tibetan Frontier, by Benno Weiner. Cornell University Press, 2020.

Making It Count: Statistics and Statecraft in the Early People's Republic of China, by Arunabh Ghosh. Princeton University Press, 2020.

Tea War: A History of Capitalism in China and India, by Andrew B. Liu. Yale University Press, 2020.

Revolution Goes East: Imperial Japan and Soviet Communism, by Tatiana Linkhoeva. Cornell University Press, 2020.

Vernacular Industrialism in China: Local Innovation and Translated Technologies in the Making of a Cosmetics Empire, 1900–1940, by Eugenia Lean. Columbia University Press, 2020.

Fighting for Virtue: Justice and Politics in Thailand, by Duncan McCargo. Cornell University Press, 2020.

Beyond the Steppe Frontier: A History of the Sino-Russian Border, by Sören Urbansky. Princeton University Press, 2020.

CPSIA information can be obtained
at www.ICGtesting.com
Printed in the USA
LVHW012047280222
712220LV00020B/882/J